George Gibbs Northwest Array

~  ~

Full Reports, Place Names, Word List, Artifact Names, and Guide

Compiled & Edited

By

Jay Miller, PhD

George Gibbs

Cover: Color Map of Lakewood with blue line boundaries of
Gibb's homestead claim named Chetlah ~ "Rock"
and his cabin site at the blue circle
by Kurt Reidinger

All punctuation has been regularized and simplified.

© 2019

Intro

Contents

Introduction	2	
George Gibbs Biography	3	
WHS endorsement:	9	
Dall:	11	
Powell:	12	
Ke-kai-si-mi-loot ~ Queen Chief	13	
Restored ethnohistoric manuscript	16	1856 > ½ 1877 +
Railroad route ethnographic survey	117	1855
Place Names with Key to Sounds	162	
Basic 180 Word list	183	
Artifact Names	190	with updates by Zalmai Zahir
Smithsonian Guide	226	
Ke-kai-si-mi-loot ~ Family Bio	264	
References	276	
Thanks	281	
Index	282	
E sites	286	

Footnotes   # 1 - 185

Published half ~ ½ = John Wesley Powell, ed. 1877 Smithsonian Contributions to North American Ethnology. Volume I ~ Tribes of the Extreme Northwest by William H Dall, and Tribes of Western Washington and Northwestern Oregon by George Gibbs, LLD. Washington, DC: Smithsonian.

Providing essential ethnography on Washington State tribes, Wisconsin Historical Society holds the 1856 bound handwritten overview manuscript by George Gibbs, who lived for a decade in the Northwest. Half of his mss was published in 1877 edited for Major JW Powell by William Dall, Alaska naturalist, who left out a hundred pages and gave Gibbs an MD instead of his LLD {*Legum Baccalaureus*} from Harvard. In 1955 the missing pages, lacking a phrase or two, became two articles {cited below} by a prim WSU English professor.

Dall re-spelled tribal names according to linguistic conventions, a single letter for each sound, thereby changing those spellings easily recognized throughout the region because they were introduced among early settlers by Gibbs himself. Dall also wrote them in the singular, where Gibbs used a plural form for his tribal names. Dall made paragraphs of long passages, and these have been retained for readability, though marked as [no ¶] within the original text, using the symbol for the paragraph mark. Retold tales in particular are told as unindented, continuous sentences, regardless of topic or subject.

Gibbs was keenly interested in native peoples and their languages. Indeed an appendix to the 1877 federal report is his classic dictionary of the native language of Puget Sound, which he called Niskwalli and we now call Nisqually ~ Tx^{w}əlshootseed ~Southern Lushootseed. Gibb's ethnography and linguistics provide the baseline for all research in the region, as well as providing crucial evidence in federal court cases confirming tribal treaty rights to local fish, shellfish, game animals, and other resources. It is a great pity, therefore, that many of us were unaware of the greater value of the entire manuscript.

* Footnotes are identified as

eec = Ella E Clark, *gg* = George Gibbs in originals;

jm { } = Jay Miller, *zz* = "Zeke" Zalmai Zahir added to text

GEORGE GIBBS
(1815-1873)

The eldest child of a distinguished Northeast family, Gibbs spent an adventurous decade in the Northwest, which he abundantly chronicled it in notes, diaries, letters, manuscripts, and massive publications. But his efforts took a toll. Short and burley, he suffered severely from gout as he got older. Yet when told to keep his feet elevated, he disobeyed doctor's orders to continue writing and editing his own materials and language materials from the Smithsonian.

George was born 17 July 1815 after his parents had been married for five years. His father, Colonel George (1776-1833), was 39, and his mother Laura was 19 and daughter of Oliver Wolcott, Whig Federalist politician. The Gibbs family traced its American origins to James who left Bristol, England, in 1670, and his son George who put down roots. The grandson George (1735-1803) founded the family fortune by running 70 trading ships of the firm of Gibbs and Channing out of Newport, Rhode Island. After he died, his widow Mary (nee Channing) established the family in Boston. Half of her eight children died young. Living with her were two daughters, Sarah, unwed, and Ruth, married to her cousin Rev. William Ellery Channing. Sarah, in particular, was a staunch Episcopalian, and maintained the family chapel and cemetery at "Oakland" in Rhode Island. William, a brother, became governor of Rhode Island.

As a young man, the colonel visited China and Russia, with the family hope that he would learn the trade. Instead, he turned to scholarly interests in geology and mineralogy. Family funds bought him the finest mineral collection in the US, which eventually went to Yale University. Upon marriage, he became a gentleman farmer at Sunswick Manor, on Long Island, where his children were born. He easily sailed his sloop across into downtown Manhattan ~ New York City. The family had wealth, power, and connections throughout the Northeast.

Laura, the mother, was daughter of Oliver Wolcott, Secretary of the Treasury and strong Whig, allied with George Washington, John Adams, and Alexander Hamilton. Wolcott was head treaty negotiator when New York Iroquois were forced to cede homeland to the US just after the successful American Revolution, accomplishing by threat what US forces had not been able to do by scorched earth tactics. Whigs lost favor with the election of Thomas Jefferson and appointment to the Treasury of Albert Gallatin, who became famous for his study of North American native languages later in his life. Gibbs, Channing, and Wolcott family fortunes were even more compromised by the election of populist, Irish-born, Indian-hating Andrew Jackson in the 1830s and 1840s.

Laura had seven children. George was eldest, followed by Mary (1917, died 1820), Elizabeth {Tuckerman} (1819 – 1906), Oliver Wolcott (1822 – 1908), Alfred (1823 – 1868), Laura Wolcott {D'Oremieulx} (1827 – 1902), and Francis Sarason (1831 – 1882). Elizabeth married a city businessman, Laura married a professor at West Point Military Academy, Oliver, better known as Wolcott, became an MD and professor, Alfred graduated West Point for an Army career, becoming a brigadier general, and Frank speculated in Chicago. Alfred's fellow officers often helped George.

After some schooling by his family and occasional tutors, George was sent to newly-founded Round Hill School at Northampton, Massachusetts. Its curriculum was based on languages, mostly taught by European native speakers. The boys were also allowed to set up "Crony Village" where they lived outdoors and hunted with bows and arrows. This training with its freedoms had a long lasting impact on George's scholarship. He graduated at age sixteen.

From this prep school, George went on to enroll at Harvard Law School, delaying his degree until 1838 by taking a grand tour of Europe with his Aunt Sarah in 1834. He served as law librarian, completing an inventory and catalogue that also set a standard for the rest of his life. He joined a law practice in New York City, but soon turned most of his attention to the New York Historical Society, where he mixed with the great Americanists of the day. They included Albert Gallatin, Henry Schoolcraft, and John L Stevens, who traveled through Middle America with the artist Frederick Catherwood recording Maya sites. In 1843, George became librarian of the society, completing an inventory of manuscripts and maps. He also urged that they concentrate on American materials, doing that well instead of scattering their energies. As a result, the fame of this organization has been assured for over a century.

With news of gold in California, the withering of his law office, and a sense that life was passing him by, George and John Ruggles left on 20 March 1849 for Fort Leavenworth, where his brother Alfred and the Mounded Rifle Regiment, marching west, provided safe escort. George carried the map drawn by John Fremont in 1845, amending it as he saw the need. Later, he also added details from an 1828 map by Jedediah Smith he inspected at Fort Vancouver. When his invaluable document was discovered in the American Geographical Society in 1953, it received great cartographic fanfare.

The overland journey ended at Oregon City, and George looked around for a local base. He chose Astoria, made famous in the history of the fur trade by Washington Irving, to set up a law office. He soon became assistant collector of customs, earning $2000 a year, and invested in lots, expecting the tiny port to soon grow, but that did not happen.

Ever the lawyer, he damaged his career in 1850 by insisting that the Hudson Bay Company pay duties on shipments from Victoria to Fort Nisqually, though the customs office was far away at Astoria, at the mouth of the Columbia. He insisted the new Oregon governor and judge take passage on an American vessel instead of the free passage offered by HBC. During resulting bitterness, he wisely resigned his lucrative job, which later allowed him to return to it a few years later.

He next joined the treaty commissions set up for the Willamette Valley tribes of Oregon. George used his fluency in Chinuk Wawa (pidgin, jargon) to collect vocabularies from many of these badly decimated communities. He prepared a useful map of the Willamette with Edward A Starling, briefly serving as the first BIA agent on Puget Sound.

Many of his family had settled in San Francisco, providing him with a base there. In 1851, George finally went to California, intent on finding gold. Instead, he was repeatedly diverted by his academic talents. He was hired by the California treaty commission, serving with Redick McKee's delegation assigned to the northern territory between Golden Gate and Oregon west of the Sacramento Valley. Local conditions were harsh. Clear Lake Pomo were living in naked squalor. After his initial shock, he recovered enough to take down word lists and ethnography. Local ranchers were no better. *Vaqueros* entertained the commission's detachment of dragoons by tying grizzlies to bulls to force a fight to the death. Yet his research interests remained foremost. His diary was filled careful notes on local geology, flora, fauna, and habitats. Along the Klamath River, he could finally use his WaWa to good purpose.

One instance of Gibb's fluency, as well as his sense of humor, appears in the memoirs of an friendly army officer, Erasmas Darwin Keyes (1810-95) in Fighting Indians in Washington Territory (1988), extracted from his Fifty Years' Observation of Men and Events (1884): 18.

We had another gentleman, Mr. George Gibbs, who was in civil government employ and who was a member of the officers' mess at Steilacoom, and who is worthy of mention for the reason that he possessed many accomplishments and amiable qualities. Gibbs devoted much time to the dialects of the aborigines, and became a master of the Chinook jargon. All unwritten languages are difficult to learn, but he was able to speak them so well that he astonished the Indians themselves. The Chinook dialect is made up of the distorted and truncated words and phrases of the Russian, English, French, and native languages. It was remarked that Gibbs could speak Chinook better than any other man, white or red. He came down to San Francisco, and one morning put on the dress and headgear which he had worn among the savages. In that rig he entered a fashionable shop to make purchases. He inquired for various articles, but none of the shopmen could comprehend him. They sent out for linguists of various nations and tribes, of which there were many in the city, but not one could speak Chinook. Gibbs wore a long beard and a serious countenance, and appeared anxious to make himself understood. Finally, after babbling his jargon for half an hour, he walked away, leaving the wondering crowd to conjecture his nationality.

Only once did Gibbs try to turn his research interests into business ones. The ancient Pacific trade valued dentalia (tusk) shells, dredged from deep water off the west coast of Vancouver Island. Fully aware of the high regard natives along the Klamath had for these tapered, tube-like tusk shells, George sent samples to his brother, who was in business in Shanghai. He asked Frank to find Chinese to make enough porcelain copies to string 5000 fathoms but nothing ever happened.

In 1852, the departing Whig President Millard Fillmore (VP before the death of Zachary Taylor) appointed George to be customs collector at Astoria. Though he knew he would soon be replaced, Gibbs used this steady salary to pay off debts. His luck held.

In 1853, he was hired by Captain George McClellan for the survey for the northern route for a US transnational railroad. McClellan was a classmate of George's brother Alfred. The large survey staff included Gibbs as geologist and ethnologist, Lt Johnson K Duncan as draughtsman and assistant astronomer, Joseph Minter as personal aide and engineer; Lt Henry C Hodges as quartermaster; Lt Sylvester Mowry as meteorologist, Dr James G Cooper as surgeon and naturalist; and AL Lewis as guide. Remarkably well equipped but over cautious, this survey under accomplished.

Yet George was tireless at collecting word lists wherever he went, as well as corresponding with educated locals and carefully interviewing long residents like Fr Marie-Charles Pandosy at the Yakama mission and Fr Joset at Fort Colville near Kettle Falls. He fully inspected any documents, books, and personal archives he encountered, keeping notes and copies for the future.

In January 1854, Governor Isaac Stevens hired George to prepare a topographical report on Puget Sound. Alexander Anderson, an aged HBC employee then in Seattle, provided background information for the larger region. Particularly crucial information relates to the Swaal, Washington's Athapaskan speakers who fled an Alaskan volcano about AD 800 and lived on the Skookumchuck tributary of the Chehalis River and in Willapa Hills:

Writing in February, 1856, Gibbs states the result of his inquiries as follows:[1]

"Of the Willopah tribe formerly inhabiting that river and the head waters of the Chihalis, there are, I believe, but two families left; from a man belonging to them I obtained the following:

"He called his people O'whil-lapsh, the termination of which I should, however, judge to be of Chihalis origin. Their territory is called Whilap-a-hai-you. The vocabulary was taken down in some haste, and, besides, being incomplete, is not always altogether correct. Enough, however, is given to afford evidence of its character.

"Mr. Anderson says: 'The Kwal-whee-o-qua seem, from what I can learn, to have occupied the Willopah River and its tributaries towards the head of the Chihalis, and to have interlocked with the tribe who inhabited the country bordering on the Elokamin River. Their habits or life seem to have been very similar to those of the Klatskanai — the chase and an interior life for part of the year — resorting to the main rivers at certain periods to secure a supply of salmon.' "

George himself took a donation homestead (T 19 R 2E S 11-14, see color cover)[2] on 17 May 1854 near Fort Steilacoom, close to friends in the US Army and Masonic Lodge #1. He named it Chetlah {čəƛəʔ = rock}. Like his father, he was a gentleman farmer, hiring the family of William Lane to do the actual labor. His land was within the region still claimed by HBC as part of Fort Nisqually. Resettled in DC, Gibbs would end his public career as a lawyer involved in US negotiations under perdonal attack by the British HBC for this conflict of interest as they were seeking legal reparations for their lost land, improvements, and revenues.

To fill in native language gaps, he kept up a barrage of letters requesting information from informed locals such as missionaries, doctors, traders, and military. He relied on William Tolmie at Fort Nisqually, William McNeil at Fort Simpson, Dr George Stuckely at Fort Dalles, Seth Lount at Fort Orford, UG Warbass at Cowlitz, and James Swan at Shoalwater Bay.

By the end of the year of 1854, Gibbs was serving on his third treaty commission, having drafted the form used by Gov Stevens throughout Washington Territory in 1855. Based on treaties with the Omaha and Missouria, George is credited, because of what he had seen happen to starving natives in California, with adding clauses about native rights to salmon, shellfish, plants, and hunting as a way of allowing Indians to feed themselves and hold off destitution and damage on the expanding frontier. In the immediate aftermath of these hasty treaties and unreasonable demands to relocate peoples, the Treaty War flared up. While Gibbs was away, concerned Army friends removed George's writings from Chetlah to the fort for safekeeping.

Gibbs held ironic public offices in Olympia. He briefly was acting governor between the time Stevens left for Montana and Charles Mason took over. The legislature elected him brigadier general of the Washington militia, but, at the outset of the Treaty War, Mason put a career army officer in charge. Because of these reshufflings, Gibb's was later criticized for his seeming inactivity.

---

[1] Franz Boas and Pliny Goddard, Vocabulary of an Athapascan Dialect of the State of Washington, <u>International Journal of American Linguistics</u> III: 39-45 1924-25. See Also, Report of the British Association for the Advancement of Science, 1899, p. 59. *jm*

[2] T-ownship, R-ange, and S-ection (36 units each of 640 acres measured 1 mile by 1 mile) of the General Land Office (GLO, now BLM) grid, often surveyed from a basic Meridian line that was eventually integrated into the overall pattern grid. *jm*

In 1855, as relief, Gibbs helped concoct a naturalist hoax that amused readers of several newspapers: The prock (*Perockius Oregoniensis*) was a newly discovered mammal that had adapted to steep mountainous living by having shorter legs on its uphill side!

When visiting his homestead, his worker reported criticism of the war by local Métis men, HBC employees married to native women. Ever the lawyer, Gibbs had Lane swear out an affidavit on 9 March 1856. Stevens later misused it in accusing Métis of disloyalty. This malicious campaign helped to drive Steven's aide Doty, son of a Wisconsin governor, to suicide. George felt even more compelled to uphold the letter of the law when Gov Stevens had the chief justice arrested in his own courtroom and declared martial law in two counties.

Thereafter, these two men became embittered and Gibbs lost his official support, and retired to Chetlah intending to farm and write. The Lanes tended his fields, and a Nisqually named Jack cooked. It is also likely that Jack was the source for the words that later became Gibb's Nisqually Dictionary.

For a fourth time, Gibbs joined a survey, this time a joint US-British venture along the border with Canada, under Archibald Campbell. Staff included G Clinton Gardiner, John Grubb Parke, and Caleb Kennerly. Many staffers had been "snakers", naturalist students of Spencer Baird before he took charge of the Smithsonian. The military escort included Lt August V Kautz, a German-born army officer with descendants enrolled among the Nisquallys; and Lts George Pickett and Philip Sheridan, of later Civil War fame. Indeed, several of these men left children among local tribes, particularly while camped at Chilliwack (Chiloweyuck). Son by a Haida wife, James Pickett, in particular, became locally famous as an artist and newspaperman. In 1858, Gibbs finally went up the Skagit River, having previously relied on interviews with locals to learn about upriver conditions before the treaties. The lower river was blocked by a logjam two miles long until dynamited away in 1870.

The boundary survey shipped specimens of all kinds to the Smithsonian in bulk. Among them, unknown until a few years ago, was Mutton, the 18-month old wooly dog pup that had been Gibb's pet until it chewed up one too many mountain goat pelts and was itself collected, prepared, and sent by Kennerly, who left a child at Lummi among the Kinleys.

When the field survey disbanded and moved to DC for the write up phase, George went along, returning to the Northeast after eleven years away. He arrived at his mother's home in New York City on 10 January 1861. He wrote up his portion in DC until 30 May 1862, when he was released after five years devoted to this federal effort.

He turned next to working on native language materials at the Smithsonian, while offering advice and publishing a guide to philological [ethnographic and lingusitic] research, and a basic 180 word list (See p182, p226). He also edited and published his own materials on Lummi and Klallam, Straits Salish languages, as well as a Yakama grammar by Oblate Fr Pandosy. He assembled dictionaries of Chinook WaWa, which he learned and used in Oregon, and of Nisqually (southern Lushootseed), probably supplied by his native cook Jack.

An 1864 treaty between the US and Britain allowed for payment of indemnities for the loss of Ft Nisqually and surrounding lands to Americans who had crowded in, Gibbs among them. These funds were to be paid to the Hudson Bay Company (HBC) and its subsidiary Puget Sound Agricultural Company. The British claimed $4,281,936 but the 1869 final settlement was for $650,000. By the end, Gibbs produced fourteen volumes of testimony and accounts. As noted, he finally had to defend his role as a homesteader at Chetlah after a personal attack based on conflict of interest by the HBC late in the proceedings.

Two years before he died, following family tradition, he married his first cousin, Mary Kane Gibbs, on 11 April 1871. They moved to New Haven, in the Yale neighborhood, where he intended to finish many projects. Instead, his wife became his nurse until he died 9 April 1873 and was buried in the Rhode Island family cemetery beside the chapel maintained by his Aunt Sarah (see website on last page).

Over 58 years, Gibbs was predominately a scholar who supported himself in government employ which drew upon his legal training. He was gifted with the ability to organize diverse materials of himself and others, though he failed to publish all of it. Childless, his materials passed back to their original institutions or went to collateral family lines, such as the manuscript heavily edited in 1877, passed on with other family papers to the Wisconsin Historical Society in Madison by a grand niece living in Milwaukee.

Thus, despite being assembled by a life-long organizer, Gibbs family materials are today scattered from the Wisconsin Historical Society to archives at Harvard, New York Historical Society, and DC (several locations). Coming from the East and returning there after his decade in the Northwest, he was driven by great insight and scholarly motivation. His friends shared his concerns and protected his papers during the Treaty War. Eventually they became valued gems in major archives of the East.

Gibbs was a more-than-adequate artist, surveyor, map maker, and tracker. He left an extensive collection of artifacts, augmented by family travel in Mexico and elsewhere. Native languages were ever his keen interest, supporting related work on place names, literature, and cultural traditions that have not survived well in their own communities.

Overall, Gibbs was an organizer; building on his talents as lawyer, observer, artist, surveyor, map maker, interviewer, archivist, linguist, and synthesizer.

Matthew T Blessing - WHS
Mon, Jan 5, 2015 at 7:59 AM

    Dear Professor Miller: Thank you for your letter. By all means, we welcome a modern historical editing of George Gibbs' manuscript. As you know, the manuscript is in the public domain. Your project is also the very reason why public historical societies exist. We would, of course, request one complimentary copy of the completed work for the WHS Library-Archives collections. Please let me know if you need any additional support or permission statement. Good luck with this important project.

All the best, Matt Blessing
State Archivist and Administrator for the Library-Archives
Wisconsin Historical Society, 816 State Street Madison, WI 53706
(608) 264-6480 matt.blessing@wisconsinhistory.org
Web site: www.wisconsinhistory.org

Collecting, Preserving, and Sharing Stories since 1846

    Very much a man of his times and colleagues, we can look to the work of George's friends for context and example.[3]

> Surgeon George Sukeley … was with us on nearly all our scouting expeditions. He was a man of genius and devoted to science. His activity of body and mind was extraordinary, and he was equally admired by the army, the citizens, and the friendly Indians. He collected and forwarded to the Smithsonian Institute a vast number of beasts, birds, fishes, reptiles, and insects peculiar to the country we were in; likewise many bones, jaws, and skulls of dead Indians. He also sent the head of an enormous wolf, which one of the sentinels shot while on post at Muckle- [18] shoot Prairie. He had in his employ an old squaw who was able to tell him the Indian names of every quadruped, snake, worm, bug, insect, fish. creeping, swimming, flying, or burrowing animal that he found, and many that he did not find, but which she discovered and brought to him. If Cuvier or Agassiz had known of the existence of that squaw they would have gone half round the world to consult her, for she was an unexampled genius and a veritable she Aristotle.

---

[3] Erasmas Darwin Keyes (1810-95), Fighting Indians in Washington Territory (1988), extracted from his Fifty Years' Observation of Men and Events (1884): 17-18.

Gibbs Major Works:[4]

1834 The Judicial Chronicle. Cambridge, MA: J Monroe & Co.

1846 Memoir of the Administrations of Washington and John Adams, edited from the papers of Oliver Wolcott, Secretary of the Treasury. NY: W Van Norden.

1853 Indian Nomenclature of Localities in Washington and Oregon Territories [West of the Cascades]. 14pp. ms # 714. [SI 248] DC: National Anthropological Archives.

1853 California Languages. Henry Schoolcraft federal report in five volumes, Volume III.

1854 Pacific Railroad Reports: Reconnaissance of the Country Lying upon Shoalwater Bay and Puget Sound 1:465-473 (1 March); Geology of the Central Portion of Washington Territory 1: 473-486 (1 May).

1856 Tribes of Western Washington and Northwestern Oregon. Full Manuscript. Madison: Wisconsin Historical Society.

1858 Vocabularies, Washington Territory. Manuscript No. 227, National Anthropological Archives, Smithsonian Institution, Washington, D.C.

1862 Grammar and Dictionary of the Yakima Language by Fr Pandosy. NY: Cramoisy Press.

1863 Instructions for Research Relative to the Ethnology and Philology of America. Smithsonian Miscellaneous Collections VII: 1-51.

1863 A Dictionary of the Chinook Jargon, or Trade Language of Oregon. NY: Cramoisy Press. DC: Smithsonian Miscellaneous Collections VII (10).

1863 Alphabetical Vocabularies of the Clallam and Lummi. NY: Cramoisy Press.

1863 Alphabetical Vocabulary of the Chinook Language. NY: Cramoisy Press.

1873 Physical Geography of the North-Western Boundary of the US. Journal of the American Geographical Society of New York 3, Part 1: 134-157; 4, Part 2: 298-415.

1877a Tribes of Western Washington and Northwestern Oregon. Washington, DC: Department of the Interior, United States Geographical and Geological Survey of the Rocky Mountain Region, Part II: 157-241. {½ ethnography}

1877b Dictionary of the Niskwally. {Appendix to ½ ethnography}. Smithsonian Annual Reports for 1866, 1870 Contributions to North American Ethnology 1: 285-361.

* Stephen Beckham 1969 George Gibbs, 1815-1873: Historian and Ethnologist. UCLA: History PhD Dissertation.

---

[4] *Northwest Anthropological Research Notes* 31 (1&2 1997): 95-187 reprints only the 1877 half.

William Healey Dall

William Healey Dall (21 August 1845 – 27 March 1927) was born in Boston of old English stock. His father Charles Henry Appleton Dall (1816 – 86) was a Unitarian minister, the first, in 1855, such missionary to India, though his family remained Massachusetts. His mother Caroline Wells Healey (22 June 1822 – 17 December 1912) was a teacher, transcendentalist, reformer, ardent feminist, and friend of Henry David Thoreau. In high school, Dall settled on the study of mollusks and, in 1863, enrolled at Harvard and studied with Louis Agassiz, Jeffries Wyman, and Daniel Brainerd. Employed at Chicago, he continued his study with Robert Kennicott (1835 – 1866) at the Chicago Academy of Sciences Museum, who took him along on an expedition to map a telegraph line route between North America and Russia by way of the Bering Sea. The ship captain was whaler and naturalist Charles Melville Scammon (1825 – 1911), exploring the coast of Siberia with stops in Russian Alaska.

Kennicott died of a heart attack on 13 May 1866, seeking a route along the Yukon River. Dall resolved to finish the work of Kennicott, at his own expense, until, luckily, the U.S. purchased Alaska in 1867 and his exploration collections benefited the Smithsonian. Moving to DC, he catalogued these thousands of new specimens and, in 1870, published *Alaska and Its Resources*, as he was appointed Acting Assistant to the U.S. Coast Survey (renamed US Coast and Geodetic Survey in 1878). His later collections were sent to specialists for analysis: shells to Agassiz, plants to Asa Gray, and artifacts to the Smithsonian, which published his Alaskan ethnography beside his heavily-edited Gibbs.

Dall married in 1880, joined the US Geological Survey in 1884 based at the US National Museum, and, in 1899, led the elite scholarly team of the Harriman Alaska Expedition. In a sense, his editing of Gibbs provided background for his own later study of Northwest geology and fossils (1890, 1892, 1895, 1897, 1901, 1910). At death, he is eulogized as Alaskan pioneer, anthropologist, coast pilot, malacologist, paleontologist, zoologist, nomenclaturist, and poet.

Ever on the alert for unique features of native languages, Gibbs noted Tsmshyan's 8 counting systems from data supplied by fur traders and military, which editor Dall fumbled:

NOTE ON THE USE OF NUMERALS AMONG THE T'SIM SI-AN
By George Gibbs, MD {LLD}
The numericals given elsewhere appear to be simply used in common counting. In counting *men*, a different set are used, as is the case in the Nikwalli [Niskwalli]. And I suspect in counting salmon, still another; as the word "kig-geet t'de kep'h" is given for 30 in such a case. [Vocabulary of Chymshien Language, by Dr. John Kennedy, Chief Trader, Hudson Bay Company [HBC], obtained in 1854 and given in 1860 to George Gibbs by Capt WA Howard, BAE ms 276c]

Indeed, Sm'algyax ~ Tsmsyan counts: 1) by general & abstract #s, 2) beings & animals & flat things (skins, mats, clothes), 3) humans (*-ool*), 4) by length (*-gn ~ -xn < gan* = tree), 5) canoes (*-gantk*), 6) humans aboard canoes (*-daat*), 7) by volume & fathom (*-on < an'on* = hand ~ arm), and 8) by linear unit (*-gaay < gayk* = chest ~ wing) (Dunn 1995: 38-40).

1877 Acknowledgement (excerpt)

John Wesley Powell

The contributions in this volume from the pen of Mr Gibbs will, it is believed, be found to be of exceeding value. On every page are exhibited evidences of his thorough and conscientious work, and it must ever be a matter of deep regret to American linguists that Mr Gibbs was not spared to complete his labors, and to give to all this great collection of linguistics that better finish that would have resulted from his editorial skill.

It seemed proper that a biographic notice of Mr Gibbs should appear in the introduction to this volume, and I had commenced the preparation of such a notice, but when I learned that a "Memorial of George Gibbs" had been written by John Austin Stevens, jr, and published by the New York Historical Society, and subsequently republished in the Smithsonian Report for 1873, I recognized that this task had been performed far better than I could do it myself.

To Mr WH Dall I am indebted not only for his valuable contributions, but also for his kindly painstaking assistance in the general preparation of the volume.

The valuable contributions from the pens of Dr William F Tolmie and Rev Father Mengarini are but a part of the material in my hands collected by these gentlemen. I hope that the method of publication adopted will meet with their approval.

Mr JC Pilling has rendered me valuable assistance in his proofreading of the greater part of the volume — a work which he has performed with care and skill.

For the last ten years I have habitually laid before Professor Henry all of my scientific work, and have during that time received the benefit of his judgment on these matters, and to a great extent I am indebted to him for advice, encouragement, and influence. In expressing my gratitude to the Professor, I beg also to express the hope that the results of my work will not wholly disappoint him.

JW POWELL.

KE-KAI-SI-MI-LOOT
(1790s – 1875)
Queen Chief

Throughout the Northwest, rank trumped gender so elite women of the nobility had commanding roles. Few have entered the written record, such as Angeline ~ *Kikisiblu*, daughter of Chief Seattle; Chehalis Queen Susan ~ *Kwəntal'uc'łn*, sister of Chief *Yawnish*; *Yagʷałiw* ~ *Yagʷało* (Ya-gwa-thiyu) – often attended by body guards as daughter of the Skagit Prophet married to Samish Chief *Pətius* at Bayview; and Sally, widow of Tsenahmus, a Chinook chief.[5] Better known in the written record is the woman named Ki-kai-si-mi-loot, nicknamed Queen and well known to Dr William Tolmie at Fort Nisqually. More recently called Ms Chief by Murray Morgan, he misidentified her as Chinook.[6] She entered the US historical record in the 1840s for her crucial aid to the Wilkes Exploring Expedition, who called her "squaw chief", particularly during their survey of Gray's Harbor. Briefly introduced here, her more complete biography appears in an appendix.

According to Wilkes (1844: Volume #5), Passed Midshipman Henry Eld, assisted by George Colvocoresses (1852), was placed in charge of the survey of Grays Harbor, departing from US ships anchored off Ft Nisqually in Puget Sound, where Queen was hired to provide horses and porters to carry their canoes and gear across the Black River portage into a tributary of the Chehalis River.

> On the same evening [19 July 1841] he arrived within a short distance of the portage; and the next morning Mr [George] Colvocoressis went, with the sergeant and boy, to an old squaw chief who had promised at Nisqually to be their guide to the Sachap [Satsop] river, and to furnish horses and men to cross the portage. They returned at an early hour, without either horses or Indians, but with a promise that they were to be furnished the next day. The next morning they found that the chief had arrived with five horses and a number of Indians, and was ready to transport the baggage. Some time, however, elapsed before an arrangement could be made for the large canoe, which was thought to be too heavy to transport; but this was finally settled by the same personage offering another in lieu of it, which, though of smaller dimensions, was accepted. Ten

---

[5] Queen Susan was sister of Chief Yawnish; Yagʷałiw, daughter of the Skagit prophet and wife of Samish Chief Petius at Bayview; ; as well as unnamed Sneatlum women from Penn Cove, and "Damasq" of the Puyallup at Minter. *jm*

[6] Scanewa was the Cowlitz high chief, beheaded by Klallams in 1828. A family tree lists his father as Xniva, sister as Cynthia (~ Kwe'-caith, stuck dumb thereafter at seeing his returned corpse), and son Tyee Dick ~ Elac-ac-ca married to Tyee Mary, a neice ~ daughter of Leschi (Fitzpatrick 2004: 126). Her siblings were a sister Sophy (buried in 1850s with pomp first at Ft Nisqually), and two brothers, Qun-us-up-am ~ George and Tom ~ Hky-you-yah. Of her descendants, Del McBride says Queen is a neice of Scanewa; Cecelia Carpenter (1986: 169) names her as What-co-blote, Sophy as Hup-ah-sootse, and says Tom was killed by his father-in-law for abusing his wives (daughters ~ sisters). Murray Morgan (1979: 61) wrongly names her as Princess Charlotte, Chinook Chief Concomly's daughter married to a Cowlitz chief. See #6. Her fuller evolving bio is in <u>Pacific Plateau Portrayals</u> 2015.

Indians were furnished to transport it and the rest of the articles, and they were soon in a condition to move. This despatch [sic] was principally owing to the directions and management of this squaw chief, who seemed to exercise more authority than any that had been met with; indeed her whole character and conduct placed her much above those around her. Her horses were remarkably fine animals, her dress was neat, and her whole establishment bore the indications of Indian opulence. Although her husband was present, he seemed under such good discipline as to warrant the belief that the wife was the ruling power, or, to express it in more homely language "wore the breeches" [5: 121].

The companion report by Colvocoresses provides an estimate of her age and more detail about her family and slaves:

8 P.M., we have just seen a Squaw Chief, of the Sachal tribe, who has promised to meet us at the first "Portage" and act as our guide to the Sachal River....

On the following day we made an early start, and by 8 o'clock we reached the Portage. The chief woman was there awaiting use, with her horses, five in number; they were large, fine-looking animals, and in excellent condition, which is not generally the case with Indian horses. She also brought with her ten men, who were to assist in carrying the small canoe. The large one, she declared, was too heavy to transport, and if we would let her have it, she would give us a smaller one in return, when we arrived at the Sachal River, which offer we very thankfully accepted. In less than an hour all the arrangements had been completed, and we proceeded on our journey, the Indians bring up the rear.

It is due to the Chief Squaw to say, that we owe this [speedy] dispatch principally to her; through her husband was present, she made all the bargains, and gave the Indians their directions. She is a woman of great energy of character and exercises greater authority over those around her than any man chief I have met with since I have been in the country. She is about fifty years of age [1841], and dresses very neat for an Indian woman. [1852: 240, 243]

About 5 P.M., we were overtaken and passed by our old friend, the Squaw Chief, and her husband. She informed us that they were going to pay a visit to a sister [Sophy], who was resident on the banks of the Chapel River. Her canoe was large and handsomely painted, and was paddled by five slaves, two of whom were women. [1852: 246]

As they tried to reach their goal, she again came to their rescue:

On the 31st, after passing two elbows in the river, the cape on the south of the entrance to Gray's Harbour was seen. The flood tide was very strong against them, so that they made but slow progress, and as they opened out the harbour and entered it, they found a strong southwest wind blowing, which caused a short and disagreeable sea, that very nearly swamped their small canoe, and obliged them to run for the lee shore. Here all the things were taken out and placed to dry, on one of the huge trees that had been brought down by the freshets. From this awkward situation they were relieved by the old squaw chief [#5: 133 and her husband, who passed them quickly in a light canoe], who had preceded them from Nisqually. She came over in her large canoe, with ten Indians, and offered to carry the [137] party over to the weather shore, where they could encamp in a less exposed place. The offer was gladly accepted and they were taken over to the village [5: 136-137].

Over a decade later, she came to know George Gibbs, who was compiling a dictionary and ethnography of tribes along the route of the US northern railroad, and was especially concerned with tribes in Puget Sound and western Washington territory. He homesteaded at Steilacoom (See cover), teaching this spelling to other settlers, taking down words from his Nisqually cook, and with a woolly dog pet named Mutton, whose pelt is at the Smithsonian.

Though she provided Gibbs with her human and spiritual pedigree, he relied more on her residence near Ft Nisqually than her intertribal blood ties, as shown below. She also narrated a fuller version of the great regional epic of Moon[7], and other stories dropped from the 1877 edited summary. All are restored herein.

Ke-kai-si-mi-loot, an old woman of the Nisqually, daughter of To-was-tan,[8] a former chief and related to half the nobility of the country on one side or the other, not content with her human pedigree, which, however, she could only carry back three generations, informed me that she was sprung from four generations of Skookams: *Tshit-no-wehtsh, Ai-yah-hose, Hutl-kwus-keh-nam, & Tsul-tsah-lup-tu*,[9] after which they became Indians, *Ke-uch-keh-nam* being the first. How far back this was she could not say (Gibbs in Clark 1955: 315).

Her spirits' pedigree confirmed her fame as a native doctor ~ shaman. Her human pedigree is traced here in footnotes to famous Cowlitz chief Scanewa, and (great) neice Catherine (Mrs Dan) Mounts, who buried Queen and her sister Sophie on the hill above their farm on Mounts Road on Nisqually Delta.

---

[7] For many Puget Sound tribes, especially the Snoqualmie, this epic establishes the stellar pedigree of chiefly families throughout this region and beyond. *jm*

[8] To-was-tan was married to Cynthia ~ Kwe'-caith, sister of Scanewa, so Queen was, by English kin terms, cousin of his son Tyee Dick. For natives, however, all cousins are called brothers and sisters. *Tyee* is the Chinuk Wawa jargon word for a "boss, leader, or chief". *jm*

[9] *Skookum* is the Chinuk WaWa word for "strong, dangerous, powerful," including types of powerful spirit beings, such as "*A-yah-hase* is a demon half deer and half snake with two heads and two pairs of horns" (Gibbs in Clark 1955: 315). *jm*

Gibbs, George (1815-1873)
Report to Hon. I I Stevens, 1856,
    Governor and Superintendent Indian Affairs of Washington Territory
On the Indian tribes of the Western District
By George Gibbs {Now in Wisconsin Historical Society, Madison}

Olympia, WT 1856

Sir,

    In pursuance of your instructions to embody the information concerning the Indian tribes of this District, collected by me while the treaties were in progress, into a report answering the "Inquiries" of Mr Schoolcraft,[10] I have the honor to submit the following.

    Some modification has been made in form, in order to present the subject more consecutively, and I have thought best, instead of applying his questions to each tribe separately, to assume the Nisqually as a basis, merely pointing out analogies or differences between them and others, as they have suggested themselves.

    I would further state, that the report having been in great part prepared before the commencement of the existing disturbances, I have completed it according to the original intention, without reference to that subject.

I have the honor to be &c.
Geo Gibbs

Hon I I Stevens

---

[10] Henry Schoolcraft (1851-57) used standardized ethnographic questions for six huge but jumbled volumes printed by the US government. Gibbs (1863) prepared another Smithsonian guide for ethnography and linguistics, with 180 basic words (see p226). *jm*

Tribes of Western Washington and Northwestern Oregon

By George Gibbs, MD {LLD}[11]

CONTENTS

Page #s

	here	<Gibbs>	[Dall]	
Geographical distribution	17	3	163	
Notices of particular tribes	22	15	170	
Population	27	35	181	
Tribal organization and government	31	40	184	
Property	30	43	186	
Slavery	32	46	188	
Retaliations	34	49	189	
Wars	34	57	190	
Food	36	56	193	
Fur-trade	39	63	197	{fused}
Society, marriage, and domestic relations	39	63	197	
Sepulture	41	68	200	
Feasts	44	77*	205	
Gambling	44	78*	206	
Medicine and diseases	45	80	207	
Domestic manners	46	85	209	cf 63
Names	47	87	210	
Peculiar customs	48	88	211	
Flattening of the head	48	88*	211	
Arrival of puberty	49	90*	212	
Measures of value, time, &c	49	92	213	
Houses	50	95	214	
Canoes	51	96*	215	
Clothing, utensils, &c	53	102*	219	
Domestic animals	54	106-8	221	
Symbolic writing	55	100	222	
Mounds and earthworks	55	109	222	etc

---

[11] Gibbs trained as a lawyer at Harvard; not an MD; an error widely repeated. As noted, after he died in 1873, his 1856 report was re-edited and chopped in half as Dall 1877: 163-241. Inserted <angle> [square] {curved} brackets herein indicate <page #s> in Gibbs' handwritten manuscript, [page #s] in printed Dall 1877, {additions by *jm*}.

Migrations	56	111	223	
<Mythology>	58	115	295	
<Future State>	71		315	
<Cosmology>	73		318	
<Natural Phenomena>	76	155	321	
<The Deluge>	76		322	
<Origin of Mankind>	77	157	323	
<Tamanous>	80	161-181	125	
<Tales>	88			
<Spilyai>	88	182	140	
<Wattatash>	90	187	143	
<Slokwalm ~ Sloqualm>	91	190	145	
<Kwyeema ~ Why-ee-ma>	93	195	149	2nd column >>
<Snow Peaks>	95	201	152	
<Yapoolla ~ Yahpohalla>	96	203	154	
<Josup>	98	207	156	
<The Dead Hunters ~ Seal Hunters>	100	213	160	
<The Mokwatatum ~ Mo-kwo-tah-oom>	101	215	162	
<Tis-ai-lukam ~ Tis-ai-luck-han>	100	218	164	
Notices of early travelers	104	223	223	
Early visits of white men	111	243	236	
Table showing relations of tribes named	114		241	
* Added at end of list		250		

GEOGRAPHICAL DISTRIBUTIONS [163]

<3> In the Western district of Washington Territory, – that is to say, between the Cascade mountains and the Pacific,- there is found, compared with the extent of country occupied, an extraordinary diversity in the aboriginal tongues. Mr Hale, the ethnologist, who accompanied Captain Wilkes's expedition, recognized among them eight languages belonging to five distinct families, and to these are now to be added six other languages which escaped his observation. In addition, there are dialects of several but partially intelligible, even to those speaking the same general language.

As might be inferred, the tribes inhabiting this district are divided into bands having far less connection with each other than is the case with there Indians of the prairie, where a more wandering life bringing them continually into contact serves to keep up an identity in the common tongue. With all this diversity of speech, there is notwithstanding a general resemblance in character, manners, and habits throughout the district, but modified by geographical position and by other causes operating on both the physical and moral condition of the race. [no ¶]

Among nations whose life is almost altogether sensual, the character is affect to a more perceptible degree by exterior circumstances than among the cultivated. Scarcity or abundance of food, its nature, the modes of obtaining it, the occupations and amusement of life, <4> climate, dress, all, to a marked extent, operate not only upon individuals, but upon the tribe.

Except upon the strongest evidence, it could hardly be believed that the [164] Flathead of the Rocky mountains, whose virtues approach him more nearly to the ideal savage of romance than any other upon the continent, was the kinsman, if not the progenitor of the Niskwalli; or the "Comanche" a relative of the Snake "Diggers".[12]

In a geographical view, the district presents three natural divisions: the Columbia River, the Coast, ad Puget Sound; to which might perhaps be added a fourth, in the prairie country between the Kowlitz River and the Puyallup. The Cascade Range, which separates the latter from the great interior basin has a general elevation of from five to seven thousand feet, much broken however by ridges and elevated points; the great volcanic peaks; four of which, Mt Adams, Mt St Helens, Mt Rainier, and Mt Baker, lie north of the Columbia: towering far above all. The width of this range varies from fifty to seventy-five miles. It is timbered on the east side with pines and larch; on the west, with fir, spruce, and the white cedar of *arbor vitae*. The forest country on the western side may be said to extend to the ocean, the prairies occupying a comparatively small area. The skill of the Indians not enabling them to cope with the forest, they have been confined for the most part to the borders of the rivers and sound, to the coast, and the small <5> prairies between the sound and the Columbia.

The banks of the Columbia, from the Grand Dalles to its mouth, belong to the two branches of the *Tsinūk nation, [* Chinook of authors] which meet in the neighborhood of the [Cowlitz] Kowlitz River, and of which an almost nominal remnant is left; upon the elevated plateaus lying south of Mt Adams and Mt St Helens, and upon the southern and western slopes of the later, are the Klikatats and the Tai-tin-apam; on the [Cowlitz] Kowlitz, the tribe of that name, once numerous, but now almost extinct; and in the mountains north of the Lower Columbia, between Shoalwater Bay and the heads of the Tsihalis, the tribe of *Willopah*, (Owhillapsh,)[13] or, as termed by Mr Hale, Kwalhioqua, now reduced to a handful. These along belong to four of the five families of languages above mentioned: the Tsinūk together forming one; Klikatat and Taitinapam belonging to the *Sahaptin*, of which the Walla-Walla and Nez Perce are the leading types; the Kowlitz to the western branch of the *Selish* or Flatheads, and the Willopah to the same division [165] with the Tahkali or Carriers, living on the headwaters of Frazer River, and the Klatskanai, Umkwa {Umpqua}, and Tū-tūten {Tututni} of Oregon.

The position of the [Chinook] Tsinūk previous to their depopulation was, as at once appears, most important. Occupying both sides of he great artery of Oregon for a distance of two hundred miles, they posses the principal thorough fare between the <6> interior and the ocean, boundless resources of provision of various kinds, and facilities for trade unequaled on the Pacific. From the Dalles to "Cape Horn", below the Cascades, the river flows westward through a pass in the mountains, and with but a narrow margin occasionally intervening; but father down it opens into what Lewis and Clarke denominated the Wappatū Valley, connecting with the valley of the Willamette by that river, and by the Kowlitz with the Tsihalis country and the basin of Puget Sound. Through this district it runs northward, the course of the valley tending with it until it is again diverted by the Tsinūk mountains to its original westerly course. Toward the mouth it spreads into extensive bays, the north side lined with precipitous rocky bluffs of that range, while on the south the mountains which separate it from the Twallatti plains close in and unite with the Coast Range.

---

[12] Indeed, a racist term for equestrian speakers of the sparse Numic branch of Uto-Aztecan. *jm*
[13] Properly the Swaal, Kwalhioqua is their name in Chinookan. *jm*

From the Dalles to the Cascades, the navigation is uninterrupted. At the latter point, which is the dividing ridges of the mountains, a series of rapids occurs, below which the influence of the tides is felt, and the river may be considered as navigable to the sea. The immense quantities of deposit annually brought down during the freshet occasion, however, extensive sand-bars, which are scattered at intervals to its mouth, encumber its estuary, and <7> to a great degree create the difficulties of its entrance. The banks of the Columbia, where elevated above the freshets, are clothed with evergreens, fir and spruce predominating, and the same vegetation extends over the general face of the surrounding country, which, joined to its rocks of basalt and volcanic conglomerate, throw an aspect of gloom over the landscape. It is only in the early summer when the cottonwood and maple of the low grounds are in fresh leaf that the prevailing monotony is broken. The freshets of the Columbia overflow not merely the low islands, but most of the alluvial country bordering the river. They take place during the summer commencing in May or June according to the mildness of the [166] season, and subsiding toward the end of July. Freshets also occur on its tributaries, but these are more directly the effect of rains and are highest in the winter, whereas those of the Columbia arise from the melting of snow in the Rocky mountains. The two principal branches on the north, below the Cascades, are the Kathlapūtl Wiltkwu, or Lewis River, and the Kowlitz. The floods of these rivers have an important influence upon Indians economy in their relation to the salmon fisheries, which furnish the most important staple of subsistence.

The mouth of the Columbia might <8> perhaps more correctly be considered with the coast section, with which it is intimately connected; portages leading from Baker Bay to Shoalwater Bay, and thence to Gray Harbor. The first of these is an extensive but shallow piece of water, about twenty-five miles in length, separated from the sea by a narrow strip of lowland. [no ¶]

Several streams flow into it, of which the most noticeable is the Willopah, which has a rich alluvial valley of some extent. The southern end of this bay is Tsinūk territory, and it was formerly their principal winter quarters. The north end belonged to the [Chihalis] Tsihalis, and the [Willopas] Willopah occupied the mountain country lying behind it. It was a district admirably suited to Indian habits, furnishing great quantities of fish and clams, and the neighboring forest abounding in game. A few miles to the north lies Gray Harbor, the estuary of the Tsihalis. Its extent is considerable, being some twelve miles in length from east to west, and about the same in its greatest width. This also is the country of the Tsihalis Indians who extended up the river to the Satsop, where they were met by bands to whom the name of [Upper Chihalis] Upper Tsihalis is collectively given. North of this there are not land-locked harbors, the streams entering the sea directly and without estuaries; of these there are several, the largest being the Kwinaiutl {Quinault}, the Loh-whilse, and the [Kwillehyute] Kwillehiūt. What is known <9> of this section is chiefly from the journey of Messrs. Simmons and Shaw, who follow the coast down from Cape Flattery, in the summer of 1855. The rivers take their rise in the Coast or Olympic Range, the Kwinaiutl in a lake of some size. South of Point Grenville, the sand-beach stretches along the coast, affording easy land communication and enabling the Indians to maintain a few horses, but between that and Cape Flattery the chose is more rocky and [167] broken, spurs from the mountains putting down to the sea. There is, however, some intermediate tableland. The shore is, with the exception of the immediate beach, covered with forest. The interior of the peninsula is a pile of abrupt mountains, upon some of which snow lies perpetually.

The coast North of the Tsihalis tribe is successively occupied by the <u>Kwinaiult</u> {Quinault}, the [<u>Kwillehyūte</u>] <u>Kwillehiūt</u> {Quileute}, and the <u>Makah</u>, the first speaking a dialect varying considerably from the Tsihalis, the second a distinct language, the root of which is probably also in the Selish, and the third the language of Nūtka Sound. The Makah territory extends from the southern Cape Flattery, called by themselves Osett, around Cape Klasset, and up the Straits of Fuca, as far only as the Okeho River. These last, in accordance with the rude interior of their country, are confined almost entirely to the coast, and seek their substance from the sea itself. <10> [no ¶]

The Kwinaiutl find their supplies in the streams, and to a certain extent in hunting, while the Tsihalis properly belong to the bays, from which they obtain winter salmon and shell-fish, and trade with the interior for kamas roots and berries. Trails are said to exist from the Chahlatt River to the Elwa on the straits, and from the Kwillehiūt to the Pishtst and the Okeho.

Pursuing the Straits of Fuca, the mountain barrier comes in like manner to the shore until reaching the neighborhood of False Dungeness, leaving only a few coves for habitation. [*] From thence to Port Townsend a strip of more local character, some of it valuable for cultivation, border the coast and bays. Only a few streams, and those of inconsiderable length, empty into the straits. Along this tract from the Okeho River to Point Wilson, the [<u>Clallams</u>] Klallam, or <u>S'klallam</u> are located, a tribe connected with those of the southeastern part of Vancouver Island. They are as may be supposed almost exclusively marine, depending mainly for support upon fish or the commodities which they get in exchange; but less venturous than the Makah, they do not pursue the whale, or voyage beyond the mouth of the straits.

The interior basin, reaching from the forty-ninth parallel southward and embracing the islands, Bellingham Bay, and the waters of Admiralty <11> Inlet, Hoods Canal, and Puget Sound, forms the third section, whose remarkable feature is the series of bays and inlets which penetrate it in every direction. [168] The country included in his basin though considerably broken preserves near the water a very general level of about two hundred feet, rising higher and generally in tables toward the Cascade mountains. Its eastern side is intersected by numerous rivers which have their origins in that range, interlocking with others emptying into the Columbia, and running in an oblique course toward the sound. The principal of these, commencing at the north, are the Nūksahk {Nooksack}, which at the mouth takes the name of Lummi; heading in Mt Baker, which it partially encircles, and emptying by two mouths into Bellingham Bay and the Gulf of Georgia; the Skagit and Stoluch-whamish, emptying into the shallow bays lying between Whidbey Island and the main; the Snohomish, of which the Snokwalmū is the principal branch, emptying into Part Gardner; the Dwamish, the upper part of which is known generally as White River, heading in Mt Rainier and falling into Elliott Bay; the Puyallup, heading in the foot-hills of the mountain and emptying at Commencement Bay; and the Niskwalli, rising on its south side and discharging into Puget Sound. All these streams have low deltas of greater or less extent at their mouths, as well as alluvial bottoms, the <12> more north ones the most extensive. Farther up they run through narrow, timbered bottoms, bordered by high bluffs, the escarpments of the tablelands, until at the foot of the mountains they are canyoned. It is by these streams, and the depressions or passes occurring at their sources, that the Indians of the interior obtain access to the sound for the purposes of trade. They are none of them navigable except by canoes, nor even in that way for great distances. Their course is rapid, and they are subject to frequent overflow, being alike affected by the heavy rains and by the rapid melting of the snow on the mountains. The principal freshets arise from the former cause and occur in winter. The greater part of the country is timbered, but there are open prairies on

Whidbey Island, and from the Puyallup around the head of the sound. These last are of gravelly soil, and extend, with the intermediate belts of timber, to those on the upper waters of the Tsihalis and the Kowlitz. A distinguishing feature in this district is the number of lakes, some of considerable size, which are scattered through it. The largest of these are those near Bellingham Bay and that emptying into the Dwamish. The western side of Hood Canal, like the Straits of Fuca, is [169] bordered by mountains, which from the western wall of this basin. No streams of any size fall into it except the Skokomish, which enters at the elbow. The mountain group thus included between the Tsihalis, the coast, the Strait of Fuca, and Hoods <13> Canal, and known as the Olympic Range, would seem to have been once an island forming part of a chain with Vancouver and Queen Charlotte Islands. The Indians occupying this basin have all sprung, unless an exception be allowed in the Tsemakum, from the great Selish root, and are usually mentioned as the Niskwalli nation. They are divided into a vast number of small bands, having little political connection, but gathered into families, allied by similarity of dialect and by relationship. These, with their constituent, will be hereafter specified.

From these three principal divisions, an inferior or subdivision might perhaps be separated in the prairie country just mentioned, the facilities for grazing offered by this tract have induced in the occupants equestrian habits, which distinguish them from their neighbors. The number of their horses is, or course, inconsiderable, as compared with the tribes of the great plains, but has been sufficient to create an exception to the otherwise universal aquatic life of the coast region. The bands included are chiefly the Niskwalli proper and the Upper Tsihalis.

In former times, before the diminution of the tribes and the division of trade to the posts, there were numerous trails across the Cascades by which the Indians of the interior obtained access to the western district. Of late, many of these have fallen into disuse, becoming obstructed with timber <14> and underbrush which they have not industry enough to clear out.[14] In fact all their trails thorough the forest, though originally well selected, have become excessively tortuous, an Indian riding around the fallen trunk of tree after tree sooner than clear out a road which he seldom uses. The old Klikatat trail across the mountains to Vancouver had become impassable, and was cut out by Captain {George} McClellan in 1853. Another led from one of the branches of the Yakama, south of Mt Rainier, to the Kowlitz River, which in like manner has been almost abandoned, and the north trails from the Winatshapam and Tselann {Chelan} Lake to the Sto-loch-wha-mish and Skagit seem to altogether so. The two most used at present are those by the Nahchess and the main Yakama or Snokwalmū passes, the former of [170] which is the route of the United State military road from Steilacoom to Walla Walla. The trade between the two districts was once considerable. The western Indians sold slaves, haikwa [dentalia, tusk shells], kamas, dried clams, &c, and received in return mountain-sheep's wool, porcupine's quills, and embroidery, the grass from which they manufacture thread, and even dried salmon, the produce of the Yakama fisheries being preferred to that of the sound.

It will be noticed that north of the country more immediately bordering upon the Columbia, the whole of the western district is inhabited by tribes derived from a single stock, with the exception <15> of the western point of the peninsula occupied by the Makah. The extensive family to which Mr Hale has given the name of Tsihali-Selish, from its extreme

---

[14] Aboriginal trails were maintained through continuous usage and seasonal use of controlled fire, but, as Gibbs himself noted, epidemics so thinned the native population that the landscape assumed the uncared-for appearance of "wilderness" that setters wrongly assumed was "natural" instead of their own fault. *jm*

western and eastern members thus stretches from the Rocky mountains to the Pacific. On the south, its territory s are bounded by those of the Sahaptin and [Chinook] Tsinūk families. On the north, it has in the interior the Tahkali, belonging to the [Athapascas] Tinneh. The northern boundary upon the coast is not so definitely ascertained, but in my opinion will be found in the neighborhood of Johnston Straits, upon the Gulf of Georgia, this including the [Nanaimook] ~ Nanaimūk, [Cowichan] ~ Kowichin, Songhus, and Sokes [Sooke, T'Sou-ke] of Vancouver Island, and Kwaitlen of Frazer River. The subject of their migrations will be noticed hereafter.

NOTICES OF PARTICULAR TRIBES

Of the river Indians, and generally of those with whom no treaties have been made, very little is to be added to the observations contained in my former report. In that paper, the Klikatat were treated as belonging to the eastern division of this Territory, to which their original location and affinities attach them. As, however, they are here spoken of as connected with the western division, some explanation is necessary. After the depopulation of the Columbia tribes by congestive fever, which took place between 1820 and 1830, many of that tribe <16> made their way down the [Cathlapootl] Kathlapūtl (Lewis River), and a part of them settled along the course of that river, while others crossed the Columbia and overran the Willamette Valley, more lately establishing themselves on the Umkwa. Within the last year (1855), they have been ordered by the superintendent of Oregon to return to their former home, and are now chiefly in this part of the Territory. The present [171] generation, for the most part, look upon the Kathlapūtl as their proper country, more especially as they are intermarried with the remnant of the original proprietors. No correct census has at any time been made of the Klikatat, but they are estimated at from 300 to 400, exclusive of the Taitinapam.

Of the Willopah (Kwalhiokwa {Swaal}) or, as they call themselves, Owhillpash, there are yet, it appears, three or four families living on the heads of the Tsihalish River above the forks. According to the account of an old man, from whom the vocabulary was obtained, the Klatskanai, a kindred band, till lately inhabiting the mountains on the southern side of the com, and now also nearly extinct, formerly owned the prairies on the Tsihalis at the mouth of the Skūkumchuk, but, on the failure of game, left the country and crossed the river. Both these bands subsisted chiefly by hunting. as before mentioned, they are of the Tahkali sock, though divided by nearly six degrees of latitude from the parent tribe. The fact of these migrations of the <17> Klikatat and Klatskanai within a recent period is important, as indicating the direction in which population has flowed, and the causes inducing this separation of tribes.

At the council held on the Tsihalis in February, 1855, an opportunity was offered of ascertaining with sufficient correctness, the numbers of these Indians, as also the particulars of the tribes intervening between them and the Makah of Cape Flattery. The name Chihalis, or Tsihalis, strictly belongs to the village on the beach at the entrance of Gray Harbor. The word itself signifies *sand*. It has, however, now become applied to all the bands inhabiting the bay and river. The Lower Tsihalis, or those from the mouth of the Satsop down, including the villages on the Whishkah and Wanūlchi, and the few on Shoalwater Bay, numbered in all but 217.

These differ very little in anything except language from their Tsinūk neighbors. There were formerly five principal villages of the tribe on the river, seven on the north, and eight on the south side of the bay, and even within the recollections of American settlers the population was very considerable. Ka-ko-an, belonging to the Tsihalis village, a very old man, seems to have been the principal chief, and his son, Tū-le'-uk, now claims, in his place, to be the head of the tribe. [172]

The [Upper Chihalis] upper Tsihalis, who for the present <18> purpose may be mentioned here, are a connecting link between the Kowlitz, the Lower Tsihalis, and the Niskwalli. By the Indians on the sound they are known s Stak-ta-mish, or inland people; by others, as Nū-so-lupsh, a name apparently referring to the rapids in their stream, as the same is applied to the Upper Kowlitz, and by the Willopah as Kwū-the-ni. Their country included generally all that drained by the Tsihalis above the mouth of the Satsop, embracing some of the most fertile land in the T territory. This tribe also is verging on extinction; the total number, as near as could be ascertained, being 216. their principal chief, at the time of the settlement by Americans, was Tsin-nit-ieh, a man of rather extensive influence. Since his death they can scarcely be said to have had one, though Gowannus is recognized by the agency as the nominal head. No treaties have as yet been concluded with any of the preceding.

The Kwinaiutl, of which tribe the Kwe'hts-hū {Queets} form part, were present at the council. This tribe speaks little more than a dialect of the Lower Tsihalis tongue. They are mostly on or at the mouth of the two streams which bear their respective names. The Kwinaiutl is celebrated for its salmon, which are considered to excel in quality even those of the Columbia. The [Kwill'ehyutes] Kwillehūit were not represented at the council, though two boys belonging to the tribe accompanied the Kwinaiutl, probably sent to ascertain its <19> objects. It had been supposed previously that the different branches of the latter extended to the Makah territory, and that all of them were present by their delegation. Under this supposition, they would have been treated with as a single tribe had not the accidental discovery of the essential difference in the language led to more particular inquiry. This circumstance of itself shows the importance of ethnological investigation in the management of Indian affairs. In classifying the languages of the district, I have provisionally placed the Kwillehūit, as well as the [Chemakum] ~ Tsemakum, or whom mention will be made hereafter, among those of the Selish family, conceiving the analogy to be sufficient to authorize the conclusion. The very great dissimilarity between them and the other adjacent tongues is, however, recognized by their neighbors, who say that they "speak like birds," a phase commonly used in regard to languages absolutely foreign. There [173] are two bands of this tribe, the Kwillehuit or Kwe-dee'-tut, and the [Hooch] ~ Hūch ~ [Hoh] or Kwāāksat. They are good seamen, and more nearly approach the Makah in daring than any of the others.

The Kwillehūit and Kwinaiutl were included in a treaty separately, made subsequent to the general council of the coast tribes on the Tsihalis. The place for reservations were by that instrument left to be fixed by the President. No settlements whatever have as yet been made in their country, <20> nor is it probably that there soon will be.

Of all the tribe s west of the Cascades, the Makah exhibit the most marked and characteristic traits, differing from the sound Indians in features and habits as much as language. Their intercourse with the white have been very limited, and that not of a kind t make much change in their original customs. Physically, they have the type of the Nūtka Indians. The expression indicated ferocity ad treachery, for which indeed they have a wide reputation. The beard and moustache are well developed, and are not extirpated. The complexion, as is indeed the case with all these tribes, varies considerably, some being much darker than others, without reference to the intermixture of blood. Flattening the head, though prevalent, is not carried to a great excess. In many respects, they are superior to their neighbors, being far more enterprising and exhibiting greater skill and industry in the manufactures; and they are more moral, for they prostitute only slaves. This tribe had a considerable infusion of white blood, a Russian vessel having been cast away near here, as it is supposed, some thirty-five or forty years since, and the crew, being strong enough to protect themselves, having lived among the Indians for some time before they were relieved. Several individuals were present at the council who in their features, complexion, and yellow hair <21> bore the strongest proof of the Sclavonic origin.[15] They have four principal or winter villages: Neeah, at the site of the old Spanish fort on Neeah Bay (Port Nuñez Gaona); Waatch, on the south side of Cape Flattery; Tsū-yess, in a cove or indentation a few miles south of it; and Osett, at the Flattery rocks. Another village on Neeah Bay has been abandoned since the prevalence of the small-pox in the fall of 1852, and the Klasset and Tatooche Island villages are summer resorts. It is stated on the authority of Yallakūb, or Flattery Jack, that previous to the [174] sickness the tribe could muster 500 fighting men. The total of both sexes and all ages is now reduced to little more than that number. Both Yallakūb and Klehsitt, or the white chief, died during that winter. The later, a Russian half-breed, was the head of the tribe; Jack being however the best known, from his speaking a little English, and his greater familiarity with traders.

The [Neah] Neeah village, at the time of our visit in January, 1855, consisted of two block of four or five houses each built close together. The largest single house was about seventy-five feet long y forty in width, and probably fifteen feet high in front, the whole constituting one room. The frame consisted of heavy posts set in the ground, supporting rafters, some of which were at least eighteen inches in thickness at the butt. The labor of raising them in their position, <22> with no aid from machinery, may be imagined. The sides were formed of planks placed horizontally, and secured by upright poles, inside and out, at a few feet apart, to which they ere tied through small apertures by withes. The roof, like those of the Sound Indians, was made of boards, guttered out and lapping one over another. Each house is occupied by several families, their respective portions being separated by a partition of two or three feet high. Chests of quite large size, and very neatly made considering the tools employed, contained the personal chattels of the owners. A raised platform ran around the house, on which the inhabitants sat, slept, or worked; and overhead were shelves and poles on which their property was stowed. A more miscellaneous assortment could hardly be found at a pawnbroker's. Sealskins full of oil, baskets of dried halibut and salmon, flitches of blubber, whaling apparatus, paddles, bundles of mats, articles of all sorts from wrecked vessels, boxes and bags of every description, hung, lay, or stood in endless variety and confusion. Some of the other houses were nearly as large. Into one, a canoe thirty-six feet in length had been introduced for the purpose of repairing, nor did it occupy any inconvenient room. Mr Goldsborough, who visited the village in 1850, informed me that the houses generally were on an even larger scale at that time; that Flattery Jack's home was no less than one hundred (100) feet in length, <23> and that abut twenty women were busily engaged in making bark mats and dogs'-hair blankets. One of the blocks is partly surrounded with a stockade of [175] puncheons twelve or fifteen feet high, strengthened by very large posts, into which a tie-beam is mortised.

The Makah are, as has been mentioned before, almost exclusively maritime in heir habits; their country being very small, broken, and rocky. They pursue the whale in their canoes even out of sight of land, and attack him with a daring that would not disgrace New England fishermen. On one occasion, a canoe was gone five days. The men succeeded in killing the whale, and subsisted on the blubber, chewing some roots which they had with them for want of

---

[15] Cf Kenneth Owens, The Wreck of the *Sv Nikolai* 1985. *jm*

water. After all, they were compelled to abandon the fish. Their tackle consists of a harpoon, the point formerly edged with shell, now usually with copper, very firmly secured to a lie, and attached lightly to a shaft about fifteen feet long, to which also the line is made fast; a seal-skin float is attached by another line, and serves to buoy the whale when struck. The scene of the capture is described by eye-witnesses as very exciting, then canoes being sometimes engaged, the crews yelling and dashing their paddles with frantic eagerness. When taken, the whale, buoyed up with floats, is towed in triumph to the village and cut up. They formerly tried out the oil by placing the blubber, <24> after it had become softened, into boxes, and melting it out with heated stones. The oil is kept in the paunch of the whale, or in seal-skins and bladders, and is used as an article of food as well as for trade. The season commences in March. The Makah were till lately in the habit of purchasing oil from the Nittinat also, and have traded in a single season, it is said, as much as 30,000 gallons. Previous to becoming whalers, the young men go through a species of probation, probably similar to that of the Tamahno-ūs {Tah-manawus}. A portion of them only attain the dignity of whalers, a second class devote themselves to halibut, and a third to salmon and inferior fish, the occupations being kept distinct, at least, in a great measure. The larger class of canoes generally belong to a single individual and he receives a proportionate share of the booty from the crew. The halibut season is from March to May, when the salmon fishery commences. This last is by trolling. Very few of the fall salmon are taken. Cod are obtained at the entrance of the straits, and other kinds of fish are abundant at all seasons, among which is the Kūshkao, apparently a species of perch, of very good quality. Muscles and echini of large size are also [176] abundant. Sea-otter are not obtained at the cape, but the Indians purchase them of the Nittinat, and carried them to Victoria for sale. Formerly they raised a large quantity of potatoes; but since the sickness they have neglected this provision.

The Makah bore the nose as well as the <25> ears, and both men and women wear ornaments in them, generally; in the former, a small triangular bit of shell, in the latter, larger pieces. The men for the most part wear nothing but a blanket; the women, a breech-clout, and blanket of dogs' hair or down, or a cedar bark robe. A few of the men, at the time of the council, had bear skins tied around the throat with the fur out; and they sat on the ground, the skins encircling them and covering the face to the nose, they made a very picturesque appearance. Their hats, when they wear any, are of the conical form common along the coast. Their finest manufactures are the blankets already mentioned. Those of dogs' hair and down are common to other parts of the sound, more particularly those which have least communication with the whites, as homespun articles here, as elsewhere, give place to "store goods" with advancing civilization. The cedar blankets and robes are known almost exclusively to be their own; they are very nicely made, and quite pliable. Their dishes resemble those of the northern Indians, of which many specimens have found their way to the States; long, shallow trays serving to hold the common mess, and smaller square ones for the individual portion.

The Makah before they were broken by sickness carried their war-parties to some distance. They are still on bad terms with the Soke {Sooke} and Psong of Vancouver Island, as well as with their immediate neighbors to the south, the Kwillehūit. They chastised <26> the [Chamakums] Tsemakum of Port Townsend before the Klallam attacked them, and not long since threatened the Klallam also, but the difficulty was arranged by King George, the Klallam chief, giving his sister to the white chief in marriage; a regal settlement of difficulties worthy of European diplomacy.

The occasion of the treaty made with them by Governor Stevens, in January last, the Makah were first brought into official intercourse with the whites. Previous to that time, they had declined to receive papers from the agent, Colonel Simmons, being under apprehensions that they would [177] back the small-pox. By the governor's direction, they, on that occasion, named two subchiefs from each village, from whom he selected an Osett,[16] named Tse-kau-utl, as head chief. This treaty secured to them the point of the peninsula, including the site of the old Spanish fort, on Neeah Bay, and the Watch village on the coast.

The [Clallams] Klallam I consider to be another branch of the Selish, though of a more remote origin than the Niskwalli. Their opposite neighbors of Vancouver Island, the Soke or Tsohke of Soke Inlet, and the Tsong of Songhu {Songhees} or Victoria belong to the same connection. The tribe is still a numerous one though like others of the district, considerably reduced. A few families have removed to, and are permanently settled on, the island. Their proper country lies on the straits between the Okeho River and Point Wilson; but, after the reduction <27> of the Tsemakun, many of them established themselves at Port Townsend. The Klallam were embraced in the same treaty with the Tsemakum and the Skokomish, and a common reservation made for them at the head of Hood Canal. Since the death of S'Hai-ak, or King George, Tsitz-a-mah-han, or Duke of York, has been recognized as the head chief. Their total number is now 926. Their principal villages are Okeho [Hoko], at the mouth of that river; Pishtst, on Klallam Bay; Elwa, at the mouth of a stream so called; Yinnis, at False Dungemess; Stehtlum, at New Dungeness; Kahkwaitl, at Port Discovery; and a recent one at Kahtai, or Port Townshend.

The [Chemakums] Tsemakum are reduced to 90 souls. Their original country embraced Port Townshend, Port Ludlow, and Port Gamble. The tribe probably was never a very large one, but has been noted among all is neighbors for its pugnacity. It has been successively engaged in wars with the Makah, Klallam, Toan-hūch, Snohomis, and Dwamish, in all of which it suffered severely. Their present chief is Elsakweoit. These as before mentioned have, like the Kwillehūit, been classed with the Selish tribes. Singularly enough, while their languages exhibit greater resemblance to each other, notwithstanding their relative position, than do either to their immediate neighbors, the Tsemakum is literally an unknown tongue to the rest; not an individual, it is said, out of the tribe being <28> acquainted with [178] it, a circumstance very unusual among Indians. In their modes of subsistence, habits, &c, they do not differ noticeably from their neighbors.

There remains on these waters what may be termed the Niskwalli nation, which is thus divided, pursuing the geographical order: [no ¶]

1st. Skokomish, of whom the Toanhūch[17] seems to be another name only, said to mean in the Klallam tongue "a portage". Of these, there were formerly several bands, as the Kwūlseet [Quilcene] and others, whose names are preserved in those of different localities. They occupy both sides of Hood Canal above Port Gamble, and number 200 souls. Their chief is now Hol-hol-tin, better known as Jim. As already mentioned, the Skokomish were embraced in the same treaty with their neighbors, the Klallams and Tsemakums. Their language constitutes a distinct one, differing so far from that of the Niskwalli as not to be generally understood. The

---

[16] Ozette, a native village buried by an Orphan Tsunami caused AD 1700 mudslide, called the "American Pompei," was excavated by Dr Richard Daugherty and the Makah Nation. *jm*

[17] Twana is the name for all of the natives of Hood Canal, with Skokomish the densest concentration of river villages with more survivors to provide the name for their new reservation at the river mouth. Their ethnography by William Elmendorf (1960) is the single best description for the Puget Sound region. *jm*

Skwawksin, or Skwawksnamish, who occupy the isthmus between Hood Canal and Case Inlet, in some respects more properly belong to this connection than to the Sound Indians."

2^d. The bands occupying Puget Sound and the inlets opening into it as far down as Point Pully. These all speak the same dialect, the Niskwalli proper, and were all included in treaties made at Shenah-nam, or Medicine Creek, December, 1854, since ratified by the Senate. They number collectively <29> [eight hundred ninety three] 893. A division might be made of these into three subtribes, the first consisting of the S'Hotlemamish of Case Inlet, Sahehwamish of Hamersly Inlet, Sawamish of Totten Inlet, Skwai-aitl of Eld Inlet, Stehtsasamish of Budd Inlet, and Nūsehtsatl of South Bay or Henderson Inlet; the second consisting of the Skwalliahmish or Niskwalli, including the Segwalitsū, Steilakūmahmish, and other small bands; and the third of the Puyallupahmish, T'Kawkwamish, and S'Homamish of the Puyallup River and Vashon Island.[18] The first are properly salt water Indians; the second are for the most part like the Staktamish, or Upper Tsihalis, equestrian in their habits, and the last are River and Sound {canoe} Indians.

Three reservations were assigned to these bands as permanent homes, each consisting of about two section of land; one being the small [Squaxin] island at the mouth of Hammersly Inlet or Skūkim Bay, another upon the sound near Niskwalli, and a third upon Commencement Bay {Tacoma Puyallup}. These are all upon [179] the water, and are suitable for fishing stations. As, however, none of them afford pasture land, it will be desirable that when negotiations are concluded with the Upper Tsihalis some provision be made of a tract suitable for animals, to which all those possessing them can resort in common. By the treaty Kwi-e-mihl and Sno-ho-dum-sit were designated as head chiefs of <30> the bands embraced within its provisions.

Below these is the division of which the Dwamish and Sūkwamish {Suquamish} are the principal bands, occupying Elliot Bay, Bainbridge Island, and a portion of the peninsula between Hood Canal and Admiralty Inlet. Their head chief is Se-āā-thl, or, as it is usually pronounced Seattle, from whom the town on Elliott Bay has been named. In this connection are also the Samamish, Skopahmish, Sk'tehlmish, St'kamish and other small bands lying upon he lakes and branches of Dwamish River, who are claimed by the others as part of their tribe, but have in reality very little connection with them. The aggregate number of the whole was by census 807, which probably falls a little short of the truth. They differ but slightly from the Niskwalli in language. These tribes were included with all the others of the eastern shore and the islands in the treaty of Mikleteoh {Mukilteo} or Point Elliott. A reserve of two sections was retained for them at Port Madison.

3^d. The Snohomish, with whom are included the [Snoqualmoo] Snokwalmū, Skiwhamish, Sk'tah-le-jum, [Quehtlmamish] ~ Kwehtl-ma-mish, and Stolutsawhamish, living on the Snohomish and [Stoluchwhamish] Stolutswhamish Rivers. The Snohomish tribe itself occupies only the country at its mouth and the lower end of Whidbey Island; the upper part of the river belonging to the Snokwalmū, &c. They number 441 souls, and the other bands, collectively, <31> 556. At the time of the treaty they were all placed under Patkanam, the chief of the latter. It is observable that though the connection between them is most intimate, the Snohomish assimilate in dialect to the next tribe, the Skagit, while the Snokwalmū speak the Niskwalli in its purity. In the treaty of Point Elliot, the reservation for this division was fixed at two sections on a small creek emptying into the bay formed by the mouth of the Snohomish

---

[18] These tribal names, in Gibb's spelling, appear on the US treaties and are updated in Wayne Suttles, *Northwest Coast* 1990 #7: 487, See Jay Miller, *Minter Bay* 2015. *jm*

River. A central reservation of one township, to include the former, intended for the general agency of the Puget Sound district, and as an ultimate home for [180] all the tribes, was contemplated at the same place. The small bay known as Tulalip Bay upon which is now a saw mill, affords an excellent site for this purpose, and the land in the neighborhood, being easily cleared and of good quality, would enable the Indians in a great measure to subsist themselves. The Snokwalmū and other upper bands of this division possess a few horses, and are much intermarried with the Yakama Indians, here indiscriminately called Klikatat. They hunt as well as fish; their neighborhood to the mountains and more active and energetic character giving them a superiority in this respect. One of the two principal trails across the Cascade mountains, that by way of the main Yakama, passes through their country; the Nahchess trail leading from White River.

4th. The Skagits, including the <32> Kikialu, Nūkwatsamish, Tow-ah-ha, Smali-hu, Sakumehu, Miskaiwhu, Miseekwigweelis, Swinamish, and Skwonamish, occupy the remaining country between the Snohomish and Bellingham Bay, with the northern part of Whidbey Island and Perry Island. With them a different dialect prevails, though not so distinct but what they can be understood by those already mentioned. They altogether amount to 1,475, and have been assigned Goliah as head chief. This division have no horses but are altogether canoe Indians. With the exception of the islands and the immediate shore of the main, their country is altogether unexplored. They formerly had some communication with the Indians beyond the mountains; but it is supposed to have been discontinued in consequences of obstruction to their trails. The Skagit reservation, as agreed upon in the treaty, was the peninsula forming the southeastern extremity of Perry Island.

5th. The Samish, Lummi, [Nooksahk] ~ Nūksahk, living around Bellingham Bay and the Lummi River. The two former on salt water, the last exclusively river Indians, who as yet have had very little connection with the whites. Collectively, these might be called the Nūh-lum-mi. Tsow-its-hūt was recognized as their common chief by the treaty, and a reservation made for them on an island at the forks of the river. Altogether they number 680. The languages of the <33> Lummi, at the mouth of the river, and of the Nūksahk, a few miles higher up, differ so much as to be almost unintelligible to one another. The latter seems to approach more nearly to that of the Frazer [181] River, and, in fact, their principal intercourse is with Fort Langley and the Indians in that direction. The above tribes were also treated with at Point Elliott. It is believed that there is no other permanently located on the main shore south of the boundary line; but some of the Vancouver Island Indians cross over in the fishing season. The name of tribes living to the north of the Niskwalli, cited by Mr Hale on the authority of a Canadian, it may be mentioned are recognizable in those of Puyallup, [Suquamish] ~ Sukwamish, Skagit, and [Cowitchin] ~ Kowitain or [Kawitshen] ~ Kawitshaen.

With these end the Niskwalli nation. The enumeration here given may be relied on as substantially correct. It was taken by Colonel Simmons while distributing presents, and when almost all the Indians were got in. The result is, for the Niskwalli connection, a total of 5,242; for the total population of the Sound and Straits of Fuca, 6,258. Adding to this the most recent enumeration, or estimate, of the coast and Columbia River tribes, the Indian population of the district may be assumed at 8,687.

This total, as well as the details, differs considerably from the estimate made in January, 1854, and, indeed, from the census taken in the winter of 1854-55, <34> while the treaties were progressing. It seems to be pretty certain that the lower tribes, instead of diminishing, are on the increase. This is to be attributed in some measure to their being at peace among themselves and protected by the settlements from northern invasion, and to the fact that no epidemic diseases have recently attacked them. As regards the apparent proportion between men and women, no deduction can be drawn, for the reason that the women are counted with the tribes to which their husbands belong. <35>

POPULATION

In my report to Captain McClellan, I made an attempt to compare all the estimates of the Indian population of the Territory which was within my reach. Since then, an actual count or census of most of the tribes in this part of the T territory has been twice attempted, once by myself and once by Colonel Simmons. In considering the different statements which have been made from time to time, I am well satisfied that none of them can be taken as the basis of any accurate calculations respecting the ratio of increase or diminution, and I am further inclined to the opinion that the aggregate former population, taking one period with another, has never been very much greater than within our knowledge of it. In arriving at [182] any conclusion, it is necessary to regard no merely the actual facts of increase or mortality known to us, but the capacity of the country to furnish subsistence, the modes of obtaining it followed by the Indians, their general character and habits, their fecundity, their wars, and various other circumstances directly or indirectly bearing upon life. That the estimates, even of residents, cannot be relied upon with confidence, has been made sufficiently evident by the discrepancies in our different attempts[,] at an actual enumeration[,] and <36> those of travelers, like Lewis and Clark, are likely to have been still wider from the fact. Still, as no other data exist upon which to found any pinion, we are driven to assume these for the purpose of discussion.

The population of the Columbia, below the Cascades, was very probably at its height early in the present century. None of the early writers mention the indications of previous mortality as remarkable in extent; and this negative evidence is almost conclusive when taken in connection with their subsequent multiplication between 1820 and 1830. Lewis and Clarke, in 1806, estimated the total number at about 8,500, which is within the bounds of probability. They in fact seem to have rather underestimated the four lower bands of Tsinūk, whom they place at 1.100 souls, whereas Mr Irving, on the authority of the fur-traders, but a few years later, gives their number of warriors along at 554, a force requiring a much larger total. The same period may also be assumed as the date of greatest prosperity of the tribes on the coast and on the Kowlitz and the Tsihalis rivers. The estimate of the former, founded on Indian authority and aided by the reported number of houses, gives a total of 4,300, not a excessive one, if the Makah are included, as seem to be the case. Of the Kowlitz and Upper Tsihalis, who are not mentioned by them, 4,000 may be admitted as the extreme. <37> [no ¶]

According to Vancouver, it would appear that the Sound tribes had suffered from some great calamity previous to his visit in the spring of 1792. In all those waters from Port Discovery to head of the sound, during a minute survey, he did not met with over 1,200 Indians, at the least half of these must have belonged to the Skagit and Snohomish. The season of the year was too early for them to have left the water in search of roots and [183] berries; and those that he saw manifested no alarm at his presence, which would induce the idea that other had fled in consequence of his approach. Beside the quantity of bones which he met with in different places, and more particularly the neglect which they were treated, indicated the recent presence of some pestilence.

As nearly corresponding with the time when Lewis and Clarke supposed the small-pox to have visited the Dalles, it is not improbably that his disease had prevailed here also, though Vancouver does not speak of its marks upon the survivors as being very recent. War could not have been the cause of such widespread effects, as their hostilities never resulted in such bloodshed within a short time, though acting as a steady check on population. After Vancouver's visit, there must have been a very considerable increase {in deaths}, which according to Indian account, has been since, at two or <38> three different times affected by epidemic diseases. [no ¶]

In the district referred to, there are at this time over 5,000 Indians; and while the tribes lower down the sound are increasing, as appears by the number of children, others in more intimate connections with the whites have greatly fallen off, and some are nearly extinct. It would seem, therefore, as if constant fluctuations from natural causes, not arising out of the settlement of the country, had existed among them from an early time, and the inference would be that their total number had never greatly exceeded that which they have reached since the discovery. Too great stress is not to be laid upon the assertions of the Indians themselves that they were once a great many, for their ideas of number are vague at the best, and the recollections of any former mortality would probably be exaggerated, while the after-increase would be disregarded. I should consider a population of 8,000 for the tribes within the Straits of Fuca as the utmost which they have ever reached. Mr Finlayson, of the Hudson Bay Company, made a count of the Klallam in 1845, and ascertained their number to be 1,760. Taking this as their maximum at any once time, the total number of Indians in this Territory, west of the Cascade mountains, dur <39> ing their most flourishing epoch, and on the supposition that the condition existed simultaneously to all of them, would amount to 26,800, or about three times their present number.

This seems to me as great a body as the country could have supported according to their modes of life, and certainly is in itself formid [184] able. It is most probable however, that the whole were never at once in the same condition of prosperity, but that fluctuations occurred among different tribes at various times.

Mr Hale, to whose work I have only recently had access, does not tough upon the Sound tribes, with the exception of the Niskwalli (Skwale); and the estimates furnished by Captain Wilkes in the same year (1841), although covering a portion of the deficiency, are yet very incomplete, and do not coincide with the others to those mentioned by both.

The census of a portion of the Sound tribes, made by Dr Tolmie in 1844, and published in the former report, is, though undoubtedly more accurate than the above so far as it goes, but a very partial one. I have endeavored to combine all these, on the assumption that no great changes had taken place in that interval, but without being able to arrive at <40> any valuable result as regards details. It seems probable, however, that the total population of the western district at that time reached 15,000, and that the tribes most exempt from diminution since have been those of the eastern shore of the sound below the Puyallup river. [no ¶]

The more recent estimates of General Lane, in 1849, I have passed over as being mere estimates, and not entirely complete. They cannot aid in any way in drawing accurate conclusions. [no ¶]

On one point connected with the subject of population, a fact of ethnological importance may be referred to, viz, the very small number of indigenous half-breeds. Notwithstanding the length of time that the fur companies have occupied the country, and the almost universal connection of its employees with naïve women on permanent terms, the number of metifs [French > *metis* = mixed] is hardly appreciable.

TRIBAL ORGANIZATION AND GOVERNMENT

No division of tribes into clans is observable, nor any organization similar to the eastern tribes, neither have the Indians of the territory emblematical distinction resembling the totem. Among some of the northern tribes, as I am assured by Mr John Work, of the Hudson Bay Company's service, these exist. As regards the chiefdom, it is theoretically hereditary but if on the death of a chief the eldest son is objectionable from stupidity or bad rep <41> utation, it is said that the tribe sometimes set him aside for the [185] next. If a chief's sons are too young to govern, his brother or next relative succeeds him and continue chief till his death, when the office reverts to the son of the elder. It is not unusual to find men living as chiefs over the mother's tribe instead of the father's. This is the case with Seahtl among the Dwamish. The reason seems to be that on the death of the father [,] the children, if young, are often carried back by the mother to her own people and brought up among them. It des not appear that the title in such cases descends in the female line. With the exception of a very few men of whom reputation for courage or sagacity is considerable, and whose influence in consequence extended over a tribe, their nominal chiefs have no control beyond their own petty bands, nor is it potent even then. Wealth gives a certain power among them, and influence is purchased by its lavish distribution. There is no class of braves, or warriors, and no distinction between war and peach chiefs. The decision of all questions of moment depends upon the will of the majority interested, but there is no compulsion upon the minority. To this fact, as will elsewhere be noticed, seems to be due in some degree, the splitting up and subdivision of tribes, in fact, society is perfectly democratic, because in the absence of government or authority, it cannot <42> be otherwise. There is no priesthood aside from the tamahnous men or doctors, who have by virtue of the office an important part to play as leading the ceremonial incantation which accompany proceedings of general interest.

In their councils, every one has the right of speaking, and assent or dissent is ascertain by exclamation or silence. Some of them are effective orators, though in general their eloquence is of a very noisy and vociferous kind.

The women are present at, and join in, these talks, speaking in a low tone, their words being repeated aloud by a reporter. On occasions of less ceremony, they sometimes address the audience without any intervention, and give their admonitions with a freedom of tongue highly edifying. In a few instances, matrons of superior character, "strong minded women" have obtained an influence similar to that of chiefs. Sally, the widow of Tsenahmus, a Tsinūk chief, well known on the Lower Columbia, enjoys great authority among the Indians and general immunity from the whites. The queen, an old lady of the Tsihalis, who patronized Captain Wilkes's party in 1841, yet rules her neighbor [186] hood with undisputed sway, and on occasion of the late council "put in her oar" with considerable effect against a removal. After the talks, time is <43> generally taken by the assembly to consider the matter in hand before a final action is decided. The feasts at which their principal consultations generally take place will be mentioned hereafter. They are given by some leading chief or rich man, who takes the office upon himself with a view of bringing himself conspicuously before the public. [centered .]

Property

As far as I can gather the views of the Sound tribes, they recognize no individual right to land except actual occupancy. This seems to be respected to this extent, that if a man has cleared a spot of land for cultivation, he can hold it on the return of the season for planting from year to year, as long as he sees fit. So in their villages, the site of a house pertains to the individual a long as he leaves any vestige or evidence of a building on it. Among the Tsinūk and Lower Tsihalis, the right may have been carried somewhat further, but unsettled land away from their usual haunts are but little regarded. Tribes are, however, somewhat tenacious of territorial right, and well understood their respective limits; but this seems to be merely as regards their title, and they never, it is believed, exclude from them other friendly tribes. It would appear also that these lands are considered to survive to the last remnant of a tribe, after its existence as such has in fact cease. There seems to be, in some instances, <44> a vague claim by chiefs to territorial sovereignty, as for example among the Makah, where any wrecked property floats ashore the proprietor claims from the finder a portion of it, and it is said payment is exacted for the use of particular pieces of ground. Cases have been mentioned of a claim by a chief to ownership of the shore country occupied by his tribe; but these do not seem to have any foundation in acknowledged right, or to be actually maintained. Sneetlum, the former chief of the Skagit, is said to have made such pretensions. As regards the fisheries, they are held in common, and no tribe pretends to claim from another, or from individuals, seigniorage for the right of taking. In fact, such a claim would be inconvenient to all parties, as the Indians move about, on the sound particularly, from one to another locality, according to the season. Nor do they have disputes as to [187] their hunting grounds. Land and sea appear to be open to all with whom they are not at war. Their local attachments are very strong, as might be inferred with regard to a race having fixed abodes, and they part from their favorite ground and burial place with the utmost reluctance. [no ¶]

As regards the right of property in houses or goods, their ideas are naturally clearer. The maker of anything is its necessary owner until he voluntarily parts with its possession. So also the captor of fish or game, the one who digs roots or raises vegetable; but it <45> is not probably that they have ever speculated upon the origin of this right nor would their minds comprehend any abstract reasoning upon the subject. They have customs, however, in some respects peculiar to themselves. Not only do the men own property distinct from their wives, but (which is a consequence following on polygamy) their wives own each her private effects, separate from their husband as well as from the others.

He has his own blankets, she her mats and baskets and generally speaking her earnings belong to here, except those arising from prostitution, which are her husbands. On the decease of a man, his property is immediately taken possession of by his relatives, and what is not destroyed or displayed at this grave is divided among them, his sons if grown up taking a part; his wives get nothing whatever, nor young children, but unless appropriated by the men, return to their own people, taking the later with them. Another custom in respect to property is that the seller of a horse, slave, or woman guarantees life and safety for a time. If they escape or die within perhaps a month or two, the purchaser can demand back the price. As a general thing, they do not dispose of property before death. Instances happen of course when they express the wish that individ <46> uals should have particular articles, but is not always regarded. Judge

Ford informed me that one day the Indians announced to him the death of a man near by.[19] The next they told him that he was alive again, and that he said he had not disposed of his horses to suit him, and had come back for that purpose, that he had not done so and was going to die again, which he accordingly did during the day, and that time in earnest. This sort of *coma* preceding death, I should be remarked in explanation, seems to be not uncommon. [188]

Slavery

Slavery is thoroughly interwoven with the social polity of the Indians of the coast section of Oregon and Washington Territory. East of the Cascades, though it exists, it is not so common; the equestrian habits of the tribes living there probably rendering it less profitable or convenient that among the more settled inhabitants of the coast. Southward it ceases, so far as my observation has gone, with the Siskiou mountains, which divide Oregon from California. Many of the slaves held here are, however, brought from California, where they were taken by the warlike and predatory Indians of the plains, and sold to the [Calapooyas] Kallapūia and [Chinooks] Tsinūk. The system probably originated in wars, all prisoners becoming slaves as a <47> matter of course, though as usual they have some fanciful modes of accounting for it. Thus some of the Sound Indians told Colonel Simmons that the first was made on the occasion of a great feast, when one of the guests criticized the cooking of the fish. The others, disgusted at his ill-breeding, debated upon his punishment. Some were for killing him; but it was finally decided to make him a slave, that he might always serve his insulted host, which accordingly was done. However this may be, the occasions of making them have since greatly multiplied. Thus, if one Indian was wronged another, and failed to make compensation, or if a debtor is insolent, he may be taken as a slave. Their mode or procedure is characterized by their wonted deliberation. The plaintiff comes with a party to demand satisfaction, and hold out to the other the option of payment or servitude. If no satisfaction is given he must submit unless he is strong enough to do battle. And this slavery is final degradation. This rule of once a slave always a slave extends so far that if the debtor should have given up some relative in his power, and subsequently redeems him, he becomes his slave in turn. If a man purchase his father or mother, they become his slaves, and are treated as such. The children of slaves by <48> others are slaves likewise. And the children of a man by his own slaves are but half free; they do not rank as *seahb-viri*.[20] Even if one purchases his own freedom, he is yet looked upon as an inferior. A distinction is to be made as regards women, that whereas in one sense they are always slaves or property, yet when a man sells away his sister or daughter, she, if born of free parents, becomes the wife of the creditor or purchaser, [189] and as such does not follow the rule of distribution, but on the death of her husband returns to her tribe or family. The number of persons thus held upon the Sound is less than farther north, but probably amounts to one-tenth of the population. Many of them belong to distant tribes, and other belonging to these are held elsewhere. The system has been the cause of constant disturbance among themselves, as well as of wars with heir neighbors; for not only were the latter often made for the purpose of obtaining them, but the occasional escape or stealing of slaves created difficulty and led to retaliation. For this reason, it was thought expedient in the treaties with the Sound tribes to stipulate its abolition.

---

[19] Sidney Ford was a Chehalis pioneer; John Slocum of Squaxin revived to found the Indian Shaker Church with his wife Mary; Chief Atwin Stockum of Cowlitz also revived. *jm*

[20] Lushootseed *s'iab* = honored, noble < from *iab* = treasured + Latin *vir(i)* = man (men). *jm*

The life of a slave was entirely at the disposal of his master or mistress, and it <49> was formerly customary among most of the tribes to kill part at least on the death of the owners.

At [Chinook] Tsinūk, as lately as 1850, an attempt was made to starve a little slave girl to death, who had been given to a child in the family, previously deceased, and her life was only saved by the intervention of the citizens, who offered to pay her price, representing that it would be as good to destroy the value in merchandize, and adding the weight of a threat in case of refusal. [no ¶]

Dr Tolmie informs me that the course of the slave trade has always been from south to north; the only exception in his knowledge being that the Kowlitz Indians, formerly a very strong tribe, used to make forays on the Sound and carry their prisoners to the Columbia river.

Retaliation

The law of life for life is fully recognized, subject, however, to compromise on payment of damages. The procedure is about as follows: If one Indian has taken another's life, the revenge is not immediate; it is talked over for some time, perhaps months, during which any overture for settlement can be made. If nothing is offered, the relatives of the deceased, with a sufficient party of their friends, proceed to the murderer and make a demand on him for satisfaction. If he or his friends can make up a sufficient amount of goods to appease the next of <50> kin, the affair is settled, the other friends being paid something for their trouble in the matter, and some return is then usually made by them in token that peace is restored. If the murderer cannot himself make a suitable recompense, or his friends will not [190] assist him, they then take his life, and the affair stops, no hostility being provoked anew by the act. The amount to be paid as blood-money depends upon the importance of the person killed; women being of less value than men. Ten blankets will generally pay for a common person. Occasionally, the individual sought for, instead of compromising, makes fight, especially if a chief or a man of influence, in which case a *quasi* war arises between the two tribes or factions. It generally terminates without much bloodshed, and leads to an amicable arrangement. This system of retaliation, which is carried out in every matter, and takes the place of civil process for debt, as well as actions for torts or criminal prosecutions, has worked much mischief among the Indians, and been one source of slavery, as well as the breaking up of the tribes. The principal cause arises in the event of death under the hands of the doctor, as he always receives his fee in advance, and on the understanding that he is to cure his patient. So, if not successful in his conjurations, he is <51> [C]alled upon to refund, perhaps with damages, or in case of failure, is set upon and killed in turn. Should the patient, however, on his death-bed, attribute his fate to the malignant tamahno-ūs of the practitioner, his friends do not trouble themselves with any preliminaries, but dispatch him at sight. [centered]

Wars

Until the influence of the white came to be sensibly felt, and their numbers thinned by disease, a state of petty warfare prevailed between many of the different tribes. Even now among those who have been less intimate in their new relations, some such condition of things exists, and jealousy of each other is universal. It has been a matter of great amusement among travelers to be told by every successive band that just beyond them the Indians were very bad; any worse than the last, however, never being reached, but like an *ignis fatuus* [ME "fools fire", will o' the wisp], keeping a little ahead. Their wars among themselves, it is probably, were never very blood. Ross Cox gives a very graphic account of the Tsinūk method, which was probably not far from correct. Having once determined on hostilities, they give notice to the enemy of the day on which they intend to make the attack, and having previously engaged as auxiliaries a number of young men whom they pay for that <52> purpose, they embark in canoes for the scene of the action. Several of [191] their women accompany them on their expeditions, and assist in working the canoes. On arriving at the enemy's village, they enter into a parley, and endeavor by negation to terminate the quarrel amicably. Sometimes a third party, who preserves a strict neutrality, undertakes the office of mediator, but should their efforts fail in procuring redress, they immediately prepare for action.

Should the day be far advanced, the combat is deferred by mutual consent till the following morning, and they pass the night intervening in frightful yells and making use of abusive and insulting language to each other. They generally fight from their canoes, which they take care to incline to one side presenting the higher flank to the enemy; and in this position with their bodies quite bent the battle commences. Owing to the curve of the canoes, and their impenetrable armor, it is seldom bloody; and as soon as one or two men fall, the party to whom they belong acknowledges themselves vanquished and the combat ceases. If the assailants be unsuccessful, they return without redress; but if conquerors, they receive various presents from the vanquished party in addition to their original demand. The women and children are always sent away before the en <53> gagement commences. [no ¶]

The same description will apply to most of the battles on the Sound, except where northern tribes are concerned, who are more warlike and ferocious. Most of those which have been witnessed by early settlers consisted chiefly in howling at night and firing their guns, beyond bullet range, in the day; their faces are painted in accordance. But these are some instances of more determined conduct. The now almost extinct tribe of Tsemakum, living on Port Townshend, were, by the common report, very troublesome neighbors, and on bad terms with all. They were first broken by the Makah, who partake of the superior courage of their race. They are said also to have had a great fight with the Snohomish many years ago, and some seven years since were attacked and their fort destroyed by the Sukwamish, under Seahtl. In these affrays, as well as in a fight between the Klallam and Snohomish, a number of lives were lost. But the real method of warfare among them was by murder, overpowering individuals by numbers, or killing them by stealth and unawares. In this way, their wars, so to call them, were kept up. [192]

The armor mentioned by Cox consisted of an elk skin shirt, remarkably thick, doubled, and thrown over the shoulders, with holes for the arms. It descends to the ankles and from the thickness of the leather is perfectly arrow proof. The head <54> is covered with a species of helmet made of cedarbark, bear grass, and leather, and is also impenetrable by arrows. The neck, therefore, is the only vital part of the body exposed to danger in the action. In addition to the above they have another kind of armor, which they occasionally wear in place of the leathern shirt. It is a species of corset formed of thin slips of hardwood, ingeniously lace together by bear grass and is much lighter and more pliable than the former; but it does not cover so much of the body. Neither is any longer used in this Territory.[21] [no ¶]

---

[21] {* written along left margin, inserted here: The above was written before the breaking out of the existing [Treaty] war, in which it is unnecessary to say that they have displayed a hardihood and pertinacity for which credit was never given them.} *jm*

The Sound Indians, but more particularly those on the Straits of Fuca, sometimes fortify their dwelling by stockades made of heavy puncheons twelve or fifteen feet high, set in the ground, and strengthened by large posts and cross pieces.[22] These were loop holed, and calculate very well to serve even against muskets. [no ¶]

Bow and arrow, and a heavy club carved at the end, were their original weapons. They have gone almost entirely out of use, not being often employed even for game except among the Makah, who still adhere to them. The arrows are pointed with hard wood or bone, and resemble in every respect the figures in the third volume of Mr Schoolcrafts's work. They are in no respect equal in workmanship to those of the interior or the coast of Cali <55> fornia. [no ¶]

None of the western tribes within my observation have pursued the practice of scalping the slain nor do they wear scalp-locks. The Indians on the Straits of Fuca and thence northward decapitate their enemies, as was noticed by Vancouver. While surveying Port Townsend, he saw on one of the low point of Craven Peninsula, "two upright poles set in the ground, about fifteen feet high, and rudely carved. On the top of each was stuck a human head, recently planted there. The hair and flesh were nearly perfect and the head appeared to carry evidence of fury or revenge, as in driving the stakes through the throat to the cranium, the sagittae, with [193] part of the scalp, were borne on their points some inches above the rest of the skull. Between the stakes a fire had been made, and near it some calcined bones were observed, but none of these appearances enabled us to satisfy ourselves concerning the manner in which the bodies had been disposed of." No suspicion of cannibalism exists against any of these tribes.

It is most probably that the fire had been the usual cooking-fire of Indians, and that the heads were those of enemies slain by the Tsemakum, and set up in this manner in defiance on leaving their camp. It is possible that they may have burned the bodies; but such a practice has not been noticed and certainly never was common among them. <56>

FOOD

The principal food of the Indians on the west side of the Cascades may be briefly set down as fish, roots, and berries. Game furnished to but few of them any considerable item. There are mountain-sheep or, more properly goats, in the higher parts of the range: but they probably never constituted any important article of food, their wool being the principal object of their capture. Elk and deer are hunted to a certain extent, chiefly by the bands nearest the mountains; and the Snokwalm, in fact, kill more of the later on the island than do the Sound Indians themselves. Lewis and Clarke speak of game as having rather furnished an article of luxury than of support to the Tsinūk, though abundant in their country. A hunter is, in fact, looked upon with respect by almost every tribe in the district. [no ¶]

The roots used are numerous; but the wappatū, or sagitaria, and the kamas are the principal. These are found in great quantities, the former in ponds, the later in the prairies, particularly such as are wet; and they were formerly a great article of trade with the interior. Besides these, the roots of the [balsam] sunflower and fern are largely used, and a smaller white roots of rather insipid taste. From the fern, they make a species of flour which is baked into bread. The kamas season is in the latter par of May and June, and then as well as in the fall when sunflower is dug, the prairies are dotted over with <57> squaws, each armed with a sharp stake and a basket, busily engaged in digging them. At these times, camps are generally found near the

---

[22] See Jay Miller, First Nations Forts, Refuges, and War Lords around the Salish Sea 2011. *jm*

skirts of timber which border the open lands for the convenience of [194] gathering and preserving. The kamas is baked in the ground, a hole being firs dug and heated with stones, and the root covered over with twigs and earth. There are numerous other roots and plants use in their fresh state. [no ¶]

Of the berries, such as the strawberry, salmon-berry, raspberry, and others which are not suitable for drying, are consumed at once; but the huckleberry, of which there are several kinds, sallal, &c, are dried and stored for winter's use. The salmon-berry, a large and somewhat coarse species of raspberry, is abundant in the river bottoms, and grows to about an inch in length. There are two varieties, the yellow and purple. It obtains its name from its ripening about the same time with the height of the salmon season on the Columbia, and its association with that fish in Indian superstition. Acorns in those section of the country where they oak is found are gathered and stored for winter. But the great staple of food through a vast portion of the country west of the Rocky mountains, as well in the interior as on the coast, is the salmon, which frequents in extraordinary quantities almost every river from the Sacramento northward, and pursues his way to the very base of the Rocky mountains. <58> Of this there are several kinds, no les than six, it is supposed, entering the Columbia alone at the different period of the year, and others being found in other localities. The salmon, which enter that river in the spring and are the only once prized as food by the whites, do not seek either the small river s of the coast or the lower tributaries near its mouth for the purpose of spawning, but push directly up the principal branches, such as the Willamette, the Snake, &c, to the colder waters of the mountains. In this they are assisted by the simultaneous occurrence of the freshets which enable them to overcome the obstructions with greater ease. In some of the forks of the Columbia they penetrate to the main chain of the Rocky mountains; but in others, as the Snake, they are stopped by impassable barriers. Later in the season inferior kinds are abundant, and these also succeed in forcing their way up the large branches, but in addition, leave detachments in every creek that enters the coast, every brook which unites with the rivers, ad even in the slough formed by rain in the prairies. It is at this season that the coast Indians lay up their winter supplies; for those late species possessing little fat are the easiest dried for keeping. The Indians of the [195] interior preserve the former kinds also, which after a stay in the fresh water have lost their superfluous oil, and these are [∨ actually] often actually <59> traded to those Indians at the mouth of the river or on the Sound. The Dalles was formerly a great depot for this commerce. It seems that the spring salmon ascend only those river s which take their rise in snow or which are subject to spring freshets. Thus they are found in the Sacramento, the Klamath, the Columbia, and in the Kwinaiutl, where there is a variety considered the finest [blueback sockeye] on the coast. In the bays however, they do not enter, at least in any numbers; and in Puget Sound, though taken in some of the streams rising in the Cascades, they are by no means abundant nor so large as in the Columbia. The other kinds are, however, found in great quantity. [no ¶]

The spring salmon are taken on the river s with the seine; at the rapids and in the small streams either with the scoop-net or with a gig. The latter is usually forked, the points or barb attached loosely by a thong so as to give play to the fish. On some of the rivers where the depth permits, weirs are built to stop their ascent.

The fish are split very thin, the backbone being taken out and then a slice on each side, and all parts even t the heads are preserved. No salt is use, nor are they properly smoked; but a small fire is kept beneath the poles on which they hang, to hasten their drying. The quantity put up at some of the principal fishing grounds was <60> formerly immense, and even now is very considerable.

Besides salmon, sturgeon is taken in the Columbia, and a variety of other fish, though the two former only are staples of food. In the Straits of Fuca and part of the Sound, halibut is found; rock-cod, and several other species are abundant everywhere. The true cod is sometimes taken within the Sound, but mostly without the headlands. Off the Strait of Fuca, about fifteen miles are banks upon which the Makah are in the habit of fishing for these and halibut. What salmon are taken by this tribe are chiefly got by trolling. Among the Klallam and some others, the flesh of the dog-fish is boiled, and when dried, pounded to the consistency of four.

Shell-fish in great variety exist I the bays and on the coast, and many of these are dried for winter stores. Seals are also occasionally captured and regarded as a great luxury; but a yet greater prize is the whale. The [196] Makah alone of all these tribes venture to kill it in whaling style. The Kwillehūit take it by means of harpoons buoyed with seal-skins, which they leave to mark its course until it dies, and the more southern Indians content themselves with the animal when it drifts ashore dead, as occasionally happens. The blubber is cut up and preserved by partially smoking, or the oil dried out and saved in the paunches of animals. <61> [no ¶]

As the salmon form the most important staple of subsistence, so with them are connected the greatest number of superstitions. These have, with many tribes, in a measure died away, but till of late years were rigorously maintained. Messrs. Lewis and Clark, mentioning the capture of the first salmon at the Dalles, in 1807, an occasion of great rejoicing as a harbinger of the school, state that "in order to hasten their arrival, the Indians, according to custom, dressed the fish and cut it into small pieces, one of which was given to each child in the village." At the mouth of the Columbia, the first salmon taken could only be eaten by the medicine-men. The next was eaten by the inhabitants of the lodge. The taking of the "first fish of the season" was, in fact, everywhere the occasion of a feast. The salmon dance was performed, and the anticipation of plenty lightened the hearts of all. The earlier fish could not be obtained at any price by a white man, unless they were first cooked lest he should open them with a knife instead of a stone, or cut them crossways. The heart was always roasted and eaten, for fear a dog should eat it, when no more salmon would be taken. Restrictions upon women during menstruation and pregnancy were stringent, and there were numerous other details observed, such as eating particular parts with the rising and <with the 62> falling tide, consuming the fish before sundown, &c. On the ripening of salmon-berry, however, these rules were abated, the incoming of the schools being by that time rendered certain. The feasts have of late been discontinued, and the salmon dance neglected. In all these respects, the Niskwalli had the same observances as the Tsinūk. [no ¶]

To the above is to be added, as a limited resource, the potato, which is more or less cultivated by all. The estimate formed by Colonel Simmons, in 1854, of the quantity raised by all the Sound tribes was somewhat over 11,00 bushels of potatoes; no proportion, however, existing among the various tribes of the amount to the population. [197] [no ¶]

With all these sources of subsistence, the greater part of which is afforded spontaneously by the land or water, nothing but indolence or want of thrift could lead to want among the population even greater than we have reason to believe at any time inhabited this district. But they were at particular seasons, undoubtedly straightened for food, and much more formerly than now when they obtain assistance from settlers in compensation for service. No instance of cannibalism has ever occurred to the knowledge of the whites. [no ¶]

To the necessity of seeking the different article of food at different times is to attributed chiefly the constant locomotion of these tribes. not only do they at one time frequent the prairies or marshes for roots, at <63> another the forests for berries, and again the sounds and river s for fish, but they have particular points at which they seek the last at various seasons; and although they have their permanent villages where their winter residence chiefly is, and their potato grounds, they are seldom to be found all gathered there together except on special occasions.

The fur-trade

This may be said to be extinct in the western part of the Territory. The Hudson Bay Company continue to purchase the few skins brought to them, but they make no account of the trade. Beaver are again abundant on all the streams because no longer sought for. Black bear, land-otter, muskrat, mink, and a few others exist, but are only occasionally brought in for sale.

[SOCIETY
MARRIAGE AND THE DOMESTIC RELATIONS]

It is not unusual to find on the small prairies human figures rudely cared upon trees. These I have understood to have been cut by young men who were in want of wives, as a sort of practical intimation that they were in the market as purchasers. Generally speaking, these Indians seek their wives among other tribes than their own – whether from motives of policy or an indistinct idea of physiological propriety, <64> it is difficult to say; more probably the former. It seems to be a matter of pride, in fact, to unite the blood of several different ones in their own persons. The expression, "I am half Snokwalmū, half Klikitat", or some similar one, is of everyday utterance. With the chiefs, this is almost always the case. [198]

Domestic affection cannot be considered strong among these races. The ties between parent and child, husband and wife, seem little closer than between more distant relatives, or even others of the same tribe. Indeed, the term "*naika tilicum*",[23] my relation, or one of my people, is more often in their mouths than any denoting nearer kin. Mothers, it is true, show a certain degree of affection toward their children; but even this is subject to exceptions, or rather is itself an exception, as might be expected in such a general state of profligacy. Men have a certain pride of offspring, but it is rather as an evidence of virility on their own part than arising from parental care. As an evidence of this condition of things, the occurrence of infanticide, now less common than of old, is a sufficient proof. Grandparents [grandparents and grandchildren use the same terms for each other] seem to have a greater attachment to their descendants than do the immediate progenitors. On the part of the children, the affection is still less. [As an evidence of this condition of things, the occurrence of infanticide, now less common than of old, is a sufficient proof. Grandparents [grandparents and grandchildren use the same terms for each other] seem to have a greater attachment to their descendants than do the immediate progenitors.] Between husband and wife there is probably as little. A strong sensual attachment undoubtedly often <65> exists, which leads to marriage, as instance are not rare of young women destroying themselves on the death of a lover; but where the idea of chastity I so entirely wanting in both sexes, his cannot deserve the name of love or it is at best a temporary duration. A young man, desirous of obtaining a wife, usually cohabits with her for a time before purchasing her, during which he is gathering together the necessary amount of property to be paid, or perhaps the courtship commences in this way – the girl wishing a husband, and taking a straight forward mode of attracting one. The condition of the woman is that of slavery under any circumstances. She is the property of her father, of her nearest relatives, or of her tribe, until she become that of

---

[23] Chinuk WaWa = "my kin ~ friend ~ ally." *jm*

her husband. She digs the roots and prepares them for winter, digs and dries clams, cures the fish which he catches, packs the horses, assists in paddling the canoe, and performs all the menial offices. The more wives a man possesses, therefore, the richer he is; and it is an object for him to purchase others as his means increase. The accession of a new wife in the lodge very naturally produced jealousy and discord, and the first often returns for a time in dudgeon to her friends, to be reclaimed by her husband when he chooses, perhaps after propitiating her <66> by some presents. The first wife almost always retains a sort of predominance in the lodge; and the man, at least after his appetite for a subsequent one is satisfied, usually [199] lives with her. Wives, particularly the later ones, are often sold or traded off. Divorce is unknown, for the simple reason that the marriage tie, if so it can be called, has no force, except in the will of the husband. [Marriages among nobles were alliances between families and factions and so expected to survive at all costs.] A man sends his wife away, or sells her at his will. On the death of a brother, the survivor generally takes his wife; so also the father sometimes takes the wife of his son, and even the son his father's subsequent wives. [to protect the children] They are, however, often sold or returned to their own people. Prostitution is almost universal. An Indian, perhaps, will not let his favorite wife, but he looks upon his others, his sisters, daughters, female relatives, and slaves, as a legitimate source of profit; and this seems to have been a trait of the coast tribes from their first intercourse with the whites. Occasionally, adultery forms the cause of difficulty; but it is then only because the woman is reserved for the time being to the husband's use, or because he fears to be cheated of his just emoluments. Cohabitation of unmarried females among their own people brings no disgrace if unaccompanied with childbirth, which they take care to prevent. <67> This commences at a very early age, perhaps ten or twelve years. The practice of abortion is to be considered in its connection. This is almost universal, and is produced both by violence and by medicines. Certain plants are known to them which effect it, and it is generally believed by the whites, that they know of others which produce sterility at will. [no ¶]

The ceremony of a wedding among the Tsinūk is thus described by Ross Cox, and is much more correct than most of his remarks upon Indian manners: "the negotiations preceding a marriage are short, and the ceremony itself simple. When a young man has made his choice, he commissions his parents or other relatives to open the business to the girls' relatives. They are to receive a certain quantity of presents; and when these are agreed on, they all repair to the house intended for the future residence of the young couple, to which nearly all the inhabitant of the village are invited. The presents, which consist of slaves, axes, beads, kettles, *haikwa*, brass and cooper bracelets, &c, are now distributed by the young man, who, in his turn, receives an equal or perhaps greater quantity from the girl's relatives. The bride, decorated with the various ornaments common among the tribe, is then led forth by a few old women and presented to the [200] bridegroom. He receives her <68> as his wife; and the elders, after wishing them plenty of fish, fruits, roots, and children, retire from the house, accompanied by all the strangers."

SEPULTURE

The common mode of disposing of the dead among the fishing tribes was in canoes. There are generally drawn into the woods at some prominent point a short distance from the village, and sometimes placed between the forks of trees or raised from the ground on poles. Upon the Columbia river, the Tsinūk had in particular two very noted cemeteries, a high, isolated bluff, about three miles below the mouth of the Kowlitz, called Mt Coffin, and one some distance above, called Coffin Rock. Mr Broughton, one of Vancouver's lieutenants who explored the river, makes mention only of several canoes at this place. And Lewis and Clarke, who noticed the mount, do not speak of them at all; but at the time of Captain Wilkes's expedition, it is conjectured that there were at least 3,000. A fire, caused by the carelessness of some of his party, destroyed the whole, to the great indignation of the Indians. Captain Belcher,[24] of the British ship *Sulphur*, who visited the river in 1839, remarks, "in the years 1836 <69> (1826), the small-pox made great ravages, and it was followed a few years since by the ague; consequently Corpse Island and Coffin Mount, as well as the adjacent shores, were studded not only with canoes, but, at the period of our visit, the skulls and skeletons were strewed about in all directions." This method generally prevailed on the neighboring coasts, as at Shoalwater Bay, &c. Farther up the Columbia, as at the Cascades, a different form was adopted, which is thus described by Captain Clarke: "About half a mile below this house, in a very thick part of the woods, is an ancient Indian burial-place; it consists of eight vaults, made of pine or cedar boards, closely connected, about eight feet square and six in height; the top securely covered with wide boards, sloping a little so as to convey off the rain. The direction of all these is east and west, the door being on the eastern side, and partially stopped with wide boards decorated with rude pictures of men and other animals. On entering, we found in some of them four dead bodies care [201] fully wrapped in skins, tied with cords of grass and bark, lying on a mat in a direction east and west; the other vaults contained only bones, which, in some of them were piled to the height of four feet; on the tops of the vaults and on poles attached to them, hung brass kettles and frying-pans, with holes in their bottom, baskets, bowls, sea-shells, skins, pieced of cloth, hair-bags of trinkets and small bones, the offerings of friendship or affection, which have been <70> saved by a pious veneration from the ferocity of war or the more dangerous temptations of individual gain. The whole of the walls, as well as the door, were decorated with strange figures cut and painted on them; and besides these were several wooden images of men, some of them so old and decayed as to have almost lost their shape, which were all placed against the sides of the vaults. These images, as well as those in the houses we have lately seen, do not appear to be at all the objects of adoration in this place; they were most probably intended as resemblances of those whose decrease they indicate; and when we observe them in houses, they occupy the most conspicuous part, but are treated more like ornament than objects of worship. Near the vaults which are still standing, are the remains of others on the ground, completely rotted and covered with moss; and, as they are formed of the most durable pine and cedar timber there is every appearance that for a very long series of years this retired spot has been the depository for the Indians near this place." Another depository of this kind, upon an island in the river a few miles above, gave it the name of Sepulcher Island. The Watlala, a tribe of the Upper Tsinūk, whose burial place is here described, are now nearly extinct; but a number of the sepulchers still remain in different states of preservation. The position of the body, as noticed by Clarke, is I believe of

---

[24] See Robert Boyd, <u>The Coming of the Spirit of Pestilence</u> 1999. *jm*

universal observ <71 ance> ation, the head being always placed to the west, [The reason assigned to me is that the road to the *me-meh-oose* *illahee*,[25] the country of the dead, is toward the west] and if they place them otherwise they would be confused. East of the Cascade mountains, the tribes whose habits are equestrian, and who use canoes only for ferriage or transportation purposes, bury their dead, usually heaping over them piles of stones, either to mark the spot or to prevent the bodies from being exhumed by the prairie-wolf. Among the Yakamas we saw many of their graves [202] placed in conspicuous points of the basaltic walls which line the lower valleys, and designated by a clump of poles planted over them, from which fluttered various articles of dress. Formerly these prairie tribes killed horses over the graves, a custom now falling into disuse in consequence of the teaching of the whites. [no ¶]

Upon Puget Island, all the forms obtain in different localities. Among the Makah of Cape Flattery, the graves are covered with a sort of box rudely constructed of boards and elsewhere on the Sound the same method is adopted in some cases, while in others the bodies are placed on elevated scaffolds. As a general thing, however, the Indians upon the water placed the dead in canoes, while those at a distance from it buried them. Most of the graves are surrounded with strips of cloth, blankets, and other articles of property. <72> Mr Cameron, an English gentleman residing at Esquimalt Harbor, Vancouver Island, informed me that on his place there were graves having at each corner a large stone, the interior space filled with rubbish. The origin of these was unknown to the present Indians. [no ¶]

The distinctions of rank or wealth in all cases were very marked; persons of no consideration, and slaves, being buried with very little care or respect. Vancouver, whose attention was particularly attracted to their methods of disposing of the dead, mentions that at Port Discovery he saw baskets suspended to the trees containing the skeletons or young children, and, what is not easily explained, small square boxes containing apparently food. I do not think hat nay of these tribes place articles of food with the dead, nor have I been able to learn from living Indians that they formerly followed that practice. What he took for such I do not understand. He also mentions seeing in the same place a cleared space recently burned over, in which the skulls and bones of a number of persons lay among the ashes. The practice of burning the dead exists in parts of California and among the Tshimsyan of Fort Sampson. It is also pursued by the Carriers of New California [Caledonia], but no intermediate tribes, to my knowledge, follow it. Certainly those of the Sound do not at present. It is clear, <73> from Vancouver's narrative, that some great epidemic had recently passed through the country, as manifested by the quantity of human remains uncared for and exposed at the time of his visit, and very probably the Indians, being afraid [203] of contagion, had burned a house in which the inhabitants had perished, with the dead in it. This is frequently done. They almost invariably remove from any place where sickness has prevailed, generally destroying the house also. At Penn Cove, Mr Whidbey, one of Vancouver's officers, noticed "several sepulchers formed exactly like a sentry-box. Some of them were open, and contained the skeletons of many young children tied up in baskets. The smaller bones of adults were likewise noticed; but not one of the limb bones was found, which gave rise to an opinion that these, by the living inhabitants of the neighborhood, were appropriated to useful purposes, such as pointing their arrows, spears, or other weapons." It is hardly necessary to say that such a practice is altogether foreign to Indian character. The bones of the adults had probably been removed and buried elsewhere. The corpses of children are variously disposed of, sometimes by suspending them, at others by

---

[25] Chinuk WaWa = "dead land, land of dead." *jm*

placing in the hollows of trees. A cemetery devoted to infants is, however, an unusual occurrence. [no ¶]

In the case of chiefs or men of note, much pomp was used in the accompaniments of the <74> rite. The canoes were of great size and value, the war of state canoes of the decease. Frequently one was inverted over that holding the body, and in one instance, near Shoalwater Bay, the corpse was deposited in a small canoe, which again was placed in a larger one and covered with a third. Among the Tsinūk and Tsihalis, the tamahno-ūs board of the owner was placed near him. The Puget Sound Indians do not make these tamahno-ūs boards, but they sometimes constructed effigies of their chiefs, resembling that person as nearly as possible, dressed in his usually costume, and wearing the articles of which he was fond. One of these, representing the Skagit chief Sneestum, [Sneetlub] stood very conspicuously upon a high bank on the eastern side of Whidbey Island. The figures observed by Captain Clarke at the Cascades were either of this description or else the carved posts which had ornamented the interior of the houses of the deceased, and were connected with the superstitions of the tamahno-ūs. The most valuable articles of property were put into, or hung up around the grave, being first carefully rendered unserviceable, and the living family were literally stripped to do honor to the dead. No little self-denial must have been practiced in parting with articles so precious, but those chiefly interested fre [204] quently had the least to say on this subject. The graves of women <75> were distinguished by a cup, a kamas stick, or implement of their occupations, and by articles of dress. Slaves were killed in proportion to the rank and wealth of the deceased. In some instances, they were stared to death, or even tied to the dead body and left to perish thus horribly. At present, this practice has been almost entirely given up, but till within a very few years it was not uncommon. A case which occurred in 1850 has been already mentioned. Still later, in 1853, Toke, a Tsinūk chief living at Shoalwater Bay, under took to kill a slave girl belonging to his daughter, who, in dying, had requested that this might be done. The woman fled, and was found by some citizens in the woods half starved. Her master attempted to reclaim her, but was soundly thrashed, and warned against another attempt. [no ¶]

It was usually in the case of chiefs to renew or repair, for considerable length of time, the materials and ornaments of the burial place, with the common class of persons, family ride or domestic affection was satisfied with the gathering together of the bones after the flesh had decayed, and wrapping them in a new mat. The violation of the grave was always regarded as an offense of the first magnitude, and provoked sever revenge. Captain Belcher remarks: "Great secrecy is observed in all their burial ceremonies, partly <76> from fear of Europeans; and as among themselves, they will instantly punish by death any violation of the tomb, or wage war is perpetrated by another tribe, so they are inveterate and tenaciously bent on revenge should they discover that any act of the kind has been perpetuation by a white man. It is on record that part of the crew of a vessel, on her return to this port {[the *Columbia*]}, suffered, because a person which belonged to her {[but not then in her]} was known to have taken a skull, which, from the process of flattening, had become an object of curiosity." He adds, however, that, at the period of his visit to the river, "the skulls and skeletons were scattered about in all directions; and, as I was on most of their positions unnoticed by the natives, I suspect the feeling does not extend much beyond their relatives, and then only till decay has destroyed body, goods, and chattels. The chiefs no doubt are watched, as their canoes are repainted, decorated, and greater care taken by placing hem in sequestered spots." [205]

The motive for sacrificing or destroying property on occasion of death will be referred to in treating of their religious ideas. Wailing for the dead continued for a long time, and seems to be rather a ceremonial performance than an ac of spontaneous grief. The duty of course belongs to the women, and <77> the early morning is usually chosen for the purpose. They go out along to some place a little distant from the lodge or camp, and in a loud, sobbing voice, repeat a sort of stereotyped formula, as for instance, a mother on the loss of her child.[26] [no ¶]

Ah seahb!	*Shed-da*	*bud-dah*	*ah ta bud*!	*Ad-de-dah*!
Ah chief!	My	child	dead!	Alas!

When in dreams they see any of their deceased friends this lamentation is renewed.

FEASTS

Various occasions are made the subject of festival, of which the arrival of the first salmon of the season was one; marriage, where the parties were of note; the ceremony of piercing the ears and nose of children; and others of like character. These were always accompanied by singing, dancing, gambling, and the distribution of presents by the host. But the greatest of all was when some one, desirous of securing or extending his influence, gave a grand *potlatch*.[27] This was generally some chief, or what was equivalent to it, a man of wealth. Some have been known to save all their means for years, accumulating property of value, *haikwa*,[28] beads, blankets, and other articles, until they possessed sufficient to make an ostentations display. Then all his friends from his own and adjacent tribes were invited, an immense house built for the express purpose, <78> quantities of food prepared, and during the feast, which lasted for several days, the whole of his stores distributed to his guests; sometimes particular articles being given to individuals, and again others thrown indiscriminately to the crowd, who snatched at and tore or cut them to pieces, that each might secure a token. These great affairs have gradually fallen into disuse among those tribes most nearly associated with the whites, but still take place with the more remote, as the Klallam, Lummi, &c; on a smaller scale, however, they are everywhere practiced. [206]

GAMBLING

There are several games, the principal of which is the same. In one, a small piece of bone is passed rapidly from hand to hand, shifted behind the back, &c, the object of the contending party being to ascertain in which hand it is held. Each side is furnished with five or ten small sticks, which serve to mark the game, one stick being given by the guesser whenever he loses, and received whenever he wins. On guessing correctly, it is his turn to manipulate. When all the sticks are won, the game ceases, and the winner receives the takes, consisting of clothing or any other articles, as the play may be either high or low, for simple amusement, or in eager rivalry. The backers of the party manipulating keep up <79> a constant drumming with sticks on their paddles, which lie before them, singing an incantation to attract food fortune. This is usually known as the game of hand, or, in jargon, *It-lu-kam*.[29] Another, at which they exhibit still more interest, is played with ten disks of hard wood, about the diameter of a Mexican dollar, and

---

[26] This phrase is sobbed in Lushootseed. *jm*
[27] Chinuk Wawa from Nootkan = "invitational, inviting." *jm*
[28] Chinuk Wawa = dentalia ~ tusk shells. *jm*
[29] Also, Chinuk Wawa *mamook itlokum* = "to gamble, make ~ play hand game." *jm*

somewhat thicker, called, in the jargon, *tsil-tsil*; in the Niskwalli language *la-halp*.[30] One of these is marked and called the chief. Another, a mat is spread on the ground, at the ends of which the opposing players are seated, their friends on either side, who are provided with the requisites for a noise, as in the other case. The party holding the disks has a bundle of the fibers of the cedar bark, in which he envelops them, and, after rolling them about, tears the bundle into two parts, his opponent guessing in which bundle the chief lies. These disks are made of the yew, and must be cut into shape with beaver tooth chisels only. The marking of them is in itself an art, certain persons being able by their spells to indue [imbue] them with luck, and their manufactures bring very high prices. The game is counted as in the first mentioned. Farther down the coast, then highly polished sticks are used, instead of disks. [no ¶]

The women have a <80> game belonging properly to themselves. It is played with four beaver teeth, having particular marks on each side, *meh-ta-la*.[31] They are thrown as dice, success depending on the arrangement in which they fall. [no ¶]

Each species of gambling has its appropriate tamahno-ūs, or, as it is called upon the Sound, Skwolalitūd, that is, its patron spirit, whose coun [207] tenance is invoked by the chant and noise. The tamahno-ūs of the game of hand is called by the Niskwalli, *Tsaik*;[32] of the disks, *Knawk'h*. It would seem that this favor is not merely solicited during the game, but sometimes in advance of it, and perhaps for general and continued fortune. Colonel Simmons informed me that he saw an Indian at the Falls of the Fenalquet die from exhaustion and overexcitement while undergoing a performance intended to secure this tamahno-ūs. He had lain for several days in a lodge without eating, while his friends shouted and drummed until death himself "jumped the game" on him. [no ¶]

Of horse racing it is unnecessary to speak.

MEDICINE AND DISEASES

Besides the regular practice of the tamahno-ūs men, who may be considered the faculty, the Indians used a number of plants as medicines, somewhat as herb doctors intrude their nostrums in the States. Among these is the root of the Oregon <81> grape (*Berberis aequifolim*), a decoction of which serves as a tonic, and is also their remedy for venereal. A decoction of the white flowering or poisonous [death] Kamas furnished an emetic, and that of the cucumber vine (*Sicyos Oregonus*) both an emetic and cathartic. The root of a species of [licorice] fern growing among the moss which covers the limbs of the maple and other trees in damp situation is chewed as an expectorant, and is made into a tea as a remedy for gonorrhoea. The herbs used to produce abortion or effect sterility, I do not know. A power made from the tail of the rattlesnake, as first noticed by Dr George Suckley, United States Army, is employed by some tribes for the former purpose, aw to expedite natural labor; but violence is oftener resorted to by the women of the coast. Small-pox the coast tribes do not pretend to treat with medicine; but, as mentioned in my report to Captain McClellan, those of the interior claim to have remedies for it. The inside bark of the skunk-wood chewed up serves as a poultice, and the juice of the colt's-foot as a fomentation for bruises and sprains. Women during their periods of menstruation bind the twigs of the hemlock-spruce round their bodies, but this would seem to be a species of charm. These

---

[30] Cf *slahal*, played with sticks and pairs of marked bone cylinders, not disks. *jm*
[31] Cf *tala* = "dollar, money." *jm*
[32] A spirit of plenty, luck, abundance. *jm*

twigs are also used as a bed for the sick. For gonorrhoea, the females also smoke <82> themselves over a fire made of certain [208] plants or wood. They have no styptics. Swelling produced by injuries they sometime scarify. Sores that are slow in healing are cauterized, and they employ moxa[33] by the application of coals of fire, and the powder left by worms under the bark of trees is also strewn over to dry them up. This, and also potter's clay dried and powdered, is used for chancres. Suction by the mouth is employed as a topical remedy to alleviate pain, and this too is part of the practice of the tamahno-ūs doctors. Their sweat-houses are partially excavated in the ground, just large enough to contain the body of one person, and covered with boards and earth, the heat being produced by hot stones; after the operation they plunge into cold water. Fractured limbs are bandaged and splinted with strips of wood. [no ¶]

Of diseases to which they are subject, venereal in its different forms and the small-pox are assumed to have been introduced by the whites; the latter, it is true, indirectly, it having reached here through other and more distant tribes. According to Mr Dunn,*[34] "it commenced among the tribes residing between the sources of the Missouri ad the Mississippi. Thence it spread it devastation northward as far as Athabasca <83> and the three horns of Great Slave Lake, and westward across the Rocky mountains, through the whole region of Oregon T territory, spreading to a vast distance along the shores of the North Pacific." The date of this visitation he does not mention. Lewis and Clark supposed that it had swept the Columbia some third years before their arrival, or about the year 1780 [1782]. There have been several returns of it since, the last in 1852-53, when the coast tribes particularly were ravaged. To thee imported disease, the measles are probably to be added, which are scarcely less fatal than the others. The great mortality produced by congestive fever between 1820 and 1830 upon the Columbia has been mentioned by various writers. This the Indians, though doubtless erroneously, supposed to have originated from an American vessel. Among indigenous diseases, consumption is one of the most destructive; their carelessness in regard to dress, the slight shelter from rain and exposure permitted by their wandering habits, and the dampness of the climate for a large part of the year, rendering it exceedingly common. And it seems to have become more so, since the partial change in their habits [209] by association with the whites. A very common eruptive disorder attacking the throat, and commonly supposed to be from syphilis, has been recognized by Dr CM Hitchcock, late surgeon United States Army, as the "yaws", very common in the <84> West Indies, and known among the Cherokees and others of the Atlantic States. Sore eyes and blindness occur, as also paralysis. Diarrhoea is a common and often fatal disorder, particularly among children. <85>

DOMESTIC MANNERS

The head of the family and his principal wife occupy the first place near the fire, and it I an impoliteness t pass before them. They are also first served at meals. Where a man has several wives, each has his own fire in the lodge, and takes care of her own children. the one with whom the husband sleeps for the time being, though in the same house with the others, provided the articles of food, which it belongs to the women to furnish, and cooks them herself. The man's business is to do the hunting (of which, however, west of the Cascades, there is but little, game

---

[33] 'Moxa' ~ cautery ~ moxibustion is the application of flames to a powder to burn an ailing body part as a counter irritant. *jm*

[34] Inserted < *The Oregon Territory, &c, by John Dunn, late of Hudson's Bay Company>. *gg*

not being abundant enough to form an item in the general economy), to catch the fish, make canoes, split the planks of the lodges, and put them up or remove them, lasso the horses, and in fine to attend to such thing as are deemed manly occupations among savage nations. That of the women is to get roots and prepare them for winter and cure the fish; on the salt-water, to dig and dry clams, load and assist in paddling the canoes, and, on the prairie, to pack and unpack the horses, make the camp, cultivate the potato-patch, and generally everywhere to do the drudgery.

There does not seem to be any particular government of children, nor any difficulty growing out of their origin in different mother. Children continue to suckle often [till] three or four years [of age], a practice which probably has its effect in lessening the fecundity of women.

Common conversation in the lodge is, as might be supposed, on tribal subjects, relating to their own common concerns, dogs, horses, &c., the little occurrences of the day, what each has been doing, every trifle being thus know to all. The future is rarely a subject of attention. They are, on the other hand, fond of reciting their former actions, or speaking of persons deceased, relating what each knows of them, as one civilized would discuss the char [210] acters of history. It an Indian has been on a journey, perhaps the night ensuing that of his return the others come to his lodge. They ask no questions, but sit quietly, and when he sees fit he commences a history of what he saw and heard, even to the minutest details. The one who remembers the most, or is the best carrier of news, has a corresponding importance. They are exceedingly lewd in their common talk, the most indecent subjects being coolly discussed and jested upon. When a couple of canoes met, for instance, they always stop to talk, to exchange news, and generally to "chuff" one another, in a style that would electrify a Thames waterman.

Their first meal when at home, is generally about ten or eleven o'clock; the previous night, till a late hour, having probably been spent in gambling, tamahno-ūs making, or some other amusement. From that time forward, cooking goes on with very little <87> interruption, on behalf of some member of the family until bed time.

Names

Names are given to children when they begin to walk and talk, and are generally family appellations, though not in the first instance that of the father, but rather that of the grandfather on either side, or, if there are several, of the uncles. These are changed in after life; sometimes in honor of a deceased relatives; sometimes in commemoration of an event. On the death of an Indian, his name is not mentioned for a long time. If spoken of, it is as "he that is dead"; but after some two or three years, when the grief of his family is supposed to be assuaged, his son, perhaps, summons his friends, gives a feast, and announces that he has taken his father's name. On occasion of the council at Neeah Bay, an Indian named Ko-bet-si, who received a commission as a sub-chief, changed his to Ko-bakh-sat. At the Tsihalis council, An-nan-in-ta, the son of Tsinnite'h, a former great chief of the Upper Tsihalis, announced that he had taken that of his grandfather, Wa-kwin-nam.[35] They are unwilling to speak their own name; a sentiment for which I a never able to obtain a reason. Nor do they use name in calling one another. They attract attention by the word "Do-teh!" look here! If hailing a stranger, or if a friend, "Kug-wej-oh!" you there! Many, but <88> not all their names, have signification, as Squū-shum, smoke or fog, the name of a sub-chief of the Snokwalmūh. The termination *kanam*, common t all the tribes on the Sound, but to which they attach [211] no meaning, I believe to be

---

[35] Dale Kinkade, <u>Upper Chehalis Dictionary</u>, Appendix B ~ Personal Names 1991: 336-337. *jm*

a derivation from the Selish word "*keine*", {-*qin* suffix for} head, which pervades many proper names throughout the eastern district; as, *Oki-nakeine*, *Tsemakeine*, the latter signifying a springhead or water source. As the names of the father's and mother's families are alike perpetuated in this way, and as different tribes intermarry, similarly in the names of persons cannot be assumed as proof of similar origin. They are all exceedingly fond of receiving "Boston names", and particularly court such as are understood to belong to distinguished chiefs. In consequence, brevet titles of all the generals of the Army, living and dead, are worn by *tyees* of the different tribes. A few of English origin, bestowed in former times, are also highly valued.

The Sound Indians certainly, and I believe the others, give names to their dogs, but not to their horses, except the descriptive ones arising from color. The name of one dog was explained to me to mean *dirt*.

PECULIAR CUSTOMS

Flattening the head &c – the process of flattening the head, has been too often described to need <89 repetition> repletion. It is continued for about a year when most excessive, and is confined to children of free parents; slaves not enjoying the privileged distortion, for a different reason, it is not performed on the offspring of whites by Indian mothers, it being a matter of pride to assimilate them to their fathers. The only reason for this practice that I could ever obtain was from a Klallam Indian, to the effect that *Dokwebudl*[36] ordered them to do it in the first place to make them handsome. The operation does not appear to affect the intellect, judging from a comparison with adjacent tribes who do not use it. It is supposed to be the cause of squinting in some cases; but its effect upon the general health is not observable.

The custom is most universal, and carried to the greatest extent among the tribes on the Lower Columbia and Puget Sound. Those immediately east of the Cascades, and near the river, practice it to a limited degree only. It extends, according to Dr Tolmie, through the Haeltzuk [Heiltsuk] connection as far north as Milbank Sound, in latitude 52° N., where the custom of distending the lips commences in its stead. Southward it reaches to the Coquille River, latitude 43° 10´ N., upon the coast, and about thirty miles back. In departing from the center, gradually diminishes in degree [212] and is, on the outskirts, limited to the women. <90>

In comparative examination, it should be remembered that as slaves are for the most part obtained from broad skulls, formed among the addicted to the practice, which are not compressed, may be assume to be of different origin, and, on the other hand, those very much altered, which are met with among the northern tribes, are probably less so. The care bestowed on the disposition of the dead will, however, generally indicate his rank, and therefore his nationality. These observations are important where deduction are attempted to be drawn from differences in crania, but are likely to be over looked by those unacquainted with the habits of these tribes. It will be seen that the custom is a local one; that within a particular district it is common to tribes of the most different families; and that beyond it other tribes of the same families do not practice it at all. [centered]

---

[36] Lushootseed name for the Transformer ~ Changer ~ duk^{w}ibəł. *jm*

Arrival at puberty

The first prominent event in a woman's life, her becoming fit for marriage, as seems to be the case with most savage tribes, is a period of ceremonial observance among these Indians. With those of the district, the girl usually retreats to some secluded spot and fasts. The region of her abstinence is said to be a great merit; but that it may not be carried too far, some old squaw, who is acquainted with her hiding place, carries her when needful a little water and dried salmon. The time is, with some tribes, <91> as the [Callapooyas] Kallapūia of the Willamette Valley, occupied in throwing up small piles of earth or stones, a practice having probably a mystical significance akin to a tamahno-ūs. The subsequent recurrences of her periods are, in like manner, seasons of retreat from the tribe, although less formality attends them. The most peculiar, as well as universal, observances are those connected with their food. This, the first object of care and anxiety with people who depend upon natural productions for their subsistence, seem to have in their minds a relation to many events; and more especially those of a sexual character, or the privation of particular kinds of foods, may have been shown by experience to be requisite to speedy recovery of health. Among the fishing Indians, the salmon, during the early season of its capture, is, so to speak, tabooed to women undergoing menstruation. Among those who live by game, elk an deer meat are equally prohibited, and similar restrictions are, to a more limited extend, imposed on pregnant [213] women. I know, however, of nothing like periods of purification. Some of the coast tribes, as those at Humboldt Bay in cal, make a practice of bathing, the women accompanying the young girl on the occasion, but this is in consonance with their general habits. The observance has been absurdly considered as a Jewish rite, and cited in proof of the preposterous idea that they are descendants of <92> the Isrealitish tribes. It seems natural enough that such a custom should prevail among Barbarians, however disconnected. With their limited field for mental exercise, the speculative powers are likely to be most active upon points of this very nature; periodicity being a fact which attracts observation and suggests at once the idea of cause. The refined objects of a difference in sex being foreign to their minds, that event which announces fitness for sensual purposed is, of all others, the most important.

Among the [Wascos] Wasko, at the Dalles of the Columbia, it is stated the event is celebrated more publicly. As the period approaches its close, the father of the girl makes great preparations, invites his friends, and has a general feast, which reaches its height on her re-appearance. The young men who wish to buy wives are then ready, with their horses, &c, to treat for the purchase.

MEASURES OF VALUE, TIME ETC

Distances were only marked by days' journeys, or their fractions, as made on horseback or in canoes. Measures of length were probably all referred to parts of the body, the principal being the extent of the outstretched arms, which was used in valuing their money, the haikwa, or wampum of the Pacific. This shell, a species of *Dentalium*, was procured <93> on the northern coast by letting down long poles, to which was attached a piece of wood filled with spikes, or teeth, between which the sell became fixed. Its price depended entirely upon its length; forty to the fathom being the standard value. When shells were so short that it require more to make up the required length, they were of very inferior account, but rose proportionately with increased size. A fathom of forty was formerly worth a slave, and even now will bring five dollars in money. Single shells were shown me on the Tsihalis for which the owner refused a dollar apiece. This money is, however, becoming scarce, and is far less used than formerly, [214] at least by the tribes who have much intercourse with the whites. It was the universal currency through an extensive district. On the Klamath river, it is valued even more highly than on the Sound and the Columbia; and those aboriginal peddlers, the Klikatat, frequently carry it to Southern Oregon for sale. The relative value of skins, I understand, to have been fixed by the fur-traders, who assumed the beaver ["made beaver"] as a unit of computation. The Indians are now all well acquainted with our coins, from the eagle to the dime, for which there are corresponding names in the jargon. [no ¶]

There does not seem to have been any system of keeping accounts peculiar to them or <94> extending beyond the simplest idea. Their computation was by visible objects, as the fingers, small pebbles, or bits of stick, and very probably noticed sticks, the most primitive of all records. In their dealing with the traders, however, they speedily comprehend the more ordinary weights and measures, to which, in the jargon,[37] names were applied; as, *ikht ill*, one weight for our pound; *ikht slik*, or *ethlon*, one yard or fathom; *ikht tamaulikh*, one tub or bushel; *ikhtle sack*, one sack. I have never met with mnemonical signs or pictorial help to memory.

Time was measured by moons, say from full to full and by warm and cold seasons; one warm and one cold constituting the year. Names for the intermediate seasons exist, though I am not certain that the same signification is attached to them as with us. Mr Hale assigns appellations to the various months in the language of some of the Flathead tribes. The Indians on this side of the mountains also had a name for each moon, by which, as they say, they could know how long it would be before the salmon came, &c. Beyond a few days, they did no apply that period as a measure, for instance, not as determining the length of the moon; nor can I learn that they had any times corresponding to our week or to part of a moon.

With tides and their periods of recurrence, those who live on the saltwater are, of course, familiar; I have not been able to ascertain whether they have speculated on their cause.[38] <95>

HOUSES

The planks of their houses are split from the tree with a tool made of elk-horn, or with wooden wedges, driven by a stone mallet, and are then [215] adzed down to the requisite thickness. Some of these boards are of great size. One that I measured was 24 feet long and 4 ½ in width. They are, in preference, split from the *arbor vitae*, or as it is usually called, cedar, but sometimes from the fir. There is some variety in the form adopted; the houses of the Tsinūk usually sloping each from a ridge-pole in the center, while those of the Sound Indians have but one pitch. They are usually intended to accommodate several families, and frequently a whole village was under the same roof. An excavation of a foot or more in depth is made through the center of the house, in which the fires are built, and where the cooking is done; the raised portion left on either side being covered with boards or mats to serve as a seat, and the bunks for sleeping placed against the sides, sometimes in two tiers. At one end of the house, there is frequently a platform for dances or the tamahno-ūs. The houses of the Makah have been already described, and the better class of houses on the Sound differ from them only in size. But the

---

[37] Chinuk WaWa developed to facilitate trade so these are crucial terms. *jm*

[38] Interior people, especially Yakamas, were once notorious for camping on low tide beaches, only to be driven away at high tides because they did not know about tides. *jm*

triumph of their architecture is displayed in the buildings erected for festivals. These were of extraordinary size and strength, considering <96> the means at their disposal. Mr HA Goldsborough measured one at Port Madison, erected by the brother of Seat'hl, some forty years before, the frame of which was standing in 1855. This was 520 feet long, 69 feet wide, 15 feet high in front, and 10 in the rear. It was supported on puncheons, or split timbers, 74 in number, from 2 to 3 feet wide, and 5 to 8 inches thick, carved with grotesque figures of men, naked and about half size. The cross-beams were round sticks, 37 in umber, 60 feet in length, and from 12 to 22 inches in diameter. There was another similar house at Dungeness, built by King George, and one at Penn Cove, by Sneetlum, similar but somewhat smaller than this. They were erected for special occasions and afterward dismantled.

CANOES

Various descriptions of canoes are used by the different tribes, suited to the waters on which they dwell. Those generally used on the Columbia above the Dalles are mere dug-outs, of very rude shape and finish, and though well enough adapted for carrying, have no particular merit. These are also used on the Kowlitz and Tsihalis, and generally those streams [216] which are shallow and obstructed by rapids, as being fitter for such waters than the sharper and more elegant varieties. Below the Dalles, several kinds were formerly common, one <97> of which, nearly straight on the gunwale, and ornamented at the bow with a carved figure-head, representing some bird or animal, seems to have been chiefly used round the Willamette and Kowlitz. A small and light canoe, of simple form, but very graceful, was used principally among the marshy island toward the mouth of the river, for hunting sea-fowl. Another kind, particularly mentioned by Lewis and Clarke, is now almost entirely confined to Puget Sound. It varies greatly in size, some of them being as much as thirty-five feet long, the stern being rounded and rising to a point, the bow terminating in a kind of billet-head. The one by far the most used at present, and the most elegant in shape, is, however, that which has popularly obtained the name of the Tsinūk canoe, the bow of which rises high and projects forward, tapering to a point, while the stern is sharp, cut off perpendicularly, ad surmounted by a block. These canoes are usually painted black outside and red within, and ornamented along the gunwale with the opercula[39] of a sea-shell,* [* *Pachypoma gibberosum*] set in rows. This kind is by no means confined to the river, but is employed far to the northward also. These are admirable sea-boats, with the exception that they are exposed to be boarded by a stern sea. A modification of this is sometimes employed by the northern Indians for a war-canoe; the beak <98> being very high, and flared out at each side, so that, when bow on, it presents a shield against arrows, and to a certain extend against balls. The management and appearance of a first-class canoe on the Columbia River is this described by Messrs. Lewis and Clarke:

> "The fourth and largest species of canoe we did not meet with till we had reached tide-water, near the grand rapids below, in which place they are found among all the nations, especially the Killamuks, and others residing on the sea-cost. They are upward of fifty feet long, and will carry from eight to ten thousand pounds; weight, or from twenty to thirty persons. Like all the canoes we have mentioned, they are

---

[39] Door hatch ~ hardshell cover for closing the passage where the soft snail body lives. After eating them, minks and others leave these lids in handy piles for humans to use. *jm*

cut out of single trunk of a tree which is generally white cedar, though the fir is sometimes used. The sides are secured by cross-bars, or round sticks, two or three inches in thickness [217] which are inserted through holes made just below the gunwale, and made fast with cords. The upper edge of the gunwale itself is about five-eighths of an inch thick, and four or five in breadth, and olds outward, so as to form a kind of rim, which prevents the water from beating into the boat. At each end, also, are pedestals, formed of the same solid piece, on which are placed strange, grotesque figures of men and animals, rising sometimes to the height of five feet, and composed of small pieces of wood, firmly united, with great ingenuity, by inlaying <99> and mortising, without a spike of any kind. The paddle is usually from four feet and a half to five feet in length, the handle being thick for one-third of its length, when it widens and is hollowed and thinned on each side of the center, which forms a sort of rib. When they embark, one Indian sits in the stern and steers with a paddle, the others kneel in pairs in the bottom of the canoe and sitting on their heels, paddle over the gunwale next to them. In this way, they ride with safety the highest waves, and venture, without the least concern, in seas where other boats could not live an instant. They sit quietly and paddle with no other movement, except when any large wave throws the boat on her side, and to the eye of the spectator she seems lost; the man to windward then steadies her by throwing his body toward the upper side, and sinking his paddle deep into the wave, appears to catch the water, and force it under the boat which the same stroke pushed on with great velocity. In the management of these canoes, the women are equally expert with the men; for in the smaller boats, which contain four oarsmen, the helm is generally given to the female. As soon as they land, the canoe is generally hauled on shore, unless she be very heavily laden; but, at night, the load is universally discharged, and the canoe <100> brought to shore.

"Our admiration of their skill in these curious constructions was increased by observing the very inadequate implement with which they are made. These Indians possess very few axes, and the only tool employed in their building, from felling of the tree to the delicate workmanship of the images, is a chisel made of an old file, about an inch and a half in width. Even of this, too, they have not learned the management, for the chisel is sometimes fixed in a large block of wood, and, being held in the right hand, the block is pushed with the left without the aid of a mallet. But under all these dis [218] advantages, these canoes, which one would suppose to be the work of years, are made in a few weeks. A canoe, however, is very highly prized. In traffic, it is an article of the greatest value, except a wife, which is of equal consideration, so that a lover generally gives a canoe to the father in exchange for his daughter."

The canoes employed by the more northern Indians are sometimes even of greater size and more solid construction than this. They are also better adapted to sea-going, as they are free from the incumbrance {sic}. With them, the Indians venture from Queen Charlotte Islands, and even from Sitka, as far sough as Puget Sound, bringing, <101> besides their crew, their whole worldly property, by no means an inconsiderable cargo. One which I saw in Victoria carried three masts, and was estimated at no less than seventy feet in length.

The usual method of constructing canoes is to cut or burn the tree down and into a suitable length, rough-hew the outside, cut out the inside with a hatchet and chisel or hand-adze, then turn it over and hew the outside to correspond with the inside. When in this state it is filled with water, which is boiled by means of hot stones, a fire being made all around the canoe on the outside. This is for the purpose of spreading the canoe, which is too narrow for its depth, and the thwarts are put and secured by cords passed through small holes in the side to keep it in shape. The prow of the Tsinūk canoe, and projecting parts of others, which are too large to be cut from a single tree, or would cross the grain, are mortised in and secured by cords in like manner. Should, unluckily, knots or other defects appear in the sides, the piece is cut out and another set in in its place. This is done by boring small holes, though which the patch is firmly sewed with twine, and which are then plugged. The seam is caulked with pitch and cedar-bark, scraped to the consistence of tow. When finished, the outside is slightly charred, and painted with coal made from rushes and <102> mixed with whale-oil. The inside is colored with a chrome, which, when burned, becomes red.

In constructing their canoes, the Indians use no lines or artificial aid. The whole is modeled by the eye. Of course, there is a great difference in quality, according to the skill of the builders, and particular persons have a high reputation for their superiority in this respect. [219]

CLOTHING, UTENSILS, ETC

The introduction of European or American articles has, in great measure, done away with their own. Almost all the Indians of the district are now principally clothed like the whites, and avail themselves of many of their tools and utensils; but their original manufactures possessed a great deal of merit. The ordinary dress of the men, when they saw fit to use any, was a deer-skin shirt, leggings, and moccasins, which, among the prairie Indians, was often embroidered with the quills of the porcupine. On the coast these quills were scarce, being obtained from a distance and by exchange, and since the opening of trade with the whites they have used beads and various colored threads. The skins are well dressed, being worked over a frame and softened with the brains of the animal. Before being used, they are smoked over a fire of green <103> twigs, which prevents them from permanently shrinking or becoming hard from wet. They also wore on occasion robes made of the skins of small animals, such as the rabbit, sewelell (*Aplodontia leporina*) [mountain beaver],[40] muskrat, &c., or of larger ones, as the cougar and beaver. Fur caps, of a form suited to the fancy of the wearer, were used occasionally; but the most noticeable covering was a broad, conical hat, with the inner rim fitting the head, made of a tough grass resembling hemp, which came from the interior. This was made water-proof, and painted with figures. The women universally wore a breech-clout of strands gathered round the waist and falling usually to the knee, which served the purpose of concealment. With the men no idea of immodesty existed. Decency had not even its fig-leaf. The clout was sometimes made of twisted grass, at others of cedar-bark, hackled and split into fringe. Of later years, they have adopted the dress of the whites, and it is only in remote districts, or among old people too poor or too obstinately attached to the habits of their youth to change them, that one now sees this pristine type of the petticoat: "A garment of mystical sublimity."

---

[40] Utterly misnamed, mountain beaver are neither, though they do make "baseballs," see Jay Miller, Herman Haeberlin Regained, Appendix G ~ Mountain Beavers 2015 [2005]: 37. *jm*

The Indians of the Sound and the Strait of Fuca attained considerable skill in manufacturing a species of blanket from a mixture of the wool <104> of the mountain-sheep and the hair of a particular kind of dog, though in this art they never equaled the more northern tribes, some of whose workmanship equaled the common kind of Mexican serape. Vancouver describes the dogs as "resembling those of Pomerania, though, in general, somewhat [220] larger". Their usual color is white. The wool is obtained from the hunting tribes next to the Cascade Mountains, and is an article of trade. The two being mixed are twisted into yarn by rolling upon the thigh, and the warp is formed by stretching these singly over a frame, tying the ends together. The woof is then passed through with a long wooden needle. The Klallam and Sound Indian do not make much use of colors in ornamenting their blankets, but those farther north introduce quite complicated figures of several colors. Another kind of robe, usually square and worn over the shoulders, is made by twisting in with the hair or wool the down of sea-birds, the whole being hand-woven in the same way as the last. This makes a very thick and warm tuff. The Makah alone manufacture the cedar-bark into texture suitable for weaving. For this purpose, the inner bark is selected, boiled or macerated, and then pounded and hatcheled {hatcheted} out. The bark is made to form the warp; the woof being made of grass thread. This stuff is pliable, and makes a convenient <105> outer garment. Very pretty capes, edged with the sea-otter skin, are made of it. This tribe also are the principal manufactures of the cedar mats, which are used on the Sound. These are entirely of bark, formed into narrow strips, and woven son the floor. They are thin and perfectly even in texture. The other tribes employ for mats two kinds of rushes, the flat or common cat-tail, and other round or tulé. These are used for a great variety of purposes, as to line their canoes, for beds, covering for goods, temporary huts &c. In fact, an Indian's roll of mats is his constant traveling companion. Of baskets, they make, or rather did make until lately, an almost endless variety, many of them of beautiful texture, tasteful shape, and ornamented with colored figures. Some were used as pails, and even to boil in, being filled with water, and heated stones thrown in. Cups, dishes, platters were carved from wood by the Makah in a very neat manner. Larger bowls, holding over a quart, were made from the horns of the big-honed sheep, and spoons from that material and those of the mountain-goat. These last articles probably came from the north, but found their way, in the course of trade, far down the cost, and even into California. The nets and seines, manufactured from the grass imported from beyond <106> the Cascade Mountains, deserve mention as very well made, the twine being perfectly even and well twisted. The [221] bows and arrows and defensive armor have been mentioned in another connection.

In all their native manufactures, the Indians of this Territory were not wanting in skill, although they were far behind the northern races, whose ingenuity is, in fact, extraordinary among savages [no ¶]

DOMESTIC ANIMALS

The horse and dog constitute the only ones, except that a few individuals may perhaps own a little stock. Umtuts,[41] a Klikatat, living at the mouth of the Kathlapūtl, until recently killed by his tribe, alone possessed a good herd. Generally speaking, the Indians west of the

---

[41] Chief Umtuch was shot by mistake, though the circumstances are cloudy, see Nathaniel Reynolds, "More Dangerous Dead than Living": The Killing of Chief Umtuch 2007. *jm*

mountains do not keep them. Their horses, ˅also˅ are few, comparatively, and of modern introduction.

The date of the introduction of the horse among the tribes in the eastern district cannot be arrived at with any certainty. The Snake, Nez Perces, and Spoken had, according to Lewis and Clarke, immense numbers at the time of their visit. Garry, chief of the later tribe, informed me that they first got theirs from the Flatheads, who, he believed, procured them from the Snakes; and there can be but little doubt that they were first brought northward by the later in their intercourse with <107> the Comanches. The Cayuse added to their stock by theft from the Spaniards, as Franchère mentions seeing them with Spanish brands.

Dr Suckley considers the dogs to be of two breeds, one resembling the coyote, or prairie-wolf, and very probably crossed with that animal, which is the kind used for hunting; the other, a long-bodied, short legged, turnspit-looking cur, which is the peculiar property and pet of the women. To these are probably to be added a third, the dog used by the Skagit, Klallam, and others of the lower part of the Sound and Gulf of Georgia, which is shown for it fleece. Vancouver mentions these as resembling the Pomeranian dog. They are of pretty good size, and generally while, with much longer and softer hair than either of the others, but having the same sharp muzzle and curling tail as the hunting-dog. Among some of the tribes of Northern cal, as on the Klamath river, there is a variety with a broad tail, not more than six or eight inches in length, which appears to be [222] natural, and not the result of docking. This I suppose to be a distinct one. The Indian dogs are much valued by their owners, particularly those employed in hunting. <108>

SYMBOLIC WRITING

I am not aware how far this may be carried among the Sound tribes. Probably there is no great essential difference between them and their neighbors of the plains in this art. It may perhaps be best explained by an example given me by a veteran mountaineer, Dr Robert Newell, of Champoeg. A party of Snakes are going to hunt strayed horses. A figure of a man, with a long queue, or scalp-lock, reaching to his heels, denoted Shoshonee; that tribe being in the habit of braiding horse or other hair into their own in that manner. A number of marks follow, signifying the strength of the party. A foot-print, pointed in the direction they take, shows their course, and a hoof-mark turned backward, that they expect to return with animals. If well armed, and expecting a possible attack, a little powder mixed with sand tell that they are ready, or a square dotted about the figures indicates that they have fortified. These pictographs are often an object of study to decipher the true meaning. The shrewder or more experienced old men consult over them. It is not every one that is sufficiently versed in the subject to decide correctly.

There are I believe no permanent symbolic writing below the Cascades like those which occur upon some of the rocks on the Columbia river above them, and attributed by the present Indians to the *Elip Tilikum*, or primeval race.[42] <109>

MOUNDS AND EARTHWORKS

Mention has been made in my former report of a circular work on the Yakama River, the construction of which these Indians disclaimed. That was the first of the kind which had ever

---

[42] WaWa = "first folks ~ people". *jm*

fallen under my observation, or which I had been informed of within this T territory or Oregon. Since then, Dr Newell has informed me that, in some parts of the Willamette Valley, as on the Twallatti plains, for instance, there are indubitable earthworks, some of them of various forms, of which he mentioned the letter L. None of them, to his knowledge, presented the figures of animals. I am aware of none on the Lower Columbia or Puget Sound which deserve the name. [223] Inclosures for garden patches were sometimes made by banking up around them with refuse thrown out in cleaning the ground, which, after a long while, came to resemble a low wall, and in some cases, as at the old Snohomish fort on Kwultsehda Creek[43], they made external ditches, which were filled with pointed stakes and covered over; but these do not belong to the class spoke of. Near the house of Mr Cameron, at Esquimalt, Vancouver Island, I noticed a trench, cutting off a small point of rock near the shore, which seems to have been about six feet deep and eight wide. Governor Douglas informed me that these are not <110> unfrequent on the island; that they generally surrounded some defensible place; and that often an escarpment was constructed facing the sea, but that the earth was thrown indiscriminately on either side of the ditch. The present Indians have no tradition of their origin. He supposes them to have been made by their ancestors, and the authors forgotten by heir descendants. There are also, near Victoria, a number of small mounds, which I was unfortunately unable to visit. Governor Douglass mentioned that one had been dug into without finding anything. Some of the gentlemen of this company supposed them to be kamas ovens.

Until examination has been made, both of these and the works in the Willamette Valley [Twallatti {Tualatin} plains], the question may be considered as still open, whether any works analogous to those of the Ohio Valley and other States exist on the Pacific Coast.* {[* <111> In connection with the subject, reference may be made here to the mounds noticed by Sir Edward Belcher in parts of the Sacramento Valley, which, he states, were raised by the existing race of Indians, for the purpose of elevating their houses beyond the reach of inundation. Whether such a motive governed the mound-builders of Ohio, under any circumstances, I am uninformed.]}

MIGRATIONS

The various tribes, as a general thing, claim for themselves to have sprung from the identical country which they now occupy, and their legends, so far as I have been able to collect them, give no account of remote changes of place. A Tsinūk story, related elsewhere, point to a northern origin for the ancestors of the tribe, but not for the people themselves. In reply to direct interrogatories upon the subject, they invariable state that they have always lived where they now do; but this is far less satisfactory than indirect evidence, as they are quick at suspecting some object in regard to their lands. [224]

Mention has already been made of the movement of part of the Klikatat southward at a very recent period, and of the statement, by the Willopah, that the Klatskanai had likewise changed their location. In addition, I have been informed that the Tsemakum and Toanhūch once lived on the upper waters of the Niskwalli and Kowlitz rivers, and the Satsop and the Stall upon the south fork of the latter; but the Indians who made this statement declared that their own people, the Staklamish, had never moved. *Their* country, they said, was the "navel of the world". On the other side of the mountains, it is well known that the Snakes have, in modern <112> times, been driven southward; and Dr Suckley was positively assured by aged Indians that the

---

[43] Quilceda ~ "sturgeon" is now the location of a huge outlet mall owned by Tulalip Tribes.

Klikatat and Yakama, branches of the Sahaptin Family,*[44] had pushed their way into the country formerly occupied by members of the Selish. This latter extension, being to the northward as well as westward, it is out of the usual line of travel. Sufficient investigation has not been made yet to determine with certainty the routes followed in many cases; still less to ascertain the relative periods at which the various offsets from the great families have moved. Some have, in all probability, after a temporary stay in one place, passed over others of an earlier date, and located themselves beyond. Thee subject is capable of much curious speculation and possibly of a near approach to a correct conclusion.

If I may hazard a conjecture at present, it is that the Tah-kali and Selish families, with, perhaps, the Shoshonee and some others, originated east of the Rocky mountains; that the country between that chain and the great lakes has been a center from which population has diverged; that these two tribes crossed by the northern passes of the mountains; and that their branches have since been pushing westward and southward. Whether the southern branches of the Tahkali have been separated and driven on by the subsequent irruption <113> of the Selish, or whether they have passed over their heads, can, perhaps, be ascertained on a severe comparison of the different dialects into which each has become divided; it being reasonable to infer that those which differ most from the present are oldest in date and emigration.

The route of the Selish has obviously been along the courses of the two great river s, the Frazer and the Columbia. By the former, they seem to [225] have penetrated to the sea, while, on the latter, they were stopped by the Sahaptin and the Tsinūk. Some branches undoubtedly crossed the Cascade Range, at different points, to the Sound, and the country intermediate between that and the Columbia. And the [Salish] Tilamūk have overstepped that boundary and fixed themselves on the coast of Oregon. They southern limit of the Tahkali is not yet ascertained. Mr Hale identified the Umkwa as an offshoot. Lieutenant Kautz[45] has lately shown the Tū-tū-ten to be another, and it is possible that some of the California languages may also be assimilated. [*]

Dr Newell states that, since he was first in the Indian country, all the great tribes have been gradually breaking up into bands. Whenever two chiefs attain abut an equality of power and influence, jealousies arise, which lead to a separation of the tribe. These are fomented by many causes, <114> the chattering of the women, or course, among others. Before the introduction of firearms, the range of the different tribes was more limited than now. They did not travel so far from their own country. This last is less applicable to the coast tribes than to those of the interior. The former are, however, even more split up, and those of the Sound country perhaps, most of all. The influence possessed even by those claiming to be head-chiefs has become almost nothing; and, in case of any disagreement in the band, the dissatisfied party move off to a little distance and take the name of the ground they occupy, or any one desirous of establishing a band on his own account induces a party of his immediate followers to accompany him, and start, as it were, a new colony. It is to this separation, and to the petty hostilities, which often grew out it, that we must mainly attribute the diversity of dialects prevailing.

---

[44] [* The Yakama are elsewhere {wrongly} referred to the Selish – [Ed. Dall]] {because many were bilingual in Salish. *jm* }

[45] Augustus Kautz – Germany-born, career army officer married to Kitty and friend of Gibbs – became an ally of William Tolmie defending Leschi, her kinsman, against his railroaded "judicial murder" by hanging. Leschi was exonerated by a special court in 2004. *jm*

MYTHOLOGY[46][47] <115>

It is a much less easy matter than might be supposed to obtain a clear idea of the Indian mythology, partly from imperfections in the means of communication with them, partly from various other causes. Not merely have their teachers, where they have had intercourse with priests of any denomination, desired to extirpate the recollection of their former superstitions, but the Indians themselves are prone to mix up a little biblical knowledge with their own legends, thus rendering it as difficult to distinguish between the original fabric and the subsequent additions as it was with the coats in the "Tale of a Tub." Again our modes of viewing and approaching the subject are so diverse from theirs that we are liable to misapprehend them; and not understanding the motive for inquiry, they on their part are apt to look upon it as impertinent.[48] Beyond this, it is probable that their ideas are not systematized even among themselves, but are wrapped up in fables, the origin of which is lost. It will be seen that the imagination has among them a vast deal more activity than the reasoning faculty.

It has very often been stated that the Indians of the Pacific Coast had no idea of a divinity before their acquaintance with white men, and in one sense this may be true, but I am satisfied that the belief in one or more superior or supernatural beings was universal and that generally some creative agency <116> was ascribed to them. It does not in my opinion necessarily follow from this idea that they recognized or understood any particular duty or obligation to worship or offer sacrifice.[49] [296] Neither does the belief in a future state of existence follow of course from

---

[46] Here begins the missing half of the handwritten manuscript published in two parts by Ella Clark, with this remark: The original copy of "Tribes of Western Washington and Northwestern Oregon" constitutes pages 3-114 and 223-250 of a manuscript which a grandniece of George Gibbs, Mrs JJ McGrath of Milwaukee, gave to the State Historical Society of Wisconsin in 1949. Pages 115-223 of the manuscript contain the following account of the mythology, religion, and folk tales of the Indians of the region. Part one was published in December 1955 Oregon Historical Quarterly 56 (4): 293-325.

For further information about Gibbs' life, see Vernon Carstensen's introduction to Pacific Northwest Letters of George Gibbs, Oregon Historical Quarterly LIV ~ 54 (Sept 1953): 190-99. eec

[47] Two remaining sections of the manuscript, "The Tamah nous" and "Tales," were published in the June 1956 Oregon Historical Quarterly 57 (2): 125-167. eec

[48] Other 19th century students of the Pacific Northwest Indians, including some who spoke Indian languages, mentioned similar difficulties. See, for example, the statement of GB Kuykendall, government physician on the Yakima {Yakama} Reservation in the 1870's, in his "The Indians of the Pacific Northwest," in Elwood Evans' History of the Pacific Northwest (Portland 1889), II: 60-61; and a statement by Rev. John McLean, missionary, in his "Blackfoot Indian Legends," Journal of American Folklore III (1890): 296. eec

[49] A little-known evidence of the idea of sacrifice (as well as of right and wrong) among the Indians of the The Dalles area is found in a legend recorded by Jeremiah Curtin and by Edward Curtis. It tells of human sacrifice to a "superior being" ~ Winter. About 25 miles below The Dalles, a little girl was placed on a block of ice and pushed into the river, to appease Winter, who was prolonging cold weather because the child had killed a snowbird. In a short time a chinook wind began to blow. (For the full story, see Edward Curtis, The North American Indian VIII: 147-149, or the present editor's Indian Legends of the Pacific

this, or where admitted is it necessarily connected with one of rewards and punishments for conduct in this life. But I am inclined to think that among most tribes, invocation, if not adoration, was in some form employed and that though not strictly speaking idolatrous, they occasionally addressed prayers to visible as well as invisible objects. That this was so with the Flatheads the evidence of Father Mengarini, which will presently be mentioned, is conclusive. Several of their observances, moreover, have the semblance of propitiation, as their throwing food to the Tatathlia, painting their faces on the arrival of the first ships, "to please Doquebutl," [duqʷəbuɬ] etc.[50]

None of their languages contain, so far as is known, a word conveying the abstract Idea of Deity, and the terms introduced for the purpose naturally involve in their minds [297] white man's God, in the Chinook phrase Sah-hali Tyee, liberally the "chief above," no apt rendering of Great Spirit having been found. So also as to the phrases for heaven. Devil and Hell. A slight admixture of hypocritical humility is moreover visible in "Christianized" Indians, which serves still farther to render explanation difficult. They always stand ready to assure the inquirer that "formerly they <117> knew not God.' It is also to be noticed that among Savages there is as great a proportional difference in education as among whites, a difference very perceptible in the purity of the language they use and in the pronunciation of words, and undoubtedly greater in their familiarity with legends, traditions, and matters of belief, owing to a greater or less opportunity of learning from the old men, or their individual interest or memory. The young men of the present day, especially when corrupted by familiarity with the whites, are very deficient in this branch of the "humanities.'

In this report I shall not attempt to dissect the tales in which their mythology is embodied but rather to present them so far as obtained, in as near their savage dress as possible. The foundation throughout all the tribes of the Selish race from the Rocky mountains to the coast, as well as the Sahaptin and Chinook families, seems to be the same. What further range it may have I am unable to say. It may be thus stated: The world was originally inhabited by different

---

Northwest (University of California Press 1953): 201-203. Hereafter cited as Indian Legends).

Father DeSmet reported an attempt at what he called "human sacrifice" among the Indians of the same area — sacrifice to the spirits of the dead. It is possible, however, that he did not know a custom reported by other early travelers; in some tribes (the Chinook, for one), after the death of a master or a master's son, a slave was killed, to accompany him and to serve him in the spirit world. Probably such a victim could not strictly be called a sacrifice. "In the course of the last summer," Father DeSmet wrote from Walla Walla in July 1846, "and almost before the faces of the Protestant ministers, a child was devoted to the *manes* of one of its companions, who died the day before. The victim was tied so cruelly that the cords entered its flesh, and exposed upon the rocks, where it would soon have perished had not a Mr Perkins, a humane man, succeeded, though with difficulty, in ransoming it' (*Life, Letters, and Travels*: 559). The rescuer was probably Rev HKW Perkins of the Methodist mission at The Dalles. *eec* {See works by Robert Boyd. *jm* }

[50] *Gibbs' note:* Mr Dunn in his "Oregon Territory" published by John Minto in London in 1844 and "British North America" gives an account of the Chinook ideas of religion which I believe to be mostly imaginary. I certainly have never been able to trace any such theory myself. His mention of idols and of sacrifices in particular appear to be incorrect. Idolatry strictly speaking seems to have been unknown. *gg*

beings, some of whom are extinct, or converted into inanimate objects, others are represented by the existing brute creation, birds, animals, etc. Many, if not all of these, possessed supernatural powers, which were variously employed, for good or ill according to their dispositions. One of these, who in no way appears to have differed from the rest except in his vocation, gave to the world its present form, fitting it for the habitation of man. <118> On the appearance of the human race, another beneficent being destroyed the giants and demons who persecuted him [man], or converted them into animals, taught mankind the arts of life and gave him fire. The stories embodying these acts vary considerable in detail with the different tribes, as may well be expected from oral traditions, often confounding the attributes or functions of [298] the two, and have but little regard to keeping or consistency. According to most of them the last mentioned personage became the moon.

The first, who among the Chinooks is called Talipus and by the Klikatats — Spilyai, both signifying prairie wolf, seems to be identical with the Smeow of the Spokanes and the Hoddeh or Whunneh of the Upper Chihalis and Nisquallies; while the Kannum or Ecannum of the Chinooks is the Watteetash of the Klikatats, the Stoqualm of the Nisquallies and the Spikani of the Selish or Flatheads, these two latter names signifying the sun or moon. The word Watteetash according to some accounts is however a generic name, including all the *Elip Tilkum* or primeval race.

The Chinook legend was originally mentioned by Franchere,[51] from whom others have taken the account. It is substantially that the Talipus created mankind, but left them imperfect, and that an inferior but beneficent being, Ecan-num, opened their eyes and mouths and taught them the arts. The editor of <119> the recent translation of Franchere's work has fallen into an error in supposing Ecannum to be the representation of Lucifer and associating this idea with the oriental devil worship. The history of Spilyai, among the Klikatats, is as finished a theme as that of the German Reinecko Fuchs,[52] than whom he is hardly a more reputable character. Innumerable tales are related of his various adventures or pranks, some of which I have added. In personal appearance he is described as having had the head of a man past middle age, his hair grizzled, with the body of a prairie wolf. He does not appear to have been the creator of the earth in Klikatat (*Leechahm*) but simply to have fitted it for the habitation of man. He broke down the obstructions which altogether prevented salmon from ascending the rivers and instead created rapids and cascades which would merely detain or compel them to leap so they could be taken, for he said, "presently there would be people who would bake fish.' [299] [no ¶]

He likewise directed where the different tribes should live, one on one side of the falls, the others opposite. He also ordained where roots should grow. According to some "authorities" he instructed the Indians in different modes of catching fish, as with the seine at Chinook, the dip net at the cascades, and also first built scaffolds to stand on while fishing and erected houses to smoke them in.[53] He first dried salmon without smoking, pounding them up and put them Into bales covered with rushes as <120> is done at the Dalles. These things he did not of his own knowledge, but from the teaching of his two sisters, who dwelt within him and knew anything afar off. At the first start people were foolish and knew nothing.

---

[51] Gabriel Franchere, <u>Narrative of a Voyage to the Northwest Coast of America in the Years 1811 ... 1814</u> (New York 1854): 258. *eec*

[52] Reynard the Fox was the trickster hero of a large cycle of tales and poems popular in Europe in the Middle Ages. *eec*

[53] For characteristic myths about Coyote as culture hero of tribes along the Columbia River, see Ella Clark, <u>Indian Legends</u> 1953: 88-102, 105-107, 110-116, 172-175. *eec*

The exact limit of Spilyai's creative functions did not seem to be fixed. One story made him the creator not of man, but of the *Elip Tilikum*, who at first had no eyes, mouth or orifices to the nose or ears. They could not talk aloud, but talked inwardly with their hearts. Watteetash looked at these and said that this was not good. He accordingly opened their eyes, mouths, etc., with a flint knife and gave them fire. These Indians did not believe Spilyai to be the creator even of the former inhabitants of the world, but that they existed of themselves.

Spilyai was immortal, or if his form was destroyed, it was only for a time. If he was thrown into the water and sunk, he talked under the water and at night came out. So if a great fire was built over him he was all burnt but his heart, which continued to talk, and at night he was restored again. Some relate that it was he who converted all the Skookums or demons into stones and animals. As an offset to his great services to the human race he had some great vices. <121> All agree inconceding his libidinous propensities, which created great scandal in primeval society. He was in the habit of taking women from the Elip Tillkum and getting children by them, who were always wolves, and in consequence of this, some greater power became angry and changed the whole to stone, [300] Spilyai included: others however say that he transformed himself. It was his will or pleasure to be stone.[54] Subsequent to the creation of man, according to the first version, he and his family were again changed into prairie wolves, who were about every where "looking for something.' There are in all these stories references inferential if not direct, to some higher power, probably corresponding with the Amotkan of the Flatheads of whom an account will presently be given, but I have never been able satisfactorily to reach the conception. One Indian informed me that he supposed Spilyai to be chief only on the earth, and that there was another above. [no ¶]

The Indians have no fear to kill the prairie wolf. [no ¶]

The benefits of imparting the arts of life and bestowing fire upon the Indians are ascribed by some of the tales not to Spilyai, but to Watteetash, who was represented as in form like a man; not old, but a grown man and handsome. He also, according to this version, destroyed the demons and took care of everything. This last agrees with both <122> the Chinook story and the Skattamish tale of Snoqualm, or the moon. Others of the Klikatats state that the Watteetash is a generic name and embraces all the *Elip Tilikum*. It is possible that with that tribe, Spilyai was originally the sole agent and that fragments of stories from others may have become ingrafted. As things are there is certainly great confusion in their faith, and it would be alike desirable for them and for all future ethnologists if a council, similar to that of Nice, should be held at cheques, for instance, to regulate it.

The following account of the mythology of the Flatheads was sent me by the Rev Gabriel Mengarini, SJ,[55] who for some years was missionary among them. It is particularly Interesting as throwing the identity of their opinions with those of the coast tribes. [301]

The earth, according to them, is not spherical, but flat and surrounded with water on ail sides, like an island in the midst of a lake; and heaven or sky is nothing else than a huge hollow mountain, covering the earth, as the covering of a kettle. Before the creation of this Skomeltem

---

[54] For Coyote myths about curious rock formations in the Tieton valley and along the lower Columbia, see Kuykendall: 68-69. *eec*

[55] This seems to be an error for Father Gregory Mengarini, who, in 1841, assisted Father DeSmet in establishing a Jesuit mission among the Flatheads of what is now western Montana. Father Mengarini mastered the Salish language so thoroughly that the Indians could not tell him from one of them by his speech. *eec*

(an obsolete word meaning mother, and which has been superseded by the word *skpi*), a very powerful woman who too existed by herself, begot a son without cooperation of man, and the son undertook to create heaven and earth and men, and for his <123> dwelling he chose the summit of the covering, viz.: heaven, whence he took the name of Amotkan[56] which means "he who sits on the top of the mountain.' Skomeltem, his mother, afterwards remained alone on another land beyond the waters; for besides one globe they thought that Amotkan created other globes under, above and around us.

This Amotkan[57] was then considered as this invisible God who has also many sons though having no wife, and when for the first time the Indians saw the whites, they considered them as the actual sons of Amotkan, and consequently immortal until one of them was killed by the Blackfeet.

The first generation of mankind became very wicked and turned a deaf ear to the admonitions of Amotkan, who in his wrath drowned them all in a general inundation. Amotkan undertook a second creation of a set of people twice as tall as the first ones, but proving worse they were all destroyed by fire from heaven. The third generation being as bad as the first, was destroyed through a general pestilence. The fourth would also have been annihilated on account of their crimes, had not Mother Skomeltem interceded with her son on behalf of mankind. The wrath of Amotkan was appeased at <124> the prayers of his mother and he promised never to destroy his creations any more.

But until that time the world was in perfect darkness, there being no sun; and the people being persuaded that the only cause of their wickedness was their darkness, they held a general council for the purpose of enlightening the world, but as everyone refused, *Sinchlep* (the small prairie wolf), being the smartest of all the animals, undertook and succeeded in doing so [302] a very little less than the actual sun, and the people were very glad; but the animals of the time had the power of speaking and Sinchlep being very cunning interfered too much in the secret business of the people, and in passing by during the day, published the actions which the people performed in secret, wherefore the people in anger took Sinchlep by the tail, which in that time was very long, brought him to the ground, and prevented his being sun any more. The *crow* then offered himself to take the place of Sinchlep but being naturally so very black, gave very little light, and unable to endure the ridicule of the people, he retired with shame. Finally Amotkan sent out one of his sons called *Spokani* to enlighten the world. Before doing so, Spokani wished to marry with a woman of the earth. In coming down from heaven he landed just in the camp of the Flatheads: but the people seeing him, though very handsome, so different from themselves, refused <125> him admittance into their lodges, Spokani, very much displeased, left the place,

---

[56] *Gibbs' note: Eh mooto,* third person of a verb signifying "to sit high," changed in composition to *Ah moto kan,* "head" or "mountain." *gg*

[57] Some Coeur d'Alene families, in pre-Christian times, prayed daily to *Amotken,* their chief deity. They asked him particularly for plenty of game, berries, roots. In their first-fruits or harvest ceremonies, they thanked *Amotken* and held out to him on a tray or in a basket an offering of the first berries or first roots. The offering was held toward the highest mountain in view, where *Amotken* was said to live. The Flathead Indians directed similar ceremonial offerings to *Amotken.* (James Teit, The Salishan Tribes of the Western Plateau, 45th Annual Report, Bureau of Ethnology (Washington 1930): 184-186, 383-387).

At the present time, according to Julia Antelope Nicodemus, *Amotken* among the Coeur d'Alene Indians refers to the president of the United States. *eec*

and seeing near the place a small cottage inhabited by a family *of frogs,* he went in, complained of the people and showed his desire to marry one of the frogs. There was one, very large and fat, and she thought herself very happy to become the wife of Amotkan [*sic*] and with one jump she became one flesh, or incarnated with the cheek of Spokani, and matrimony was then celebrated and consummated. The people on seeing the cheek of Spokani so disfigured, and enraged at the presumption of mistress frog, tried with sticks to kill her, until very much ashamed, she prayed her husband to leave the earth, and since he had come to make himself Sun, to go up immediately, which he did; but to revenge himself [for] the contempt of the people, he does not allow them to see him clearly during the day, when he covers himself with a shining robe, crosses the waters under the earth and then only shows himself, with his wife Frog on his cheek.

Thus with these Indians the sun and the moon are the same thing, and this notion accounts for their having but one and the same name for both, viz.: the word Spokani, and so <126> also the spots on the moon are nothing else than a frog. Having heard this story, I inquired of them (there were several chiefs among others present) whether they really believed the fable and they answered that they did, not knowing better. Then I asked them what they thought when they saw the sun and the moon at the same time during the day. They were all startled, looked at one another in surprise, then up as searching for the sun and the moon, joined in a general laugh, and covered their faces as ashamed, and one of them looking at me with only one eye, across his fingers, said, "Well, we were all beasts, and sure enough not one of us has ever observed and remarked what you say now." Since that time it was agreed to call the moon by the name of Spokani Skukuez, meaning the moon of the night.

As to the immortality of the soul, the end of the world, the recompense or punishment after death, they have the tradition that man in dying, dies only half, viz.; the body; the other half (which anciently they did not know how to call, but afterwards their ancestors called Singapens) does [303] not die; but the Singapens of the good ones goes to stay with Amotkan, though without knowing to what particular bliss, and the Singapens of the wicked goes to another place, not determined, having no <127> other punishment than to be deprived of the company of Amotkan. For wicked they intended liars and thieves, for lying and theft were among the Flatheads the two, if not exclusive, at least the greatest sins.[58] Moreover they said that the earth and the people have one day to come to an end, and that after this last day, all the dead shall come to life again, and shall be placed in another land, better than the present, and that after such epoch the people shall die no more.

Notwithstanding the power and nobility of Amotkan and Skomeltem, they are not the deities which the Flatheads worshipped, but Spokani, the sun – After him came as geniuses animals of every kind, the beaver, the crow, the deer, etc., etc.; but Sinchlep, the prairie wolf, was regarded as the most powerful and favorable to mankind. To show the power and favor of Sinchlep, their ancestors reported that there was a time when a large portion of the earth was inhabited by a set of giants, terrible men, who killed everyone they met with, for which they were called *Natliskeliguten,* which in the ancient language means killers of men; that Sinchiep in

---

[58] Cf Father DeSmet (Life, Letters and Travels: 227-228): The Flatheads "are scrupulously honest in their buying and selling; they have never been accused of having committed a theft; everything that is found is taken to the lodge of a chief, who cries {out the names of} the articles and returns them to their owner. Slander is unknown among the women; lying is hateful to them beyond anything else". Governor Stevens and Lt John Mullan wrote in similar vein about the Flatheads. *eec*

pity for the smaller people, went through all the earth, killed every giant, and converted them all into large stones; and even of late, when the Flatheads in crossing the mountains saw a basaltic rock standing upright on the top, they said to one another, "Keep aside, there is *Nathskeliguten*, <128> killed by Sinchlep," and every large piece of Silex they saw around was for them the fragment of an arrow of the killers of men. As it happens oftentimes that one or more of those prairie wolves come at night to howl near the village there are still many particularly of the old women, who believe that Sinchlep in howling foretells them the arrival, by the next day, of somebody, friend or foe, provided he howls only three times.[59] [304]

The worship which our Indians rendered to the Sun consisted in raising up towards it a morsel of meat or roots, before eating them, and saying: <129> "Sun, have pity on us, so that animals and fruits may grow abundantly." In their particular distresses and desires, each one prayed to whatever his eyes met with, be it a tree or a stone. In worshipping the sun our Indians were not so fervent as the Blackfeet are even now, who not satisfied with offering a parcel of their food, very often cut off large pieces of flesh and offer them to their *Natosa* (the Sun) particularly when they go to war. I have asked an old man, well nigh a hundred years of age, if he prayed when he was young, and what did he pray. "Oh yes," he answered. "Every morning my mother brought me into the woods, and having found a dry pine tree, broken and rotten from old age, she told me, 'Now, my son, scratch yourself well to that tree, and pray'; and so I did, saying: 'Oh! my good tree, have pity on me and let me live as long as you lived'; and I repeated always the same prayers. My mother did the same at another tree, not far from mine, until our sore shoulders compelled us to put an end to our prayers.'

Generally the prayers of our Indians consisted in asking to live a long time, to kill plenty of animals and enemies, and to steal the greatest number of horses possible, and this was the only instance when to steal, not only was not a fault but a great merit and bravery, since no man could ever hope to become a great chief unless he had killed at least seven Blackfeet and stolen twelve horses. <130> As it happens rather often that both people and animals are killed by thunder, so they regarded it as an evil genius, and the rainbow was for them nothing else than the same thunderbolt looking down for prey amongst the people, and the Indians believed that the only means to avoid being killed, was to make off immediately, and go to encamp at some miles distant.

The remainder that may be said about the Flatheads, is so common with other tribes of Indians that I think it quite useless to repeat here what you have already acquired elsewhere.

---

[59] *Gibbs' note:* Lt R Arnold, 3r*d* artillery, mentions a circumstance connected with the indirect or inferential transmission of intelligence by the prairie wolf that deserves notice in this connection: While in the Flat-head camp in 1853, waiting the arrival of Gov Stevens from beyond the Rocky Mountains, he one morning asked the Indians if they had yet heard anything of him. They said. Yes, that he had come through Hell-gate pass the last night. As this was thirty miles off, he asked them how they knew it. They said the coyotes howled as they used to when the Blackfeet came in. Mr Edward Lander, one of the party, in fact reached the village the same evening, having camped within the pass the one preceding. The coyotes had undoubtedly smelled the meat, and the howling of those near his camp had been taken up and passed from one to another. *gg*

According to Mr WH Ganey, among the Nez Perces, each man has a particular divinity, equivalent to the tamahnous[60] of the Chinooks, whom he worships. These are animals, birds, etc. He prays to these for material aid, as for instance, if a hunter, he bathes and invokes the eagle to aid him in [305] pursuit of game. They make no idols but set up a wing or feather, a skin, etc.

Do-kwe-butl: The Snohomish, Clallams and other tribes upon the lower part of the Sound have a deity called Do-kwe-butl or No-kwe-mutl,[61] whom I suppose to be identical with Amotkan. Of him I was not able to get a connected account. He is said to live upon the Eastern edge of the world. He made the land and rivers. He also made the sun, moon and stars and created men, or rather <131> at his bidding men came into being. Formerly all animals were men, but they became wicked, and he metamorphosed them to the forms they now bear, as wolves, crows, etc. If he got angry with the present race, he would do so with them. No-kwe-muti is particularly mentioned as having given names to everything, to the different countries, grounds, and rivers, to all the fish and animals, and as having fixed the places to which fish should come.

One Indian stated that there were two No-kwe-mutis, one good, the other bad, and in connection with the story of the eclipse that the good one sided with the Ant, the bad one with the Bear.

Beside this personage there are among the Indians of the Sound, two others of importance. One is Scotam, a great female chief who lived in the sun's road in the West. She is powerful for mischief and brought the smallpox and other diseases among the Indians. The other is Smee-ow, a great man chief, whose home is on the sun's trail in the East, and who was at war with Scotam. The details of their operation I could not follow, but they made medicine against one another. Scotam hardened her flesh so that she was proof [306] against knives, arrows, etc., but Smee-ow finally prevailed by means of an herb from the root of which he made a medicine which it would seem killed her <132> and since then the Indians use it as a remedy against the smallpox. The name of Scotam's country is *at-hlan-ole-gwan-hw*; that of Smee-ow and Doque-butl is *k-kole-gwan-hw*.

The name of Smee-ow {*Spiyaw*} occurs also in the Spokane Walhalla.

---

[60] *Tahmahnous* or *Tamahnams*, in the Chinook jargon {Chinuk WaWa}, refers to anything supernatural {Chinookan = "*tah*"}; it is often used for the Indian's individual "guardian spirit" or "spirit power," a topic to which Gibbs devotes twenty pages in the second half of his manuscript. *eec*

[61] Rev Myron Eells, an early missionary among the Snohomish [Skokomish], translated these words as "the Changer." In Snohomish traditions, the Changer "came once to create, a second time to change, and will come again to make the world over when it becomes old.' ("The Twana, Chemakum, and Klallam Indians of Washington Territory," Annual Report of the Smithsonian Institution for ... 1887, Part I: 681). In Makah traditions recorded by James Swan, the two men-who-changed-things (the *Ho-ho-e-ap-bess*) were the brothers of the sun and the moon. In a Skagit creation myth are two Changers; one before the flood and one after the flood. *eec* {duk^{w}ibuł is the Changer for native Puget Sound. Skagit also have four beings (Fire, Shield, Baby, Knife) in their genesis, as well as Sun and Moon and a hill named "heart" formed by the petrified coiled rope used by the pregnant mother to escape from the Sky world. *jm* }

Elip Tilikum. Although inferior in point of rank to the above named savage divinities, the primitive inhabitants of this world, or demon race, take a more conspicuous place in the Indian superstitions, associated as they are with so many immediately surrounding objects. Not only all animals, but almost everything remarkable in the natural world represents one of these Pre-Adamites.

The great snow peaks, isolated rocks along the shores, the boulders upon the prairies, the columns of basalt and pinnacles of volcanic conglomerate occurring in the mountain region, the large old firs and cedars, all once lived as people, and were converted by a higher power into their present forms. The word "Skookoom" signifying in Chinook sturdy or powerful, is also applied to these beings, but in a more remote restricted sense refers to those especially who were hurtful to the human race. They all possessed extraordinary power of magic, and even in their present shape to some extent retain it, for which reason they are frequently propitiated in some way. <133> [no ¶]

In relating the different stories concerning them, the Indians are very anxious to impress the idea of their personality; that they were really people, at that time, and were afterwards transformed, but the mixed character of their original and subsequent shape always runs in a very amusing manner through the whole. These stories are told with excessive minuteness of detail, each circumstance being separately narrated, as for instance, each of the five times anything is said or done is particularized, and the personages all speak in dramatic form. Much of the spirit and many of the finer "points" suggestive to the Indian mind, are necessarily lost in translating, particularly as the language of narration is an imperfect one, but the recital evidently gives [307] immense satisfaction to Indian listeners.

It is to be understood that no trace of the doctrine of metempsychosis exists in these fables. The transformation was confined to the individuals extant at the time, and in the case of animals their descendants are simply what they seem to be, wolves, jays, rattlesnakes or what not, and so also of the smaller or more recent growth of trees. Yet all animals understand the Indian language in virtue of their progenitors. An amusing instance of this notion occurred at the council grounds on the Chehalis river. When the party arrived in camp, a blue jay, interrupted in his avocation of stealing potatoes from a field <134> close by, flew into a tree and commenced chattering vehemently. One of the Indians snatched a gun, ran out and shot him and on being asked why, answered that the bird was abusing him. The Jay plays a conspicuous part in all the tales, having a high reputation for cunning and newsmongering. The reputation of the crow for sagacity would not appear to be as high as he deserves, judging from a story related to me. They, it stated, formerly when paddling their canoes, always used the edge of their paddles, until one day accidentally the steersman turned his blade flatwise and found that to be the best way. Dogs were originally deer hunters, that is, a part of them hunted, as is now the case. The huge wolf and the rattlesnake rank as among the worst of the Skookooms.

The bones of the mammoth have been discovered in the Willamette valley, but I could not learn that any tradition existed respecting it. An Indian of whom I inquired said he knew nothing about them but he supposed they were the bones of the Skookooms who formerly inhabited the lakes.

Among the various kinds of Skookooms who do not appear to have left any legal heirs are the following, most of whom probably are known by different names among all the tribes. *Tat-at-hlia,* <135> so called by the Klikatats, were ogresses of gigantic stature who carried kettles on their backs as women do kamass baskets. They were painted and had great eyes. When they caught a child they put it into the kettle with water and boiled it with hot stones.

They have all been changed into stone. Of this class were the two wicked women [308] who stand on the bank of the Columbia below the mouth of the Winatshapam, as narrated in my former report.[62] On the Willamette just above Rock Island, is a prominent rock which the Indians propitiate as they pass in their canoes, throwing pieces of bread toward and saluting it. That, I suppose, to be another, and they are met with elsewhere. Dr Tolmie[63] is of opinion that these rocks may be the representatives, not of many Tatathlia, but of those of different tribes. Of this I cannot speak with certainty. The Indians informed me that they threw bread to the Skookooms in order to conciliate them. That they never did so towards Spilyai and Wattee-tash, but only to the evil ones who formerly killed and eat [ate] people. By giving them bread they were appeased.

Chan-a-hop is a great bird that lives by the lake on the south fork of the Cowlitz, near Mount St Helens.[64] It feeds upon men, and cannot be killed with arrows or bullets. It is very probably the same that was sent to eat out the brains of the Tat-at-hlia. He is known to the <136> Klikatats and Nisquallies by the same name.

A-yah-hase is a demon half deer and half snake with two heads and two pairs of horns.[65] He lives everywhere in the mountains and bears the same name with the Klikatats and the Nisquallies.

Kwak-wa-etai-mewh. These are a little people who live in the North. They eat the haiqua.[66] The shape of their mouths, or rather perhaps beaks, allowing them to pull the meat from the shells. Beds of these shells lie around their lodges like those of clams around the houses of the Sound Indians. Their [309] flesh is proof against knives or arrows, but is vulnerable by feathers and in their own wars with the geese, etc., they got pierced with them. In the story of the "Seal Hunters" given below, these beings figure. An Indian informed me that in his father's time there was a slave among the S'Homanish who had lived with them and cured many of their wounded with gum. They are notwithstanding their size very strong, and one of them can paddle a great canoe by himself and catch it full of salmon, halibut and sturgeon.

---

[62] In "A Report on the Indian Tribes of Washington," in Reports of Explorations and Surveys ... (Washington 1855) I: 411. The *Winatshapam* is apparently the Wenatchee River. *eec* {Sahaptin *-pam* = "people of" + *wana* = "river"; their own Salishan name is Pesk^{w}aws. *jm*}

[63] William Fraser Tolmie, physician and naturalist, came from Scotland in 1833, as an employee of the Hudson's Bay Company. In 1843 he was made superintendent of the Puget Sound Agricultural Company, a subsidiary of Hudson's Bay Company, at Fort Nisqually, near the present site of Tacoma. In 1859 he was transferred to Victoria, where he lived until his death in 1888 (Washington Historical Quarterly VII (October 1916): 321). *eec*

[64] Presumably inspired by once resident condors, called *yakessilth+nos* "sharp nose" in Chinuk Wawa. *jm*

[65] These are very powerful horned snake ~ alligator beings, greatly feared unless a family inherits antidote counter magic to befriend them. *jm*

[66] Also spelled *hiaqua* and *hykwa*. Chinuk jargon for shells that were used for ornaments and for money. *eec* {especially dentalium or tusk shells *jm*}

Mo-kwa-tah-oom are the inhabitants of the land of bones, or the dead world. These are described in a Staktamish legend.

Hweh-kwa-deh of the Sound Indians, *Nah-ween-at-hlah*[67] of the Klikatats is the thunder bird, the sound of whose wings produces the noise. <137> He has sometimes been seen by the medicine men. He is very fierce, casting fire at whatever he is angry with, whether men or animals, rocks or trees. There is supposed to be but one. The Klikatats say that a long time ago the Nez Perces made a large hole in the ground and filled it with water, which they heated by stones. A great many persons, several tens, were sitting around it when the fire came and they all died. The figure of the bird in the act of carrying off a whale has already been mentioned. St-plah (Klikatat) are a gigantic race, having very long hair. They are of both sexes. They inhabited lakes and when they saw anyone looking down into the water, rose suddenly, seized and took them down.

Among the Staktaminish [Upper Chehalis] a race of demons inhabited the lakes called *Pissah,* which seemed to be the same as the *Jugwa* or *Zugwa* of the Nisquallies. Whether identical with the St-plah or not, I cannot say.

Kelo-samish, or *ke-loh-sumsh*, gigantic hunters, inhabiting the Cascade Range and [are] known to both Klikatat and Sound Indians. In one of the Snohomish tales, they are connected [310] with the story of the deluge.

Among local tales of the Upper Chihalis, relating to the Pissahs,[68] the following will serve as specimens, given me by SS Ford, Esq. <138>

There was once a lake at the forks of the Chihalis, the neighborhood of which was haunted by a Pissah or demon, in the shape of an enormous bear. This animal was a terror to the Indians, as it devoured all whom it saw, and no one was able to kill it. Finally a very powerful Tahmahnous man volunteered. He went to the lake, found the track of the bear and stuck an arrow at the edge of the water. Following the trail, he then planted arrows in the ground at short distances, where he could easily recover them and, on reaching the bear, shot at and wounded him. He then fled, the bear pursuing, and as he came to each arrow, turned and discharged it still flying, till he reached the water, where he plunged in and changed himself to a salmon, of which the lake was full. The bear on reaching the lake and finding that the man had disappeared, drank it dry, swallowing all the fish. The man then assumed his natural form and with a flint knife, cut the bear to pieces severing his heart strings, and finally released himself. All the Indians in the country were summoned to see the dead monster. They went to work and skinned him, and so large was his hide that the pieces covered all the prairies around. One ear alone covered Ford's

---

[67] The Klikatat word for the Thunderbird is spelled *Eenumtla* in a myth recorded by Kuykendall (p67). The word for thunder in a Nisqually ~ Puyallup myth has been spelled *Enumclaw,* a name given by the Indians to a mountain near Chinook Pass and by white people to a village near by. *eec* {Enumclaw is a Yakama word. jm}

[68] This word has been glossed as "danger" though they are usually described as ogress sisters, and sometimes giant cougars. The dark textures of their hides well describe the thick humus layers of these prairies where they are supposed to have been spread out. *jm*

prairie, which contained by survey several sections of land. The pieces, they kept many years. The lake never reappeared but there <139> is a prairie in its place.[69]

Another prairie on the West side of the Chihalis, also formerly a lake, was frequented by *pissahs*, and the Indians went to the top of a hill overlooking it, heated a great number of large stones and threw them in, thus drying up the water and dispersing or destroying these monsters. One of the stones is still visible on the surface of the ground, and the Indians who have still much fear of approaching the [311] place, always leave a leaf of the Satlal {salal?}, or of the Oregon grape, by the stone on entering the prairie, and a small pile of them may usually be seen round it. Another prairie on the same river, called the Nah-chall is avoided, because at night noises (*swi-li-tchin*) are heard there, sometimes like the war of the surf (which it possibly is), at others more resembling distant explosions. The occurrence of these sounds is no fiction. White men themselves have heard them.

One class of demons, represented by stones and the only ones upon which I have noticed carving, are connected with the weather.

The Multnomah stone, as it is called, is a block of basalt standing in the alluvial land of Multnomah or Sauvies island in the Columbia river. The tradition about this, firmly believed by the Indians, is that if any one touches it, rain will soon follow. Gov Douglas of the <140> Hudson Bay Company informed me that he visited it with an Indian or half breed, and that wishing to satisfy himself, if the block was movable, he pushed it forcibly. The guide, much alarmed, begged him to desist, telling him that it certainly would rain, and singularly enough a violent storm arose shortly after. It is needless to say that this was attributed entirely to the wrath of the Skookoom. Another four-sided prism of basalt, having a rude resemblance to a human face carved upon one angle, stands in his garden at Victoria, which was looked upon by the Kawitchin tribe as possessing great power over the weather. Yahotowit, an intelligent Klikatat, stated that the Multnomah stone was not the only one that produced rain. There are a great many in different places. They were a race of Skookooms[70] who have been changed to stone, and if any one sits down upon them, as a squaw when out gathering berries, it speedily rained. The occurrence of rain out of season, in a country where for several months it scarcely ever falls, is very likely to be attributed to some such supernatural cause.

A block of basalt, sculptured in similar manner to the Kawitchin stone, was lately found by Mr Alex Abomethy [Abernethy] in an old burial ground opposite Oak Point on the Columbia. It was entirely covered with moss, and was [312] unknown <141> to the surviving Indians of the tribe. This gentleman informed me that at his brother's residence, Green Point, just below Oregon City on the Willamette, there is a stone near the river bank which belongs to this class of demons. In this winter of 1849 when the great freshet took place, a deputation of Indians came from up the river to see it. Governor Abomethy [George Abernethy] found them looking round and asked them what they were doing. They told him of this stone and that if it was left uncovered, the river would rise and wash away everything. They did find it bare and covered it over with earth. In the spring of 1850 a second freshet took place and another delegation came down, found it again exposed, covered it up and cautioned him to keep it so, or every thing would be carried off.

---

[69] A variant of this story is part of the Nisqually creation myth recorded by Myron Eells in 1890; the skin of the bear's ear covered Mound Prairie in the Nisqually Plain (Religion of the Indians of Puget Sound, <u>American Antiquarian</u> XII: 68-84). *eec*

[70] Chinuk WaWa: "strong ~ powerful." For stone images, see Wilson Duff (1975). *jm*

In crossing the mountain passes of the Cascades, they are unwilling to talk, lest as they say the Skookoom of the place should send rain and snow. Mr Tinkham, one of Gov Steven's Surveying party, noticed upon the summit snow shoes hung upon the trees when he crossed in the winter of 1853-54. The Indians had left them in going over and as he understood would not use them again. His guides told him not to take them. They were possibly a propitiatory offering.

It would appear that in order to produce rain or snow, it is only necessary for one possessing <142> the tamahnous to blow into the air, splattering the saliva at the same time. This process however is I presume most effective during the wet season.

The isolated rocks of sandstone which occur scattered along the shores have been the subject of particular attention by the inventors of Indian tales. Almost every one remarkable from its position or suggesting any fancied resemblance, has its appropriate story. Near the boundary between the Makahs and Clallams on the straits of Fuca called Seh-tok, a long time ago, it is related, the Clallams went down to Neah to bake salmon, and when they returned a man remained at this place with his two sisters and slept with them, but becoming ashamed of what he had done, turned from them, when the Great Spirit changed them into stone. The rock representing the man has its head inclined [313] towards the water. Their dogs, also become stone, lie around them.

Near Pishtst (Clallam Bay) there are a number of Indians and a whale. These men had taken a whale but not killed him, and in order to tow him ashore more easily, cut off his fins and tail, when for their cruelty the whole were converted to stone. My informant added that in old times the Indians were very bad and the Great Spirit used to come down and punish the worst in this manner. As they are not so bad now, the miracles <143> have ceased.

The well known land mark in the Columbia River, called Pillar Rock, was once a young Chinook. He had fallen in love with a Klatskanai girl, with whose people the Chinooks were at war. To prevent his visiting her, his people hid their canoes, whereupon he attempted to wade the river. They called to him to come back, but he turned and abused them, and for his impiety was thus transformed.[71]

A pile of rocks near the island in Shoalwater Bay represents a wicked tamahnous man, his wife and child. This magician first introduced among the Indians the scourge of *lice,* and as a punishment those insects by order of the Great Spirit dragged him and his family into the water, where they became lasting monuments of a just retribution. Unfortunately the lice did not perish with them.

One other race of beings I have classed separately, as they in particular are supposed to infest the earth, and do not appear to have been properly *Elip Tilikum*. They are *Tsiatko*, in the Upper Chihalis, *Steh-tathl;* in Klikatat *Sheahah*. The belief in these beings is apparently universal among the different tribes,[72] though there is a great discrepancy in their accounts of them. By some, the Tsiatko are described as of gigantic size, their feet eighteen inches long and shaped like [314] a bear's. <144> They wear no clothes, but the body is covered with hair like that of a dog, only not so thick. Others describe them as of natural size and resembling men,

---

[71] For other myths explaining the origin of Pillar Rock, see Indian Legends: 100-101; Charles Wilkes' Narrative of the U. S. Exploring Expedition (Philadelphia 1844) V: 120. *eec*

[72] Traditions about giants called *tsiatko* [Sasquatch, Bigfoot] were reported by Marian Smith in The Puyallup ~ Nisqually (Columbia University 1940): 119-130. Giants appear also in the folklore of the Nez Perce, Spokane, Coeur d'Alene, and Flathead Indians. *eec*

except that they gibber and chatter, one Tsiatko making noise enough to represent a dozen persons. They are said to live in the mountains, in holes under ground, and to smell badly. They come down chiefly in the fishing season, at which time the Indians are excessively afraid of them. At the report of Tsiatko they all run for their houses, fire their guns and shout. They are visible only at night, at which time they approach the houses, steal salmon, carry off young girls and smother children. Their voices are like those of the owl, and they possess the power of charming, so that those hearing them become demented, or fall down in a swoon. A Klikatat informed me that he believed they were not *Elip Tilikum*, or of the demon race, but came afterwards, and that part of them are still men and dwell beyond the mountains where they hunt and are very hospitable, while the others steal at night. They are sometimes seen spearing fish themselves. Dr Tolmie states that an Indian woman, married to a Canadian, who lived at Fort Vancouver, some twenty years ago, told a story of having been taken prisoner by the Tsiatkos and carried into the woods between the fort and the mill. Lash-high and Swatiltoh, a couple of Nisqually Indians, once pretended to have <145> wounded a Tsiatko and tracked him by his blood for some distance. They also said that near where he was shot at a piece of mountain sheep blanket was found. Another Indian told Judge Ford that he had shot at and wounded one while carrying off a young girl and all the next day tracked him by his blood. At the approach of night he espied him sleeping against a tree, but the Tsiatko started and ran and he found it impossible to follow him.

Dr Tolmie states that a tribe of Indians living on the Fraser's River Mountains, a wandering hunter race like the Klikatats, known as Stay-tahl, are called Tsiatko by the Snohomish and are sometimes confounded with the boggles of that name, a fact that explains the Klikatat account.

There are others of this class of beings "too numerous to [315] mention" to some of whom references occur in the different legends which are given below. The suggestion of Dr Tolmie concerning the Tatathlia, viz., that it is not a class, but an individual having different representations in different localities may be true as regards some of these also, but as to others there is no question that they form a race or tribe.

Ke-kai-sl-mi-loot, [Ke-kai-si-mi-loot] an old woman of the Nisqually, daughter of To-was-tan, a former chief and related to half the nobility of the country on one side or the other, not content with her human pedigree, which however she could only carry back three generations, <146> informed me that she was sprung from four generations of Skookams, Tshit-no-wehtsh, Ai-yah-hose, Hutl-kwus-keh-nam, & Tsul-tsah-lup-tu, after which they became Indians, Ke-uch-keh-nam being the first. How far back this was she could not say.

Future state: The belief in a future state, I presume to have been common among all the tribes, although it very possibly was not universal, so far as individuals were concerned. The most intelligible account that I have obtained is that there are two countries of the dead.[73] They remain in the first until the flesh and bones have entirely disappeared, during which time they

---

[73] *Gibbs' note: Moo-kwo-tah-o-mich* and *Skwi-ah-ha-so-mich,* in the language of the Upper Chihalis. gg

For another early account of "The Indians' Idea of the Soul and the Future State," see Kuykendall: 94-95. For modern ethnographers' studies of the topic, see the monographs on Northwest tribes, published chiefly by the University of Washington and Columbia University. eec

revisit the earth at night, and are seen by men. In particular they come to their friends in dreams and urge them to follow, and when this occurs the Indians go out in the morning and lament. After the entire dissolution of the body they pass to the second country, crossing a river by the way and from this time they are lost. The road to the land of the dead is by the West, for which reason the head of the corpse is placed towards the setting sun. This view was given by an old woman of note among the Waktamish and appears to me to be the primitive one. Others speak of two worlds, one a good one in which the <147> sun always shines and salmon, game, etc., are abundant; the [316] other cold and dark and where the inhabitants suffer from hunger and thirst. This last account was confirmed by Yahotowit, a Klikatat, who however added that there was a great difference of opinion, some thinking that when they died, then was the end of it. Whether it may not be simply the Indian version of the Christian heaven and hell, it is difficult to decide positively. It would appear from Father Mengarini's account to have been indigenous among the Flat-heads at least.

There is a Klikatat story about Spilyai, founded on the unnatural conduct of one of his sons, which I did not succeed in obtaining, but which seemed to indicate that prior to that time, i.e., the time of the story, the souls of all persons went to one place, but subsequent to it, by a decree of Spilyai, some went up and others down. The Klikatat word *tumnah*, which means "heart," also signifies apparently the mind or organ of thought and the soul or life.

A resident of Astoria, a man of strict veracity married to a native woman, told me that his wife when sick many years before became insensible, and was supposed for some hours to be dead. Preparations were in fact made to bury her and considerable property was cut or burned. On her recovery she said that she had been to the "*mameloose illahee*,"[74] that <148> she saw there many persons, some of whom she had known, others who were strangers. That it was a good country and they seemed to be happy and well off, with good canoes, clothes, etc., and plenty to eat. She talked with them and they told her they did not want her yet, she must go back. Other instances are known of persons claiming to have visited the nether world and returned, Lash-high the Nisqually chief among them.

The custom, universal I believe among the American tribes, of depositing household utensils, implements of war, etc. with the body, is not to be assumed as a proof that these articles are intended for their use in the other world, or even as implying necessarily their faith in its existence. [317] [no ¶]

Garry the Spokane chief assured me that his people placed by the grave the property of the deceased that they might not be reminded of him. "If," he said, "a father has lost a son whom he loved, he kills his horse, because whenever he saw it he would say, 'That is my son's horse and he is dead.'" But though this is in some instances the notion, the principal one is undoubtedly ostentation. Several intelligent Indians of the Sound tribes stated that the canoes and other things were placed by the dead merely to please them, not because they would get them again, for every thing was new in that country. Father Mengarini <149> states that with the Flatheads the ceremony of killing horses at the grave is intended only to do honor to the deceased and not with a view to use. On the other hand, Mr WH Gray of Clatsop, formerly

---

[74] In the Chinuk Jargon {WaWa}, *mameloose ~ memaloose* means "dead ~ death"; *illahee*, "land ~ country." Memaloose Island, in the Columbia River, was one of the burying grounds of the Indians. *eec*

secular agent of the ABCFM,[75] informed me that the Nez Perces used to burn as well as kill horses and that they informed him that they did this for the use of the dead in the other world.

The Chinooks say that the dead revisit the earth at night and would be very angry if they found their property in use by others, for which reason it is put by their graves. They value these things much, and come to look after them. It seems however permissible to purchase from the dead; for a resident on the Bay was allowed to take some boards which covered dead canoes, on replacing their value in white cloth. Certain persons possess the power of seeing the dead, and a singular instance of this superstition was narrated to me by Mr James G Swan[76] as coming under his own observation. [318] [no ¶]

An Indian named Charley, who had "found his tamahnous," was one night sitting m his house, himself and another resident being in bed, and a bright fire burning, when the Indian's dog commenced jumping up and down and wagging his tail as If fawning on some one. He ordered the Indian to put the dog out, but Charles stood transfixed and exclaimed that there was a mameloose, or dead man in the <150> house, asking if Swan did not see him. Mr Swan laughed and asked who it was. He said it was George, another Indian who had recently died there, and two others with him, that George had asked him what he was doing on his ground and where his brother and sister were, and that he was very angry at his, Charles', being in that place. The next day Charles told some other Indians of what had occurred and they came to Mr S and insisted upon his sending Charles away. Mr Swan was fully persuaded that the Indian's terror was not counterfeited and that he believed in what he said. He added that the dog's share in the transaction, however, puzzled him.

Cosmogony: Their idea of the earth appears every where to be that it is round and flat, and surrounded with water. As to the sun and moon, although there is much confusion in the tales told by different tribes, they all clearly spring from a common origin. The subject belongs more properly to mythology, and some of their legends will be found at length under that head. The Snohomish story is as follows: — [no ¶][77]

---

[75] American Board of Commissioners for Foreign Missions (an agency of the Congregational, Presbyterian, and Dutch Reformed churches). WH Gray arrived in the Oregon Country in 1836, with Marcus Whitman and Henry Spalding, to establish the mission near Fort Walla Walla and a mission among the Nez Perces. In 1843 Gray became secular agent of the Willamette Mission. *eec* {He was difficult, and famously injected emetics into melons at Waiilatpu to discourage theft. *jm*}

[76] James Swan accompanied Governor Stevens in 1855, while he was making treaties with the Makah and other tribes of the Olympic Peninsula. For several years he lived among the Makah as teacher and as dispenser of medicines for the government. In 1857, he published The Northwest Coast: or Three Years Residence in Washington Territory; in 1869-70, he published The Indians of Cape Flattery, through the Smithsonian Institution. The latter was edited by George Gibbs. *eec* {See works by Ivan Doig and George Miles on Swan, and Patricia Erikson for Makah. *jm*}

[77] The Gibbs (1877: 350) Nisqually Dictionary summaries this star lore, noting more precisely: "*The Belt and Sword of Orion*, le-li'-yi-wās. They represent three men taking fish. *The Great Bear*, kwa-gwitsh (*the elk*). The four stars which form the animal are followed by three Indians and a dog. *The Pleiades*, s'ho'-dai, represent toad-fish. *The Hyades*, hud-da'-lu-sid, *a scraper for smoothing mats. The Morning Star* is le-he'-lĕl-lūs (*day-light has

The moon (*sloqualm*) was first made, and formerly lived upon the earth, but it was too hot and burnt everything, so Doquebutl ordered it to go above and be for the night. Its woman asked it where she should go if he ascended, and the moon answered, into its ~~eyes~~ face. She entered and the moon <151> went up and stays there. The moon was then like a young child, always wetting itself. Doquebutl took his clothes and dipped them in the moon's urine, made them up into a ball, and put it above for the day, and this was the sun, Kloquatl. He then made the Evening star, *Klah-hil-lel-lus* ("twilight," or "dark is come") to be the moon's youngest brother and always follow it; and the Morning star, *Le-heh-lel-lus* ("daylight is come") to bear the same relation to the sun. Singularly enough the sun and moon were confounded [319] by some tribes, only one name existing for them.[78] With regard to eclipses, some of the Sound Indians explained them by saying that the sun had particular roads in which to travel, but occasionally he missed his way, and being ashamed of himself, drew his blanket before his face. A Klikatat on the other hand told me that the sun and moon stopped to talk. The occurrence is one of general alarm and anxiety, as they fear lest hereafter there should be no light.[79] It is said that a long time ago the sun became angry, and hid himself for a while, and that it may possibly happen again. Concerning this is the following story which I obtained from a Snohomish Indian. While the sun was absent the bear and the ant, or rather their prototypes among the Elip Tllikum, made tamahnous in relation to it, the first wishing that it should shine only in intervals of six months, <152> the latter that there should be alternate day and night. The one danced and sang, "one warm, one cold"; the other, "Sun come presently, sun come presently." He proved strongest in magic and the sun appeared. Whereupon the former became an actual bear, that his wish of sleeping all winter might be fulfilled. The latter in his excitement had tightened his belt so that his waist became very small, and he was turned into a pismire.[80] The Klikatat have the same story, but they substituted the frog for the ant.

The Chinooks believe that great chiefs become stars and that falling stars indicate the death of such a one. If with trains, they are female chiefs, the train representing the woman's dress. A slight modification of this was rendered by a Klikatat who said that the common falling stars were merely going after women, and that meteors were chiefs, or [320] rather the hearts of

---

come). *The Evening Star*, kla-hai-lal-lūs (*twilight has come*). These two are respectively the younger brothers of the sun and moon. *Falling stars*, *meteors*, klo'-hi-ĕtl, o-hwēt'-lil. They indicate the death of some chief. If the meteor leaves a train, it is a female." *jm*

[78] Typically, native languages use the same word meaning 'orb,' with 'night orb' for 'moon', 'day orb' for 'sun.' The Milky Way appears as a river or pathway in some stories. The Upriver Halkomelem liken it to the glittering chest of a winter dancer's tunic covered with shiny, speckled decorations (Galloway 2009 I: 228). Thanks to Dr Tony Nugent. *jm*

[79] An eclipse, said the Makah Indians, is "caused by a fish ... which attempts to eat the sun or moon, and which they strive to drive away by shouting, firing guns, and pounding with sticks upon the tops of their houses. If not driven away, the fish would eat all of it" (Swan, The Indians of Cape Flattery: 89-90).

The Queets Indians of the Washington coast, one of them told me in 1950, believed that during an eclipse the sun or moon was being eaten by Fisher, who stayed in the sky world when the earth people went up to rescue their chief's daughter. In {his} boyhood, the Queets used to frighten Fisher away with much noise. *eec*

[80] Ant won because of her greater sacrifice by so tightening the belt around her waist that she was almost cut in two. *jm*

chiefs about to die. Several of the constellations have specific names. The latter call the Great Bear *Spilyai* or the prairie wolf; the Sound Indians, *Quag-witch* (a deer[81]); according to them it represents two Indians and a dog, chasing one. The Chihalis and Chinooks give it names corresponding with the last. On the Sound the belt and sword of Orion (*le-lee-ye-was*) is supposed to be three Indians catching fish, the sword representing the fish. The Pleiades (*S'Hodai*) is a school of fish of the Cotters {*cottids* ~ sculpiny} family. <153> Other constellations are Edad {*yidad* = grillwork}, a fish weir; H-dahhe-set {*xdaxəsət*}, the needle with which they make mats, etc.[82] The stationary character of the Pole star or its relations to the Pointers, I believe they have never noticed.[83]

The Nisquallies have the following tale, indicating the idea that the stars are men:[84] — Two girls once went out to dig for roots and remained all night. While lying by the fire they looked up at the stars, chattering and wondering what they were. One said perhaps they were men, and she would like such a star, pointing to a particular one, for a husband. The other said she did not like that one, but such another. The stars *were* young men, and taking the girls at their word, came down and carried them off to the upper world. They found this like their own; they had the same roots to dig and the same tasks. One of them had a child by the star. After a while they became tired and pined for their own country, and one day when engaged in their usual occupation of seeking roots they dug a deep hole and finding the air come through, commenced making a rope of hazel twigs. The husband of the one who had the child scolded her for not bringing more roots, but she excused herself by pretending that the infant had cried so that she could not work. The women <154> continued their occupation, and when the rope was long enough, descended by it to the lower world. The father of the star child, anxious to recover his son, followed and demanded it, but the woman refused to give it up, and eluded [321] his pursuit. He then employed the blue jay, who was very cunning, to get it for him. The Jay

---

[81] The Lushootseed words for 'deer' are {*sqigʷəc*} or {*hupt*}, with concentric wave distributions that suggest {*hupt*} is the older term. This Gibbs spelling is closer to the word {*kʷagʷičəd*} for elk, and indeed his dictionary (Gibbs 1877: 350), as just noted, has "The Great Bear, kwa-gwitsh (*the elk*). The four stars which form the animal are followed by three Indians and a dog." *jm*

[82] Lushootseed for mat needle is {*saxʷƛakʷtəd*}, cattail mat needle is {*ƛakʷtəd*}, weir is {*stqalikʷ*}, and salmon weir is {*cəlusəd*}. *jm*

[83] Contra Gibbs, Chief William Shelton at Tulalip told and carved star stories all his life. In "Lifting the Sky," he told of the creation of the Big Dipper. *jm*

After human faults caused the sky to collapse, creating confused diversity, leaders decided that all the people species should learn the single word "y'haw" {*yəhaw̓*} to shout in unison as they thrust up long poles at the same moment to push the sky back into place. They succeeded on their fourth try. Because it had been so close, many people had been wandering into and out of the sky world and some became constellations at the moment it sprang back into place. Three humans, one with a dog, were chasing four elk. These hunters became the handle of the Big Dipper and the four elk its corners. The dog remains beside the middle hunter. Stars forming a Skate had been two canoes, each with three paddlers, pursuing a fish.

[84] This theme of "Star Husbands" occurs in tribal tales all the way from Nova Scotia to the Washington coast and Alaska. Several variants have been recorded from the Indians of Puget Sound and the Olympic Peninsula. *eec*

entered into conversation with the woman as she rocked her child on the end of a stick, and having succeeded in attracting her attention from it, substituted a piece of wood and carried off the infant to the father, who took it to the world above. The mother was much incensed, but could not recover it.

Another version of the story is that the women first dug down to a lower world, to which they descended, and looking up from thence saw the stars above them, two of which they selected for husbands, and they afterwards returned by their rope. Hence they concluded that the stars were in like manner *people,* and that there was an upper as well as a lower world. <155>

Natural phenomena: he aurora borealis (*Ug-was-seh-akat*), a phenomenon by the way not so frequent as in the Eastern Atlantic States, they dread as the forerunner of sickness. Thunder, Hwch-kna-deh, has already been noticed. As to the echo, I could not learn that they had any superstition, a crew of Indians whom I questioned appearing to understand its cause tolerably well. Of the rainbow they only said that the rain made it.

At Shoalwater bay, where evidences of elevation and depression of the land, apparently at no very ancient date, are visible, the Chinooks, it is said, have traditions of earthquakes that have shaken their houses and raised the ground, but I could not learn whether any superstitions were connected with the occurrence. The volcanoes are an object of awe to the tribes in their vicinity, and enter largely into the legends, particularly of the Klikatats. It seems that violent emissions of smoke and ashes from these have been a rare occurrence, for the eruption of Mount St Helens in 1842 caused great alarm. Previous to that time the Klikatats were in the habit of visiting it, but since they have been afraid to do so. The mountains at present active are Baker, St Helens and as it has recently been ascertained Mt Hood and probably Mt Rainier also, though to a degree hardly perceptible from below. The Indians on Puget Sound state [322] that another smaller peak to the north of Mount Rainier <156> once smoked.

The deluge: eferences to a deluge or general flood of their respective countries seem to be universal, but so far as appears, are connected with the extinction of a former and demon race, not of the present. In the account given me by Father Mengarini of the Flatheads this is distinctly stated. An allusion to it appears in the Klikatat tale of "Iosup." A story was told me by some Skagits to the following effect. Doquebutl once got angry and made the water come over the country. At that time there was a people living at the mouth of the Skagit river called Skah-ka-jet. When the flood came they took their canoes and sat there till the water dried up. One of them then went into the mountains to kill wild sheep, all the animals having taken refuge there. He saw one and shot it. The rest had in the mountains been turned into Kelohsamish, of whom mention has been made elsewhere, and they seeing and not recognizing him for one of themselves, shot him.

Captain Scarborough, an old navigator of the Hudson's Bay Company, informed me that among the Tongass Indians of Russian America he had heard a story of the deluge. The few people who survived, ascended a mountain. When it subsided a black bird flew out and came back with a pine branch. Some of these tales have however too much of the flavor of Genesis about them for absolute credence.[85] <157> The scripture account of that event and its cause is

---

[85] In the traditions of several tribes of Washington, the Deluge was sent because of the wickedness of the people. "When the earliest missionaries came among the Spokanes, Nez Perces, and Cayuses, they found that those Indians had their traditions of a flood, and that

one of those which would be first related by a Christian to savages, and would take the strongest hold upon their minds, but it is [323] probable that the visible changes in the Earth's surface, and the ancient existence of water in places where is now dry land and mountains, would not escape the observant eyes of the Indians. Sea shells, and the bones of marine animals, found at great elevations alone might suggest the idea. It is very certain that they have recognized the features of once existing lakes in the numerous small prairies of the Chihalis and elsewhere, in which they are unquestionably correct.

Of the creation of mankind, there are probably as many stories as there are tribes. Some of them are referred to in the tales. The Snohomish say that Doquebutl first made their country and that of the Skagits, and a man and woman to each, and in time the world grew and the people increased in numbers and divided into tribes. Snohomish were made of the heart of some animal, the Suquamish of the liver, the Clallams of the right hand and arm to the elbow, the Vancouver's Island Indians of the upper arm, the Skagits of the bones, the Klikatats of the feet, and the Indians of the upper part of the Sound of the mouth, wherefore they have very large mouths now. A different version given me by <158> Winaput, a chief, was that there were originally five people: the Sno-homish, Skagits, Suquamish, Cowitchins and Sklallam. Doquebutl did not make them, but they grew from the ground like trees and when they became many separated into tribes. Both men and women grew together. This is not to be construed as giving their opinion that foreign tribes like the Klikatats or Makahs sprung from them, but merely that the latter are omitted from the story, perhaps because the narrator did not feel the need to account for them.

Among the Clallams the following account of their origin was given me. First of all there was one man, where he came from they don't know, but he was alone. One *Sunday* he was thinking why he should have no wife, and he went into the woods and found a fir log with the dry rot, red and yellow. He brought this home and carved it in the figure of a woman and then went out and shot a deer and taking out its entrails, heart, tongue, and teeth put them into the figure. The next day he killed an eagle, put its eyes into the woman's head and moved the eyelids over them. He then commenced tickling [324] her under the arms and round the breasts until she began to laugh a sort of giggling laugh. The figure was in a bent posture with the legs open and the arms extended as if embracing. That night he took her to bed with him and again <159> tickled her until she laughed, and her arms closed round him. The day after he went into the woods to hunt and on his return at night found that his new wife had brought forth a boy. On the second day she gave birth to a girl. It was not then as now, but they grew up very fast. The children of this couple paired and from them came the Clallams. Still another account was given by an Indian of the same tribe. In the first place there were two people at Pishtsh, one of their villages, two at Jennis and two at each other place. At some of these points there were two men, at others two women. The men travelled in search of women and when they had found them built houses and begot children. These children intermarried, brothers with sisters, until they found there were other people at the Skagits, where they went among them and got wives.

---

one man and his wife were saved on a raft. Each of these three tribes also, together with the Flathead tribes, had their separate Ararat in connection with the event" (Eells, Traditions of the 'Deluge' among the Tribes of the Northwest, American Antiquarian I (1878): 70-72).

For stories about the Great Flood, with Mounts Shasta, Jefferson, Rainier, Baker, and certain peaks in the Olympics as the Ararat, see Indian Legends: 11, 14, 31, 42, 44. *eec*

A Makah Indian narrated the legend of the origin of that race to Capt. E. S. Fowler,[86] from whom I received it. There was once a different people at Neah Bay, and among them a very old man and woman. It happened that another tribe attacked them, and the man being too old to fight, fled with his wife to a cave in the rocks. They remained there some days, till thinking the danger over, they came out and found that both parties had disappeared entirely, not leaving a trace behind. All <160> the houses and fishing apparatus had disappeared likewise. After getting something to eat, they returned in despair to their cave, and at night, hugging close to each other, the old man found his vigor to revive and his wife conceived. She soon bore a son and then a daughter, and these were the ancestors of the Makahs. Being destitute of utensils they went to work; the woman dug clams and the man fished, hunted, and made arrow points and hooks of bone, which he sharpened on the sandstone found at Neah. [325]

A Chinook account of their origin was given me by Mr Swan of Shoalwater Bay, to this effect: — An old woman and two young girls came from a country *far to the North* to Chinook. The girls one day were wishing for husbands, that they might have children, when a man appeared and told them if they would look into the other world, they should see their husbands. He made the earth open and they looked down and saw two young men, all apparently of fire. They were frightened and told their mother, who was also alarmed. At night the young men came and stayed with them. In the morning they went up above, and became stars, and the girls followed them, but their children became the Chinooks and peopled the country. This is evidently a version of the star story of the Nisquallies. It is interesting as pointing to a Northern origin of the Chinook race. <161>

Judge Ford received from an old Indian of the Upper Chihalis, a theory of the Indian extraction much less exalted. The man asked him if he knew why the Indians were inferior to the whites, as they seemed to be in every way. Judge Ford accounted for it from natural causes, but the Indian gave his own account, whether original with himself or traditional, it is very difficult to decide; he however averred that it was the latter. All men were once white, but became bad and the Great Spirit caused a flood which destroyed them. One woman alone taking with her a little dog fled to a high mountain and there took refuge in the top of a tree, where she stayed three days, when the water came to a stand. A muskrat then came to the surface, bringing earth with it, by which she knew that the danger had passed. By and by the water subsided and she came down. The dog was the father of the Indian race, which accounts for their fondness for that animal and their always keeping many of them, which the white men do not.[87]

THE TAHMAHNOUS

This is the Chinook term applied generally not merely to those incantations intended to remedy disease by methods other than the direct administration of medicine or to effect a particular object, as to invoke good or ill fortune upon any undertaking, but to everything which

---

[86] After years of seafaring life, much of it on Puget Sound, Captain Fowler settled at Port Townsend in 1857, where he held various territorial and county offices. He was a warm friend of Gov Isaac Stevens. *eec*

{Indeed, the Olympic Peninsula was originally Chimakuan territory before Nootkans moved over from Vancouver Island to become Makah. *jm*}

[87] *To be continued. From* December 1955 (LVI) issue of the *OHQ*: 125 <161-2>. *eec*

has supernatural properties.[88] The conception itself is vague and clumsy and not [126] readily under <162> stood through an imperfect medium of language like the Jargon. It differs in many respects from what is called the Medicine of the prairie tribes, but like that its origin is to be traced in the almost universal desire of mankind to gain a knowledge or acquire a power beyond their actual sphere of existence, a desire which has exhibited itself in so many forms among all nations and in every age, which animated alike the magician, the astrologer, and the alchemist and which in our own day and country prompts a species of conjuring not less astounding in its absurdity or success than that of the Indian charlatan. That the tamahnous men are for the most part as completely their own dupes as the most innocent Spirit rapper is unquestionable, and what is not less so, is that they can produce many of the phenomena of mesmerism.

According to the Chinooks, every man has a good and a bad tamahnous, something analogous to an attendant spirit or angel who influences his fortunes and the character of his life, but as I understand it, in order to obtain control over these spirits the individual must go through a certain ceremonial which comparatively few adventure.[89] This is of course [127] a necessary

---

[88] A study of this important concept in Indian religion is presented by contemporary ethnographers in their monographs on the tribes of Washington and Oregon. Shamanism, emphasized here by Gibbs, was but one aspect of a spiritual concept. The native words for the supernatural have been variously translated by "power," "tutelary," "guardian spirit," "spirit power." Some ethnographers use the word "power" for both the giver and the skill or quality bestowed upon the person. Though details differed somewhat in the various tribes, a few facts about the religion of the Puyallup ~ Nisqually of Puget Sound will show that almost every aspect of Indian life was dominated by their concept of the supernatural.

"The supernatural gave to every man or woman certain abilities, skills, attitudes, personality traits, likes and dislikes .... Adult life without power was inconceivable, and childhood was viewed as a period of preparation for the reception of power.' The powers themselves — the spirits of animals, birds, inanimate objects of nature, abstract elements — "were anxious to make contacts in the world of humans.'

Thunder power, for example, enabled a certain man to bring thunder and rain against his enemy and kept him from being killed in a war with the whites. Power from the Thunderbird on Mount Rainier, one of the strongest powers, "meant wealth and it healed wounds so that the person who had it was very brave.' Wolf power and cougar power made a good hunter. Grizzly bear power made a man gruff, likely to be "mean," and always brave. Power from the top of a tree, which sings when the wind blows, made "a person attractive and a good singer, jolly, so [that he] takes the lead on social occasions." Loon "was a great fishing power and made a man a good hunter and brave too.' Other types of power gave ability to prophesy; still others, skill in healing the sick (Smith, _The Puyallup ~ Nisqually_: 56-75; See also Walter Cline {Leslie Spier, ed}, "Religion and World View," in The Sinka'ietk or Southern Okanogan of Washington: 131-82).

Gibbs' account of the preparations for the power quest and of the vision announcing the power is essentially the same as those of contemporary ethnographers. *eec*

{tah = Chinookan word for power, spirit, energy. *jm*}

[89] But note a recent statement about the Chinook: "Both boys and girls were sent on guardian spirit quests, though the latter were in the minority. The quest was neglected completely by only a small percentage of boys, though success eventually came to perhaps but half of those keeping vigil .... Shamanistic power was acquired in the same fashion as any other power."

initiation to the profession of a Doctor or a Magician but is not confined to them; chiefs and young men of ambition or energy sometimes also "seek their tamahnous." It would seem <163> that some men on the approach of death first see it, a diseased imagination, for instance, suggesting a cause for their decease which is taken for a communication with the spirit. For this object there are certain places which alone are suitable, generally some elevated and remarkable point consecrated to the superstition.[90] The narrows on the Willopah River was one which the Shoalwater Bay Indians frequented. The aspirant, after purifying himself by washing, went up into the mountain and built a fire by which he watched, fasting, day and night. Becoming physically exhausted and his imagination wrought to a pitch of high excitement and desire, he "saw visions and dreamed dreams." In this state the first living object that presented itself as a bear or bird, etc., was adopted as the emblem of his tamahnous. On returning to his lodge, an early task was to represent this in some suitable form, as by painting or carving upon a board. This device was placed in some conspicuous situation in the lodge during the life of the owner, and after his death near his grave, so that, as they state, anyone who had before seen it might know that it was such an [sic] one's grave. One that I met with on the Willopah River, which some irreligious white man had converted into the door of a log cabin, was painted with human heads and hands and with cockle shells, and according to the Indians had belonged to a famous doctor. <164>

Of a similar character to these boards were the designs painted on the sepulchres described by Lewis and Clark and the mouldering images that kept company with the dead within.[91] The Chihalis, the Makahs and the Clallams all make [128] these designs, but I believe none of the Puget Sound Indians.[92] In one of the Makah lodges at Neah Bay there is a representative painting which I presume to be of this character, but which from its size and position in the lodge was clearly not intended to be removed. Two or three boards have been worked down to

---

(Verne Ray, Lower Chinook Texts, University of Washington Publications in Anthropology, VII (1938): 78-80).

And among the Puyallup ~ Nisqually: "One prepared for and did not seek [power], one accidentally became receptive and it came unasked, or it came unsought to those who would not normally have been considered fit subjects." (Smith, The Puyallup ~ Nisqually: 58). *eec*

[90] In western Oregon, Spirit Mountain was a favorite spot among the Santiam Indians, and vigil on Mount Jefferson brought guardian spirits of special power. Saddle Mountain, the home of the Thunderbird, was favored by the Clatsop. On White Mountain in northeastern Washington are numerous piles of stone which Indian boys left as proof to their elders that they had been there on the solitary vigil. *eec*

[91] In the vicinity of the Cascades of the Columbia, Captain Clark found an ancient burial place, consisting of eight vaults made of pine or cedar boards. "The whole of the walls as well as the door were decorated with strange figures cut and painted on them, and besides were several wooden images of men, some old and so decayed as to have almost lost their shape ... they were most probably intended as resemblances of those whose decease they indicate" (Elliott Coues, History of the Expedition under the Command of Lewis and Clark 1893, 11: 682. *eec*

[92] Among the Puyallup ~ Nisqually a person with a certain abstract power "placed painted boards before his house. He also painted himself when giving sings, which he did frequently" (Smith, Puyallup ~ Nisqually: 70). *eec*

an even face, neatly joined and fastened with cords so as to appear like one [board], five by twelve feet in size. The upper part was painted with the figure of an eagle, having its wings extended and covering the whole length of the plank. Beneath was a monstrous fish which the bird grasped in its talons. It is intended to represent the great Thunder Bird as he was once seen carrying off a whale; and is very well executed.[93] The peculiar figures which characterize the paintings of the northern Indians are embodied in this, which I have never noticed among the other tribes, and which one might also imagine to be significant.

With the Sound Indians, as far as I have been able to learn, the idea is somewhat different. No private especial tamahnous belongs to the individual, but there are powers which govern different transactions and are invoked accordingly. These are all of the <165> primeval, or demon race, who inhabited the world before this creation of man, all of whom possessed supernatural powers. The word Ske-lal-li-tude {sqəlalitut}, also apparently used for luck, or fortune, is applied to all of these, and to incantations of every description. The one most usually sought, the one which chiefs, ambitious of wealth and power, and young men of ardent and aspiring minds, [129] who would fain make their way in savage society, without working for a living, particularly covet. Is the Le-youtl-mah, the tamahnous of success or good fortune. Especial localities were also adopted to this purpose, as there the beneficent being dwelt or attended to receive his aspirants. The method of seeking him will be most readily gathered from the account of a Snohomish Indian of the mode in which his father S'hootst-hoot, an old chief yet living, obtained his wealth and eminence. When a young man and very poor, he went up the Stoluch-wamish River with his sister. She had dug and dried many cloves, and as the Indians there had none, traded them for the wool of the mountain sheep, with which she made a blanket and gave it to her brother. But after wearing it awhile, he became ashamed and said to himself, "Shall I then always depend on my sister for a living?" So he determined to seek Le-youtl-mah. He went to a place near Skagit head, the southeastern point of Whidbey's Island, washed himself perfectly clean, even to his nails, ears and neck, rubbed his <166> teeth to free them from food, watched and fasted three days. At the end of that time he fell into a trance, in which a man with a very handsome face and bright eyes appeared to him and told him to go down to a point jutting out into the water and do as the chief should tell him who lived in the house under the water. This, as he saw, was a very fine house with a smooth floor and containing everything that could be desired. S'hootst-hoot did as he was directed. He cut a cedar withe and fastened it to a large black stone — a white stone would not have answered, as a fish might swallow it and carry him off — and dove at the place pointed out to him, where the water was about fifteen feet deep, but the stone broke the house to pieces and all its contents floated to the surface. He himself rose faint and exhausted and could not have reached the shore had not Le-youtl-mah pushed him towards it. As he stood by the beach looking for the place which he seemed to know but could not exactly fix upon, the water rose to his breast. He stepped back and it rose again, and again he moved away. It rose a third time, and he then saw and recognized the place for which he had before struggled and again swam for [130] it, but he was three times washed back. The fourth time he succeeded and found the Le-youtl-mah. That is, he saw him. It was the same figure that first appeared to him and who now led him ashore again. <167> From that time his good fortune followed him always at two places, Skagit head and another near it.

---

[93] What seems to be a sketch of this design is given in Swan's *The Indians of Cape Flattery*: 9. It had been in a chief's lodge and was "afterwards placed at the base of a monument erected over his body." *eec*

The way in which they benefit by this, according to their own account, is that other Indians are seized with a desire to make them presents. They never want for food, or blankets, or slaves. Gifts are showered upon them. The son of Hts-Stuch-tam, or S'Homahmish, informed me that his father was always finding dead seals and porpoises. It is, however, only chiefs (Se-ahm) {si'ab} that is, freemen of some rank or distinction, who find Le-youtl-mah. If others seek him, wash and fast and reach his house, he asks them who they are, and tells them they are not of his people, but must seek some other Skelatitude. Some have lied about finding him who never did, and these died. It is necessary that the seeker should be chaste and particularly should not have had connection with a woman out of season, as no matter how much they wash they would be detected by the smell. The number of those who ventured upon the ordeal was, I imagine, always limited, as but few have been pointed out to me as having passed it. Among them are Chow-its-hoot,[94] chief of the Lummi, and Hat-ya-watst, Gen{eral} ?? Em Pierce's father.

Kwi-han, a young Satsop Indian, related that when he was a boy, his father took him to the mountains to hunt, and having killed an elk and cut it up, his father told him to stop and seek his tamahnous. <168> He hesitated, but his father still advising him, he finally stopped, built a fire, washed night and morning in the brook, rubbing himself down with spruce twigs, and kept watch all night, jumping backwards and forwards over the fire and shouting. But he saw nothing. Probably faith was not strong enough or his constitution was too strong.

The parentage of Hy-outb-mah is mentioned in the legend of Sisailuchan. It would seem that he was one of the Elip Tilt-kum or primeval race. His house is full of slaves and property of all kinds. [131]

The Sound Indians state that once a Chemakum woman, very pretty and young, went to Point Willow to bathe. She washed her hair with urine (savash soap) and was dressing it over the water when one of Le-youtl-mah's [sic] slaves saw her, rose and carried her down with him. When a canoe upsets, the Indians see her come up bearing a child in her arms, with seaweed growing from her nostrils.

The tamahnous of medicine is among the Nisquallie called *Sho-nahm* or *Sho-mahb* {$x^w dab$}, a name given also to the professors themselves. The mode of gaining this power is generally similar to the other. The seeker fasts and washes himself in some sequestered brook, rubbing his body with herbs. He lies down in the brook and the water overflows him, when he falls into a swoon. On his recovery he can see diseases in the body. Dr Tolmie informed me that <169> the small lakes in the Nisqually plains were once considered the especial haunt of the Sho-nahm. As might be expected, these medicine men have a strong hold upon the superstitions of the Indians, an influence of late, however, much weakened by familiarity with the whites and their mode of treating diseases. The Indian Sho-nahm or doctors are not only physicians skilled in cure, but necromancers who can bring calamity or death at will. They are thus often hated as well as feared and not seldom fall victim to the revenge of those whom they threaten. In curing diseases the practice seems to differ considerably, whether from adherence to particular systems or not is a matter difficult to decide upon. One operation which I witnessed was as follows: The doctor was a wild-looking old fellow, dark-skinned and much wrinkled, with a shock of matted hair, which he now and then swept from his eyes and tied in a knot in front. His dress was parti-colored, made of a blue and a red flannel shirt cut up and sewed together in parts. The patient

---

[94] Famous for two house panels displaying one of his powerful spirit helpers as an engraved disk with incised diagonals to the right and left, each leading to a smaller circle. It is said to be the sun carrying two sacks of treasures. One panel survives at the Bellingham museum. *jm*

was a young woman, sick of consumption, and according to my unprofessional opinion, bound to die with or without assistance, so that if the doctor's own life, as well as his reputation, were at stake his course was nearly run. The woman lay upon a pile of mats in a lodge with one female attendant near by and a dozen men ranged on <170> either side to assist the operation by driving away the [132] spirit of the disease. Their paddles were placed before them and each was provided with a short stick. A small fire of bark was kept up at either end of the hut and a pan of water was placed by the side of the practitioner. When everything was ready, he commenced with a short jabber, the others striking up a chant in which I could recognize no particular words, and keeping time by beating with their sticks on the paddles. Dipping his hands into the water and blowing upon them, he stooped over the woman, whose chest was uncovered, and commenced sucking the spot where I presume the pain was seated, his whole frame heaving as if with the violence of his exertions. After a few moments he placed his hands to his mouth, spat into them and, clenching his fists, squeezed out the saliva into the pan, jabbering and gesticulating, occasionally holding up his fists joined together, with one thumb upward, that the rest might see he had brought away part of the disease. Then he again washed his hands in the pan, motioned for a while as if hauling something from 'the woman, and blowing upon his fists, commenced sucking. At times he threw his hands upwards as if casting the disease into the air, using many contortions. Joining occasionally in the chant, singing solus for a few moments, or talking to the others, apparently explaining the progress of the operations. <171> The sweat meanwhile poured from his face and arms. This performance lasted for perhaps an hour, during which the patient remained quiet, merely covering or uncovering herself as required. He then ceased for a short time while she sat up and in a low, plaintive voice told how she felt and, as nearly as I could learn, what she had dreamed when in the temporary stupor into which she had fallen from time to time. In these dreams they place great faith. The doctor listened to this very attentively, responding now and then with a gentle ah! and wearing as benign an expression as his visage could be twisted into, interrupting her only to explain to the friends around the highly beneficial effects springing from his treatment. It seemed from her gestures that the seat of pain had now moved from the chest to the throat, and he accordingly commenced again, sucking at that point. The spot acted upon in the first instance had [133] become very red, like a scald, but no actual blister was raised nor had the blood followed, as was sometimes the case. The termination of the performance is usually the production of a small black stone or bit of wood, previously concealed, and which the doctor wrenches from the body, exhibits for a moment, and then casts into the fire, or throws away. <172> The Indians showed no unwillingness that we should witness the performance, though formerly they stopped if intruded upon by whites, nor was their own conduct indicative of much respect. On the contrary they seemed highly amused with my curiosity, and made a good many, doubtless very waggish remarks on it. I should mention that it is not in order to stand up during the ceremony, as the practitioner is supposed to blow his evil spirit into the air, from which it might enter the body of any person standing erect, or if he did not, the fact might discourteously give the lie to his theory. They, however, allowed me to stand over the patient, either in the charitable hope that I might succeed to the cast out a devil or thinking that as a *Boston* [95] I was proof against it.

If a doctor becomes sick himself, he usually charges it to the bad tamahnous of some other and rival medicine man. An old practitioner at Steilacoom, who had lived longer than

---

[95] Chinook term for a white man of the United States. *eec* {especially from the American port of "Boston." *jm*}

usual in his profession, was wiser in his generation and attributed his illness to the spirit of the Black Hand. The fees of the medicine men are in proportion to the wealth of the patient or the magnitude of the disorder and consist of blankets, guns, *hiaqua*, and other articles. If he fails and the sick man dies under his hands, his own life is forfeited unless he succeeds in appeasing the wrath of his friends. The profession is therefore a dangerous one, and the love of power, <173> the influence maintained over the crowd, is probably the great inducement to follow it. It may be mentioned that the foreign physicians are very apt among the Indians, as among some others, to enjoy a greater reputation than their own, those of the wilder tribes, the "Stick Indians" in particular, being supposed to have the most potent familiars.[96] It would [134] seem, however, that the powers of the medicine men have become greatly enfeebled in modern times, the age of miracles having passed away among the Chinooks as well as elsewhere. Nothing has occurred of late years, like the following, of which I have been "credibly informed.' Once a great magician came from the far North with his brother to the Chinook country. The brother was drowned in Shoalwater Bay, which seems then to have been a lake, and in order to recover the body, he sent the Indians into the mountains to gather stones and build a great fire. When he had heated the stones, he cast them into the lake and dried it up so that he found the body, which in order not to lose it again he put it into his own belly. The stones are visible at this day at what is called Rocky Point. The doctor afterwards went over to Chinook and treated some women who were sick, but his medicine not suiting them, they became angry; and an old woman, also skilled in magic, employed her powers against him, telling the people that he had his brother in his belly. <174> She caused him to swell up and as he sat on Scarborough Hill, she opened him with a knife and then converted him and his brother into rock.

The numerous lakes in the prairies between the Nisqually and the Puyallup were formerly all haunted, and were the especial resort of young men seeking the inspiration of the Shonahm.[97] If they had been chaste, they sometimes received the afflatus. If not, the spirits destroyed them. A lake lying about five miles back of Fort Nisqually was called Nis-jug-wa (Jug-wa is a fright or monster). Another above Steilacoom is called the lake of the Black Hand, because from it a gigantic sable hand was seen to arise.[98] [135]

The Klikatats seek the tahmahnous by wandering in the mountains night and day till they meet it. It may be a bird, a deer, or any other object that has formerly been a Skoo-koom. The seeker must have been chaste, but he may take a wife afterwards. Some find the Tamahnous of becoming rich or chiefs; others, of being doctors. The Tamahnous within the doctor tells him the nature of the disease, in what part of the body it is. The doctor then seeks it out in the shape of a

---

[96] "A race of tall Indians, called 'wild' or 'stick' Indians, was said to wander through the forests .... Their homes were hollowed like the sleeping places of animals .... It was largely because of this lack of any houses or villages that they were characterized as 'wild,'" (Smith, Puyallup ~ Nisqually: 129). A young Quinault – Chehalis told me that they were called "Stick Indians" simply because they lived in the woods. *eec* {In Chinuk WaWa, '*stik*' means "wood, forest, trees." *jm* }

[97] Crater Lake also "was held to be very potent for this purpose" — of becoming a shaman. (EC Curtis, North American Indian XIII: 177). *eec*

[98] Judge James Wickersham of Tacoma published this story about Lake Steilacoom in 1898. Because of the strange hand, Indians never fished or swam in the lake. (Nisqually Mythology, Overland Monthly, 2nd Series XXXII: 345-351). *eec* {This spirit hand is confirmed in the 1920 place name study of TT Waterman. *jm* }

small object, which is black, green, red, etc., according to its nature. This he throws to a distance.

Sometimes, though not often, women find the tamahnous of medicine. Among the Wascoes, <175> according to Doctor Suckley,[99] when one of these dies, one of her female descendants, if she has any, is bound to take up the profession. The ordeal is similar to that undergone by the men. The wife of a well-known citizen at The Dalles was the granddaughter of a doctress and was when a girl compelled to attempt it. She went to a brook to wash and saw the apparition of her relative, shrieked and fainted, and when she returned to her senses ran back and could not be persuaded to return. She, however, was always afterward the object of consideration from her tribe.

Allusion has been made to mesmerism as akin to the phenomena of the tamahnous, and there appears to be no doubt that to a certain extent the power of inducing a state resembling the magnetic slumber is possessed by some of these men, nor that it does in certain cases bring with it relief. Evidence on this point from witnesses of undoubted veracity is abundant. A remarkable instance was related to me by Dr Suckley and by Lieutenant Archibald Grade (5th Inf[antry].), both of whom were present at the time. An Indian named Tomasowtt, a great medicine man at The Dalles, was the operator. The patient was a young girl who had a spinal affection. The Wascoes had had a dance which lasted five days, and the whole band were assembled in a lodge, at one [136] end of which there was a board platform somewhat raised. Tomasowtt stood upon this, dancing, swinging and shouting, <176> and tearing off, as his excitement increased, one article after another of his clothing, until he stood perfectly naked. At length he exclaimed, "I feel a wind coming which will make me strong enough to put her to sleep." And becoming apparently exhausted or weak from his exercise, he grasped the pole, which supported the roof, at the same time stooping so as to bring his back into a horizontal position. His knees shook under him and his voice subsided into a low, monotonous song. The girl was then brought in and laid upon him, with her back to his, her head lying over his shoulder and kept in her position by a couple of squaws who held her legs. She had on only a shift. Meantime the people present kept on singing and pounding upon boards, and the man continuing dancing and singing. In a short time, perhaps ten or fifteen minutes, the girl went to sleep. She was then laid on the floor, and the Doctor kneeling by her commenced a low, wailing cry. The Indians stated that no one but he could awaken her. As the slumber passed off, she commenced crying, then singing louder and clearer and finally got up and danced with all her strength.

Mr WH Gray assures me that before any knowledge of mesmerism had reached Oregon, he had seen a third person made a medium by an Indian doctor at Clatsop. The patient was an old woman, afflicted with cancer in the breast. The doctor influenced a young man so that he had perfect control <177> over his actions, by means of singing and gesticulating, all the rest present accompanying as usual. He kept him in this state for an hour, not saying much to him. While in it, the man communicated the result of the disease, that the patient would die, which the doctor announced to the crowd. The person mesmerized, on his recovery, said that he had been to the other world; he had seen various persons in his travels there, whom he had known before, among them the spirit or the old woman who had arrived there but had not got settled. In a case like this, it may be remarked, there could be no vengeance taken on the practitioner.

On inquiring from various Indians, they have all assured [137] me the patients in these cases could only be awakened by the doctors themselves and that any other person might prick

---

[99] Dr George Suckley was physician & surgeon of the Pacific Railway Expedition of 1853. *eec*

them with knives or pins without their feeling it. A peculiar state or sleep or temporary insensibility seems indeed generally to follow from the operations of the Medicine Men, the dreams of the sick during the period being one of the chief means of diagnosis.

But a still more extraordinary power is claimed by a few, that of communicating self action to inanimate objects. The first person from whom I received this information was Mr James Strong of Cathlamet,[100] who had witnessed the performance of To-tilikum, the chief at Woody Island, near that place. <178> Two large carved sticks or poles were used for this purpose, which were manipulated by the Indian for some time and with great violence, the usual accompaniment being kept up by the spectators. At length a rapid and tremulous or waving motion was communicated to them, the operator holding them near one end. The Indians informed him that no one but the man himself could arrest this motion. Mr Strong was suffered after a time to attempt it and failed in doing so, but was not satisfied as to the cause. I have never been fortunate enough to see this exhibition, which very few persons pretend to understand. It does not appear to be a branch of medicine, but simply of magic, and its knowledge is confined entirely to the tribes on or near the coast and sound. Ho-hoke or the Raven, a Cowlitz Indian, and a very old man living on the Puyallup, are the only others who have been named to me as possessing it; but every Indian with whom I have spoken on the subject in various parts of the district corroborates the story of the "Skookum sticks.' The Klikatats state that they have not the power themselves, but have seen others exercise it among the Chinooks. The sticks are bars of cedarwood, carved and painted, and are sometimes smeared with grease and feathers. The motions of the operator in conferring the property upon them are described [138] as mesmeric passes. The sticks are not necessarily held by him, <179> but may be by others, and the fingers of those grasping them become clenched so that they cannot be disengaged unless the exhibitor blows on them, when they loose their hold but remain stiff till soaked in warm water. Neither can as many men as can seize the sticks stop their motions. The operator alone is able to do this, which he accomplishes by throwing out his hands, and blowing at the same time, when they cease.[101] Such is the universal assertion of the Indians themselves; and the facts are certainly not

---

[100] James Strong "began to live among the Indians upon the Pacific Coast in 1850, learned one of their languages, and for six years traveled and lived among them" — from the preface of his book, Wah-kee-nah and Her People (1893). *eec*

{Wahkeenah, a Yakama girl, was raised in his family before she married. Because Strong provided her native family with financial compensation she is sometime in error called a slave, but that misunderstands and demeans her opportunities. *jm*}

[101] Kuykendall (p91) heard about an old medicine man, at or near The Dalles, who "was quite famous for his exploits in 'dancing the stick.' When all the people had gathered in a lodge for one of his séances, he would begin 'to sing his tahmanomash song'. After singing four times, any person present was invited to take hold of the stick. As the old man sang and kept time by swinging his arms, the person holding the stick was jumped around by the stick, which began hopping about. As the tahmanowash man warmed up and sung and gyrated more vehemently, the violence of the dancing increased. The dancer was instructed to hold the stick still; but the more he tried, the more violently he was jumped up and down and around the lodge .... At last... he fell over in a state of cataleptic rigidity, still clinging with a deathgrip to the stick .... Indians familiar with the performance describe the sensations experienced while holding the sticks as being like that produced by the

more incredible than other performances of which we hear, wherein imagination is acted upon by will.

There is another kind of tamahnous, said to have originated among the Clallam and the knowledge of which is confined chiefly to the Indians on Hood's Canal and the western side of the Sound, or rather to the fraternity in whose breasts its mysteries are deposited. Not being initiated, I can only give its character upon report. It is variously called S'Heena, S'Hin-hin and S'hehn, heh-nim. Both men and women and even children are received, and previous chastity is not apparently required. None are admitted into the lodge during the early part of the ceremony, which lasts five days, several perhaps undergoing it at once. During this time the novitiates are *actually dead*. On the fifth day, they are brought out with a rope around the waist, and are raised up by five persons, [139] holding them on their fingers' ends <180> and hoisted into the air five times. They then come to life and immediately are started on a keen run, one holding the rope, and driven through the woods until sundown, when they are taken to the water and bathed. Bloody froth and mucous issues from their mouths and they are like drunken men, sometimes for days. Those previously initiated are meantime painted black and powdered with down and perform all sorts of wild antics. The performances conclude with dancing. The Indians claim for the adepts extraordinary powers. For instance, I was told that if one of them was angry with a man, he would shoot him dead. All efforts to extract the ball or arrow would be in vain. The friends of the victim would inquire who did it, but no one would reply, until S'Hin-hin himself came forward and perhaps said, "I killed him, because he has been abusing me." He would then stoop down, draw out the arrow, and the dead man would immediately come to life. Again if one of them lost anything, he would call on the others, perhaps three or four of them and they would search all the lodges until they found it. The offer was recently made to induct me and finish the business in twenty-four hours, but being uncertain whether I might not fail in coming to life again — I waived it.

Indians who are not among the initiated look upon this tamahnous with great fear. <181>

There are various other kinds of incantations performed on the Sound for specific purposes, some of which require no previous ordeal or preparatory rites and which anyone may use at pleasure. Those insuring success in gambling are noticed elsewhere. *Steh-him* is the magic of *bounes fortunes* and its song brings success with women. *Tsaik,* {*ceyk* = 'plenty, abundance'} besides being the tamahnous of the game of "hand," brings fair wind and abundance of *haiqua* or Indian money. In procuring wind, they dash the spray with their paddles in the direction towards which they wish to go. *Tobe-shah-dad* {*tubšədəd* 'warrior, fierce'} brings good weather and stops the wind. The *Gil-meh-hu* is the salmon dance and intended to make the fish plenty. The power to affect this is, however, first sought like that of the Teyoutlmah, and the adept conducts the dance in which the rest join. [139]

In seeking a good tamahnous or Skelalitude, they never get a bad one — or the reverse.

It will be seen that the whole resolves itself into the idea of obtaining by these wild rites the aid of the supernatural beings, who are supposed to possess certain functions or powers. Singing and dancing and noises generally seem to be the means by which their favor is caught, and the repeated expression of a wish or utterance of a demand enforces their compliance. [no ¶]

The number five is a magical one, <182> as will at once be detected in the various legends. A question asked five times must be answered, or an order given [must be] obeyed,

---

interrupted electric current. Their muscles were thrown into a state of tonic spasm, so that they found it impossible to let go." eec

however unwillingly, provided the party be possessed of power. The tamahnous is wound up in everything relating to them. A man's very whims are his "tahmahnous." All their amusements and occupations are connected with it; and almost all natural objects around them, as representing the great magicians of the primeval earth, are tahmahnous.

TALES

THE HISTORY OF SPILYAI
(Klikatat)

When Spilyai started upon his travels, there were very high falls upon all the rivers so that the Salmon could not get up. They were confined in a great lake, which belonged to five sisters. Spilyai saw that this was not good and he concluded to lower the obstruction and enable the salmon to pass. Accordingly he disguised himself as a child, and came to the water-side where one of the sisters was washing herself, crying. She supposed him to be one whose people had been upset in a canoe and took *him* home, where he speedily became a pet. The four older sisters did not suspect his true character, but the youngest knew him and wondered, saying to herself, "That is Spilyai. What does he want?" She did not, however, communicate her suspicions to the rest. They gave him some fish <183> to eat and were astonished at his voracity. He ate up everything in the house. The youngest sister was confirmed in her suspicions by this. When the women went to dig roots, they set Spilyai up erect in his cradle, but as [141] soon as they were gone, he freed himself and resumed his natural shape, putting on his head five bowls made from the horns of the big horn sheep. Every day for four days he worked away at the dam, digging it down, at night taking the form of a child again. On the fifth day towards evening, the sisters felt in their hearts that something was wrong, and said to each other, "Let us run and see what is the matter at our house." [no ¶]

They found the child gone and heard the rushing of water. They hurried to the dam and there was Spilyai at work enlarging the hole with his stick and the salmon leaping at it. Each [sister] was armed with her kamass stick,[102] which she broke over his head. But he was not afraid and worked till the hole was finished. They asked him why he had done this. He answered: because it did not suit him that they should keep all the salmon till they died, that they ought to be satisfied with part and let the rest go up for other people. He ordered that thenceforth the great fish, as the whale, etc., should go to the sea, and the small ones, such as salmon, should ascend the rivers. And [he] went away after <184> changing the sisters to Wheet-wheet or sandpipers.

After this he traveled up the river till he became hungry and wished for something to eat, so he consulted his own sisters whom he always carried in his belly,[103] taking them out when he

---

[102] Stick used in digging camas roots or bulbs, one of the Northwest Indians' most important vegetable foods. *eec* {Dibbles pry up both roots and seafoods without big impacts, see Jay Miller, Dibble Cultivating Prairies to Beaches: The Real All Terrain Vehicle 2005. *jm*}

[103] Cf. Kuykendall (p. 65): "A most singular myth connected with Coyote was that he had three sisters that lived in his abdomen. These sisters were in the form of berries that grow in the mountains. These sisters were very wise, and were oracles to Coyote; whenever he found himself unable to accomplish his designs, or was in doubt about how to proceed, he called out these sisters and asked them what he had better do, or how he should manage. They are

wanted their advice, as they were very wise. They [141] told him to catch some salmon and eat them. The salmon were now running; Spilyai stopped at a point of land projecting into the river and called the salmon: "Come, my people. I made you and you are my people. I am very hungry. Have pity on me." So the salmon rushed towards the shore and he extended his paws, but they jumped over them, splashing his face with water and he caught none. He made five ineffectual attempts as he went along, at one time trying to haul his blanket like a seine, but they still escaped him. Becoming very hungry, he again took out his sisters. They were quite angry, being cold, and were cross with him, whereon he blew into the air, ordering it to snow. Then they became frightened and told him to go to a sandspit and take a stick, and as the salmon passed, to strike them on the back of the head. Upon this he suffered the women to return and did as he was told. He killed two salmon, split them, spread them with sticks and set them up before the fire to roast. As he watched them he fell asleep and the grey wolf (*hah-lish*) came <185> with his four brothers and, seeing him asleep, said, "It is Spilyai. Let us steal his salmon.' So they took it and greased his mouth and paws with the skin, and went a little way off. When Spilyai awoke and found his salmon gone and himself still hungry, he wondered how it could be, but he saw that his face and hands were greasy and finally concluded that he must have eaten his fish and forgotten it. So he caught two more, put them to the fire and fell asleep again, with the same result. This occurred five times, the wolves watching him and playing the same trick. In despair Spilyai again had recourse to his sisters, who said, "You fool, Spilyai! You were fast asleep, and Hahlish has stolen your fish. But see! He has got a pile of eggs there a little way off and has fallen asleep himself. Do you go and steal them, in turn." [no ¶]

So Spilyai went and as he came up, he said, "Are you asleep?" No answer. "Are you fast asleep?" a little louder. Still no answer. He then took all the eggs, the whole pile, and eat them up, daubing the faces of the wolves with a little, and went away. When the wolf awoke he, in turn, wondered what had become of his eggs, and finally concluded [142] that he must have eaten them himself.[104]

On his way up the river (the Columbia) Spilyai stopped at Wasco, where The Dalles now are. <186> There were then no rapids in the river by which the Indians, who had just been created, could catch fish. So he said to the chief, "Give me a girl to sleep with tonight, and in the morning I will build you a dam. You are all to go to sleep yourselves.' The chief did so and gave him his choice of many girls, for the people were already numerous. Spilyai stayed with one and towards morning built The Dalles. The next night he stopped at Waiyum, and on being shown the same civility, made the Falls, and on the third night Wanwanwie (the mouth of the John Day's River). When he came to Walla Walla, the chief there had two daughters and Spilyai

---

represented as always being unwilling to give the desired information; and then Coyote would threaten to send rain upon them, when they would yield and tell what he wanted to know. When he would urge them to give him information, they would say, 'If we tell you, you will say that you knew that yourself before'; and when they finally gave the desired information, he always said, 'Yes, my sisters, that is what I thought; that was my plan at first.'" *eec*

{Overly polite and modest, these siblings (sisters ~ brothers) of Coyote were feces or, as one elder prefers, "his poops." *jm*}

[104] In the variant of this tale still told by the Nez Perce, Coyote painted Fox with the egg yolks, spread yellow over the back of Owl, and changed the appearance of Raccoon and Wolf with charcoal and ashes from the fire. *eec*

made the same offer for the use of one of them for a single night. To show that he was in earnest, he built the dam in advance; but the chief would not consent or else the girl was unwilling, and he broke it down again. A huge rock standing in the river is the witness of his revenge. In this way he traveled, taking maidenheads and creating rapids every where.[105] <187>

THE WATTETASH
(Klikatat)

Wattetash had a son born to him, and his wife invited everyone to come to a feast, and had a great deal of singing and dancing. Among those present were five Skookoom [143] women from beyond the sea (or where the surf breaks). One of them said to the mother, "See, my breast is sick, it is so full of milk. Lend me your child to suckle, and I will give it back to you." So she took it, and she and her sisters slipped off secretly, and carried it with them. Watteetash and his people searched everywhere for the child, till at last he concluded it had been stolen by Skookooms. The sisters took the child to their house, where it grew and became a man, and they fed him on frogs, which were their food. By and by, he became a man, and of great stature. And he said to himself, "How is it that I am different from these people? They are black, and I am white." [no ¶]

One day when he was making arrowheads, the Blue Jay came to him and stood talking. He threw the chips of stone that he had in his hand, at the jay, and a piece struck him m the eye. The Jay said to him, "Why do you treat me so, when I come to talk to you and tell you about your relations? Take the stone out of my eye and I will tell you all about them." He did so and the Jay told him how he had been stolen, and that his haiqua which he had on at the time <188> was hidden in his cradle and hung up to the roof of the lodge. The Jay told him to get the haiqua, put it on, and come with him, and he would show him the way home. He proposed to start in the morning when the sisters went out to dig kamass. Accordingly the next day they started, but the young man was afraid to go through the surf, and the Jay took him under his wing and brought him along over the sea. When he reached the country on this side, he found the people fishing for salmon, making a ring by standing in the water and bending their bodies so as to touch their heads like the slats of a weir. They had no fire but put their salmon on sticks and stood them up as if before one, and then they danced and made tamahnous. Unless they danced very high and a long time, the fish did not become cooked. The young man pitied them, saying, "See how tired my people are." Then he went and cut a tree, and split it up, and showed them how to make weirs, and he taught them how to make fire with two sticks, turning one rapidly between the hands, with the point upon the other. Thus he traveled everywhere, teaching [144] them how to

---

[105] In variants of this tale as told by several tribes along the Columbia, Coyote was responsible for forming the waterfalls along the Gorge, Celilo Falls, Dry Falls of the Columbia, Steamboat Rock, the Ginkgo Petrified Forest, Lake Chelan, Okanogan and Spokane and Kettle Falls; and for most of the fishing equipment and skills of the Indians (Indian Legends: 91-98, 105-107). *eec*

Gibbs' note: The falls of the Spokane River, which are impassable by salmon, were made by him [Coyote] to prevent the fish from going to the Coeur d'Alene country, where he had been refused his fee. *gg* {Chelan Falls is another consequence of refusing Coyote "a wife for the night." *jm*}

fish and make fire.[106] After a time he came to a house and asked for water, and an old man went down to get it; but the white salmon (the hook-nosed or winter salmon, an inferior sort) came up and opened <189> its mouth as if to bite. The old man ran back and said there was a skookoom[107] in the water that wished to eat him.[108] Watteetash told a young man to go with him, and show him the skookoom. He went into the water, and when the salmon came up to bite at his feet, he struck it with a fish spear and said, "See, it is not a skookoom but a fish. When you are hungry and can not get the other kind, eat this."

He finally reached his father's house. His father called all his people and told them that his son had returned. There was a great rejoicing, and the young man then made his tamahnous five days, washing himself and at the end of the dance, put on his blanket. But the sisters had followed him, and when they saw him said, "There is our child," and called to him to come. He refused, and they changed him into a loon and returned to their house. According to this account, Spilyai himself turned all the skookooms into animals, stones, etc. The version given below, received from a Stakta-mish, or upper Chihalis woman, named Ki-kai-si-mi-loot, is the more popular one. <190>

THE STORY OF SLOQUALM (THE MOON)
(Stak-tamish)[109]

Hoddeh[110] (who is the same as Spilyai) first went to the Falls above Stehchas (Olympia)[111] where he made the ground barren, and ordered that there should be no kamass, on

---

[106] Several tribes of Puget Sound and of the Olympic Peninsula told variants of this tale: The stolen child became the Changer; brought back to the earth by Blue Jay, the Changer transformed the world of the ancients to its present form and taught the people their arts and crafts. The footprints of the Changer, old Indians say, can still be seen along Hood Canal and on the shores of Chuckanut Bay. *eec*

[107] Chinuk WaWa for "strength, strong power." *jm*

[108] *Gibbs' note:* In the absence of the article it is difficult to ascertain through the imperfect medium of the jargon whether this is an individual name or one of a race, a Watteetash. I am inclined to think it is the latter. *gg*

[109] The Stak-ta-mish, "forest people," are commonly called Upper Chehalis, They "belonged to the coastal division of the Salishan linguistic family" (Bureau of Ethnology, *Bulletin* 145: 426). They lived along the upper Chehalis River, in what is now southwestern Washington.

A variant of this story of the moon is included in Thelma Adamson's *Folk-Tales of the Coast Salish,* Memoirs of the American Folklore Society (1934): 158-72. *eec*

[110] *Spilyai* is Coyote. In his Nisqually Dictionary, Gibbs (1877b: 338) says "Mythological characters: *Hwun-ne, Hun-ne,* or *Hod-de* is probably the same as the *I-tal-i-pas* of the Tsinuk, the *Spil-yai* of the Klickatats and *Sinch-lep* of the Flatheads (*the prairie wolf*), and as the *Smi-an* (*badger*) of the Spokans; the western representative of *Manabozho,* the Great White Hare of the Algonkins.... The name of *Hod-de* or *Hun-ne* is very probably derived from *hōd, fire,* which according to some accounts, he introduced." {Throughout herein, native words are *italicized*, Spirit Names are capitalized.} See Honne ~ The Spirit of the Chehalis, George Sanders and Katherine van Winkle Palmer, reprinted 2012, preface by Jay Miller. D and N interchange in some Salish languages. *jm*

the [146] the shores of the Sound. He then went to the hoosolupsh, or upper Chihalis country, carrying a basket of it upon his back, which he planted everywhere on the prairies. He built a dam or weir on the Chihalis for salmon, and when he had caught a male, he opened it, took the milt, and wished five times that it should become a child to him, but corrected himself and wished for a wife.[112] Shortly after, he went down to the water and saw two women (sisters) sitting there. They had sprung from the milt of the salmon. He called to them as his wives; but they corrected him and said that they were his children. They did not wish to be his wives. He still persisted, and they became afraid and ran into the woods. They came to the house of an old blind woman called Yuknkwalt-tum, who was rocking her grandchild in a cradle suspended be a branch to a cord. The child's mother, Smalleh, was absent on the other side of the hills. This child was born, as was its mother, without the aid of a man. The girls stole the boy, leaving a piece of rotten wood in his place, and went away. When the old woman <191> found it was gone, she called five times to her daughter, whose heart on the fifth call became sick[113] (that is, she became alarmed) and she came to her mother. The old woman directed Smalleh to carry her, in pursuit of her child. She shortened the distance, so that she came up with the fugitives five times; but on their laughing, Smalleh dropped her mother each time, so that finally they escaped and carried the boy off. At each place where the old woman fell, there became a lake. These lakes are the upper prairie in the Chihalis. Smalleh, on the loss of her son, took some of her own urine, and mixing it with water, drank it, and became with child of another. When the first boy grew up he took the girls who had stolen him as wives, and had a great many children by them, among whom [are] the Cedar and the Sucker fish. One day while he was making arrow heads of flint, the Blue Jay came to him, chattering as usual. The [147] young man threw the dust from the arrowhead into his eyes. The Jay asked him why he did so. He had come to tell him who his relations were. After some talk, the man agreed to accompany the Jay, and they started together, but as his children cried, he wrapped them up in his blanket and left them in the house. <192> His wives were then absent, and on their return, they tried to follow him; but he pushed up the earth behind him into mountains and prevented them. He was angry with them because they had stolen him. On his way he came to a country full of demons called T'Hot-yookh, who were in the habit of eating men. They took him and put him under a great fire to bake him as one does kamass; but he came out unhurt and he drove the demons into the fire, when they burst with a noise like a gun. After setting at liberty all the Indians whom they had taken prisoners, he traveled on until he met another demon, a woman who emasculated and killed all the men that slept with her. Sloqualm[114] – for that was his name – proposed to stay with her, but she refused him. He asked her five times and finally prevailed. When they went to bed, he told her to shut her eyes. She wished to know why, and he told her that he always made the women with whom he stayed do so. He then took a stone chisel and hammer and split her open, and restored to life all the people she had killed. Thus he went on his way destroying demons until nothing bad was left; they were all dead. There were many such. Fire was once a demon, and it was everywhere. The earth and stones were all fire; but <193> Sloqualm put it out, and ordained that when men

---

[111] *Stehchas* is the newer native name for Olympia, referring to the impressive "splicing connector" causeway built by Americans across Budd Inlet. The older Lushootseed name for the native village there is "black bears" (Hilbert, Miller, and Zahir 2001: 305-9).

[112] While the Moon epic is widely known, this crucial episode only appears in Adamson (1934).

[113] In WaWa, *sik tumtum* means "sick ~ troubled at heart".

[114] *Sloqualm {M = B}* is Lushootseed noun-forming S + ɫuk^{w}alb "sky orb ~ sun ~ moon ~ day".

wanted to warm themselves, they should make a small one. He changed the earth and made everything good. Finding some Indians standing in a stream, so as to intercept the salmon, and that they were chilled with the water, he built a fire to warm them and constructed a weir. They had before then used their hands for a wedge in splitting wood and their heads as a mallet; but he showed them to use tools. The crow had defiled them as they stood in the water, and he turned him black. He came to the beaver and called him, "My grandfather," and gave him his blanket of fur, and taught him to build a house. The beaver said to him, "Oh, Chief! I have no house. Take pity [148] on me! Thank you." Still pursuing his journey, he killed an elk, dried the meat, tied it up in the skin, and carried it with him. When he came to a house, he threw off his load. There were five houses, with five nice young women. He told them each in turn to carry his load. They first washed and dressed themselves, and then came to him; but none of them could lift it. There was a sixth woman, all dirty and foul. She was poor and a common person, while the others were high-born (*Seahb*, "chiefs"). She took up the load and followed him, and the five were ashamed. <194> As they went he brought on a storm of rain, and they stopped at each of the five houses; they were all wet; they next tried the poor woman's house. It was a miserable house, but perfectly dry. This woman's name was Swak-keuk (the frog). Her grandmother, Chole-swoeh, washed her and smoothed her hair, and Sloqualm slept with her, for he said, "The one who carries the load is my wife." They were now not far from his mother's. His woman carried five sacks with her. When he reached his mother's house, she knew him. His younger brother was grown up, but she had never ceased to cry for his loss. The poor woman remained in the house as his wife. He and his mother talked together five days, and he asked her what her wishes were. He proposed to his brother to become the moon, and accordingly the young man started and went out five times into the night; but each time he became afraid and returned. Sloqualm finally said to him, "Do you become the sun, and I will be the moon," and his mother said, "Good! Let it be so!" [no ¶]

So he told his brother to go round above during the day, and below in the night. It is the urine of which the sun was made that <195> causes the eyes to smart when we look at it. He himself also went up above with his woman, who may be seen with him, carrying his five sacks in her hand. (The Klikatats also point out the figure in the moon as a frog holding a bag of *ictahs* (various articles of property: in Wawa); but they say that the moon tries to throw it off, for if it was not for the frog, it would be warm at night, as well as in the day.) When there is no moon, his mother cries and is very unhappy; but when he re-appears the Indians are pleased, for [149] he made everything good and watches over them. His mother and grandmothers are now rocks in a prairie on the Chihalis, and whenever the Indians go there, they throw stones at them. If the stones bound off, they say there will be no moon; but if they rebound towards them, there will be. As to Hoddeh, he went over to the Columbia River, and is always traveling, giving food of different kinds at different places and teaching games.

THE STORY OF WHY-EE-MA
(Klikatat)

There lived a man named Whyeema (the War Eagle) and his wife at Whulats, in the Yakima country; and opposite to them, on the other side <196> of a stream, lived Kwy-a-wih, (the Cougar) and his wife. The war eagle had a son, who in the fashion of those times grew to manhood in five days. The cougar had a daughter, who also grew up. The young eagle became a great hunter; he made a bow and arrows from the horns of the big horn sheep, with which he could shoot through five animals at once. Every day he used to go out and hunt a different kind of game. The first day he killed five of the big horn and, removing the entrails, brought them all home on his shoulders, two on the left and three on the right, holding them by the fore feet and not using a rope. His bow and arrows he carried on his head. When he got home, he threw the animals down in the house, and his father skinned them and dried the meat. They were very fat. The young man then took the skins and chewed them, and forthwith spit them out, already dressed soft. The next day, he went out again and saw ten antelopes lying down, asleep in two bands. He crawled up the dry bed of a stream and shot an arrow through one band of five, killing them all, and carried them home in the same way. These also were very fat, as they were in those days, while for some reason the antelopes now are lean. He dressed the <197> skins of them in the same manner, and said to his father, "My father, do you make me a pair of moccasins, for I run about every day like a slave, barefooted, and my feet are sore." [150] [no ¶]

His father replied, "My son, do not talk so, I too go about everywhere barefooted." [no ¶]

Then Whyeema rolled the skins up in two bundles, put them under his arms, and pressed them to his sides, and immediately they became moccasins, one hundred and ten pairs, and all embroidered. The third day the young man killed five caribou, and brought them home, and said to his father, "My father, make me a pair of leggings, and presently a shirt with fringe, and garnishing on them.' His father answered, "My son, I understand. I know how to make them.' So he made him a shirt and leggings of caribou skin. The fourth day the young man killed five black-tailed deer; and the fifth he went after the white-tailed, for he always wished a different kind each day. He saw a band of five and followed them, but they were not real deer; they were false ones that the cougar's daughter had made to deceive him. The young Whyeema had never known a woman and did not wish to marry. He preferred to hunt. The chiefs around had all offered him their daughters, but he had <198> refused them. The cougar's daughter had seen and fallen in love with him, and she had in the same way refused all the young men of the country. She determined to catch him and changed herself into one of the deer. When he saw the deer, he shot, intending to strike it behind the foreleg; but she caught the arrow under her arm and stopped it, so that the head protruded in front, and the feathers behind. She pretended to be wounded badly, and ran over a hill, leaving a trace of blood. The young man followed and, reaching the summit, saw no deer, though there was nothing at all to hide one; but a woman standing by the water side, with her head bent down, washing and combing her hair, which was long and reached to the ground. He said to himself, "There is a woman standing. Perhaps she has seen my deer.' So he called to her, "Nah! Have you seen a deer pass by?" She did not answer till he called the fifth time, when she looked up laughing and said, "Why don't you come nearer? Are you afraid? See, I have no fur on my skin. I am not a Skookoom. If you don't come nearer, I won't tell you about your deer."

He came a little nearer, but she still told him to approach. [151] At length he came up to her, when she ordered him to come close to her, to put his toes so as to touch hers. He was bashful <199> and would not. Then she told him, "If you do not, I will not tell you about your deer. Why are you afraid of me? And you will lose your arrow too.' The arrow she had buried in the sand and stood upon it. So he stood with his feet to hers. She told him, "Closer! Press your feet against mine." He did so, for he thought to himself, "If I lose that arrow, where shall I get such another?" For it was very strong, not a common arrow, but made of sheep's horn, straightened. She saw his heart and knew what he thought, though he did not speak aloud, and she laughed and bantered him again. "Now," said she, "give me your hand.' But he would not, being ashamed, and put his hand behind him. She teased him thus five times, till he gave her his hand. Then she told him he had been so long changing his mind, he should kiss her before she told him. He was ashamed to do this too, and the girl laughed and coaxed him the more, telling him that he ought to have a wife, to take care of him and make his clothes. He resisted, however, until she bid him the fifth time, when his mind changed and he became willing to marry her. She knew it at once and said to him, "Well, then, come home with me now. Don't go to your father's today." He followed her to the Cougar's house; and as usual, at the end of five days, she brought him a son, exactly like <200> his father, with a hooked nose and all. The son grew up in five days more, and became a man. His father then asked him, "Do you know who I am?" He replied, "Yes, you are the son of Whyeemash. Your father is a great chief. I knew it when I was in the womb. But my mother is not a chief. She is beneath you. You and I are indeed chiefs, you first and I your son.' Whyeemash then said, "Let us go together from here. Today I found your mother with another man, and I shall put her away.' The young one was ashamed and at once agreed to go; but they first went to the house and sat down. Presently the woman came in, and her husband told her in a bantering manner, "Be you cook now and dress something to eat. Here is your son, grown up, and he is hungry.' She answered, "I am not a slave. Cook for yourselves [152] if you want food." He told her to go into the other house. She went, and her son then took some venison, not real deer's meat but made to look like it by means of witchcraft, cut it into a large thin slice, and put it on sticks before the fire. Then he took a small basket and filled it with his urine,[115] and called to his mother, asking her if she did not wish to eat. She said, "Yes," and asked what was in the cup. He told her that it was tea and asked if she did not know tea <201> when she saw it. She drank it and said that it was very sweet. Then she ate up all the meat which her son had cut and laid in a wooden tray. After this she proposed that they should all go together to the house of Whyeema. They started, but when she got to the door, she fell down. Froth came from her mouth and her body turned black. She was dead. Her husband divided her corpse, saying, "You wanted to go up above, but it is well that you should go down there.' He and his son then went home.

THE SNOW PEAKS
(Klikatat)

Mt St Helens, Mt Hood, and Mt Rainier were formerly people, brothers. Their names were Pahtoo, Weeist, and Wachsum, St Helens or Pahtoo being the oldest.[116] Weeist became angry with Pahtoo, for some reason, and prepared a bow and arrows, to go to war with him. The bow was made very strong, covered with glue and the sinews of the deer. He had also a long knife, like a sword. When he was ready, he went over to Pahtoo and said to him, "My elder brother, I have come to have an explanation with you. Why is your heart always sick towards your people? Why do you bend your head whenever the wind blows?" He spoke thus five times. They had many words, when Weeist drew his knife and cut off the head of Pahtoo, <202> at a blow. It flew over and fell on the other side of the mountains, and became Tahoma [153] or Mt Adams. Weelst then stamped on his neck and rounded it off, as it now is. Pahtoo was not killed.

---

[115] * Baskets of urine stand in every lodge, that being used instead of soap. *eec*

[116] In accounts of Cascade peaks, *Pahto* is Mount Adams; *Wy-east* = Mount Hood; *Tahoma* = Mt Rainier. According to Chief Jobe Charley, who has lived most of his long life in sight of Mount Adams, all snow-capped peaks were called *Pahto,* "standing high," by the Indians on the Yakima Reservation; *Wachsum* is now Mount Simcoe, west of Satus Pass. *eec*

His heart remained strong, and when Weeist returned home, he thought to himself he would serve the other brother in the same way. He therefore went to Wachsum and addressed him, "My youngest brother, why are you always behaving so badly to your people, taking their women to sleep with?" Wachsum did not answer, but said to himself, "Where has he been to see me? I have not seen him anywhere." Pahtoo then struck Wachsum's head off, which flew and lit in the Winatshapum country,[117] at the head of the river, and he stamped on his neck in the same way as had been done to himself. Not satisfied with this, however, Pahtoo, after days, returned home and made a bow and twenty arrows, straight and strong. He took these and his knife and went to Weeist. The latter [Mt Hood], it seems, after cutting his brother's head off, had stolen his son and taken him with him. He forms the elevation or shoulder of the old crater on the south side. The anger of Pahtoo was increased at seeing his son; but he dissembled and addressed Weeist, [on] another old subject of bending the head <203> when the wind blew, asking him what he looked down at. Weeist said to himself, "I do not do so. Perhaps he is still angry because I formerly cut his head off.' Then Pahtoo nourished his knife and asked him if he was not afraid. He said, "No," for his neck was very strong. Pahtoo pretended to sheathe his knife, but passed it between his legs, and immediately cut Weelst's head off, also throwing it to the Klamath country, where it now stands.[118] He stamped him down, as had been done to himself, and telling his own son to remain where he was, took Weeist's son home with him. The latter forms the shoulder on Mt St Helens. The three brothers afterwards agreed to become only mountains. They all smoke but their heads do not.[119] [154]

THE STORY OF YAHPOHALLA
(Klikatat)

A man and his wife and one son lived at the Vancouver Lake. His name was Yahpohalla (the water spider). He was very large, his foot being a fathom long, and an arm's length wide. The mother's name was T'ken. Yapohalla was anxious to become a great chief, and accordingly

---

[117] This seems to be Wenatchee country; hence the head may have become Glacier Peak. *eec*

[118] Mount Shasta? *eec*

[119] Gibbs recorded another myth about the Cascade peaks, along with some facts about them, in his report on the "Geology or the Central Portion of Washington Territory," dated 1 May 1854: *eec*

"Smoke was distinctly issuing from St Helens during our journey. This and Mount Baker are the only volcanoes at present active in the chain. Its last considerable eruption was in 1842, when it covered the country as far as Vancouver and The Dalles with ashes, and presented a luminous appearance after the smoke had cleared off. The Indians report that there were once three mountains that smoked always. Mount Hood and Mount Adams being the others. Respecting Mounts Hood and St Helens, they have a characteristic tale to the effect that they were once man and wife; that they finally quarreled and threw fire at one another, and that St Helens was the victor; since when Mount Hood has been afraid, while St Helens, having a stout heart, still burns. In some versions this story is connected with the slide which formed the Cascades of the Columbia, and by damming up the water inundated the forest, the remains of which are now visible along its margin. The date of this event Lewis and Clark fixed at about thirty years before their arrival. (Reports of Explorations and Surveys I: 475-76). *eec*

obtained five more wives from the coast. Aiaih (apparently a species of fish), one from each place where a chief lived [*sic*]. The son meantime grew and became a <204> great chief also and had a great deal of property. He knew everything (by intuition as in "second sight") and knew how to make everything. His father became jealous of him and considered in his heart how to kill him, lest his son should become a greater chief than himself. So one night, while the son was lying asleep in his bunk, wrapped in his robe, the father took a long knife and cut his head off, filling the whole house with his blood. He then called the boy's mother and, pretending astonishment, asked who had done it, what people had killed his son. She knew who it was but did not reply, for her heart was gone. Then the father said, "In the morning I will send everywhere and find who has done this.' But she said, "You need not, for you did it yourself. Now look out for me, for you will not see where I am going," She immediately slipped through a crack in the floor and went down into the water. By and by, the [155] father heard it thunder and became afraid, saying to himself that perhaps the Chief above would do to him as he had done to his son, that perhaps he would even overturn the world. So he took his son's head and put it on again, and leaped backwards and forwards over him five times, and his son came to life again. The father then asked him five times, <205> "My son, what people have done this?" But his son did not reply, but asked the father where the mother had gone. The father answered he did not know. Probably she had gone out on an occasion. He knew better, for she had been gone a whole day. The son said, "I want her to get me something to eat, for I am very hungry. I do not wish any of the food here.' [no ¶]

This he said, although he knew who had cut his head off and where his mother had gone. After repeating the question "What have you done with my mother?" five times, he disappeared, going down as she had done, through the floor. On reaching the water, he took two hairs from his head, laid them on it, and they became a canoe, which he got into and followed his mother to his grandmother's. His father meantime did not see where he went to; but rushed out of doors, looking for him, intending to shoot him with his bow. Not finding him, he went into the other lodge, where his five new wives were, and asked them. They said they did not know, he did not live there, but in the other room. There was one, his favorite, to whom he said, "Perhaps you have hid him and want to steal off with him." She answered, "Are you not ashamed to talk so? You are a chief, I am not." This was not true, however, for she was the daughter of a great chief. Meantime the son reached his grandmother's house, which was a cave under water, very strong, and the door [was] made so that she alone could <206> open it. The old woman was very powerful, a great Skookoom. She knew that they were coming, for she saw in a dream what had happened. The young man found her making arrows. There were fifteen quivers of skin, each holding the arrows, hanging round the room, which she had made for him to kill his father with. He had already determined to retaliate and at the instance of his mother returned home and stole away his [156] father's favorite wife, the one whom the father had before accused. Yahpohalla slept alternately with his five wives, five nights with each, and that night with one of the others. In the morning he went into the room, woke up the other three, and asked them where their sister was. They said they did not know, they were fast asleep, that perhaps she had gone out on an occasion of nature. He waited, asked constantly for her till night, and then told one of the others who was from Chinook to send for his brothers-in-law, all of them, to seek for and kill his son. They came in seventeen canoes, all armed, and arrived about noon, having stopped but once on the way. They stayed with Yahpohalla that night, and the next morning started early. The old man had by this time become stripped of everything, for his son came every night and put him to sleep by tamahnous, tied up some of his property, and carried it off. The seventeen canoes were all full, the men sitting two on a seat and paddling, and <207> Yahpohalla standing in the bow of the first. When they reached the place, the women had stripped themselves stark naked, throwing off each their breech clouts, and had quivers of arrows slung under their arms, and their bows ready strung. Besides himself and the three women, the young man had his five slaves, the blue jays. As Yahpopohalla approached and saw the women naked, he began to banter them, asking if they were coming to have connection with them. They told him, yes, to come on and try it. The Aiaih woman then shot him through, and he fell dead from the canoe. The others each shot, and their arrows went, every one, through all the men on one side of the canoes, for the arrows were "Skoo-koom." The rest fled in terror, but the young man, running upon the water, broke the canoes in pieces and killed their occupants, except those in one canoe, who begged him to spare them, as they were relatives of his wife and not hostile to him. These he told to go.

THE STORY OF JOSUP
(Klikatat)

Spilyai first took for his wife a star (*Hahsloh*). He was himself not a chief (or well born) but a common person. She [157] on the contrary was of very high lineage and white. He knew nothing himself, whereas she was very wise. He slept with her five nights and she became pregnant. In five days more she had a man child. Spilyai wished to kill it, for <208> he said he did not want a boy, but a girl, and proposed to cut its head off. The wife refused to let him, and kept it. In five days the boy crept; in ten days he walked upright. In a month he was a grown man and wanted a woman, but there was none. He looked about for ten days and then took the dove (Me-mim) for a wife. This was just after the deluge. It had rained for four years. The earth had been covered with water and was still soft, the mountains had been broken down flat, there were no trees, and the people were all drowned. The Star brought forth a girl, also after five days, who grew up as rapidly as her brother. One day the young man went out to hunt deer, for the earth had now become hardened, and he began to think, as he walked, where he could get another wife. It was told him from above, to take his sister and they should have many children and produce people. This young man's name was Josup.[120] Josup reflected two days upon this subject without mentioning it, and ten days after he married her. Spilyai was very angry and asked him if he was not ashamed of himself to take his sister to wife. But Spilyai knew nothing, whereas the children, by virtue of their star-mother, <209> knew everything, even in the womb. Spilyai wished to throw his son in the water, but he left him and went into the mountains. He had now two wives: the Dove and his sister. Those two and himself were the only people on the earth. [no ¶]

Josup met a man entirely white, not merely his skin but his hair and beard, although he was young. And [Josup] said to him, "Oh, my brother! I am pleased to meet you. Come home to my house.' But the young man did not answer. Josup then asked where [he] had come from, but received no reply until he had repeated his question five times, when he said, "From above.' He [Josup] asked in like manner, [158] five times, what his name was, and the stranger then told him "Hoh-hoke" (the raven), which was then white. Hoh-hoke told Josup that he could not go to

---

[120] *Gibbs' note:* The Indian who narrated this said that it was the same as his own name, Joseph, which he pronounced in that way, and unless this is a mere fancy, there is a biblical interpretation in the tale. *gg*

his house, [that] he was traveling everywhere to look for his people. Josup answered that besides him, his mother and sister, there were no people. Hoh-hoke still refused to go with him, but asked in turn what Josup's name was. This he did not know, and the other then told him to take his name. They parted and Josup, going home, saw five female mice (Hool-hool) and three crickets (Silik-silk). He took them to his house; and his mother, the Star, asked him where he had found those people. He replied, "In the mountains," and that he wished to have ten wives in order to beget children rapidly. The young man was now a great <210> chief, and his father Spilyai envied him his possessions, and proposed to get rid of him by leaving him on a high pinnacle of rock. So he said to him, "My son, you are almost out of arrows.' "Yes," he replied, "I have only five left, and tomorrow perhaps I shall use them." Then said Spilyai, "I have found the nest of Why-eima (the war eagle). Tomorrow early, come with me and I will show it to you, and you can get plenty of feathers for your arrows. There are two young ones also.' Josup said, "My father, I am much pleased. I will go with you and get them, and we will make a little house to put them in.' In the morning Josup gave his father a pair of moccasins embroidered with beads and porcupine quills, and a pair of leggings, and told him to put them on. Spilyai was very proud of them and said to himself, "Now I am a chief too.' They went out to a prairie, and Spilyai showed his son the eagle's nest upon a high tree, on a rock. But it was a deception. The bird was Spilyai's dung, and he had made the rock himself. He told his son to strip and climb the tree, which he did, leaving his clothes on the ground. Then said Spilyai, "My son, don't look down or you will become giddy and fall. Look up at the bird.' When he got half way up, Spilyai put on Josup's things and ran off, leaving his son there naked, and without anything to eat. He went back to the house and passed himself off for his son; but <211> the dove and the crickets knew him and did nothing but cry, for they were wise and knew what [159] had happened. But the mice and Josup's sister knew nothing about it. Spilyai, personating Josup, said to the dove, "What are you crying for? Do you want to sleep with Spilyai?" [no ¶]

In the morning the dove told the Star, "That is not your son. It is Spilyai.' She replied that she knew it and cried, saying, "Let him go. I don't want to see him.' She then went up above again. The young man remained five days on the rock, naked, hungry, cold, and the skin worn from his hands. At the end of this time Weh-hal-hal-lt (the spider) came down from above, on its rope, and said to him, "My son, what are you doing here, cold and naked?" Josup answered, "My father Spilyai left me here, but now he is no more my father. You are my father.' The spider asked him if he wanted to get down. He replied that he did, but could not. Then the spider made a line, twisted as large as a ship rope, with a loop at the end, and told him to get into it, and hold on fast by the rope, lest he should fall. He did so and the spider lowered him to the ground and then hauled in the rope. When he reached the earth, the spider told him that Spilyai had stolen all his goods and his wives, and that his mother had returned to her sky, so that there was no one at his house. He answered that he knew it and should follow Spilyai. He now saw on the ground some clothes and shoes, with a piece of paper <212> attached to them! He looked at the paper and saw that it was a present from his elder brother, the raven, who was no other than Watteetash, the sun's son. He therefore took the clothes and put them on. Then he started after Spilyai, who had gone off with the women. As he approached the dove, who was behind with her child astride her shoulders, the child said, "Mama, my father is coming.' She answered, "Hush, my child, your father is dead.' But the child knew that it was his father, and repeated the words five times more, with the same reply. Josup now reached them, and the child held out its hand to him, but the dove did not see him and went on crying. Then Josup punched her in the side with a stick and said, "You Spilyai woman! What are you crying for?" She turned and saw him and caught hold of his hands, kissing them. He asked her why she had followed Spilyai. She said that she [160] knew it was him, but was afraid. He asked her who cut her hair off. She told him that Spilyai was mad with [her] and did it, and informed him that the crickets knew it was Spilyai; but the mice did not, and had been making merry with him. Josup then sent her on to where Spilyai had made a fire, and built his house for the night, and hid himself. Spilyai had killed a fawn, and bringing it into camp, gave the best parts to the mice, whom he was fond of because they were white and soft; [he] left <213> one foreleg for the dove and the other for the crickets. Presently Josup, who had concealed his face in a mantle or robe made of the green slime from the water, dried, and had a club slung to his wrist, came up and disclosed himself. Spilyai was struck with terror and said to him, "My son, let me go and I will be your slave.'

THE SEAL HUNTERS

The following was translated for me by Dr Tolmie, as repeated to him by a Nisqually Indian, *Alm-cot-ti*. Once upon a time there were four brothers of the S'ho-mah-mish tribe who were seal hunters; and in pursuit of their game used to go to a certain point which the seals frequented. One of their tribe, a medicine man but an unsuccessful hunter, became envious and determined to injure them, the more that they never gave them [him?] meat. He accordingly made an image of a seal in cedar wood and placed it on the point. The brothers went to the spot as usual, each in his canoe, with his spear, and seeing the false seal, one approached and threw his lance. It struck, and the point detached itself from the wooden shaft, and the seal slid from the rock into the water, towing the canoe after him. The next brother followed and struck it, with the same results, and then the third. Suspecting that there was something wrong, they tried to detach their lines, but in vain. They stuck to the canoes, and <214> the latter continued to be hurried on. The youngest brother finally approached, but the rest told him to return to their mother and not to perish also. The cedar seal towed the brothers a long way, to an island, where it went ashore, climbed the bank, and disappeared in the woods. The brothers drew their canoes up and followed it by the [161] trail of their lines, till they found their spears stuck in a cedar tree. Returning to the shore, they saw a canoe approach with a very little man in it, and being afraid, hid themselves to watch him. He anchored his canoe out from the shore, and diving from it, brought up a salmon. This employment he continued during the day, throwing the fish into his canoe. Becoming bolder and very hungry, the brothers watched an opportunity when he went down, pushed off in one of their canoes, stole some of his fish, and got back into the woods before he came up. When he rose and put his fish into the boat, he saw that some were missing; sweeping his hand round the horizon, [he] rested it, pointing to where the brothers were hid. He then drew up his anchor, went ashore into the woods, found them and made them get into his canoe. He took them to a village inhabited by people like himself, who instead of mouths had beaks with which they could extract the meat of the haiqua. The brothers lived here some time, pretty well treated on <215> the whole, and not exactly slaves until a war was declared against the little people by the swans and geese. After a great battle, in which many were slain on both sides, the birds retired, leaving the little people pierced with feathers. The men made themselves useful in pulling these out, for the hands of the little people were not like those of men. The dwarfs, grateful for the service, determined in payment to send them home, and for this purpose hired a whale to carry them. The whale took them on his back and started, but through some freak threw them off, when they became grampuses, the dorsal fin of the fish representing the paddles and the beard (?) the brush at the bottom of the canoe. They since assist their

S'Homannish [S'Homamish] brethren by driving seals ashore, and they abstain from injuring their canoes. The mother of the young men, it is added, on the loss of her sons, went down to the eastern shore of Vashons Island, and looked for them, straining her eyes to see if they would not return. She was there turned into a rock, which the passers-by can yet see, in proof of the tale. The little men were Kwakwastaimish. [162]

THE MO-KWO-TAH-OOM

Related by Ke-kai-si-mi-loot, a Staktamish {see Bio}. A chief and his wife had a daughter who was of marriageable age. One night soon after dark, a great many canoes filled with people came to his house, and one of the visitors proposed to purchase the girl. The father, supposing them to be other Indians, agreed, the sale <216> was made and the strangers departed, taking the bride with them. They went to a far country and at length arrived at a place where there were five very large houses. There they sang and danced and finally retired to rest. In the morning the girl awoke, her head lying upon her husband's arm; and looking at him, she saw that he was a skeleton. Starting up in great alarm, she pushed him from her and looked around. All the others lay there, heaps of bones. She ran out of the house, pushing aside with her foot a number of small skeletons that were near the door, and fled. In the distance she saw a smoke and made for it. She came to a house where there was a very old and decrepit woman, bent with years, who was busy making baskets. Her name was *Slaht-la-kwo* (the screech owl). The old woman said to her, "It is always so at that house. In the night they sing and dance; in the day time they are bones.' She asked the girl how she got out — if she pushed aside the children who lay there. The girl answered that she shoved them with her foot, being frightened. The old woman told her that she had done wrong, and perhaps evil would come to her, for they were children who had no fathers or mothers. In the evening there was a great noise at the house, and all the people were saying, "What has become of the girl? She has gone out, and her husband is hurt, and <217> these children are almost killed.' By and by her man came to the old woman's house. He was much hurt. He saw his wife and said to her, "See how you have hurt me and all these children.' She went back with him. Soon after dark he got well again, and all the flesh came back upon these people. They sang and danced during the night, and she went to bed with him again. In the morning when she awoke, they were again skeletons, but she laid his arm aside gently and went out, carefully stepping over the children, and returned to the old [163] woman's. So she did the succeeding days. In five days she had a child, a boy. In the day time it was a skeleton like its father, and she never looked at it. At night it was a child with flesh like herself. Five days after, she went to see her father and mother, accompanied by a crowd of these people. She proposed to remain, and her man told her she might do so, but not to let anyone see her child during the day or lay it down, but in the night to put it on the bed. At the end of four days she concluded to go to the lake and gather moss to lay her child on; and her mother proposed to her to leave the child, as she could not watch it and gather moss too. So she did, and when she was gone, the grandmother said to herself, "What is the matter with the child, that she never lets us see it in the daytime?" Then she lifted the blanket and saw only bones. She was angry and <218> gathered them up and threw them out doors. And the child died. But if the grandmother had not thrown it away, on the fifth day it would have become like other people, except that it would never have died, nor would Indians die, but live forever. This was in the beginning when the world was new made, and it was the cause of death coming. These people were not dead Indians, but the *Mo-kwatah-oom,* another race of beings, those of the former world. The woman returned and saw her child's bones lying out of doors. The father also came with four other of his people. He took the bones and carried them off, and told his wife that now they should all die and become like the child, that formerly he had been well disposed towards them, but they had behaved ill to him and they should die for it.[121] So he came at night and killed all [164] these people except *Klukutlikik* (Beaver), who jumped into the water, dove, and became really a beaver, and *Skunneh* (Muskrat), who also dove and took her two young ones with her. These two became people and the parents of the present Indians. So they all die still. The *Slaht-la-kwo* is the screech owl. When anyone is about to die, she comes to the house to call them by name.

TIS-AI-LUCK-HAN
A Staktamish Story

There was a very old man among the *Elip Tilikum*, called *Tis-ai-luck-han,* who had a son of the same name. <219> There was also a young woman whose father, *Stra-ha-laks,* was dead, leaving her an orphan. She was very rich, having five beds and many slaves. The younger Tisailuckhan, wishing a wife, went at night to the young woman's bed. He was all covered with haiqua, of which he had five dresses. She put out her hand and felt his head and arms and, misled by the haiqua, thought he was some bad Indian and covered with leprosy, so she took a stick and struck him. He took the stick away, broke it, and left her. In the morning she found her bed covered with shells, and wondered who it could have been. The slaves came and looked and said it must have been Tisailuckhan's son. She was very much mortified, for she had wished in her heart to have him. So she took all her money and five blankets and five baskets of things and overtook him, and told him that she did not know him and begged him to come back to her. But he would not. He was very angry because his head was cut. He went on home, and she followed coaxing; but he would not even look round. She became very tired with carrying her load and sat down five times. Wherever she sat, there became a large prairie. At last she met five boys playing and asked them five times where Tisailuckhan's house was, before they could answer. They kept on laughing and playing. At last the smallest boy told her, "There it is," pointing to a cloud. The boy added [165] that he had just passed, with his head broke, and <220> was very down-hearted about it. For himself, he thought some woman had done it. The girl followed as directed, and went up and up until she came to his house, and entered. He would not speak to her, and she sat five days in the house without eating or going out. His grandmother dressed his head for him. All the time he had not slept with her. At the end of the five days she got up and went out, leaving all her things in the house. But they then brought her back and gave

---

[121] Kuykendall recorded a Wishram legend about a girl who was permitted to visit her betrothed in the land of the dead. Later when she and their child were allowed to visit the world of the living, the grandmother looked at the baby too soon, and the child died. "This very much displeased the spirit people; and they decreed that, because of this sin, the dead should never return to the living again" (Kuykendall: 81-82; Indian Legends: 195-97).

In the area of The Dalles, the Indians believed "that during the daytime the spirits of the dead remain in the 'dead-houses'" but that at dusk they "go abroad over the world. They hold spirit dances at the cemeteries; and the Indians claim to have seen strange lights at the burial places at night, and to have even heard the sound of the Indian drum and weirdly singing" (Kuykendall: 82). Readers acquainted with Burns' "Tam O' Shanter" will see a strong resemblance between an Indian and an old Scottish belief. *eec*

her food, and the young man went to bed with her. They lay there five days without getting up, when Tisailuckhan was ashamed that he had slept with her without marrying (or purchasing her formally), for he had got her with child. He took all his people and went to her house and bought her for a high price. She had a child, and when she bored his nose and ears, gave a great feast as the Indians do, and gave away many presents. Five days after this she went out with her husband and seeing lice in his hair, she said to him, "Let me look at your head. It seems as if it has been hurt.' He did not reply but left her and started for his own house. Then she told two slaves to follow her with five baskets of haiqua. Tisailuckhan was angry and thought to himself, "Why has she said this to me? She broke my head and now she is making sport of it.' So he determined to prevent her following and created five lakes behind him as he went. His wife was proud, <221> as well as himself, for she was a chief, and she said, "What have I done that he should make these lakes? Perhaps he wishes to drown the child.' Then she willed the lakes to be dried up, and prevailed against her husband, and they became dry. Tisailuckhan had meantime built a fence around his house. His wife ordered her two slaves to stop where they were, with the haiqua, and she took the child and went alone to the house. He would not admit her, and she then told the slaves to throw the haiqua into the house, for she would have none of it, and to follow her quickly. She would go past three of the prairies, and kill her child in the fourth, for why should she carry her shame, when she had no husband? On reaching the fourth prairie, she took the child and impaled it on a stick, and set it up in [166] the ground. When she got home a great many mean people commenced asking questions, such as "Where were her slaves?" She said she had left them behind, her man had shut her out of the house. The Blue Jay wondered where her child was, and told the people to ask her; but his elder brother (Snaiiw) told him to be quiet, he would make the woman chief angry. He replied, "What do I care? Perhaps she has killed it." After a while Tisailuckhan took some presents and went for his wife to buy her back. When he came to the prairie, he saw his child <222> with its blanket fluttering in the wind, and thought it was running; but on reaching it, he found it impaled. It was not dead, but died soon after he took it off the stick. He carried the body home, and buried it, and started again with a quantity of goods. This time he succeeded against her. He told her that the child was crying for her at home, and persuaded her to return, which she foolishly did. When on reaching the prairie, he impaled her on a stick as she had done the child. Five days afterwards her people left the house to carry her food. They found a great many strawberries on the prairie, as it was summer, and ate them as they went along; but the Blue Jay complained of a pain in his bowels, he was cold inside, and wondered what was the matter with him. Farther on they saw the woman, apparently coming towards them. The Jay said, "Now I will find out from that woman what is the matter with me.' It was her blood that they had been eating, supposing it to be berries. At last they came up to her and found her stuck upright on a stick. They took her off, and she immediately died. They consulted what to do and concluded that one half should go on with the provision, while the rest returned with the body. Now the woman had a sister exactly like her in the face. When the people reached Tisailuckhan's house, they told him that they had left his wife, a little way back, unwell, and proposed that he should return, which, <223> like a fool, he did. He went and saw the sister, mistook her for his wife, and stayed five days with her, when her people killed him and cut him to pieces with a great knife. Whereon these pieces of flesh fell, there came a lake, which is the occasion [167] of all the lakes in the country. The child who was killed became Teyoutlmah. The mother's grandfather was named Wakutehuts, another great Tamahnous among the Upper Chihalis.

NOTICES OF EARLY TRAVELERS

The first notices of Indians of Oregon and Washington T territory s that we have are by Vancouver, whose voyage was performed in 1792. I have quoted them much at length, because they present a view of the condition of these tribes before they had been affected by intercourse with the whites, and as suggesting a number of points which require explanting or suggest inquiry. So far as the coast is concerned, his observations are very meager; for that navigator, though seeking the great river of Oregon and [226] the Strait of Juan de Fuca, seems to have had a holy horror of land, and sedulously kept at such a distance that he made no discoveries whatever. Passing Destruction Island, he noticed a canoe or two paddling near the shore, and remarks: "It was a fact not less singular than worth of observation, that on the whole extensive coast of New <224> Albion, and more particularly in the vicinity of those fertile and delightful shores we had lately passed, we had not excepting to the southward of Cape Orford and at this place, seen any inhabitant, or met with any circumstances that, in the most distant manner, indicated a probability of the country being inhabited." Of the Klasset, or Makah, he says: "The few natives who came off resembled, in most respects, the people of Nootka. Their persons, garments, and behavior, are very similar; some difference was observed in their ornaments, particularly in those worn at the nose; for, instead of the crescent, generally adopted by the inhabitants of Nootka, these wore straight pieces of bone. Their canoes, arms, ad implements, were exactly the same. They spoke the same language, but did not approach us with the familiarity observed by the people on visiting the Resolution and Discovery, which may probably be owing to their having become more familiar with strangers." The village, he observes, which is situated about two miles within the cape, had the appearance of being extensive and populous. The manner of the Indians was very civil, orderly, and friendly. They requested permission before entering his ship, and, when receiving some presents, "politely and earnestly solicited" him to stop at their <225> village. [no ¶]

His notices of the Klallam are not much more extended, for he had but little intercourse with them. Of those at New Dungeness, he says: "The appearance of the huts we now saw indicated the resident of the natives in them to be a temporary nature only, as we could perceive with our glasses that they differed very materially from the habitations of any of the American Indians we had before seen, being composed of nothing more than a few mats thrown over cross-sticks; whereas those we had passed the preceding day in two or three small villages to the eastward of Classet were built exactly after the fashion of the houses erect at Nootka. The inhabitants seemed to view us with the utmost indifference and unconcern; they continued to fish before their huts as regardless of our being present [227] as if such vessels had been familiar to them, and unworthy of their attention." On the lowland of New Dungeness were erected, perpendicularly and seemingly with much regularity, a number of very tall straight poles like flag-staves or beacons, supported from the ground by spars. Their first appearance induced an opinion of their bring intended as the uprights for stages on which they might dry their fish; but this, on a nearer view, seemed improbable, as their heights and distances from <226> each other would have required spars of a greater size to reach from one to the other than the substance of the poles was capable of sustaining, They were undoubtedly intended to answer some particular purpose; but whether of a religious, civil, or military nature must be left to some future investigation." [no ¶]

A liberty pole or a gallows, probably, would have filled the alternative suggested. The object of these erections is mentioned by Captain Wilkes as serving to suspend the nets with which the Indian catch wild fowl. Vancouver was greatly disgusted at the small importance attached to his visit. He says further that on Mr Whidbey's landing to seek for water, the Indians continued to fish, "without paying any more regard to the cutter than if he had been one of their own canoes." The circumstance was certainly remarkable, and can only be explained by the fact that the novelty had worn off, as there is no doubt, although Vancouver supposed himself to b the first who had penetrated thus far up the straits, that Kendrick and others had preceded him. At Port Discovery, he says, "a few of the natives in two or three canoes favored us with their company, and brought with them some fish and venison for sale." "These people, in their persons, canoes, arms, implements, &c., seemed to resemble chiefly the inhabitants of Nootka, though less bedaubed with paint and <227> less filthy in their extern appearance. They wore ornaments in their ears, but none were observed in their noses; some of the understood a few words of the Nootka language [WaWa]; they were clothed in the skins of deer, bear, and some other animals, but principally in a woolen garment of their own manufactures, extremely well wrought. They did not appear to possess any furs. Their bows and implements they freely barter for knives, trinkets, copper, &c., and, what was very extraordinary, they offered for sale two [slave] children, each [228] about six or seven year of age, and being sworn some copper were very anxious that the bargain should be closed." [no ¶]

At Port Townshend he saw no Indians, but a deserted village at the side of the Tsemakum town, apparently in a state of decay. [no ¶]

A few Indians were met with at Oak Cove (Port Lawrence), and near the head of Hood Canal about sixty, including women and children, undoubtedly of the Skokomish tribe, which were all that he met with on that extensive line. "The region we had lately passed," he says, "seemed nearly destitute of human beings. Nowhere did the appearance of the party create any alarm or much astonishment, the Indians always treating them in a friendly manner, and bartering their arms and other article for iron, copper, and trinkets." The following general observations are extracted entire, as they <228> bear upon the apparent population of the country at the time. They refer more particularly to the Klallam, Tsemakum, and Skokomish. Vancouver, it may be mentioned in passing, does not seem to have sought for the names of any of the tribes, and none are mentioned in his book. Other points are omitted which appear singular. In speaking of the fish taken in the Sound, he never refers to the salmon; and, what is most extraordinary, he says noting of the custom of flattening the head. [no ¶]

> <"Having considered with impartiality the excellencies and defects of this country, as far as came under our observation, it now remains to add a few words on the character of its inhabitants. None being resident in Port Discovery, and our intercourse with them having been very much confined, the knowledge we may have acquired of them, their manners and customs, must necessarily be very limited, and other conclusions drawn chiefly from comparison. From New Dungeness we traversed nearly one hundred and fifty miles of their shores without seeing that number of inhabitants. Those who came within our notice nearly resembled the people of Nootka, [that the best delineation I can offer is a reference to the description of those people, which has before been so ably and with so much justice given to the public. <229> The only difference I observed was, that in their stature they did not generally appear quite so stout, and in their habits less filthy; for though these people adorn their persons with the same sort of paint, yet it is not laid on in that abundance, nor do they load their hair with that immense quantity of oil and

colouring matter, which is customary among people of Nootka; their hair>,[122] as before mentioned, being in general neatly combed and tied behind.

"In their weapons, implements, canoes, and dress, they vary little. Their native woolen garment was most in fashion, next to it, the skins of deer, bear, &c.; a few wore dressed manufactured from bark, which, like their woolen ones, were very neatly wrought. Their spears, arrows, fish-gigs, ??jigs [229] and other weapons were shaped exactly like those of Nootka, but none were pointed with copper or with muscleshells. The three former were generally barbed, and those pointed with common flint, agate, and bone seemed of their original workmanship. Yet more of their arrows were observed to be pointed with thin, flat iron than with bone or flint, and it was very singular that they should prefer exchanging those pointed with iron to any of the others. Their bows were of a superior construction; these, in general, were from two and a half to three feet in length; the broadest part in the middle was about an inch and a half and about three-quarters of an inch thick, <230> neatly made, gradually tapering to each end, which terminated in a shoulder and hook for the security of the bow-string. They were all made of yew, and chosen with a naturally-inverted curve suited to the method of using them. From end to end of the concave side, which when strung became the convex part, a very strong strip of an elastic hide is attached to some, and the skins of serpents to others, exactly the shape ad length of the bow, neatly and firmly affixed to the wood by means of a cement, the adhesive property of which I never saw or heard of being equaled. It is not to be affected by either dry or damp weather, and forms a strong a connection with the wood as to prevent a separation without destroying the component parts of both. The bow-string is made of the sinew of some marine animal, laid loose, in order to be twisted at pleasure, as the temperature of the atmosphere may require to preserve it at a proper length. Thus is this very neat little weapon rendered portable, elastic, and effective in the highest degree, if we may be allowed to judge by the dexterity with which it was used by one of the natives at Port Discovery.

"We had little opportunity of acquiring any satisfactory information with regard to the public regulation or private economy of these people. The situation and appearance of the places we found them generally inhabiting indicating their being much accustomed <231> to change or residence; the deserted villages tend to strengthen the conjecture of their being wanderers. Territorial property appeared to be of little importance; there was plenty of room for their fixed habitations, and those of a temporary nature, which we now found them mostly to occupy, being principally composed of crossed sticks covered with a few mats, as easily found a spot for their erec [230] tion, as they were removed from one station to another, either as inclination might lead or necessity compel; and having a very extensive range of domain, they were not liable to interruption or opposition from their few surrounding neighbors.

"From these circumstances alone, it may be somewhat premature to conclude that this delightful country has always been thus thinly inhabited; on the contrary, there are reasons to believed it has been infinitely more populous. Each of the deserted villages was nearly, if not quite, equal to contain all the scattered habitants we saw,

---

[122] Inserted from written manuscript, not in 1877 publication. *jm*

according to the custom of the Nootka people, to whom these have great affinity in their fixed habitations and in their general character. It is also possible that most of the clear spaced may have been indebted or the removal of their timber and underwood [underbrush] to manual labor [regular burning over]. Their general appearances furnish this opinion, and their situation on the most pleasant and commanding <232> eminences, protected by the forest on every side except that which would have preclude a view of them, seemed to encourage the idea. Not many years since, each of these vacant spaces might have been allotted t the habitation of different societies, and the variation observed in their extent might have been comparable to the size of each village, on the site of which, since their abdication or extermination, nothing but the smaller shrubs and plants had yet been able to rear their heads.

"In our different excursion, particularly those in the neighborhood of Port Discovery, the skull, limbs, ribs, and back-bones, or some other vestiges of the human body, were found in many places promiscuously scattered about the beach in great numbers. Similar relics were also frequently met with during our survey in the boats; and I was informed by the officers that, in their several perambulations, the like appearances had presented themselves so repeatedly and in such abundance as to produce an idea that the environs of Port Discovery were a general cemetery for the whole surrounding country. Notwithstanding the circumstances do not amount to a direct proof of the extensive population they indicate, yet, when combined with other appearances, they warranted an opinion that, at no very remote period, this country had been far more populous than <m233> at present. Some of the human bodies were found disposed of in a very singular man [231] ner. Canoes were suspended between two or more trees, about twelve feet from the ground, in which were the skeletons of two or three persons. Others of a larger size were hauled up into the outskirts of the woods, which contained from four to seven skeletons, covered over with a broad plank. In some of these, broken bows and arrows were found, which at first gave rise to the conjecture that these might have been warriors, who, after being mortally wounded, had, whilst their strength remained, hauled up their canoes for the purpose of expiring quietly in them. But, on a further examination, this became improbable, as it would hardly have been possible to have preserved the regularity of position in the agonies of death, or to have defended their sepulchers with the broad plank with which each was covered. The few skeletons we saw so carefully deposited in the canoes were probably the chiefs, priests, or leaders of particular tribes, whose followers most likely continue to possess the highest [a pun!] respect for their memory and remains; and the general knowledge I had obtained from experience of the regard which all savage nations pay to their funeral solemnities made me particularly solicitous to prevent any indignity from being wantonly offered to their departed friends. <m234> Baskets were also found suspended on high trees, each containing the skeleton of a young child; in some of which were also small square boxes filled with a kind of white paste, resembling such as I had seen the natives eat, supposed to be made of the saranna root. Some of these boxes were quite full; others were nearly empty, eaten probably by the mice, squirrels, or birds. On the next low point south of our present encampment, where the gunners were airing the powder, they met several holes, in which human bodies were interred, slightly covered over, and in different states of decay, some appearing to have been very recently deposited. About half a mile to the northward of our tents, where the land is nearly level with high-water mark, a few paces within the skirting of the wood, a canoe was found suspected between two trees, in which were three human skeletons; and a few paces to the right was a cleared space of nearly forty yards round, where, from the fresh appearance of burned stumps, most of its vegetable production had very lately been consumed by fire. Amongst the ashes we found the skulls and other bones of near twenty persons in different stages of calcination; the fire, however, had not reached the sus [232] pended canoe, nor did it appear to have been intended that it should. The skeletons, found thus disposed in canoes or in <m235> baskets, bore a very small proportion to the number of skulls and other human bones indiscriminately scattered about the shores. Such are the effects; but the cause or causes that have operated to produce them, we remained totally unacquainted, whether occasioned by epidemic disease or recent wars. The character and general deportment of the few inhabitants we occasionally saw by no means countenanced the latter opinion; they were uniformly civil and friendly, without manifesting the least sign of fear or suspicion at our approach, nor did their appearance indicate their having been much inured to hostilities. Several of their stoutest men had been seen perfectly naked, and, contrary to what might have been expected of rude natives habituated to warfare, their skins were mostly unblemished by scars, excepting such a the small-pox seemed to have occasioned, a disease which there is great reason to believe is very fatal amongst them. It is not, however, very easy to draw any just conclusions on the true cause from which this havoc of the human race proceeded: This must remain for the investigation of others who may have more leisure and a better opportunity to direct such an inquiry; yet it may not be unreasonable to conjecture that the present apparent depopulation may have arisen, in some measure, from the inhabitants of this interior part having been induced <m236> to quit their former abode, and to have moved nearer the exterior coast for the convenience of obtaining, in the immediate mart, with more ease and at a cheaper rate, those valuable articles of commerce that within these last years have been brought to the sea-coasts of this continent by Europeans and the citizens of America, and which are in great estimation amongst these people, being possessed by all in the greater or less degree."

While surveying Admiralty Inlet, Vancouver met with further parties of Indians. Of the Skokomish, he says: "Towards noon, I went ashore at the village point (southern end of Bainbridge Island) for the purpose of observing the latitude; on which occasion I visited the village; if it may be dignified, as it appeared the most lowly and meanest of its kind. The best of the huts were poor and miserable, constructed something after the fashion of a soldier's tent, by two cross-sticks, about five feet high, connected at each end by a ridge-pole from one to the other, over some of which was [233] thrown a coarse kind of mat; over others, a few loose branches of trees, shrubs, and grass. None, however, appeared to be constructed for protecting them, either against the heat of summer or the inclemency of winter. In them were hung up, to be cured by the smoke of the fires they kept constantly burning. <m237> Clams, muscles, and a few other kinds of fish, seemingly intended for their winter's subsistence. The clams perhaps were not all reserved for that purpose, as we frequently saw them strung and worn about the neck, which, as inclination directed, were eaten, two, three, or half a dozen at a time. This station did not appear to have been preferred for the purpose of fishing, as we saw few of the people so employed; nearly the whole of the inhabitants belonging to the village, which consisted of about eighty or a hundred men, women, and children, were busily engaged, like swine, rooting up this beautiful verdant meadow, in quest of a species of wild onion, and two other roots, which, in appearance and taste, greatly resembled the saranna, particularly the largest. The collecting of these roots was most likely the object which attracted them to this spot; they all seemed to gather them with much avidity, and to preserve them with great care, most probably for the purpose of making the paste I have already mentioned."

"These people varied in no essential point from the natives we had seen since our entering the straits. Their persons were equally ill made, and as much besmeared with oil and different colored paints, particularly with red ocher and a sort of shining chaffy mica, very ponderous, and in color <m238> much resembling black lead. They likewise possessed more ornament, especially such as were made of copper, the article most valued and esteemed among them." Subsequently, about eighty of the Dwamish visited the ship, whose appearance he mentions as more cleanly than that of the people on the island. The latter were undoubtedly there merely temporarily, and for the purpose of digging the roots referred to.

A party of Indians, it seems, turned the tables on Vancouver, so far as the suspicion of cannibalism is concerned, and, after subjecting some of a venison pastry to a very severe examination, rejected it with great disgust, pointing to their own bodies to indicate their ideas of its origin, he satisfied them of its character with some difficulty, and drew the inference, cer [234] tainly correct, that the character ascribed to the Northwest Indian of America in his day was, at least so far a these were concerned, unjust.

The number of Indians encountered by Mr Puget in exploring the various inlets leading to the sounds which now bears his name does not seem to have been greater in proportion than those met with in Admiralty Inlet and Hood Canal, as, though Vancouver speaks of his meeting several tribes, he does no refer to their numbers. The only difficulty had with any of the natives was met with by this <m239> gentleman in what is now called Hale Passage, which, however, owing to his prudence, did not proceed to extremities. It is remarkable that on this occasion they showed no surprise at the fire of small-arms, but merely imitated the sound of the muskets by exclaiming poo! poo! and on the discharge of the swivel shotted, instead of flying, merely unstrung their bows, and came forward with demonstrations of friendship. [no ¶]

In surveying Whidbey Island and the passages lying east of it, Mr Whidbey met with the Snohmish and Skagit. Of this district, Vancouver says, "The number of its inhabitants is about six hundred, which I should supposed would exceed the total of all the natives before seen."

Already the production of European art had begun to find their way here. Not only were he Indians tolerably well supplied with iron and copper arrow-points, but the weapons also had been imported. "The chief," says Vancouver, "for so we must distinguish him, had two hangers, one of Spanish and the other of English manufacture, on which he seemed to set a very high value." From their curiosity to know if he was all white, Mr Whidbey concluded they had not before seen any Europeans, though from the different articles they possessed it is evident a communication had taken place; probably by means of intertribal trade. <m240>

Mr Broughton's account of the Columbia River Indians is far less minute. He makes no estimate of their apparent numbers, which do not appear to have struck him as very great, merely remarking that the farther he proceeded the more the country was inhabited. It is to be noticed that the deserted villages referred to by Vancouver and his different parties were probably left for the time being. The period of Mr Broughton's visit, the month of December, was one at which most of the bands living near [235] the mouth of the river were on Shoalwater Bay, engaged in taking winter salmon. The following extract embodies his principal observations:

"The natives differed in nothing very materially from those we had visited during the summer, but in the decoration of their persons; in this respect they surpassed all the other tribes, with paints of different colors, feathers, and other ornaments. Their houses seemed to be more comfortable than those at Nootka, the roof having a greater inclination, and the planking being thatched over with the bark of trees. The entrance is through a hole in a broad plank, carved in such a manner as to resemble the face of a man, the mouth serving for the purpose of a doorway. The fire-place is sunk in the earth, and confined from spreading above by a wooden frame. The inhabitants are universally addicted to smoking. <m241> Their pipe is similar to ours in shape. The bowl is made of very hard wood, and is externally ornamented with carving; the tube, about two feet long, is make of a small branch of the elder. In this they smoke an herb which the country produces, of a very mild nature, and by no means unpleasant; they, however, took great pleasure in smoking tobacco; hence it is natural to conclude it might become a valuable article of traffic among them. In most other respects, they resemble their neighbors as to their manners and mode of living, being equally filthy and uncleanly."

Mr Whidbey's account of the examination of Gray Harbor contains even less information. The total number of inhabitants seen by him was estimated at one hundred; most of the remainder being, in all probability, at Shoalwater Bay, which, as before mentioned, was the winter ground of the Tsihalis equally with the Chinūk.

The next, and a far more valuable account of the Columbia river Indians, is that of Lewis and Clark, thirteen years later. Their description of Indian manners, dwelling, and life are accurate, and they have not like many other writers, indulged in speculation or attempted to draw inferences and assign motives for action on insufficient basis. The nomenclature assigned by them to may of the bands, with which they met or of which they obtained <m242> information, is not recognizable at the present day. There are, in fact, no generic names used by the Indians among their own tribes, but each band is distinguished by its appropriate appellation, that of [236] ground which it occupies. Generic or tribal names for others are sometimes used; but, as before mentioned, the cohesion among the bands of the same family is so small, that it is more usual to hear them separately mentioned, even by their neighbors. As these appellations differ with the different tribes, and moreover die out with the abandonment of a particular locality, it is next to impossible, after such a lapse of time, to identify all of them, except by their locality or order of succession.

Subsequent to Lewis and Clarke is Franchère, whose simplicity of narration and air of truth induces a regret that his work is not more in detail. Upon this much of Mr Irving description is based. [no ¶]

Ross Cox's adventures, though highly amusing and sufficiently accurate where description alone is concerned, are liable to give very false impression of motive and idea.

Of the externals of savage life on the Oregon coast, there are many graphic and full accounts, but a insight into their minds is not so easy to reach, and those who have most carefully sought it are likely to be most doubtful of their success. <m243>

EARLY VISITS OF WHITE MEN

The Indians at the mouth of the Columbia preserve several traditions of the early visits of white men, the first of which must have been many years anterior to the arrival of Gray. The wife of Mr Solomon H Smith, who belonged to the Klatsop, and was born about the year 1818, informed me that the first while men seen by her tribe were three who came ashore in a boat from a wrecked vessel. "They landed on the Klatsop Point (Point Adams), where one soon afterward died. They were first descried by a woman who had lost her child, and, after the Indian fashion, had gone out in the morning to mourn for it. She saw a large object lying on the beach, and, while looking at it in wonder, the seamen came ashore and approached, holding a bright kettle and motioning her to bring water. She was afraid; but they put it down and retired, when she took it and ran to the village. The Indians then came down in a body. The new-comers looked like men, except that they had long beards like bears. They had already put the sick man in a box to be buried, as he was nearly dead. The Klatsop Indians sent [237] for the others on the river, who came in great numbers. Astonished at the value of their prize and, hoping to get the whole of the metals which it contained, they set fire to the wreck, by which means they lost all. There were copper kettles on the vessel and pieces of money, having a square hole through the [centre] center. <m244>

The two surviving seamen remained as laves to the Klatsop until it was found that one was a worker in iron, of which the Indians began to see the value, when they made him a chief. Afterward the two started for their own country, which they said, was toward the rising sun. They went as far as the Dalles, where one stopped and married. The other returned to Multnomah Island and married there. He had a daughter, who was an old gray-haired women when Mrs Smith was a child. Her own father remembered the arrival of the seamen. The man who lived on Multnomah Island was undoubtedly the one mentioned by Franchère in his narrative, whose son, Soto, was alive, and a very old man, at the time of his visit.

After this visit, a vessel anchored off Mahcarnie Head {[False Tilamūk]}, in the bight at the mouth of the Nehalen [Nehalem] River. About twenty armed men, with cutlasses, came on shore, bringing an iron chest, which they carried about two miles back into the country, to a spot where an Indian trail crossed a brook on the south side of the promontory. The place was east of the trail and south of the brook. There they buried it between two rocks, letting down another on top, and cut an inscription on the rock. They then killed a man and went away. Some years ago, a party of Oregonians went to search for this box, under the impression that it was hidden treasure, but were un <m245> successful, for, although the place is ascertained within a short distance, their Indian guides would not approach it." The incident of a man being killed on the spot is probably an Indian addition, drawn from their own usages.

Another vessel, having on board a large quantity of beeswax was cast away on the spit of land to the north of the same river, the Nehalen. The crew came ashore, built a house, and lived peaceably for some time, till they began to take away the Indians '' wives. This created an excitement, and finally, when they had seduced off the wife of a chief, he assembled the tribe, and asked if they would let their wives go or fight. They decided to [238] fight, and attacked the seamen with bows and arrows and spears. They latter resisted, *throwing stones behind them and under their arms with great force*, as the Indians say, but were finally all killed. This beeswax has often been mentioned y travelers, and pieces of it continue to be found after westerly storms. This vessel was probably a Japanese junk, several of which have from time to time been cast away on the coast. It is noticeable that many of the Tilamūk differ in personal appearance from their neighbors at this day so as easily to be recognized by those acquainted with the peculiarity. Their complexion is yellower than ordinary, and their eyes more oblique and elongated. <m246>

The spot on which Lewis and Clarke's winter encampment was fixed is still discernable, and the foundation logs remained till within a year or two. It was on the west bank of a little river, called by the Indians Netul, but generally known as Lewis and Clarke's river, about two miles from its mouth. The trail by which they used to reach the coast can also be traced. Their visit produced a stronger impression than any event before the arrival of the Astoria party, and they are still remembered by the older Indians. One of these Indians told a settler that the captains were real chiefs, and that the Americans who have come since were but *tilikum*, or common people. Ske-man-kwe-up, the chief, and almost the last survivor of the Wah-kiakum band of Tsinūk, preserved with great pride the medal given him by Lewis and Clarke, until within a year of two when it was accidentally lost, to his great grief.

The [Chihalis] Tsihalis Indians retain a recollection of Gray. [Cow-cow-an] ~ Kau-kau-an, the old chief of Tsihalis Point, informed me that he had seen him. Gray gave them a musket and some cartridges, first, however, cutting off the balls. They did not know its use, but supposed it was intended merely to make a noise, and fired it off until their powder was gone, when they broke it up. Afterward they found out Gray's object. He also gave them axes and knives, the first they had seen. A few years <m247> after him came Captain Tomlinson, with whom they also traded. Gray and he used to give them a "small blanket", probably a piece of coarse cloth, for a dressed deer-skin.

Quite a number of Sound Indians remember the visits of the early ships to their waters, although, as might be expected, they have confused [239] their accounts. Lakh-kanam, father of the Duke of York, the S'kllam chief, and apparently a very old man, informed me that he was about the age of a boy whom he pointed out, or some ten years when hey first arrived. This he said had been one stick, mast, and was probably the Washington, Captain Kendrick, which entered in 1789, or the Princess Royal (Spanish), Lieutenant Quimper, in 1790. The Indian s thought it was Do-kwe-butl, for they knew nothing of the kwa-ne-tum, or white man, and they feared lest some great sickness should follow. The vessel came up to New Dungeness and anchored. The old men and women went out and called Do-kwe-butl! Do-kwe-butl! The chiefs said to one another that they ought not to be afraid, and they accordingly washed, oiled, and painted their faces as when making tamahn-oūs, thinking to please Do-kwe-butl. They all went out in their canoes to the ship, when one man, a sailor, motioned to them not to come near till they had washed the paint from their faces. They went astern and did so, and then all were <m248> admitted to the ship; but Lakh-kanam, who was small and afraid, did not go. The sailors got into his canoe, and wanted to try and paddle it, but he cried till Hai-ya-watst, General Pierce's father, who is still living, and older than himself, came down into the canoe and told him not to cry. Some one, he supposes the captain, then made them all presents of buttons and knives. The captain wanted afterward to buy one of the dog's hair blankets, and one of cedar bark. He had nothing at this time to trade with except buttons, knives, and sheathing-copper, and the shell called sea-ear (*haliotis*).[123] He traded these things for curiosities. About a year or a year and a half after, a three-masked and a two-masted vessel came in. Neither of them went farther up than Port Discovery. The two-masted vessel traded them iron hoops ad broken iron; they bought deer- ad elk-skins, and gave from eight t twelve small blankets! or a musket for one skin! They also sold shot and power. When the captain had done trading, he gave away knives, looking-glasses, and other small articles as presents.

Lakh-kanam's remembrance of prices is probably very much exaggerated by distance, the good old times being a golden age with the Indians also; but the narrative is probably substantially accurate. When he had grown up and got <m249> a wife, two more ships came.

---

[123] Also ear shell, for its shiny shape. *jm*

Several had touched at [240] Cape Flattery before the first came to New Dungeness. They came ashore at once, and put up a tent, and many of the Klallam came to see her. The name of one captain was Lelis and the other Paput. That of another still was Kelalimuk. They always wanted skins from the Indians. The Indians had no beaver, but elk, deer, and sea-otter. For a large sea-otter they gave twenty blankets. They also bought haikwa for blankets, five fathoms for a blanket. These blankets were different from the first, being heavier. The last two vessels only came up to Port Discovery. He thought they then went to Klyokwot. It was afterward that ships came up the Sound. For some time, a good many came, and then they stopped. The name of the captains given by him cannot be recognized, and very possibly were of Indian bestowal. It would seem to indicate that several trading-vessels had passed up the straits before Vancouver; but there is some confusion as to times, if the sloop was Gray's, as he could not have come up in the interim. Lakh-kanam also recollects when the white people (the Russians) lived in a house at Neeah Bay. He was then grown up. A vessel was lost there, and the Makah plundered her and behaved badly. The house was only a tent. He knew nothing of a stone <m250> house, such as the adobe building erected by the Spaniards.

Winapat, or as he is called by the whites, Bonaparte, one of the old Snokomish [Snohomish] chiefs, informed me that the first ship came up only as far as Whidbey Island. Until then a piece of iron, as long as one's finger, was worth two slaves. That ship brought it to them directly. When he was a very small boy, two ships came, one of which stopped in the Klallam country, and the other went up to the Puyallup. They carried off a chief, Tseeshishten. In this, also, there is probably some error, if the ships were Vancouver's, as he makes no mention of taking away any Indians.

TABLE SHOWING THE RELATIONS OF TRIBES MENTIONED
(After George Gibbs, by WH Dall)

1. NUTKA FAMILY: a, Makah tribe.

2. SAHAPTIN FAMILY: a, Taitinapam; b, (?) Klikata (properly T'likatat).

3. TINNEH FAMILY: a, Owillapsh; b, Klatskanai; c, Umkwa; d, Tūtūten.

4. SELISH FAMILY:

    A. (Extralimital).
    { British Columbia: a, Kaitlen; b, Billikūla
    {Vancouver Island: a, Nanaimūk ; b, Kowitsin ; c, Songhu ; d, Soke.

    B. Selish (at large): {a, Kowlitz ; b, S'Klallam ; c, Tsihalis ; d, Kwinaiūtl' ;
       e, Kwillehiūt {Kwillehiūt – typical , Kwaaksat}

    C. Niskwalli Selish

        A. Skokomish {Skwawksnamish, Kwulseet}

        B. Puget Sound Group
            I.. (Salt water.) {S'hotlmamish, Kwai'aitl, Sahewamish, Stehtsasamish, Sawamish, Nū-seht-satl'.}
            II.. (Horse) {Niskwalli *proper*, Segwallitsū, Stailakū-mamish, Skwalliahmish.}
            III. (River & Sound) {Puyallupahmish, T'kwakwamish, S'homamish.}
            IV. (Dwamish) {Sukwamish, Samamish, Skopamish, St'kamish, Sk'tehlmish.}

        C. Snohomish
            I. Snohomish
            II. Snokwalmū {Stoluts-whamish, Sk'tahle-jum, Skihwamish, Kwehtl'mamish.}
            III. Yakama
            IV. Skagit {Kikiallū, Towah-ha, Nū-kwat-samish, Smali-hū, Sakū-mehū, Skwonamish, Miskai-whū, Swinamish, Miseekwigweelis.}
            V. Lummi. {samish, Lummi, Nūk-sahk.}

5. T'sinūk family: a, T'sinūk tribes

[241]

GEORGE GIBBS' INDIEN TRIBES OF WASHINGTON

This work was originally published as a 34-page appendix [p402-436] to the comprehensive 1855 survey for the proposed northern route of a railroad across the US. It had no subdivisions and consequently no table of contents. I have created the following table of contents as a rough guide for navigating this very interesting historical document, with my own additions set between { curved brackets } *jay miller = jm*

https://books.google.com/books?id=hH9RAAAAcAAJ&pg=PA402&lpg=PA402&dq=george+gibbs+indians+railroad+report&source=bl&ots=umXnvs6Qu4&sig=HlPHiqsy8wxWrMraHlLwtLTfL8&hl=en&sa=X&ei=FkyaVK6pAcitoQSlhoDoCg&ved=0CEwQ6AEwCQ#v=onepage&q=george%20gibbs%20indians%20railroad%20report&f=false

Gibbs, George. 1855. Report of Mr George Gibbs to Captain Mc'Clellan on the Indian Tribes of the Territory of Washington. In *Reports of Explorations and Surveys to Ascertain the most Practicable and Economical Route for a Railroad from the Mississippi River to the Pacific Ocean.* According to Acts of Congress of 3 march 1853, 31 May 1854, and 5 August 1854. 33rd Congress, 2nd Session, Senate Ex Doc #78. Governor Isaac Stevens in Charge. Volume 1: J – 402-453. Washington: Beverley Tucker, Printer, for US Secretary of War.

TABLE OF CONTENTS

	#	page here
Introductory	1	115
Horses among the Klikatats and Yakimas	3	117
Several legends of the Klikatats and Yakimas	5	119
The Spokanes {Spokan}	12	128
Population Estimates of Eastern Washington Tribes	15	132
Forts and Missionaries	19	136
Suggestions for dealing with the Native Peoples	23	143
Tribes of Western Washington TABLE	28	148
Tribes of Puget Sound	32	151
Population Estimates of Western Washington Tribes	36	154 > 41 > 158

J.

INDIAN AFFAIRS

39. REPORT OF MR GEORGE GIBBS TO CAPTAIN MC'CLELLAN, ON THE INDIAN TRIBES OF THE TERRITORY OF WASHINGTON.

REPORT.

[402] In considering the general subject of the Indian tribes of this territory, two natural divisions present themselves, separated by a marked and definite boundary – the Cascade mountains – on either side of which the native inhabitants differ not less than the geographical features of the country.

It will be proper to examine them in turn, taking up the various tribes of each division in order, and appending such observations in regard to their management as the most careful inquiry practicable has suggested.

In this connection, the word "nation" will be used of the whole people speaking a common language, and "tribe" as comprehending the bands organized under one head.

And first of the interior or eastern section.

Those living between the Cascade and Rocky mountains, within the limits of this Territory, or extending into it, are, first, the Wallah-Wallah nation, under which term is embraced a number of bands living usually on the south side of the Columbia, and on the Snake river to a little east of the Peluse; as also the Klikatats and Yakimas, north of the former. The first may be, for the present purpose, classed together as the Wallah-Wallah Tribe. The greater part of their country, it will be seen, lies in the adjoining Territory of Oregon, and it is proposed should remain under the direction of that superintendency. The number of these bands was in 1851 stated by Dr Anson Dart, then superintendent of Indian affairs, at 1,093 ; a part of whom, how [403] ever, belonged to the Upper Chinooks. The whole number is since much diminished by the smallpox. The present population is probably reduced to 600, of whom the majority are in Oregon Territory. The head chief of the Wallah-Wallahs is Pu-pu-mux-mux, or the Yellow Serpent {Yellow Swan}[124] – an old man, who generally makes his residence near Fort Wallah-Wallah. His influence with his people is said to be good as far as it goes, but he does not exercise it beyond his immediate band. This tribe have been notorious as thieves since their first intercourse with the whites. They, as well as their neighbors, the Nez Perces, own large bands of horses, which roam at large, over the hills south of the Columbia, and their principal wealth consists in them. There is no wood in their country, and they depend upon the drift brought down by the stream for their fuel. Their very canoes are purchased from the Spokanes. They move about a great deal, generally camping in winter on the north side of the river. Their fisheries at the Dalles, and at the falls ten miles above, are the finest on the river. The expedition

---

[124] Though often called Yellow Serpent in English, his native name refers to the snaky neck of a swan. *jm*

passed through the Wallah-Wallah country on its return route, but no official intercourse took place with the tribe. They, as well as the Nez Perces and Cayuses, are at present included in the agency of Mr RR Thompson, of Oregon. At the crossing of Snake river, at the mouth of the Peluse, we met with an interesting relic. The chief of the band, Wattai-wattai-how-lis, in coming to visit Captain McClellan, exhibited, with great pride, the medal presented to his father, Ke-powh-kan, by Captains Lewis and Clarke.[125] It is of silver, double, and hollow, having on the obverse a medallion bust, with the legend, "Thomas Jefferson, President U. S. A., 1801;" and on the reverse the clasped hands, pipe, and battle-axe, crossed, with the legend, "Peace and Friendship."

The Klikatats and Yakimas will remain to the Washington superintendency. The former inhabit, properly, the valleys lying between Mounts St Helens[126] and Adams, but they have spread over districts belonging to other tribes, and a band of them is now located as far south as the Umpqua. Their nomadic habits render a census very difficult, though their number is not large. Dr Dart stated them at 492; since when, there has certainly been a great decrease. The number of the two principal bands, as obtained during the summer, was, at the Chequoss 135, and at the Kamas plain 84. These must have constituted the chief part, as it was the season of berries when they congregated there. Including all others within the Territory, the total does not probably exceed 300. In this, however, are not reckoned the Tai-tin-a-pam, a band said to live apart in the country lying on the western side of the mountains, between the heads of the Cathlapoot'l and Cowlitz, and which probably did not enter into the former estimate. But little is known of them, and their numbers are undoubtedly small. The head chief of the Klikitats is a very old man, named Towe-toks. He evidently possesses but little influence, his people paying much more respect to his wealthier neighbors, Ka-mai-ya-kan, Skloo, and the other chiefs of the Yakimas.

The Klikatats and Yakimas, in all essential peculiarities of character, are identical, and their intercourse is constant; but the former, though a mountain tribe, are much more unsettled in their habits than their brethren.

This fact is probably due, in the first place, to their having been driven from their homes, many years ago, by the Cayuses, with whom they were at war. They thus became acquainted with other parts of the country, as well as with the advantage to be derived from trade. It was not, however, until about 1839 that they crossed the Columbia, when they overran the Willamette valley, attracted by the game with which it abounded, and which they destroyed in defiance of the weak and indolent Callapooyas. They still boast that they taught the latter to ride and to hunt.

They manifest a peculiar aptitude for trading, and have become to the neighboring tribes what the Yankees were to the once Western States, the travelling retailers of notions; purchasing from the whites feathers, beads, cloth, and other articles prized by Indians, and exchanging them for horses, which in turn they sell in the settlements. Their country supplies them with an abundance of food. The lower prairies afford game, and the mountains a great variety of berries [204] in profusion. The business of gathering these of course falls on the women, who go out in small parties, attended by a boy or old man as camp-keeper, collect and dry the berries, or bring into the general camp what is wanted for present food. Such of them as bear keeping they save

---

[125] See Francis Paul Prucha, <u>Indian Peace Medals in American History</u> 1994. *jm*

[126] Actively volcanic, known to Cowlitz as *Lawetlat'ła* = "Smoker," its notable eruptions recurred 40,000 and 3500 years ago, again in AD 1800, 1831, 1857, and 18 May 1980. *jm*

for winter use, and also for trade, exchanging them for fish, smoked clams, and the roots which their own territory does not furnish.

Of game, there is but little left. The deer and elk are almost exterminated throughout the country. the deep snows of winter driving them to the valleys, where the Indians, with their usual improvidence, have slaughtered them without mercy. The mountain goat, and the big-horn, or sheep, are both said to have formerly existed here, but, since the introduction of firearms, have retired far into the recesses of the Cascades. The black bear alone is still found, though but rarely. The salmon furnishes to these, as to most other tribes of the Pacific, their greatest staple of food. Their neighborhood to the fisheries of the Cascades and the Dalles provides them for the summer; while, after the subsidence of the Columbia, later schools ascend the small rivers, and in the autumn an inferior kind forces its way into the brooks, and even the shallow pools which form in the prairies.

Very few attempt any cultivation of the soil, though their lower prairies would admit of it. We were informed, however, that the next season many of them intended to build houses there and plant potatoes. Their usual residence during the summer is around Chequoss, one of the most elevated points on our trail from Fort Vancouver across the Cascades, where we met them at the beginning of August. They were, at this time, feasting on strawberries and the mountain whortleberry, which covered the hills around, though during the night the ice formed on the ponds to the thickness of half an inch. Towards the end of the month they descend to the Yahkohtl, Chalacha, and Tahk prairies, where they are met by the Yakimas {Yakamas}, who assemble with them; for the purpose of gathering a later species of berry and of racing horses. The racing season is the grand annual occasion of these tribes. A horse of proved reputation is a source of wealth or of ruin to his owner. On his speed he stakes his whole stud, his household goods, clothes, and finally his wives; and a single heat doubles his fortune, or sends him forth an impoverished adventurer. The, interest, however, is not confined to the individual directly concerned; the tribe share it, with him, and a common pile of goods, of motley description, apportioned according to their ideas of value, is put up by either party, to be divided among the backers of the winner. The Klikatats themselves are not as rich in horses as those living on the plains, their country generally affording but little pasturage, and the deep snows compelling them to winter their stock at a distance from their usual abodes. The horse is to them what the canoe is to the Indians of the river and coast. They ride with skill, reckless of all obstacles, and with little mercy to their beasts, the right hand swinging the whip at every bound. Some of the horses are of fine form and action; but they are generally injured by too early use, and sore backs are universal. Indiscriminate breeding has greatly deteriorated what must have been originally a good stock, and the prevalence of white and gray in their colors is a great objection. Wall-eyes, white noses and hoofs, are more than common among them. They are almost always either vicious or lazy, and usually combine both qualities. In their capacity for a continued endurance, they are overrated. A good American horse is as much superior to them in this, as in speed; but they are hardy, and capable of shifting with but little food. Nothing is known of their first introduction. They were abundant when the country was discovered. It is probable that the Shoshonees or Snakes, a branch of the Camanches {Numic Comanche}, first introduced them from the South, and that the breed has since been crossed by others from Canada. The best are those belonging to the Cayuses and Nez Perce. The demand for horses, consequent upon the settlement of the country, has rendered the tribes possessing them really wealthy.

Their price is from $40 to $100, but they have some which they will not dispose of at much higher rates. A few of the chiefs have great numbers, and one, it is said, has offered 400, a by no means contemptible dowry – to any respectable white man who will marry his daughter. [405] The Indians ride with a hair-rope knotted around the under jaw for a bridle. The men use a stuffed pad, with wooden stirrups. The women sit astride, in a saddle made, with a very high pommel and cantle, and in travelling carry their infants either dangling by the cradle-strap to the former, or slung in a blanket over their shoulders; while children of a little larger growth sit perched upon the pack-animals, and hold on as best they may.

The horses are trained to stand for hours with merely a lariat thrown loosely around their necks, the end trailing upon the ground. With the whites they are at first as shy as are American horses or mules with the Indians; but they suffer handling from the squaws and children with perfect contentment, and hang around the huts like dogs. When camping near them we often found the horses an intolerable nuisance, from their incessant whinnying during the night. Whenever the musquitoes were abundant they posted themselves in the smoke of the fires. It is the business of the {women} squaws in travelling to pack the animals, the men contenting themselves with catching them up; and they pile on the most heterogeneous assortment of luggage with a skill that would immortalize a professional packer. In breaking horses the Indians usually blind them before mounting, often tying down their ears in addition. A strap or cord is then passed around, the body of the animal, loose enough to admit the knees of the rider. Much time is spent in soothing and quieting the beast, as the Indian has plenty of it upon his hands. When everything is ready he vaults to his back, always from the off-side, slips his knees under the girth and tightens it, withdraws the muffle, and sits prepared for a series of stiff-legged plunges, ending in a charge. If the horse throws himself – for throw his rider he cannot – the quick straightening of the leg releases the knee, and he is prepared for the emergency.

In describing the household goods of the Indian, his dogs are not to be forgotten. They vary considerably in form with different tribes, but always preserve the same general character. Quarrelsome and cowardly, inveterate thieves, suspicious and inquisitive, they are constantly engaged in fights among themselves, or in prowling around the lodges for food. The approach of a stranger is heralded by short, sharp yelps, succeeded by a general scamper. They all bear the some mysterious resemblance to the cayote – the sharp muzzle, erect ears, and stiffly curling tail. Notwithstanding their worthlessness, they seem to have a strong attachment to their owners, and an Indian camp would be a novelty without its pack of curs. Very few characteristic features remain among these people. Their long intercourse with the Hudson's Bag Company, and of late years with the Americans, has obliterated what peculiarities they may have had; nor is there any essential difference in their habits or manners from those of the Indians adjoining them. They use, for the most part, the arms and utensils of the whites, and the gun has superseded the bow. The pails and baskets, constructed from the bark of the cedars, saddles and fishing apparatus, are their principal articles of domestic manufacture; and even of such things it is almost as common to find the imported substitutes.

In regard to moral character they are much superior to the river Indians; not that perfect virtue is by any means to be expected, but they are more strict in respect to their women, particularly the married ones, and they are far less thievish.

Their mode of disposing of their dead, like that of their kindred tribes, is in the ground, but without any attempt at coffins, the body being merely wrapped in its clothing. Just before our arrival at Chequoss a man had died of the smallpox, and those who had buried him were purifying themselves. During the three days occupied in this, they absented themselves from camp, alternately using the sweat-house and plunging into cold water.

The house, which was a small oven-shaped affair, was heated with stones. The mourning is performed by the women, who live apart for a few days, and afterwards bathe and purify themselves. They have the common objection to mentioning the names of the dead, as well as their own. The practice of medicine, as elsewhere, consists in incantations, and is attended with the usual hazards; the life of the practitioner answering for the want of success, or a refusal to attend when properly feed. Besides these mummeries, however, they use certain plants as [406] medicines, among which are both emetics and cathartics. The patriarchal institutions of slavery and polygamy are yet retained among them; the number of wives being limited only by the wealth of the husband, for with them it is the woman who is sold.

A curious custom exists, exhibiting their savage ideas of equity as opposed to the common-law maxim of "*caveat emptor*".[127] If a wife dies within a short period after marriage, the bereaved husband may reclaim the consideration from the father; so also with slaves and horses. No systematic attempt has, it is believed, been made to convert the Klikatats to Christianity, although many individuals have come in contact with missionaries of some denomination. Several of those at Chequoss have had instruction from the Rev. Jason Lee and others, formerly at the Dalles.

The old chief Tow-e-toks preserved a paper on which some one made a sort of calendar or record of the days of the week. He expressed great anxiety lest, as it was nearly worn out, he should be unable to distinguish the Sundays, and requested me to prepare him a new one. He added that he was in great fear of death, and constantly "talked to the Chief above." As will readily be imagined, the remarkable features of this mountain scenery, and the neighborhood of the great snow peaks – Mount St Helens and Mount Adams – give a color to the legends of the Klikatats. They, in common with the other Oregon tribes, seem to have had no distinct religious ideas previous to those introduced by the whites, nor any conception of a Supreme Being. Their mythology consists of vague and incoherent tales, in most of which Ta-la-pus,[128] or the prairie wolf, figures as a supernatural power. Besides him there are other agents, among whom a race denominated the "*Elip Tilicum*," from two jargon words signifying "first people," or "people before," figure prominently.[129] Though trifling in themselves, yet, as specimens of what may be considered the unwritten literature of the Indians, they may not be uninteresting – the more especially as the belief in the existence of those giants seems to be of universal currency throughout Oregon. The following are among them:

In descending the valley from Chequoss, there occurs beneath a field of lava a vaulted passage, some miles in length, through which a stream flows in the rainy season, and the roof of which has fallen in here and there. Concerning this they relate that a very long time ago, before there were any Indians, there lived in this country a man and wife of gigantic stature. The man became tired of his partner, and took to himself a *mouse*, which thereupon became a woman. When the first wife knew of this, she was very naturally enraged, and threatened to kill them. This coming to the man's knowledge, he hid himself and his mouse-wife in a place higher up the mountain, where there is a small lake having no visible outlet. The first woman finding that they had escaped her, and suspecting that they were hidden underground, commenced digging, and tore up this passage. At last she came beneath where they stood, and looking up through a hole, saw them laughing at her. With great difficulty, and after sliding back two or three times, she

---

[127] Latin = "buyer beware." *jm*
[128] Sahaptin = Coyote trickster. *jm*
[129] As noted, Chinuk WaWa "first folks." *jm*

succeeded in reaching them; when the man, now much alarmed, begged her not to kill him, but to allow him to return to their home and live with her as of old. She finally consented to kill only the mouse-wife, which she did, and it is her blood that has colored the stones at the lake. After a time the man asked her why she had wished to kill the other woman. She answered, because they had brought her to shame, and that she had a mind to kill him too; which she finally did, and since when she has lived alone in the mountains.

Another story about the same place is to the effect that it was made by a former people called the Siam,[130] a name corresponding with the jargon word for grizzly bear. The mouse story appears to be interwoven with the Klikatat mythology, for besides the name of this place, Hool-hool-se, (from hool-hool, a mouse,) one of the names of their country is Hool-hool-pam, or the mouse-land. This is given to it by the Yakimas. Both versions, as well as many others of their tales, refer to their Indian Pre-adamites, the Elip Tilicum; to whom, and to the Ta-la-pus, as many wonders are attributed as among Christians to Satan.

Concerning the Ta-la-pus, this story is related by the Klikatats in connexion with a favorite [407] valley – the Tahk prairie. This was formerly the bed of a lake, the remains of which now appear in a marshy pond of some extent. The wolf, when the prairie was made, promised that it should be rich in their favorite roots, the kamas and the wapp-a-too; and likewise that the salmon should come there in abundance. But the Indians, forgetful of their obligation to him, showed no gratitude, and when they came there, spent their time in horse-racing and gambling, instead of fishing and the business of life; wherefore the wolf took away the salmon, and placed two stones upon the prairie, beyond which they should not pass.

Alas, for the perverseness of man! Notwithstanding the punishment, the Klikatats and their friends run horses and gamble there to this day.

There is also, in contrast with the gigantic race above mentioned, a story of one of diminutive size, but a span high, who lived near the foot of the St Helens, and whose footprints the Indians have seen where they held their nocturnal dances. Since the eruption of 1842, it may be mentioned, they have not ventured to ascend Mount St Helens. They have also tales connected with certain of the constellations, many of which are named. The Great Bear, for instance, is called "spilyeh," or the wolf. The Yakimas occupy the country drained by the river of that name. They are divided into two principal bands, each made up of a number of villages, and very closely connected; the one owning the country on the Nahchess and lower Yakima, the other upon the Wenass and main branch above the forks. Over the first there are three chiefs – Kam-ai-ya-kan and his brothers Skloo {Skloom} and Sha-wa-wai {showaway}. Over the latter, Te-eh-yas and Owhai. Of all these, Kam-ai-ya-kin possesses the greatest influence, none of the others undertaking any matter of importance without consulting him. Skloo is accused of being tyrannical and overbearing with his weaker neighbors, and Sha-wa-wai of being indolent and wanting in force.

Kam-ai-ya-kan is, in turn, much under the influence of the missionaries, with whom he lives altogether. The others are both intelligent, and bear very good characters. All of them appear to be well disposed and friendly towards the whites, whose superiority they have sense enough to understand.

Most of what has been said of the Klikatats is applicable also to the Yakimas, though, from the nature of their country, some difference in their modes of life is of course observable. Their name, it may be mentioned, is not an appellation of their own. It is said to be the word

---

[130] WaWa = grizzly is *siam*, a respectful Lushootseed euphemism, *s'iab ~ s'iam*. jm

signifying a black bear in the Wallah-Walllah dialect. West of the mountains, both at Vancouver and at Puget sound, they also are generally called Klikatats. Like the last, they live in rude huts covered with mate, the distance of their winter habitations from timber rendering the construction of houses inconvenient; a reason, however, which does not exist with the others. They raise potatoes, a few melons and squashes, together with a little barley and Indian corn. The latter is of the eight-rowed variety, and what we saw of it very small and stunted, the ears being not over five inches long. The potatoes were generally very fine, and of several varieties; of which we noticed the lady-finger, mercer, and blue-nose. Their gardens were, for the most part, situated in the little valleys running up towards the mountains, and near enough to the streams to receive moisture during the early summer. They were rudely fenced around to exclude animals. This invaluable addition to their means of subsistence, it should be said, they, in common with many other tribes, owe to the Hudson's Bay Company. The country around the northern or main branch of the Yakima is frequently called by them Pschwan-wapp-am, or the stony ground, and the Indians living there sometimes assume the name to themselves. Besides the fisheries at the Dalles, the Yakimas have others in their river, up which the salmon run without interruption far into the mountains. On the main fork, in particular, they penetrate to Lake Kitchelus, at the very foot of the dividing ridge. In addition to the different kinds of salmon proper, they have also the salmon-trout, two varieties of the speckled trout, the red and black spotted, both of them growing to a large size; and some other species of fresh-water fish.

The salmon they take in webs and cast-nets. The weirs are constructed with considerable skill, upon horizontal spars, and supported by tripods of strong poles erected at short distances [408] apart, two of the legs fronting up stream, and one supporting them below. There are several of these weirs on the main river fifty or sixty yards in length. The cast-nets are managed by two men in a canoe, one of whom extends it with a pole and the other manages the rope. Their canoes are of very rude workmanship, compared with those belonging to tribes of more aquatic habits, being simply logs hollowed out and sloped up at the ends, without form or finish.

Another article of food obtained from the rivers is the *unis*, or fresh-water muscle, of which there are several {large}[131] varieties. Deep beds of their shells are found near the sites of villages on the river.

Of game the Yakima country is as destitute as that of the Klikatats – so much so that ten deer skins will purchase a horse. The sage-fowl and sharp-tailed grouse are abundant. The chiefs possess a considerable number of cattle, which, in the summer, find good bunch-grass on the hills. In winter they are driven to great straits for subsistence, being compelled, when the snow lies deep, as it does in the valleys, to browse upon the tops of the wild sage, or artemisia. In horses they are well off, though not rich as compared with adjoining tribes. A portion of the Yakimas, more particularly those living on the main river, in hunters language, "go to buffalo," joining the Flatheads in their hunts; but these expeditions are probably far more rare than formerly, when, with greater numbers, they and their allies carried war against the Blackfeet beyond the mountains.[132] With the tribes on Puget sound they communicate continually during

---

[131] In ancient middens these mussel shells are six inches long. *jm*

[132] Expanding from Kittitas royal families, these horse mobile confederacies included that of Split Sun of the Salishan Sinkyuse, and of Wiyawiikt, with eight sons, of whom the best known are brothers tiyayaš ~ Teias (elder), awxay ~ Owhi, and shawaway ~ Showaway. Teias's daughter married Kamayakin, whose own brothers were Ice ~ Showaway (named for

the summer by the Nahchess and main Yakima passes, taking horses for sale to Nisqually, and purchasing "hai-qua",[133] dried clams, and other savage merchandise, on their return. The Yakimas have, like the Klikatats, during the past year suffered severely from the smallpox; the village at the Dalles in particular, the Wish-ram of evil notoriety, in Mr Irving's Astoria, having been depopulated.

Individuals among them profess to have some remedy for the disease. Father Pandozy, one of the missionaries among them, informed me that he believed it to be the root of a species of iris. He had once tasted it, and it acted as a violent emetic. The Spokanes have also another and different specific. It is known to but few persons, having been gradually forgotten since the former visitation. Recently, when it broke out in one of the Spokane villages, an old woman, who was blind, described it to her daughter and directed her to proceed towards Kam-ai-ya-kans, and that if she encountered none in her way, to get from him some of that which he used. The girl, however, did find the herb and returned with it. The mother prepared the medicine, and the smallpox was stayed, but not until it had nearly destroyed the village. We were not successful in obtaining specimens of this plant, but Father Pandozy kindly promised to save some when opportunity offered. In regard to this disease, the greatest scourge of the red man, it has passed through this region more than once, and was probably the first severe blow which fell upon the Oregon tribes. Its appearance seems to have been before any direct intercourse took place with the whites, and it may have found its way northward from California. Captains Lewis and Clark conjectured, from the relations of the Indians, and the apparent age of individuals marked with it, that it had prevailed about thirty years before their arrival. It also spread with great virulence in 1843. From the other, and no less sure, destroyer of the coast tribes, the venereal, the Yakimas, and generally the Indians east of the mountains, are, as yet, exempt. Spirituous liquors have never been introduced into their country, at least beyond the neighborhood of the Dalles.

That a population very considerably more numerous than the existing one formerly occupied this region, there can be no doubt. The estimates of Lewis and Clark gave a sum of 3,240 for the bands on the Klikatat and Yakima rivers, without including those upon the Columbia, which amounted to 3,000 in addition. The whole course of the Yakima is lined with the vestiges of former villages now vacant. A very interesting subject of inquiry has been pursued by Mr Schoolcraft, in his endeavor to follow the earth-works of the Ohio and Mississippi valley into the region west of the Rocky mountains. A careful inquiry among the officers of the [409] Hudson's Bay Company, and the most intelligent free trappers of Oregon, had satisfied me that none such existed in the country. During an examination of the lower Yakima, however, the old Indian guide who accompanied me pointed out, on the left bank, a work which may possibly be considered as belonging to the same system, although being, so far as is known, a solitary one, it is somewhat questionable.

The work consists of two concentric circles of earth about three feet high, with a ditch between. Within are about twenty cellars situated without apparent design, except economy of room. They are some thirty feet across and three feet deep, and the whole circle eighty yards in diameter. We had no time to examine it more particularly, and no tools to excavate. The ground was overgrown with artemisia bushes, but, except the form of the work, there was nothing to attract particular attention, or lead to the belief that it was the remains of any other than a

---

the uncle), and youngest Shkluum ~ Skloom. See Richard Scheuerman and Michael Finley, Finding Chief Kamiakin ~ The Life and Legacy of a Northwest Patriot 2008. *jm*

[133] As noted, tusk ~ dentalium shells. *jm*

Yakima village. Our guide, however, who was great authority on such matters, declared that it was made very long ago, by men of whom his people knew nothing. He added that there was no other like it. It is well posted for defenc{s}e in Indian warfare, being on the edge of a terrace about fifteen feet high, a short distance from the river, and flanked on either side by a gully.

Outside of the circle, but quite near it, are other cellars unenclosed, and in no way differing from the remains of villages frequently met with there. The Indian also pointed out, near by, a low hill or spur, which in form might be supposed to resemble an inverted canoe, and which be said was a ship. It deserves investigation, at least, whether any relation can be traced between the authors of this and of the mounds in Sacramento valley, yet occupied by existing tribes. In this connexion may also be mentioned a couple of modern fortifications erected by the Yakimas upon the Simkwe fork. They are situated between two small branches upon the summit of a narrow ridge, some two hundred yards long, and thirty feet in height, and are about twenty-five yards apart. The first is a square, with rounded corners, formed by an earthen embankment capped with stones, the interstices between which serve for loop-holes, and without any ditch. It is about thirty feet on the sides, and the wall three feet high. The other is built of adobes in the form of a rectangle, twenty by thirty-four feet, the walls three feet high and twelve to eighteen inches thick, with loop-holes six feet apart. Both are commanded within rifle-shot by neighboring hills. They were erected in 1847, by Skloom, as a defence against the Cayuses.[134] We did not learn whether they were successfully maintained, accounts varying greatly on this subject. In the same neighborhood we noticed small piles of stones raised by the Indians on the edges of the basaltic walls which enclose these valleys, but were informed that they had no purpose – they were put up through idleness. Similar piles are, however, sometimes erected to mark the fork of a trail. At points on these walls there were also many graves, generally made in regular form, covered with loose stones to protect them from the cayotes, and marked by poles decorated with tin cups, powder-horns, and articles of dress. During the summer the Indians, for the most part, live in the small valleys lying well into the foot of the mountains. These are, however, uninhabitable during the winter, and they move farther down, or to more sheltered situations. The mission, which in summer is maintained in the Atahnam valley, is transferred into that of the main river. There are two priests attached to this mission, belonging to the order of the Oblates, Fathers Pandozy and d'Harbomey. The stations are small log buildings, divided into a chapel and lodging-room, with a corral for horses and a spot of enclosed garden ground adjoining the one at Atahnam. The fathers informed us that they found the Yakimas not very teachable, and that they had accomplished little except as peacemakers; the Indians were lazy and cultivated the ground with but little regularity, some years not planting at all. They did not believe that a resident farmer would be of use. The Indians, however, say, and justly, that they have no tools, and but little inducement to labor, their country affording other subsistence, and the toil of planting with their own rude implements not; being compensated by the result. With proper encourage [410] ment, and assistance in breaking up the ground, they would doubtless do more. It is probably an object with the missionaries to discourage secular residents, who might divide their own influence over the natives.

The courteous attention of these gentlemen to the officers of the expedition requires acknowledgment. They furnished all the information in their power respecting the country, secured good guides to the parties, and acted as interpreters with the Indians. Father Pandozy, in

---

[134] Skloom's fortified camp on Simcoe Creek was a defense against Cayuse warriors, Theodore Stern, Chiefs & Change 1996, 2: 218. *jm*

particular, is familiarly acquainted with the Yakima tongue.[135] Kam-ai-ya-kan is the only one of the three brothers who has adopted even the forms of Catholicism, and he refuses to be baptised, because he would be compelled to put away his surplus wives, of whom he has several. Skloo and Sha wa-wai are unchanged heathens.

On leaving the Klikatat country, Captain McClellan had made a small present to the chief Tow-e-toks, and distributed some tobacco among the men. It was not, however, considered necessary to enter into a formal talk with that tribe, the object of our visit, and some other points, being casually explained to them. With the Yakimas the case was different. Their country was to become a thoroughfare for the whites, and it was very important that a proper impression should be made, and a friendly understanding established. On leaving the mountains we first encountered Skloo, a tall, fine looking, but very dark-skinned man, who came up to camp attended by Wee-ni-nah, a sub-chief, living at the village of Skin, opposite the mouth of the Des Chutes river. We had already met with an amusing instance of Indian craft, in which Skloo proved to have been the operator. A small party of Indians had come on to Chequoss, and stated that they had been told the expedition was out for the purpose of seizing the horses and cattle of the Yakimas, taking their country, and destroying them if they resisted; that Lieutenant Saxton's party had proceeded against the Spokanes for the same purpose, and that Kam-ai-ya-kan and Skloo were determined to oppose us. The report had created no uneasiness, except lest it should alarm the Indians, and prevent the necessary intercourse with them. Skloo being now questioned as to the author of the report, stated that it was a Frenchman, in charge of the Hudson's Bay Company's train, who on his way to Fort Colville had preceded Lieutenant Saxton a few days. As the story had already caused us some inconvenience, in preventing us from obtaining a guide, and as it was feared that more serious annoyance would result to the other party, Captain McClellan forwarded a complaint on the subject to Governor Ogden, at Fort Vancouver. It subsequently appeared that the person referred to was a gentleman far above the suspicion of any such conduct, and that the whole was a fabrication got up by Skloo himself, for the purpose of fishing out the object of the expedition. A short talk was held with him by Captain McClellan, explaining this to his entire content, and in turn he gave what information he possessed respecting the mountain trails. In justice to him, it should be said, the more especially as he has but few friends, that his manly deportment left a more favorable impression than did some who bore a far better character. A small present was given him on parting.

Kam-ai-ya-kan we found at the mission, and he afterwards came over to the camp at Wenass for a formal visit. He is a large, gloomy-looking Indian, with a very long and strongly-marked face; slovenly in dress, but said to be generous and honest. Captain McClellan explained to him the general nature of the American government, as far as was necessary for him to understand, and the rank that Governor Stevens, who was coming with a party across the mountains, would hold in the country. He expressed the hope that the good disposition which Kam-ai-ya-kan had shown towards the whites would be maintained; that if any injury was done by them to his people, they were not to seek revenge, but complain to the Governor, who would redress it; and that if any was suffered from the Indians, he would expect him to punish the offender. It was the intention of the whites to make a wagon road across the mountains, and many would undoubtedly pass through their country. Should they be in need, he wished Kam-ai-ya-kan to assist them. Their coming would be an advantage to his people, for they would buy their potatoes, and exchange cattle which had become tired with long travel, for his, which were

---

[135] Marie-Charles Pandosy, <u>Grammar and Dictionary of the Yakama Language</u> 1862. *jm*

fat, giv [411] ing him boot. In conclusion, he added that the great white chief had instructed him, when he met with friendly chiefs among the Indians, to give them a present as coming from him. A quantity of Indian goods were thereupon given him. Kam-ai-ya-kan made a suitable reply, in which he referred to a subject previously mentioned by Skloo – the negotiations of white men pretending to be chiefs, who were not, particularly in regard to the purchase of their lands. He had heard they would give a few presents, and then pretend they had purchased the land. Captain McClellan informed him who were the persons having the power to make these purchases, or to treat with them, with which he expressed himself satisfied.

At Ketetas {Kittitas}, on the main Yakima, we were visited by Ow-hai,[136] one of the two principal chiefs of the northern band of this tribe. His elder brother, Te-eh-yas, had gone to Puget sound, and we did not see him. Ow-hai appears to be forty-five or fifty years of age, and has a very pleasant face, with a high but retreating forehead, of which he is somewhat vain. In speaking of Kam-ai-ya-kan, he remarked that he had a big head, and thought much; adding, as he touched his own, "like myself."

He remained with us during our stay, and afterwards accompanied the party as far as the Pisquouse {Piskwaws}.[137] In a talk with him the same information was communicated, in substance, as that given to Kam-ai-ya-kan. This band trades much more with the Sound than Kam-ai-ya-kan's, and is, therefore, better acquainted with trails; the one which proved on examination the best, leading directly up the river from our camp. After the usual custom of seeking wives in adjoining tribes, they are much intermingled with the Snoqualme on the western side of the Cascades, as well as the Pisquouse to the northward. The latter, in fact, speak indifferently the Yakima and their own languages. We found the people here much better dressed than those below. The young men and women affected more of their native costume than the old. Owhai's two sons, both tall, handsome men, had their blankets and dress profusely ornamented, and the wife of one of them, a very pretty woman, wore a dress stiff with bead-work and porcupine quills. Ow-hai himself, on the other hand, appeared in a full American suit, and touched his hat by way of salutation – a compliment which he clearly expected to be noticed and returned. He, like Kam-ai-ya-kan, has adopted some of the forms of Catholicism, and professes to pray habitually, but there seemed to be a shadow of hypocrisy in his devotion. He is, however, a man of very considerable understanding and policy, and inclined to profit by the example of the whites.

On striking the Columbia after passing the mountains, between the Yakima country and the Pisquouse, Ow-hai pointed out to us one of the lions of the country, in the shape of two columns of sandstone standing together, but apart from the bluff, which was of similar material. These, he told us, were " Ahn-cotte" or, in the language of the fairy tales, "once upon a time" two women of the race of "Ellip Tilicum",[138] who lived here, and were very bad, being in the habit of killing those who passed by, the Indians begged the Great Spirit to destroy them, and He granting their prayer, sent an enormous bird which picked out their brains, and then turned them into stone. In proof of which, the narrator pointed out a hole in the top of one of the columns, from which a boulder had fallen, as the aperture broken by the bird in extracting his meal. A short distance beyond, he turned a little off the trail to point out to us another curiosity. It was a

---

[136] These are the sons of the founder of the Yakama confederacy around Kittitas, see # 121. *jm*

[137] Psk^{w}aws is a simplification into English of their Salish name; Wenatchee their Sahaptin one. Many were bilingual in this Salish territory. *jm*

[138] As noted, WaWa = "first folks." *jm*

perpendicular rock, on the face of which were carved sundry figures, most of them intended for men. They were slightly sunk into the sandstone and colored, some black, others red, and traces of paint remained more or less distinctly on all of them. These also, according to their report, were the work of the ancient race; but from the soft nature of the rock, and the freshness of some of the paint, they were probably not of extreme antiquity.

Nothing could in this connection, he ascertained from the Indians, whether they had any traditions of their own migration from another country.

With the exception of the district occupied by the Flatbows and Kootenaies, the remaining country north of the forty-seventh parcel is occupied by different tribes of the *Selish* or *Flathead* [412] nation. These may be divided for the present purpose into the following: the Pisquouse, Okinakane, Schwo-yelpi or Kettle Falls, Spokane, Coeur d'Alene, upper and lower Pend d'Oreilles, and Selish or Flathead proper.

The country of the Pisquouse lies immediately north of that of the Yakimas, and we entered it next upon our route. Under this appellation are here included the Indians on the Columbia between the Priest's and Boss rapids, on the Pisquouse or Winatshapam river, the En-te-at-kwu, Chelan lake, and the Methow or Barrier river. The name of Pisquouse, however, properly refers to a single locality on the river, known to the Yakimas as Winatshapam.[139]

The Pisquouse themselves, as has before been remarked, are so much intermarried with the Yakimas that they have almost lost their nationality. These bands were formerly all united under one principal chief, Stal-koo-sum,[140] who is said to have been a man of great note among them. He was killed a few years since in a fight with the Blackfeet, since when there has been no head of the tribe. Stal-koo-sum's son, Quil-tan-ei-nok, or Louis, was an aspirant for his father's throne, and came over to Ketetas to recommend himself to captain McClellan's patronage, under the tuition of Ow-hai, who seemed to be interested in his promotion. It was considered desirable to unite the scattered fragments of the empire under one head, if possible, and he was therefore engaged as a guide, the better to ascertain his character. It should be remarked, that though the chiefdom of the petty bands, or villages, seems to be hereditary, it does not always follow that one who has placed himself at the head of the tribe, or confederacy, transmits his power. Quil-tan-ei-nok had, as we learned, used great efforts to succeed in this object of his ambition; having gone to the Sound, and even to the Willamette valley, to procure a paper from some agent recognising his rights, on the strength of which he might silence all cavillers. In this he had been hitherto unsuccessful, and he was doomed to further disappointment. On reaching the mouth of the Pisquouse, Captain McClellan informed the Indians that it would be well for them to choose, in concert with their neighbors, a head chief, who would represent them all, and who might talk for them with the chief of the whites; that if they would agree among themselves upon a proper person, the Governor would give him a great writing, signifying his consent. In the mean time some presents were distributed; that to Quil-tan-ei-nok being the largest, that he might have honor among his own people at least. When the election came off, however, he was beaten, and by a candidate whose name had never previously been mentioned. At this place we were offered the entertainment of a horse-race, and on promising a yard of red cloth as the prize of victory, a general enthusiasm seized upon the whole tribe. Horses were sought in every direction, that

---

[139] Wenatchee Lake and River is a famous sockeye fishery. *jm*

[140] Making reference to an eclipse, the name appears as Half Sun, though Split Sun is more accurate. It became the name title of the head of the confederacy of tribes hunting bison on horseback on the Montana Plains. See works by Verne Ray, Ruby and Brown. *jm*

would stand a chance of winning, and in a short time a dozen of the best came up to the starting-point. A goal was fixed on the plain, at some distance, which they were to turn around and return; and at a signal from the chief they stripped – not the horses, but the riders; doffing their blankets and other inconvenient articles, and appearing in costumes of primitive simplicity. One rider wore a pair of moccasins, and another sported a shirt; while with a third a streak or two of red paint, judiciously disposed, gave every requisite distinction. There was some very pretty running, and still better jockeying; but as the distance was unmeasured, and nobody took note of the time, an official report cannot be given. The winner, who rode a handsome gray gelding, carried off a prize that a few years before was worth as much as his horse.

The Okinakanes comprise the bands lying on the river of that name as far north as the foot of the great lake. They are six in number,[141] viz: the T'Kwuratum {"yellow rock"}, at the mouth; Konekonl'p, on the creek of that name; Kluckhaitkwu, at the falls {sk^{w}ənt}; Kinakanes, near the forks; and Milakitekwa, on the west fork. With them may be classed the N'pockle, or Sans Puelles, on the Columbia river; though these are also claimed by the Spokanes. The two bands on the forks are more nearly connected with the Schwoyelpi than with the ones first named. The country of the Pisquouse and Okinakanes may be described together, and briefly. It is mountainous and sterile, the valleys narrow, and affording here and there spots susceptible of cultivation. For [413] grazing it is as little adapted; and there is, in its whole extent, nothing to tempt encroachment upon its miserable owners.

During Captain McClellan's examination of the Methow river, six of the bands, belonging in part to each tribe, agreed upon Ke-keh-tum-nouse, or Pierre, an Indian from Klahum, the site of Astor's old fort, at the mouth of the Okinakane, as their chief.

The occasion furnished an opportunity of making an actual count, which for these six bands gave a total of 214. The remainder would, according to our observations, raise the number of Indians south of the 49th degree, and between the Columbia and the Cascade mountains, to 550; a larger one than was expected, As the smallpox was at its height, however, this is doubtless already much diminished. During the whole route we found the disease prevailing to a fearful extent. Several villages had been nearly cut off; and we saw, at some places, the dead left unburied on the surface of the ground. These tribes have no cattle, and but comparatively few horses. They told us that formerly they had many, but that the company had purchased them for food; and they complained bitterly that the shirts and other articles given them in exchange were worn out, and nothing was left them but their new religion. At Fort Okinakane we observed a mode of disposing of the dead differing from any before noticed. They were wrapped in their blankets, or other clothing, and bound up right to the trunk of a tree, at a sufficient distance from the ground to preserve them from wild animals. Notwithstanding the climate, none of these Indians have a better shelter than is furnished by their mats. They raise some potatoes, but their main resource is salmon. These, at the time of their visit, actually filled the streams. In the Okinakane, in particular, there were myriads of a small species, which had assumed a uniform red color. They were depositing their spawn, and were in a condition eatable only by Indians, who were busily engaged in drying them.

On leaving Fort Okinakane, the new chief accompanied the party to Fort Colville in the capacity of a guide, assisted by two of his subjects; and the cavalcade was enlarged at the lake by the chief of the Saht-lil-kwu band, a religious personage, who sported the title of King George,

---

[141] Okanogans are Upriver Mid-Columbia Interior Salish speakers, see Jay Miller, Middle Columbia Salishans 1988. *jm*

and persecuted us nightly with family worship. We parted with the whole with the loss of much tobacco and few regrets. Fort Colville is the principal ground of the Schwoyelpi, or Kettle Falls tribe, one of the largest of the Selish.

According to the information received from Father Joset, of the Jesuit mission, they number from five to six hundred. At the time of our visit the greater part had gone to the buffalo hunt. They do not obtain many furs, the greater part of those taken at this post coming from the upper Columbia. The fishery at the Kettle falls is one of the most important on the river; and the arrangements of the Indians, in the shape of drying-scaffolds and stone houses, are on a corresponding scale. They take the fish by suspending immense baskets upon poles beneath the traps, into which the salmon spring. We saw here, for the first time, the canoe used upon the upper waters of the Columbia. It is of birch bark, and of a form peculiar to these rivers, being longer on the bottom than on the top. A canoe, of thirty feet in length on the floor, is open only about twenty-four feet, and gathered to a point about three feet long at each end. They are stretched on a light frame of split twigs, and are at once fast and buoyant. The mission is situated upon a high bluff above the falls, and consists of a small house for the priest and a chapel. Around these are a number of huts and store-houses belonging to the Indians; the latter raised from the ground on posts. Fathers Louis and Joset, of the Order of Jesuits, are stationed here. Our visit admitted of but little opportunity of gathering further information concerning the Indians than what has already been published. The few who were present; were assembled by Governor Stevens, who addressed them. They have no head chief of note, and there were present on the occasion only Klekahkahi, the chief at the falls; Kuiltkuiltlouis, a sub-chief; and Elimiklka, the son of a former chief of this place.

The last was highly spoken of by Mr McDonald, but did not seem to be in equal favor at the mission. We learned that but few of the original Schwoyelpi stock remained; they had gradually [414] become extinct, and their places were filled by people from the adjoining bands. The smallpox had as yet made no great inroads on this band; its general course seemingly having been up the eastern side of the Columbia. One case had, however, occurred at the time of our arrival. On the route from Fort Colville to Wallah-Wallah the party passed the old Chemakane mission, the former station of Messrs. Walker and Eels. The house was still standing, and occupied by an American. This is the country of the Spokanes, who are next to be noticed.

The Spokehnish, or Spokanes, lie south of the Schwoyelpi, and chiefly upon or near the Spokane river. The name applied by the whites to a number of small bands, is that given by the Coeur d'Alenes to the one living at the forks. They are also called Sinkoman by the Kootenaies. These bands are eight in number: the Sin-slik-hoo-ish, on the great plain above the crossings of the Coeur d'Alene river; the Sintootoolish, on the river above the forks; the Sma-hoo-men-a-ish, (Spokenish.) at the forks; the Skai-schil-t'nish, at the old Chemakane mission; the Ske-chei-a-mouse, above them on the Colville trail; the Schu-el-stish; the Sin-poil-schne, and Sin-spee-lish, on the Columbia river; the last-named band is nearly extinct. The Sin-poil-schne (N'pochele, or Sans Puelles) have already been included among the Okinakanes, though, as well as the Sin-spee-lish below them, they are claimed by the Spokanes. The three bands on the Columbia all speak a different language from the rest. Most of the Indians, at the time of our visit, were absent on their hunt, and we had no opportunities of estimating their number by inspection. Judging from those that we saw, and the information received from various sources, they probably amount, excluding those enumerated at Okinakane, to four hundred and fifty. They were a wilder looking race than the tribes to the westward. The men are generally spare, even when young, and soon become withered.

Their principal chief is Spokane Garry,[142] whose name was bestowed upon him by Governor Sir George Simpson, by whom he was sent, when about twelve years old, to the Red river for education, where he spent five years. Garry is now about forty-two years of age, is very intelligent, and speaks English fluently. He bears an excellent character, and is what he claims to be, a chief. Of petty chiefs there are, besides, an abundance, each band having two or three.

Garry himself accompanied us to the forks of the Spokane, where his band usually reside. A few lodges, chiefly old men and women, were there at the time. His own, in neatness and comfort, was far beyond any we had seen. His family were dressed in the costume of the whites, which in fact now prevails over their own. Many of the Spokanes, besides their intercourse with the fort, visit the American settlements, where they earn money by occasional work, most of which is spent in clothing, blankets, &c. The chief offered us the hospitality of his house with much cordiality – a cup of tea or coffee and bread. The "Spokane House," which is a landmark upon all the maps of this country, was an old Hudson's Bay fort, situated at his village, but has long since been destroyed.

This tribe claim as their territory the country commencing on the large plain at the head of the Slawntehus – the stream entering the Columbia at Fort Colville; thence down the Spokane to the Columbia, down the Columbia half-way to Fort Okinakane, and up the Spokane and Coeur d'Alene, to some point between the falls and the lake, on the latter. There is in this direction a question of boundary between them and the Coeur d'Alenes, which appears to be as complicated as some of those between more civilized nations. No resort to arms has, however, occurred, and the territory continues under joint occupation. An additional source of coolness between them arises from a difference in religion – the Spokanes being Protestants, or of the "American religion," and the Coeur d'Alenes Catholics.[143] The latter taunt the former as heretics, whose faith is worthless. Garry narrated to us the evils arising from this state of feeling, with a forbearance and Christian spirit of toleration which would have honored any one. This tribe have at present no missionary among them, but they seem to have been consistent to what they learned under the tuition of Messrs. Walker and Eels, of the Chemakane mission. The country of the Spo [415] kanes, though in most respects unattractive to settlement by the whites, is well suited to the pursuits of the Indian.

The high plain, which extends from the Spokane river to Lewis's fork of the Columbia, and which belongs chiefly to them and the Nez Perces, though bleak and exposed to violent winds, affords grazing for their stock and an abundance of the roots used by themselves for food, while their river supplies them with salmon. They obtain buffalo hides for their lodges, and skins of elk, carraboo, and deer, for their own clothing, in their semi-annual hunts to the eastward.

Of the larger game there is but little in their own country. The buffalo,[144] it would seem, in former times penetrated at least occasionally thus far to the westward, though now they never come through the northern passes. We were informed by an old Iroquois hunter, at Fort Colville,

---

[142] Spokan Garry was educated at the Red River settlement and lived to return to his people, unlike other students. *jm*

[143] The Couer d'Alene mission at Cataldo, built with wooden pegs not nails, still stands along Interstate 90 at the Idaho border. *jm*

[144] A painted bison image appears on the wall of a cave in Moses Coulee along the middle Columbia River south of Wenatchee. See Butler (1978). *jm*

who has been some forty-eight years in the company's service, that the last bull was killed some twenty-five years ago in the Grand Coulee.

Of the remaining tribes of the nation it will be necessary to speak even more briefly, for out journey did not bring us in contact with them, and but little can be added to what has been before published.

The Skitswish, or Coeur d'Alenes, live upon the upper part of the Coeur d'Alene river, above the Spokanes, and around the lake of the same name. They are estimated by Dr Dart as only two hundred in number, which is believed, however, to be too low an estimate. Father Mengarini, formerly missionary among the Flatheads, gives as his opinion that they reach four hundred and fifty. A mean has been adopted in the recapitulation. This tribe has also a missionary station belonging to the Order of Jesuits.

The Kalispelms, or Pend d'Oreilles of the Lower Lake, inhabit the country north of the Coeur d'Alenes and around the Kalispelm lake. Dr Dart gives their population as five hundred and twenty, which is but little short of Father Mengarini's.

The Slka-tkml-schi, or Pend d'Oreilles of the Upper Lake, a tribe who, by the consent of the Selish, occupy jointly with them the country of the latter. According to the same authorities, they reach about four hundred and eighty.

The Selish proper, or Flatheads, inhabit St Mary's or the Flathead valley, and the neighborhood of the lake of the same name. Mr John Owen, who occupies the site of the old Jesuit mission of St Mary's as a trading-post, says that there remain of these but sixty-five lodges, of about five to a lodge, giving a total of three hundred and twenty-five – a number considerably exceeding Dr Dart's estimate, which, is but two hundred and ten.

The tribe was once a very powerful one, but has been much diminished by the attacks of the Blackfeet, who enter into their country through the mountain passes, or meet them in their hunts upon the eastern side.

Their custom is to make two hunts annually across the mountains – one in April, for the bulls, from which they return in June and July; and another, after about a month's recruit, to kill cows, which have by that time become fat. In these excursions they are accompanied by that portion of the Pend d'Oreilles who live in their country, and about one hundred lodges of the Nez Perces, as well as parties from such other tribes as see fit to join them. Their country is admirably adapted for grazing, and they possess about one thousand head of American cattle, which were introduced by the worthy and zealous Father De Smet.

They are not rich in horses, but still have many good ones, though frequently robbed by their enemies, the Blackfeet. They get no salmon, but live altogether by the hunt, and do not manifest, any disposition to agricultural pursuits or fixed residence. They have no canoes, but in ferrying streams use their lodge: skins, which are drawn up into an oval form by cords, and stretched on a few twigs. These they tow with horses, riding sometimes three abreast. Their own territory still furnishes them with ordinary kinds of game – elk, moose, black and white-tailed deer, the big-horn, and bears. Beaver and otter are abundant.

The mission of St Mary's was abandoned in 1850, the habits of the Flatheads leaving the mis [416] sionaries unprotected, end proving an obstacle to effectual labor. They have at the station a village of log-houses, but notwithstanding generally prefer their own lodges. Their great chief is Kwi-kwi-kal-sih, or Victor, a man highly spoken of by the whites who have come in contact with him. The tribe, in fact, seem to be an exception among the Indians of Oregon. Their heroism in battle, their good faith towards others, and their generally inoffensive conduct, have been the theme of praise both from priest and layman. They are, however, rapidly disappearing before the murderous warfare of the Blackfeet. Should their country become a thoroughfare of travel, they will, to some degree at least, be protected from their enemies; but, on the other hand, the destruction of the buffalo and other game will render some new mode of subsistence an object of proper care on the part of the government.

The Kootenaies or Kitunahas, and the Flatbows, who now, according to Father De Smet, form one tribe,[145] called by their neighbors Skalza, or Skolsa, inhabit the country extending along the foot of the Rocky mountains, north of the Flatheads, for a very considerable distance, and are about equally in American and in British territory. They do not enter into the census of the Oregon superintendent, and they have had no intercourse with the whites except through the Fur Company. Captain Wilkes states their number at about 400. Their usual camp is situated in the Tobacco plains, where they were visited in 1845 by Father De Smet, who gives a description of their country.

The Nez Perces, or Saptin {Sahaptian}, lie to the south of the Selish, and on both sides of the Kooskooskia and north fork of Snake river.

Their country, like that of the Wallah-Wallahs, extends into both Oregon and Washington Territories. They are one of the most numerous of all these, tribes, amounting, according to the census of 1861, to 1880; since when there has probably been less decrease than among some of the others.

They are much intermarried with the Wallah-Wallahs, whose language belongs to the same family, and also with the Cayuses. They have no chief of note at present living; Towwattu, or the "Young Chief," having recently died.

Wailatpu, or Cayuse: The country belonging to this tribe is to the south of and between the Nez Perces and Wallah-Wallahs, extending from the Des Chutes or Wawanui river to the eastern side of the Blue mountains. It is almost entirely in Oregon, a small part only, upon the upper Wallah-Wallah river, lying within Washington Territory. The tribe, though still dreaded by their neighbors, from their courage and warlike spirit, is but a small one, numbering, according to the same authority, 126. Of these, individuals of the pure blood are very few; the majority being intermixed with the Nez Perces and Wallah-Wallahs – particularly with the former – to such a degree that their own language has fallen into disuse.

It was this tribe that destroyed Dr Whitman's mission in 1847. Their head chief, Pa, ?? or the "Five Crows," has since then generally absented himself from his people, as, although not concerned in the murder, he became notorious for the abduction of one of the women. These are all the tribes which enter into the Territory east of the mountains, except that a small remnant of the original tribe belonging at the Cascades of the Columbia river still exist. They are of the Upper Chinook nation. From their geographical situation, they will fall within the eastern district; and as the Klikatats frequent the fishery there, it would be desirable to comprehend them with the latter.

It would be interesting to give a reliable comparison of the Indian population at the different periods since their intercourse with the whites; but the data from which this could be drawn me too uncertain to furnish satisfactory conclusions. Messrs. Lewis and Clark give the earliest information respecting them.

---

[145] Regarded as a language isolate, Kootenay was the first to split from protoSalish near the mouth of the Fraser, settling upriver in the Interior. For de Smet, see Jacqueline Peterson, <u>Sacred Encounters</u> 1993, and Joseph Donnelly, <u>Wilderness Kingdom</u> 1967. *jm*

Their journey, however, permitted only very loose conjectures on the subject, and their division of the tribes is with difficulty to be recognised at present. The following, however, appears to be the arrangement, and it is so far intelligible as to render it certain that their locations have not materially changed within that time. [417]

Lewis and Clark's Estimate – 1806 and 1807

Names of Tribes.	Corresponding names.	Population.
Wallah-Wallah	Wallah-Wallah	2,600
Wah-how-pum	John Day's river	1,000
E-ne-show	Des Chutes river	1,200
Se-wat-palla	Peluse {Palus}	3,000
Sokulk	Priest's Rapids	3,000
Chan-wap-pan	Lower Yakima	400
Shal-tat-tos	Lower Yakima	200
Squam-a-ross	Lower Yakima	240
Skal-dals	Lower Yakima	400
Chim-nah-pun	Upper Yakima	2,000
Sha-la-la	Cascades, Upper Chenooks	1,000
E-che-loot	Cascades, Upper Chenooks	1,000
Chilluk-kit-e-quaw	Dalles	2,400
Smak-shop	Dalles	200
Cat-sa-nim	Okin-a-kanes	2,400
He-high-e-nim-mo	Sans Puelles	1,500
Whe-el-po	Schwo-yel-pi	3,500
Sar-lis-lo	Spokanes	900
Sket-so-mish	Spokanes	2,600

Mick-suck-seal-tom	Pend d'Oreilles	300
Ho-pil-po	Flatheads	600
Tush-e-pah	Koo-tames	800
Chopunnish	Nez Perces	8,000
Wille-wah	Grand Ronde	1,100
Willet-pos	Wai-lat-pu	-------
Total population		**42, 200**

Captain Wilkes' Estimate – 1841

Names of Tribes.	Population.
Cascades	150
Dalles	250
Yakima	100
Okinakane	300
Colville and Spokane	450
Des Chutes &c	300
Wallah-Wallah	1,100
Total population	**2,650**

The above furnishes a very incorrect statement even of the tribes that are given, and some of the most important are omitted altogether, No conclusion can be drawn from it whatever.

A more general one is contained in Captain Wilkes's pamphlet on Western America, as follows:

Names of Tribes.	Population.
Kitunana	400
Flatheads	3,000

Nez Perces	2,000
Wallah-Wallahs	2,200
Total population	**7,600**

Which is also much less than the actual number at that time. Yet more incorrect is the estimate [418] of Lts Warre and Vavasour, RN {Royal Navy},[146] published in Martin's "Hudson's Bay Territories, &c" in 1849, though, as regards this part of the Territory, it is not so bad as the rest:

Estimate of Lieutenants Warre and Vavasour.

Names of Tribes.	**Population.**
Wallah-Wallahs, Nez Perces, Snakes, &c	3,000
Colville and Spokane	450
Okinakane, several tribes	300
Kullas Palus, (Kalispelm,) several tribes	300
Kootenaies, several tribes	400
Total population	**4,500**

Dr Dart's Estimate – 1861.

Names of Tribes.	**Men.**	**Women.**	**Children.**	**Total.**
Wallah-Wallah	52	40	38	130
Des Chutes	95	115	90	300
Dalles	129	206	147	482
Peluse	60	62	59	181
Kanatat	297	195		492
Yakima, (estimate)				1,000

---

[146] Henry Warre and Merwin Vavasour were British secret agents who toured Oregon and Puget Sound in 1845-6, both describing locales enhanced by Warre's careful drawings. *jm*

Rock Island				300
Okinakane				250
Colville				320
Sin-ha-ma-mish, (Spokane)				232
Coeur d'Alene				200
Lower Pend d'Oreille				520
Upper Pend d'Oreille				480
Mission				210
Nez Perzes	698	1,182		1,880
Cayuse	38	48	40	126
*Total population				**7,103**

* The Pisquouse {Peskwaws} and Kootenaies are omitted, and the band of Upper Chinooks, at the Dalles, included with the Wallah Wallahs.

Estimate of 1853

Names of Tribes, &c.	Population.
Klikitats	300
Yakimas	600
Pisquouse and Okinakanes	550
Schwoyelpi, or Colville	500
Spokane	450
Coeur d'Alene	325
Lower Pend d'Oreille	480
Upper Pend d'Oreille	520

Flatheads	325
Kootenaies and Flatbows	400
Nez Perces	1,700
Cayuse	120
Wallah-Wallahs, Peluse, &c	500
Dalles bands	200
Cascades	36
Total population	**7,006**

NOTE – Of which it is proposed that the Nez Perces, Cayuse, Wallah-Wallahs and Dalles Indians remain under the Oregon superintendency. [419]

As the relations of the Hudson's Bay Company to the Indian tribes, as well as to the citizens of the Territory, is a matter of some importance, a statement of their establishments is herewith submitted.

The principal is Fort Vancouver, on the Columbia River, which is the parent establishment whence the others are supplied with goods. The post is enclosed by a stockade of two hundred by one hundred and seventy-five yards, twelve feet in height, and is defended by bastions on the northwest and southeast angles mounted with cannon. Within are the governor's house, two smaller buildings used by clerks, a range of dwellings for families, and five large two-story warehouses, besides offices. Without, there is another large storehouse, at present hired by the United States. These are all built of square logs framed together. At some little distance there is also a village of fifty or sixty cabins, occupied by servants, Kanakas, and Indians, and a salmon-house on the bank of the river. The buildings are old and considerably decayed, only the repairs necessary to keep them in tenantable order having of late years been expended. There are at present two chief factors at this post, Messrs. Peter Skene Ogden and Donald MacTavish, with a considerable number of clerks and other employees.

The company's land claim at Fort Vancouver embraces several tracts: first, the plain on which the fort and United States barracks are situated, with a small one behind it, making together a tract of about four miles square. About one thousand acres are enclosed or under cultivation; attached to which there are sheds, stabling, and a small dwelling for a farmer. Adjoining this, to the eastward, is another tract, known as the Mill claim, two and a half by three quarter miles square, on which is a saw-mill having tolerable water-power, but subject to stoppage during freshets. Besides the above, they claim two other small prairies behind the first mentioned, which are respectively a half and one mile square.

The business at this post has changed with the condition of the country since the treaty, and is now almost entirely mercantile and carried on with the settlers. American Oregon never was, strictly speaking, a fur country, and the fall in the value of beaver has annihilated what trade it once afforded. Comparatively a small amount of Indian goods are now imported, that description of merchandise being sent to the posts in their own territory by way of Victoria. What trade with Indians is carried on here is the ordinary retail trade of country stores, and for cash. The amount of their general business may be gathered from their imports during 1863. These consisted of one cargo of assorted American goods from New York, and another valued at about $19,000 from London, paying duties to the amount of nearly $24,000. A considerable portion of these were sold on commission at Portland, Oregon City, and other places in the Willamette valley.

The next post above Vancouver is Fort Wallah-Wallah, on the Columbia river, below the entrance of the Snake. There are here three or four one-story adobe buildings, with offices, enclosed by a wall of the same material some thirty-five yards on each side, having a bastion at one angle. It is almost utterly valueless except as a station where horses can be kept for the trains. There is, indeed, some trade with the neighboring Indians, chiefly in cash, but not enough to warrant its maintenance, except for the above purpose. The fort is in very indifferent repair, and the country in the immediate neighborhood a desert of drifting sand. Some eighteen or twenty miles up the Wallah-Wallah river is a so-called farm, on which are two small buildings, a dwelling-house, and dairy. There was formerly a dam for irrigation, but it is broken down. They have here some twenty acres cultivated in different spots; the principal object is grazing. The force here consists of Mr Pambrun, chief clerk, one interpreter, two traders, and six men, Canadians and Indians.

Fort Colville, upon the Columbia, above Kettle falls, is next in importance to Vancouver, though far inferior to it in extent. It is situated on the second terrace, at some distance back from the river, the lower one being flooded in part during the freshets. The buildings consist of a dwelling, three or four store-houses, and some smaller ones used as a blacksmith's shop, &c.; [420] all of one story, and built of square logs. The whole was once surrounded by a stockade, forming a square of about seventy yards on each side. This had been removed, except on the north, where it encloses a narrow yard containing offices. One bastion remains. About thirty yards in the rear of this square are the cattle-yard, hay-sheds, &c., enclosing a space of forty by sixty yards, roughly fenced in, and the sheds covered with bark. On the left of the front are seven huts, occupied by the lower employees of the company; they are of rude construction and much decayed. On the right of the square, in the rear, at a distance of a few hundred yards, are three more buildings, used for storing produce.

Besides the principal establishment, there is a cattle-post, about nine miles distant, on the stream laid down as the Slawntehus, and a grist-mill of one pair of stones, three miles off, on the same stream. The latter is said to be in pretty good order, and the water to serve all the year round. Here, formerly, the flour for the northern posts was ground from wheat raised on the company's farm. This farm was once pretty extensive, but only a small portion is cultivated at present.

Fort Colville was once the post of a chief factor, the highest officer in charge of a station, and here the annual accounts of the whole country were consolidated previous to transmission across the mountains. The present force consists only of Mr McDonald, chief clerk, a trader, and about twenty Canadians and Iroquois Indians. In former years goods were sent through this post for those north of the line, but this route is now abandoned. The amount of furs collected here is not large, and comes chiefly from the upper Columbia. They are principally bear, beaver, muskrat, marten, and fox skins. The beaver is not considered to be worth in London more than its cost when laid down there.

About fifteen Canadians are settled on claims in this neighborhood, chiefly on the Slawntehus. They are former servants of the company whose time has expired, and who intend to be naturalized.

Below Fort Colville is Fort Okinakane, situated on a level plain on the right bank of the Columbia, a little above the mouth of the Okinakane river, and not far from the site of one of Mr Astor's posts. The fort consists of three small houses, enclosed with a stockade. There were formerly some outbuildings, but they have been suffered to decay. There is no appearance of business here, and no goods on hand. One trader, a Canadian, was the only white man on the ground when we visited it. A few furs only are taken, and the post probably does not pay its expenses. It was once of consequence as a stopping place for the bateaux passage to and from Fort Colville, but is now kept up apparently for form's sake. We learned that the price of such furs as were taken here was, for a black fox-skin, a quarter of a yard of red cloth, or a red cocktail plume; for marten or red fox, ten charges of powder and ball; for beaver, otter, or bear skins, thirty charges.

Fort Kontamie, upon the great bend of the Flatbow river, and not far from the Flathead lake, is an inferior post, in charge of a Canadian as trader and postmaster, with one Canadian and a half-breed under him.

The above constitutes all the posts situated in the country east of the Cascades and north of 46°. It may be worth while to include the rest of those in American territory.

There are in Oregon and east of the mountains only two – Fort Hall, on the head of the Snake river; and Fort Boisee upon the same, nearly opposite the mouth of the Owy-hee. The latter is merely a stopping place, occupied by a trader and a few Kanakas. The former is a more important one, from its opportunities for trade with the emigrants and with the Salt lake. Of the present condition of this I am not informed; but it is only a third-rate post.

West of the Cascades, in Oregon Territory, the principal is Fort Umpqua, on the Umpqua river. This was destroyed by fire two or three years since; but to what extent, since rebuilt, I do not know. The rest consist of a house and granary at Champoegs, on the Willamette; one acre of ground below the falls of Oregon City, purchased from an American, a farmer; 640 acres [421] on Sauvies's island, at the mouth of the Willamette; with a house, dairy, and garden – the building about six years old. The old buildings at Astoria are of no value whatever.

In Washington Territory, west of the Cascades, there are, first, and the only one of importance, Fort Nisqually, on the lands of the Puget Sound Agricultural Company. It is situated at some distance from the water, on a high, undulating prairie, and is a cluster of small buildings, of no great value, within a stockade. The trade here is principally with the settlers. Besides this, there is a granary and about five acres of land two miles above the mouth of the Cowlitz river; a tract of land on Cape Disappointment, occupied by an old servant, and a small store and lot of ground at Chinook.

With the exception of Fort Vancouver, it is believed that none of these posts are worth maintaining for any other purpose than that of holding the property till a sale can be effected. The condition of the whole country is completely changed since they were established, and the company are now little else than general merchants. At all points of present importance they meet with the usual competition from our citizens; and whenever it will repay the enterprise, the same competition will follow them elsewhere. The relations of the company to the Indians are necessarily far less intimate than they have been, though not less friendly; but even the more distant tribes now frequent the towns, attracted partly by novelty, and partly by the opportunities afforded for earning money by labor. Most of them comprehend fully that the sceptre has departed from Judah, and that our own people possess the country.

The familiarity of the company's officers with the Indians and their usages, of course gives them a certain influence; but there is no evidence that this has been used unfairly, or that since the conclusion of the treaty they have ever endeavored to prejudice them against our government. So far as regards their course previous to that time, it was clear enough. As traders, they endeavored to secure to themselves every advantage of trade; as British subjects, they upheld and stood by their country while it stood by them; but in every matter between a white man and an Indian, they sustained the white, of whatever nation. The conduct of Dr John McLoughlin and of Mr Peter Skene Ogden, on more than one trying occasion, was worthy of all praise. It was the former who, on the destruction by the Umpqua Indians of the train under the command of Jedediah Smith, an American and a rival fur-trader, sent against the aggressors an armed party, and restored to him, without charge, his recaptured goods; it was the latter who, upon hearing of the Whitman massacre, instantly set out himself for the Cayuse country anti purchased the liberty of the surviving women and children. For the expenditure on this occasion, it may be mentioned, the company have never requested or received payment. Their hospitality and kindness to the early settlers drew upon them censure from home; while, in this country, those who have received most at their hands have been most bitter in their abuse.

The white servants of the company, as their time expires, settle here and become naturalized. Some of the officers, also, are already citizens, and others will follow their example. Very few will ever leave the country.

In respect to the impression which it is supposed may be created by purchasing goods from them for Indian service, it may be remarked, that any danger or misconception of this point has passed away. Very few goods have, in fact, ever been purchased from the company by government officers for this purpose, and the reason, on those occasions, has been simply because they alone had supplies of suitable kind.

The missions also require notice in connexion with Indian relations.

The Presbyterians formerly had stations among the Cayuse at Waiatpu, on the, Wallah-Wallah river, under the superintendence of Dr Whitman; among the Spokanes at Chemakane, upon a branch of the Spokane river, under Messrs Walker and Eels; among the Nez Perces at Lapwai, near the mouth of the Kooskooskia, under Mr Spalding; and at Kaima, on its headwaters, under Mr Smith. The last was maintained but a short time, and all of them have been abandoned since Dr Whitman's murder. The Methodists also once had a mission at the Dalles. [422]

The only missions now among the eastern tribes are those of the Jesuits and Oblates. There are, of the former, two priests at Fort Colville, two among the Pend d'Oreilles and two among the Coeur d'Alenes. Of the latter, there is one at Wailatpu, and two on the Yakima. The mission of St Mary's, among the Flatheads, was given up in 1851, on account of the Blackfeet incursions. The Yakima mission is not fixed, but transitory, having two regular stations, one occupied in winter, the other in the summer.

Concerning the influence of the existing missions, there can be no doubt that it is, to a certain extent, beneficial in preserving peace among the tribes as well as in settling private quarrels. Beyond a very small number, however, their control over individuals is limited. They have, unquestionably, inculcated principles of honesty and morality, which in some cases perhaps have taken root, but have essentially failed in accomplishing any great and lasting improvement. Many of the Indians have adopted certain forms of Christianity, such as the sign of the cross, the repetition of short prayers, or singing of canticles; but I have failed to notice that this has always been a proof of trustworthiness. For the rest, it is evident that the objects of these gentlemen are inconsistent with the settlement of the country, or the establishment of fixed agencies. It is not intended to be represented that they have used reprehensible means; but in the knowledge that their influence must infallibly be shaken whenever contact with the whites becomes general, it is not to he doubted that they have discouraged it.

In this connexion it may be remarked, that under no consideration should agencies be conferred on priests or clergymen of any denomination, as the desire to propagate their own peculiar tenets cannot fail to embarrass their official relations. The distinction is already drawn among the Indians between the "American" and French religions, and, as in the case of the Coeur d'Alenes and Spokanes, has already created ill feelings. Any appointments of clerical officers will necessarily be regarded as an endorsement of their peculiar doctrines; whereas all idea of a connexion of religion and government should be discountenanced.

It is a fortunate circumstance that there has as yet been little or no negotiation with the Indians of the Territory, and that their official relations with the government have been but few, and those confined to tribes on the Columbia river. The, evils arising from the want of a settled and consistent policy, from constant changes of agents, and from the rejection of treaties entered into with them, have not arisen here. The field is new, and it is highly desirable, both for the sake of the whites and the Indians, that it should be entered upon with judgment.

To remove the Indians altogether into any one district is impracticable, for the western verge has been reached. To throw the fishing tribes of the coast back upon the, interior, even were the measure possible, would destroy them; nor is there any suitable region east of the Cascades where all of the tribes now living there could be concentrated and find food. They must, therefore, remain as they are, adopting such a plan only as will remedy, so far as may be, the inconvenience of the contact.

The great primary source of evil in Oregon and the western part of this Territory is the donation act, in which, contrary to established usage and to natural right, the United States assumed to grant, absolutely, the land of the Indians without previous purchase from them. It followed, as a necessary consequence, that as settlers poured in, the Indians were unceremoniously thrust from their homes and driven forth to shift for themselves. No provision was made to support them after their former means were taken away; and finally the treaties negotiated by authorized agents of the government, in which some small patches of their own territories were secured to them, were either rejected or passed over in silence. A consequence of this has been that a natural distrust has sprung up in their minds as to the good faith of the government or its agents in making treaties at all. The policy has indeed one merit, that of economy. Bur a few years will elapse before a universal escheat will preclude the necessity of any purchase.

Excepting a few persons south of the Columbia and Snake rivers, and the Hudson's Bay Company's forts, there tire few or no white settlers within the limits of Washington Territory east [423] of the Cascades. So far, therefore, as the tribes inhabiting that country are concerned, no difficulty has as yet sprung up. It is entirely in the power of the government to obviate its future occurrence.

But in order to avoid the rejection of future treaties, a course almost impossible to explain satisfactorily, and which is rendered still more unfortunate by the length of lime required to amend or renew them, it is necessary to procure in advance from Congress some expression of its views on the subject. This is in fact requisite under any circumstances, because the law gives no power to the superintendent to make even provisional reserves, and lands set aside for Indian use may be taken up without remedy before a satisfaction can be procured. In fact, they are very likely to be so, with a view to speculation out of the government.

It is not believed that extensive reserves would be desirable for these tribes. The nature of their country and their own habits make the case entirely different from those of the prairie Indians. Although some, of them cross the mountains in search of buffalo, they are not generally hunters; nor is their country any longer a game country. They require the liberty of motion for the purpose of seeking, in their proper season, roots, berries, and fish, where those articles can be found, and of grazing their horses and cattle at large; but they do not need the exclusive use of any considerable districts. A large portion of their territory will, in all human probability, never be occupied by white men; and so far nature has provided reserves. What is necessary for them, and just in itself, is, that small tracts of good land should be set apart as permanent abodes, where they may raise their vegetables and bury their dead, secure that they will not be driven off at the pleasure of the first comer.

This is especially so, because their main resource during a portion of the year is speedily destroyed in the neighborhood of settlements. A drove of hogs belonging to one white man will consume the winter provision of a tribe of Indians. In like manner, the use of their customary fisheries, and free pasturage for their stock on unenclosed lands, should be secured.

The subject of the right of fishery, in its present position, is believed to be one concerning which difficulties may arise. It is certain that the intention of Congress never was that the Indians should be excluded from them; but as no condition to this effect was inserted in the donation act, the question has been started whether persons taking claims, including such fisheries, do not possess the right of monopolizing them. It is, therefore, proper that this also should be set at rest by law.

A tract of a mile square would, it is believed, be sufficient for each of the before-mentioned tribes, or, where deemed more convenient, four quarter-sections at different points. This amount, however, should not include the land required for agencies; and authority ought to be given to the superintendent to set aside for this purpose not exceeding another square mile, (to be in one body,) in the territory of each tribe, which shall be exempted from individual claim. It is not supposed that it will be requisite to occupy them all at once; but, in anticipation of the future settlement of the country, it is desirable to secure suitable positions, that the United States may not be compelled to buy back what is required for public uses.

No conventional arrangements, strictly so speaking, are known which need action on the part of the government; but the assurance has everywhere been given by the whites, settling among the Indian tribes, that Congress would compensate them for the lands taken. Those among whom establishments have been made for any length of time, finding themselves crowded out of their houses, and fast dwindling away, ask often when this promise will be fulfilled, for they have but a little time left to employ it, and they leave no children behind. Distrust thus attaches to the country, and the advance of settlement into new districts is looked upon with suspicion.

As regards treaties for the purchase of their lands and other purposes, it would be most advantageous simply to acquire the right of settlement at pleasure in their territory, except upon the tracts reserved for their own use, leaving the remainder as lands common to both. Payment should-be made to them in goods, for although most of them understand the value of money per [424] fectly, the former mode is preferable, as it does not furnish an inducement to go into the tons, and as it confers a greater benefit at less cost. The merchandise should consist chiefly of blankets, coarse warm clothing, agricultural tools, &c., with as few of what is termed "Indian goods" as possible. In respect to presents, the indiscriminate distribution of considerable amounts is to be avoided as useless if not injurious. Small presents are proper on the occasional visits of chiefs to the agencies, but these should be discouraged when not on business.

In negotiating treaties, as the distance from the settlements to the residences of the different tribes is very considerable, and the cost of transporting merchandise for presents to the interior would be enormous, it is recommended that none whatever be given, with the exception of a little tobacco for the council smoke, and on the conclusion of the treaty a beef-ox or two to each tribe. If the reason is explained to them, as they will of course know what to expect when the treaty is ratified, they will be perfectly contented. Should the suggestions elsewhere made be adopted, arrangements may be in progress before the first distribution, which will much reduce the cost of delivering the annuities. The estimates in other respects have been made for a small party of officers and their necessary attendants. No troops are required, and every additional person only adds to the expense and prevents celerity of movement.

As nearly two years must elapse after the conclusion of a treaty before a ratification can take place, an appropriation be made, the goods purchased, forwarded, and transported to the place of distribution in the usual course, it is recommended that an appropriation for the first payment be made in advance, that the goods may be on hand as soon as the ratification takes place. Goods for the eastern part of the Territory should be shipped to Portland or Fort Vancouver; those for the western, to Puget sound. But most of the necessary articles can now to better advantage be purchased in San Francisco than imported from the States, and it is recommended that this course be pursued.

In every treaty concluded with these tribes, it should expressly be stipulated that for offences committed against the persons or property of the whites, the chiefs in the first instance shall be held responsible for the delivery of the offender and the restoration of the goods, and that, further, the amount of all damages shall be deducted from the annuity of the tribe. The chief should receive some compensation for his responsibility, and be assured of the support of the government in maintaining his authority.

With proper judgment and care, no difficulty is to be apprehended in managing the relations with any of the tribes east of the Cascade mountains. They are none of them disposed to hostilities against the whites, and the most that is to be feared is an occasional theft. Parties of two or three might traverse the whole country without annoyance. Neither are they at variance with one another, but pass fearlessly from tribe to tribe. Petty jealousies of course exist, as they do between band and band in the same tribe; but there is no serious dissension, calculated to lead to warfare among themselves. Policy requires that some military force should be maintained in the neighborhood of the great emigrant trails, and perhaps hereafter a post may be required on the main Columbia, at or near Fort Colville; but for this there is no present necessity. Whatever force is employed should, however, be cavalry, and during the summer should be kept constantly in motion.

One principle of policy, in particular, should be observed -- the union of small bands under a single head. The maxim of divide and conquer does not apply among these people. They are never so disposed to mischief as when scattered and beyond control; whereas it is always in the power of the government to secure the influence of chiefs, and through them to manage their people. Those who at present bear the name have not influence enough, and no proper opportunity should be spared of encouraging and supporting them in its extension. This policy, long pursued by the Hudson's Bay Company, was one secret of their former great influence.

It has been mentioned that a portion of the Wallah-Wallahs, together with the Nez Perces and the Cayuses, live upon the borders of the two Territories, and partly in each. [425]

In relation to this state of things, it will be perceived that some arrangements must be made between the two superintendencies, to prevent clashing in their government. The WallahWallahs proper, and the other bands south of the Columbia and Snake rivers under the Yellow Serpent, may very well be separated from the Yakimas, as they already in fact, and together with the other two tribes, remain under the jurisdiction of Oregon. The three are intimately connected with one another. The Wallah-Wallahs and Nez Perces speak dialects of a common language, and the Cayuses have abandoned their own for that of the latter. They have greatly intermarried, their countries adjoin, and their separation would be almost as impossible as the division of the tribe itself. Their relations with the Oregon agency and people have, moreover, been of long standing, and will remain more intimate than with those of this Territory. Except the Bannaks and the Snakes, they form the only tribes falling within the eastern division of Oregon.

Treaties should nevertheless be concluded with them at once on behalf of the citizens of both Territories, and in the mean time their subsequent jurisdiction be permanently fixed.

The most judicious, and at the same time the most economical, mode of organizing the department, would probably be to divide the Territory into two districts, one on each side of the mountains, in both of which there should be a full agent. It should be his duty to visit in person, at least once in each year, every tribe in his district, pay the annuities, supervise the farmers or laborers employed to assist the Indians, and generally to act as the deputy of the superintendent. The agent should be authorized to employ an assistant or clerk, who should live with him, and during his absence on tours of inspection, manage the business of the office. When it is recollected that the Territory embraces eleven degrees of longitude by six in latitude, it will be obvious that the superintendent, especially when his duties are united with those of the executive, can not give his personal attention to distant tribes, and that the most responsible duties must necessarily be discharged by subordinates. Their pay and position should be such as to secure men thoroughly qualified, both by character, ability, and familiarity with the Indians. The pay of a sub-agent, barely equal to the lowest wages of common labor, cannot be expected to secure the efficient service of any man in such a situation, much less of a competent one. As the agent himself cannot personally supervise all the different tribes in learning the use of their tools, the proper arrangement of their crops, building fences, &c, it is recommended, further, that the superintendent, under the sanction of the department, be authorized to allow the pay of a sub-agent to not more than one person for each principal tribe of Indians who shall settle among them, and under his direction, or that of the agent, assist in teaching them. Should this, however, not be deemed advisable, the agent should be allowed to hire for at least three months during each of the first two years after the ratification of the treaty, a person suitable for the task.

Their own cattle would, among the eastern tribes, suffice for their wants in breaking up their land, and doing the requisite hauling. In the western agency the work would require to be done chiefly by hand, as the wooded country of the coast does not afford sufficient range, and the Indians have but few horses, and no cattle. Another provision ought to be made for the protection of their fields in that district. Settlers taking up lands adjoining the reserved grounds should be compelled to do half the fencing necessary to exclude their hogs and other stock, the Indians, under the direction of the agent, doing the remainder. As it is, they are exposed to the loss of their little provision, and government will probably be called upon to remunerate them for the damage.

The location recommended for the eastern agency is the neighborhood of the old Chemakaine mission, which affords good land and timber, and is both central to the district and accessible to wagons from Wallah-Wallah or Fort Colville. For the western agency, some point on or near the southern end of Whidby's island would probably be the most convenient.

The Columbia river should be constituted a sub-agency, to have jurisdiction over the scattered bands of the Upper and Lower Chinooks, and those of the Klikatats who reside either in whole [426] or in part among them. The boundaries of this jurisdiction can be served by the superintendent, as it is advised that the Indians living within it be for the most part left to the operation of civil law; the duties of the sub-agent will not be more onerous than call be performed with the necessary attention to his other occupations, and no particular residence need be furnished or designated.

In the present condition of the Territory there is great confusion as to the applicability of the laws regulating intercourse with the Indian tribes. For certain purposes it is Indian country, while for others it assuredly is not, and in every respect it is desirable that Congress draw the line of distinction.

The difference between the eastern and western sections of the Territory may require some few differences in legislation. The western portion is as yet the only one where settlements have been made ; it is there that the bulk of the population will continue to be ; but very radical amendments are demanded in the other also. The following have suggested themselves:

Act of June 30, 1834: Section 2, prohibiting trade with the Indians without license, to be repealed, except, of course, in spirituous liquors, the introduction of which into the Territory east of the mountains may continue to be illegal. West of them, however, the law as against importation is nugatory, and should be repealed. The repeal of sections 3, 4, 6, and 6, will necessarily follow. In case of the settlement of the country by the whites, there will of course be merchants and traders, and the Indians should have the right to purchase where they can get the best and cheapest goods. This they will do in any event, and the section will continue to be a dead letter, even if not repealed.

Section 7 to be limited to clothing and goods of American or European manufacture. These Indians have few peltries, and look forward to the sale of stock, horses, and potatoes, as a benefit to be derived from the incoming of settlers.

Section 9 to be repealed, and, as a substitute, the marking of cattle, horses, mules, hogs, and other domestic animals, with conspicuous ear or other marks, to be required, which marks, as in the western States, to be recorded in the office of the clerk of the county; a penalty to be affixed to the effacing of marks, adopting a mark previously recorded, forging a mark, or falsely marking animals.

Section 20. It is proposed that in lieu of the penalty here affixed, the jury shall impose the fine – not, however, to be less than say $50 for each offence; and also the term of imprisonment, if that is not repealed. One practical difficulty in the execution of the present law is, that juries are inclined to consider the amount of the penalty as too great to rest upon Indian evidence only; some other changes will follow from the amendment proposed to section 26.

Section 25. For the purpose of better defining the limits of federal and territorial jurisdiction, it is proposed that the power of the former shall extend to all cases of felony, and that of the latter to cases of *misdemeanor*; that the federal courts have also power to appoint commissioners in each county, whose duties and powers shall be the same as those of commissioners of the United States courts in other States and Territories, and who shall be entitled to the same fees as justices of the peace in the Territory of Washington.

As an additional section, it is recommended that in all cases where the military forces of the United States shall be employed against Indians, and shall take as prisoners or enforce the delivery of persons accused of any crime, it shall be competent for them to try by court-martial and inflict such punishment as the case may warrant, even to that of death. The object of this provision is, the greater impression upon the tribes produced by a speedy punishment and the saving of the great expense consequent upon the keeping of prisoners until courts can be convened at distant places. The rules of the common law, moreover, in relation to evidence, are so glaringly inapplicable to cases where Indian testimony is taken, that a conviction would be utterly impossible in most instances, if depending entirely upon it.

There is another measure which, under proper regulations, it is believed would prove of essen [427] tial benefit to the Indian, and of great convenience to the citizen – a well-considered system of apprenticeship. Neither those of the coast nor those of the interior have any objection to service; on the contrary, they all regard it as an advantage in securing a certainty of food, and the means of purchasing necessaries. Large numbers of Spokanes, Yakimas, &c., come down in the winter to Vancouver, Portland, and the other towns, to seek employment, and their number is yearly increasing. They do small jobs, and work as boatmen, porters, and house-servants, and, besides many presents of clothing, get good wages, averaging thirty dollars a month. They are, however, as might be expected, inconstant, and after a short time return to their homes, or spend their money in gambling before seeking work again. In a country where labor is as much needed as it is here, even this comparatively unprofitable kind is in demand. Were, however, a measure adopted which would give permanency to the relation of master and servant, and at the same time protect the rights of the latter, the value of Indian labor mould be greatly raised. As it is, many persons hold slaves, purchased from their Indian masters, who are to a certain extent profitable, though they are generally of the worst class. The Indians show considerable mechanical ingenuity, and would undoubtedly make good blacksmiths, carpenters, and mechanics generally. As household domestics, attendants on the saw-mills, and in many other ways, they can be employed to advantage; but it is especially as farm servants that the proposed measure would be most useful, as, at the expiration of their term of service, they would carry back with them a sufficient knowledge of agriculture to improve their condition at home. I mould therefore recommend that the superintendent of Indian affairs, or any full agent, under such general regulations as the superintendent may direct, be authorized, with the consent of the parents or next relations, to bind any Indian child as an apprentice to a citizen of good character and standing, on such terms and for such time as may be agreed upon, not, however, to extend beyond the period when the apprentice shall reach the age of twenty-one years; the contract subject to be terminated by the superintendent or agent, should he be satisfied of personal ill-treatment, immoral use, or an intention to leave the Territory. As the practical details of such a system can hardly be perfected in advance, and as abuses might arise which would require an earlier action than could be procured from Congress, it is suggested that the superintendent be vested with entire powers, subject only to the revision of the department.

These measures, it is believed, are sufficiently comprehensive to cover the whole ground, and at the same time preserve all that is requisite of the system.

The western division of the Territory remains to be considered. On the Columbia river and at Shoalwater bay are a few remnants of the once numerous Chinooks. Of these there were, properly speaking, two nations-the Upper and the Lower Chinooks; the former extending from the Dalles nearly to the Cowlitz river; the latter from thence to the ocean. As these are better known from previous accounts than any others on the Pacific, it is unnecessary to dwell at length upon them. Besides the small party at the Cascades already referred to, there are of the Upper nation but five bands, living at different points on the Washington side of the river, and one at the mouth of Dog river, in Oregon. In whatever arrangement is made, it would be well to include the whole. They number but about 200. Of the Lower Chinooks there are six or seven settlements, most of which consist of single families. The one on Chinook beach is the largest, and amounts to 66. Almost all these are, however, intermingled with the Chihalis {Chehalis}. One of their grounds is upon the south side of the Columbia, opposite the mouth of the Cowlitz, and therefore in Oregon. The total number of this tribe is reduced to about 120. There are four persons who claim to be chiefs: Ske-ma-que-up at Wahkiakum, To-tili-cum at Woody Island, E-la-wah at Chinook, and Toke at Shoalwater bay. As this last named locality has only recently been much known, a rather more particular notice of it is not out of place. It was really the principal seat of the Chinooks proper, who resorted to the Columbia mostly for their spring salmon, while they dug their clams and procured their winter supplies on the bay. It formed, in fact, a perfect Indian Paradise in its adaptation to canoe travel and the abundance of scale and shell-fish which [428] it furnished. The southern half of the bay belonged to them; the country on the Willopah river to the tribe of that name, and the upper end to the Chihalis; Trails[147] now partially obliterated and overgrown connect it with the Cowlitz, the Chihalis, and different points on the Columbia, with the people of which the inhabitants kept up a trade in dried fish and clams, purchasing in return kamas, wappatoo, and other foreign commodities. At present but few Indians remain here, the smallpox having nearly finished its work during the past year. In the winter and spring it spread with great virulence along the coast as far north as Cape Flattery. Some lodges upon the southern peninsula of Shoalwater bay were left without a survivor, and the dead were found by the whites lying wrapped in their blankets as if asleep.

Quite extensive, cemeteries are scattered along the bay, the canoes in which the bodies of former generations were deposited having out-lasted the race itself.

The Willopahs {Swaals}, or, as called by Capt Wilkes, Qualioquas {Kwalioqua}, may be considered as extinct, a few women only remaining, and those intermarried with the Chinooks and Chihalis.

Part of the Chihalis Indians still frequent the bay for fish, clams, and oysters, and, with the Chinooks living there, are employed by the whites in taking the latter for market. They bring their canoes along the coast: if the water be smooth, paddling outside the breakers; if rough, trailing them with great dexterity between the surf and the beach. They have some horses, and this beach is a favorite race-ground. The number of the tribe upon Gray's harbor, and that part of the river from the Satsop down, is supposed to be about one hundred and fifty. No settlements have been made on Gray's harbor, and only three claims takes up; but it is impossible to foresee

---

[147] See works by Helen Norton. *jm*

at what moment population may thrust itself into any district, and another season may find this occupied throughout.

There are said to be several other bands inhabiting the northern branches of the Chihalis, the Whishkah, Wynoochee, &c, between whom and the whites there has been no intercourse whatever, and who have never been included in any estimate. For the present purpose they may, with sufficient probability, be reckoned at three hundred. The Indian's of the Upper Chihalis will be considered in connexion with the Cowlitz.

Following up the coast, there is another tribe upon the Kwinaitl {Quinault} river, which runs into the Pacific some twenty-five miles above the Chihalis, its headwaters interlocking with the streams running into Hood's canal and the inlets of Puget sound. Little is known of them except that they speak a different language from the last. Still farther north, and between the Kwinaitl and the Makahs, or Cape Flattery Indians, are other tribes whose names are still unknown, hut who, by the vague rumors of those on the Sound, are both numerous and warlike. All these have been lately visited by the smallpox, with its customary desolating effects.

The Cowlitz, likewise a once numerous and powerful tribe, are now insignificant and fast disappearing. The few bands remaining are intermingled with those of the Upper Chihalis. According to the best estimates obtained, the two-united are not over one hundred and sixty-five in number, and are scattered in seven parties between the mouth of the Cowlitz and the Satsop.

The Taitinapam, a band of Klikatats already mentioned, living near the head of the Cowlitz, are probably about seventy-five in number. They are called by their eastern brethren wild or wood Indians. Until very lately they have not ventured into the settlements, and have even avoided all intercourse with their own race. The river Indians attach to them all kinds of superstitious ideas, including that of stealing and eating children, and of travelling unseen.

Upon the estimates above stated, the whole number of all the Indians south of Puget sound, and between the Cascades and the coast, would amount to about eight hundred and fifty, in place of three thousand, the estimate of Captain Wilkes in 1841 – a diminution of – per cent per annum.

In regard to all these tribes, scattered as most of them are in small bands at considerable distances apart, it seems hardly worth while to make any arrangements looking forward to permanence or involving great expense. The case of the Chinooks and Cowlitz Indians in particular [429] seems desperate. They are all intemperate, and can get liquor whenever they choose. They are, besides, diseased beyond remedy, syphilis being with them hereditary as well as acquired. The speedy extinction of the race seems rather to be hoped for than regretted, and they look forward to it themselves with a sort of indifference. The duty of the government, however, is not affected by their vices, for these they owe, in a great measure, to our own citizens. If it can do nothing else, it can at least aid in supporting them while they survive. They live almost altogether among the whites, or in their immediate neighborhood, taking and selling salmon, or doing occasional work, and for the rest letting out their women as prostitutes. No essential advantage would, it is feared, be obtained by removing them to any one location, for they would not long remain away from their old haunts, and probably the assignment of a few acres of ground for their villages and cemeteries, and the right of fishing at customary points, would effect all that could be done. Still, if they should manifest such a wish, the experiment might be tried of settling each tribe in one village at some place not yet occupied, and constituting it a reserve. This, except during the salmon season, might remove them somewhat farther from temptation.

{Puget Sound}

The tribes that inhabit the region bordering on Puget sound and the Straits of Fuca alone remain; and in speaking of them, it will be most convenient to commence with the Straits, and following up Hood's canal to the inlets at the head of the Sound, thence return northward by the, eastern shore and the islands, to the boundary line of the British provinces.

The Makahs, or Classets, inhabit the coast in the neighborhood of Cape Flattery, their country extending but a short distance up the Straits, where it adjoins that of the Clallams. Their language is said to extend down the coast about half way to Gray's harbor. This tribe, which has been the most formidable to navigators of any in the American territories on the Pacific, numbered, it is believed, until very recently, five hundred and fifty.

During the last year the smallpox found its way to their region, and, it is reported, reduced them to one hundred and fifty, their famous chief, Flattery Jack, being among the number who died. The Makahs resemble the northwestern Indians far more than their neighbors. They venture well out to sea in their canoes, and even attack and kill the whale, using for this harpoons pointed with shell, and attached by a sinew line to seal-skin floats. It is said that the year previous to the sickness, they took 30,000 gallons of oil. This was purchased chiefly by vessels. They also take a number of sea otter--the skins of which are sold at Victoria--and raise a good many potatoes.

Among their articles of manufacture are blankets and capes, made of the inner bark of the cedar, and edged with fur. Their houses are of considerable size, often fifty to a hundred feet in length, and strongly built. They sometimes place their dead in trees, at others bury them. Their marriages are said to have some peculiar ceremonies, such as going through the performance of taking the whale, manning a canoe, and throwing the harpoon into the bride's house. The superior courage of the Makahs, as well as their treachery, will make them more difficult of management than most other tribes of this region. No whites are at present settled in their country; but as the occupation of the Territory progresses, some pretty stringent measures will probably be required respecting them.

Next to the Makahs are the Clallams, or, as they call themselves, S'Klallams, the most formidable tribe now remaining. Their country stretches along the whole southern shore of the Straits to between Port Discovery and Port Townsend; besides which, they have occupied the latter place, properly belonging to the Chimakum. They have eight villages, viz: Commencing nearest the Makahs, {1} Okeno {Cheerno}, or Ocha, which is a sort of alsatia or neutral ground for the runaways of both tribes; {2} Pishtst {Pysht}, on Clallam bay; {3} Elkwah {Elwa}, at the mouth of the river of that name; {4} Tse-whit-zen, or False Dungeness; {5} Tinnis, or Dungeness; {6} St-queen, Squim bay {Sequim}, or Washington harbor; {7} Squa-que-hl, Port Discovery; and {8} Kahtai, Port Townsend.[148] Their numbers have been variously estimated, end, as usual, exaggerated; some persons rating them as high as 1,500 fighting men. An actual count of the last three, which were supposed to contain half the popu [430] lation, was made by their chiefs in January, and, comprehending all who belonged to them, whether present or not, gave a population of only 376 all told.. The total number will not probably exceed 800. That they have been more numerous is unquestionable, and one of the chiefs informed me that they once had one hundred and forty canoes, of eighteen to the larger and fourteen to the smaller size; which, supposing the number of each kind to be equal, gives a total of 2,240 men.

---

[148] Erna Gunther, <u>Klallam Ethnography</u> 1927; for recent desecration at (4), Mapes 2009.

One cause of the over-estimate so frequently made of Indians, is their habit of moving about, gathering in bodies--one day at one place, and at another the next; thus leaving the impression of great number in each. Many of the Clallams of Vancouver's island, too, visit the American side of the Straits, and swell the apparent population. The total of all the tribes in this part of the Territory has, however, been placed rather under than over the mark, for many of them live altogether off the Sound, and have not come in contact with the whites.

The head chief of all the Clallams was Lach-ka-nam, or Lord Nelson, who is still living, but has abdicated in favor of his son, S'Hai-ak, or King George--a very different personage, by the way, from the chief of the same name east of the mountains. Most of the principal men of the tribe have received names either from the English or the "Bostons;" and the genealogical tree of the royal Family presents as miscellaneous an assemblage of characters as a masked ball in carnival. Thus, two of King George's brothers are the Duke of York and General Gaines. His cousin is. Tom Benton; and his sons; by Queen Victoria, are General Jackson and Thomas Jefferson. The queen is daughter to the Duke of Clarence, and sister to Generals Scott and Taylor; as also to Mary Ella Coffin, the wife of John C. Calhoun. The Duke of York's wife is Jenny Lind; a brother of the Duke of Clarence is John Adams; and Calhoun's sons are James K. Polk, General Lane, and Patrick Henry. King George's sister is the daughter of the late Flattery Jack. All of them have papers certifying to these and various other items of information, which they exhibit with great satisfaction. They make shocking work, however, in the pronunciation of their names; the rs [R] and fs [F] being shibboleths which they cannot utter.[149]

It is a melancholy fact that the Clallam representatives of these distinguished personages are generally as drunken and worthless a set of rascals as could he collected. The Clallam tribe has always had a bad character, which their intercourse with shipping, and the introduction of whiskey, have by no means improved.

The houses of the chiefs at Port Townsend, where they frequently gather, are of the better class-- quite spacious and tolerably clean. Two or three are not less than thirty feet long by sixteen or eighteen wide, built of heavy planks, supported oh large posts and crossbeams, and lined with mats. The planks forming the roof run the whole length of the building, being guttered to carry off the water, and sloping slightly to one end. Low platforms are carried round the interior, on which are laid mats, serving for beds and seats. Piles of very neatly made baskets are stored away in corners, containing their provisions. There are from two to four fires in each house belonging to the head of the family, and such of his sons as live with him. They have an abundance of salmon, shell-fish, and potatoes, and seem to be very well off. In fact, any of the tribes living upon the Sound must be worthless indeed not to find food in the inexhaustible supplies of fish, clams, and water-fowl, of which they have one or the other at all times. They have a good deal of money among them, arising from the sale of potatoes and fish, letting out their women, and jobbing for the whites.

The Clallams, and in fact all the other Sound Indians, flatten their heads. Their canoes are of different models; the common one being that known as the Chinook canoe, the most graceful of all; some of which are of large size and great beauty. They have, besides, one called the Queen Charlotte's Island canoe, which, in a heavy sea, is preferable to the first as less liable to be boarded astern. The canoe used for duck-shooting is very pretty, and exceedingly well

---

[149] A "shibboleth" is a distinctive word that sets one language off against others, as pronunciation of the Hebrew word shibboleth ("ear of grain") distinguished Gileadites from Ephraimites [sh/s]. *jm*

adapted for the purpose. It sits low on the water, and an Indian seated in it, and gliding noiselessly along beneath the shadows of the trees, or lying beside some projecting log, would [431] need sharp eyes to detect him. Another and very large canoe, of ruder shape and workmanship, being wide and shovel-nosed, is in use among all these tribes for the transportation of their property and baggage. Among their characteristic manufactures are blankets or robes made of dogs' hair. They have a kind of cur with soft and long white hair, which they shear and mix with a little wool or the ravellings of old blankets. This is twisted by rolling on the knees into a cord or coarse yarn, and is then woven on a frame. They use the down of water-fowl in the same way, mixing it with hair, and forming a very thick and warm fabric.

The Clallams, as well as the Makahs and some other tribes, carry on a considerable trade with Vancouver's island, selling their skins, oil, &c., and bringing blankets in return. At present it is hardly worth while to check this traffic, even if it were possible; but when the white population increases, it may become necessary as a revenue measure. In any treaties made with them, it should enter as a stipulation that they should confine their trade to the American side. Apart of the Clallams are permanently located on that island, and it is believed that their language is an extensive one. The Lummi, on the northern shore of Bellingham bay, are a branch of the same nation.

This tribe have, within the last year, been guilty of the murder of three Americans, as well as of several robberies. For the first, that of a man named Pettingill, one of the two perpetrators was secured by arresting the chief, and has been in custody at Steilacoom some months waiting his trial. The other case was the murder of Captain Jewell, master of the barque John Adams, and of his cook, and was unknown till recently, as it was supposed that Jewell had absconded. In both cases the parties had considerable sums in their possession, which fell into the hands of the Indians. On learning of the last affair, a requisition was made by Governor Stevens upon the officer commanding the military post at Steilacoom, and a party promptly dispatched there to support the special agent in securing the criminals.

Some severe lesson is required to reduce them to order, as their natural insolence has been increased by the weakness of the settlements near them, and by the facility with which they can procure liquor. The establishment of a military post at some point on the Straits would be very desirable for the purpose of overawing them and their neighbors.

Above the Clallams are the Chimakum, formerly one of the most powerful tribes of the Sound, but which, a few years since, is said to have been nearly destroyed at a blow by an attack of the Snoqualmoos. Their numbers have been probably much diminished by the wars in which they were constantly engaged. They now occupy some fifteen small lodges on Port Townsend bay, and number perhaps seventy in all. Lately, the Clallams have taken possession of their country, and they are, in a measure, subject to them. Their language differs materially from either that of the Clallams or the Nisqually, and is not understood by any of their neighbors. In fact, they seem to have maintained it a State secret. To what family it will ultimately be referred, cannot now be decided. Their territory seems to have embraced the shore from Port Townsend to Port Ludlow. Still above the Chimakum are the Toanhoock [Twana], occupying the western shore of Hood's canal. They are a branch of the Nisqually nation; but their dialect differs greatly from those on the eastern side of the Sound. They amount to about 266. With them may be classed the Skokamish {Skokomish}, upon the head of the canal, who probably number 200. Neither of them have had as much intercourse with the whites as most of the Sound tribes.

Upon Puget sound, and the inlets communicating with it, are several small bands, the remnants of once larger tribes, formerly all, it is believed, under one head chief. Of these the

Squalli-ah-mish or Nis-qually is the most numerous, and deserves particular mention as having given its name to the general language. Their respective numbers will be given in the general statement.

To the north of this group, another may be formed of those inhabiting the shores of Admiralty inlet from Puyallup river to Suquamish head, including Vashon's and Bainbridge's islands, Port Orchard, Elliott bay and the D'Wamish river, and Port Madison. Most of them are nominally [432] under a chief named Se-at-tle, belonging to the Suquamish tribe, but residing principally with another, the D'Wamish. This last is the one called, on the charts of Puget sound, the Nowamish; and it should be mentioned that a very considerable difference in the spelling of almost all these names exists, arising from the fact that several letters of their alphabet are convertible; as D and N, B and M, U and G. For instance, the band in question are indifferently termed N'Wamish and D'Wamish; another clan of the same trio, the Samamish, are also called Sababish; and the name Suquamish is frequently changed into — {Suk^{w}abš}. The D'Wamish are the best known of this connexion, from their neighborhood to the rising town, named after their Chief Se-at-tie, and the whole generally bear their name, though they are by no means the most numerous. Their proper seat is the outlet of a large lake emptying into the D'Wamish river, and not on the main branch. At that place, they, and some others, have small patches of potato ground, amounting altogether to perhaps thirty acres; where, it is stated, they raised during the last year about 3,000 bushels, or an average of one hundred bushels to the acre. Of these they sold a part, reserving the rest for their own consumption. Each head of a family plants his own, the quantity being regulated by the number of his women. Their potatoes are very fine, though they have used the same seed on the same ground for a succession of years.

The jealousies existing among all these petty bands, and their fear of one, another, is everywhere noticeable in their establishing themselves near the whites. Whenever a settler's house is erected, a nest of Indian rookeries is pretty sure to follow if permitted; and in case of temporary absence, they always beg storage for their valuables. The compliment is seldom returned, though it is often considered advantageous to have them in the neighborhood as spies upon others. Some amusing traits of character occasionally develop themselves among Indians, of which an instance happened with these. A saw-mill was erected during the last autumn, upon the outlet of the lake, at a place where they are in the habit of taking salmon. The fishery was much improved by the dam, but what afforded the greatest satisfaction to them was its situation upon their property, and the superior importance thereby derived to themselves. They soon began to understand the machinery, and took every visitor through the building to explain its working, and boast of it, as if it had been of their own construction.

The southern end of Whidby's island, and the country on and near the mouth of the Sinahomish river, belong to the Sinahomish tribe. These number, including the bands connected with them, a little over 300. Their chief is S'Hoot-soot, an old man who resides chiefly at Skagit head. Above them, and upon the main branch of the river, is another band, not under the same rule, the Snoqualmoos, amounting to about 200 souls. Their chief, Pat-ka-nam, has rather an evil celebrity among the whites, and two of his brothers have been hung for their misdeeds.[150] This band are especially connected with the Yakimas, or, as they are called on the Sound, Klikatats.

It requires notice in this place, that besides the tribes, or bands, inhabiting the shores and the lower part of the rivers, there are on the headwaters of the latter, along the whole course of

---

[150] Agent Robert Fay noted Goliah (25/2/1857, #1821) was six feet tall, slim, and 36; recent elders recall he had a broken leg. *jm*

the Cascade mountains, another range of tribes, generally independent of the former, who rarely descend from their recesses, but are intermediate in their habits between the coast and mountain tribes; except the Taitinapam, however, they all belong to the general family upon whose borders they live. Those in the neighborhood of the passes own a few horses, which subsist in the small prairies skirting the base of the mountains.

The tribes living upon the eastern shore possess also territory upon the islands, and their usual custom is to resort to them at the end of the salmon season--that is, about the middle of November. It is there that they find the greatest supply of shell-fish, which form a large part of their winter stock, and which they dry both for their own use and for sale to those of the interior. The summer and fall they spend on the main, where they get fish and put in their potatoes.

Below the Sinahomish come the Stoluchquamish, (river people) or, as their name is usually corrupted, Steilaquamish, whose country is on a stream bearing their name; and still north of them the Kikialus. No opportunity has afforded itself for accurate inquiry into the numbers of [433] either. The first are said by some to amount to two hundred, while the latter may perhaps be set down at seventy-five. The next tribe proceeding northward are the Skagits, who live on the main around the mouth of the Skagit river, and own the central parts of Whidby's island, their principal ground being the neighborhood of Penn's cove. They have lately diminished in numbers and lost much of their influence since the death, a year or two since, of their chief, S'neetlum, or, as he was commonly called, Snakelum. The tribe has been long at enmity with the Clallams, who have attempted to encroach upon their lands. The Skagits raise a considerable quantity of potatoes, and have, besides, a natural resource in their kamas, which grows abundantly on the prairies of Whidby's island. Both of these are now being greatly injured by the cattle and hogs of the settlers. The kamas, it is worth mentioning, improves very much by cultivation, and it is said to attain the size of a hen's egg in land that has been ploughed. Swine are exceedingly fond of it. The Skagits are about three hundred all told; and there are other bands upon the headwaters of their river, amounting probably to as many more.[151]

Below the Skagits again, occupying land on the main upon the northern end of Whidby's island, Ferry's island, and the Canoe passage, are three more tribes, the Squinamish, Swodamish, and Sinaahmish, probably two hundred and fifty or three hundred altogether; and lastly the Samish, on the small river of that name and the southern part of Bellingham bay, estimated at one hundred and fifty. With these, according to the best information procurable during a rapid journey of inspection, the Nisqually nation terminates, the next tribe to the north speaking a dialect of the Clallams.

It is probable that that of the Samish is a by-word between the two.

The Lummi, living on a river emptying into the northern part of Bellingham bay and on the peninsula, are variously estimated at from four to five hundred. Their chief is Sahhopkan; in general habits they resemble the Clallams.

Above the Lummi, on the main fork of the river which is said to rise in and carry off the water from Mount Baker, is still another considerable tribe called the Nooksahk. They seem to be allied with the Lummi and the Skagit, and, according to Indian account, they speak a mixed language. They are supposed to be about equal in numbers to the Lummi.

The Shimiahmoo inhabit the coast towards Frazier's river; nothing seems to be known of them whatever. They are probably the most northern tribe on the American side of the line, the Kowailchew lying principally, if not altogether, in British territory.

---

[151] See works by June Collins, Sally Snyder, and Bruce G Miller. *jm*

Concerning the tribes north of the Sinahomish, nothing but estimates founded on the opinions of the few settlers in that district could be gathered, the opportunity afforded by a hasty voyage through the Sound being, of course, very limited. Steps have been taken to correct them. The general result, it is believed, will warrant the estimates furnished.

Accompanying the recapitulation of the tribes in the western district will be found the estimate of Captain Wilkes in 1841, and one calculated by the Hudson's Bay Company in 1844, which was politely furnished by Dr Wm F Tolmie, at Fort Nisqually. The latter exhibits what, according to the best information, is the decrease since that period in the tribes then known, but no adequate data then existed on which to base a reliable comparison. For the purpose of procuring certain returns hereafter, a form is herewith enclosed, and it is recommended that the agents be obliged annually to make out as fully as practicable.

Some variations from the plan suggested for the management; of the eastern district will necessarily suggest themselves in respect to the western, though it is believed they are not material; but owing to the great number of small bands into which most of the Indian population is broken up, the labor of treating with and disposing of the latter will be much the greatest. It is therefore recommended that a separate commission be appointed for that district.

In order to bring the whole subject fully before the government, estimates have been prepared, based upon the best opinions and information attainable, of the expenses of negotiating treaties with The tribes of each district; of the annual payments they may be expected to involve; of the [434] cost of establishing agencies, and finally of the yearly expense of maintaining them. It is believed that the plan suggested will prove efficient, and that the expense is but trifling, compared with the extent of the country to be purchased; the number and situation of the tribes occupying it, and, above all, of the advantage to be secured to the Territory in the quiet and effectual settlement of perspective difficulties. No plan, however well devised, can be successful without the concurrence of the citizens; and in making these suggestions, the advice of men possessed of experience in Indian relations has been obtained.   GEORGE GIBBS

To: Capt George B. McClellan
Commanding Western Division NP Railroad Exploration
I have examined the foregoing report, and fully approve of Mr Gibbs's views as therein expressed, and would respectfully recommend that they be adopted.
GEORGE B McCLELLAN,
Lieutenant Engineers and Brevet Captain Commanding, &c., &c.

The estimates, as they relate to the Indian service solely, and as they are not approved by me, are not submitted. The Nez Perces are almost exclusively in Washington Territory; and being closely affiliated with the other tribes of the Territory, accompanying them always in their annual hunt, they should be attached to the Washington superintendency. There should be three agencies in the Territory--the eastern, central, and western agencies-for reasons set forth in my reports to the Indian bureau, and which have been approved both by the department and by Congress. By a law of Congress it is made the duty of the officers of the Indian department to make all treaties with Indians. Hence, the proper commissioners will be the Indian superintendent and his agents. There are minor points which are not approved; but the report, generally, is submitted as one of ability, and as exceedingly creditable to its author.
ISAAC I STEVENS,
Governor of Washington Territory

Census of various Indian tribes living on or near Puget Sound, NW America, taken by WF Tolmie in the autumn of 1844.

Names of tribes	Men	Women	Boys	Girls	Slaves	Total population	Horses	Canoes	Guns.	Remarks
Stak-ta-mish	62	62	39	21	23	207	89	27	13	Between Olympia and Na-wau-kum river
Squaks'na-mish	33	44	28	25	4	135	5	17	7	
Se-hehwa-mish	29	23	7	30	3	92	–	14	7	
Squalli-a-mish	138	162	75	66	30	471	190	92	48	
Pu-yal-lup-a-mish	69	81	37	33	7	207				
S'Ko-ma-mish	34	22	34	28	7	118	–	34	14	
Su-qua-mish	158	102	113	97	64	525	5	160	93	
Sin-a-ho-mish	102	100	61	59	–	322	–	61	28	
Sno-qual-mook	122	153	65	25	8	373	–	36	27	
Sin-a-ah-mish	78	37	47	22	11	195	–	36	8	
Nooh-lum-mi	65	57	52	47	23	244	–	60	15	
Total						2,689				

Captain Wilkes Estimate – 1841

Tribes and localities	Population.
Chinooks	209
Pillar Pock, Oak Point, and Columbia river	300
Cowlitz	350
Chihalis and Puget Sound	700

Nisqually	200
Port Orchard	150
Penn's Cove, Whidby's island, including the main land (Scatchae tribe)	650
Birch Bay	300
Clallams at Port Discovery, New Dungeness, &c	350
Port Townsend	70
Hood's canal (Suquamish and. Toando tribe)	500
Total	3,779

Estimate of Indian tribes in the Western district of Washington Territory – January, 1854. [435]

Names of tribes and bands	Where located	Men	Women	Total bands	Total tribes	Remarks
Upper Chinooks - 5 bands, not including Cascade band	Columbia river, above the Cowlitz	–	–	–	200	Estimate. – The upper of these bands are mixed with the Klikitats; the lower with the Cowlitz
Lower Chinooks - Chinook band, Four others, (estimate)	Columbia river, below the Cowlitz, and Shoalwater bay	32 –	34 –	66 50	– 116	One of these is intermixed with the Cowlitz - the rest with the Chehalis
Chihalis	Gray's harbor and Lower Chehalis river	–	–	100	–	Estimate
Do	Northern forks Chihalis river	–	–	200	300	Estimate
Cowlitz and Upper Chihalis	On Cowlitz river and the Chihalis, above the Satsop	–	–	–	165	The two have become altogether intermixed

Tai-tin-a-pam	Base of mountains on Cowlitz, &c	–	–	–	75	Estimate
Quin-aik, &c.	Coast from Gray's harbor northward	–	–	–	500	Estimate
Makahs	Cape Flattery and vicinity	–	–	–	150	Estimate
S'Klallams	Straits of Fuca	–	–	–		
Kahtai	Port Townsend	67	88	155		
Ka-quaitl	Port Discovery	24	26	50		
Stent-lum	New Dungeness	79	91	170		
All others	False Dungeness, &c., westward	–	–	475 –	850	The last estimated
Chima-kum	Port Townsend	–	–	–	70	
To-an hooch	Hood's canal	123	109	265	–	Some of the women omitted in the count, but estimated
Sko-ko-mish	Hood's canal – upper end	–	–	200	– 465	Sko-ko-mish estimated
Guak-s'n-a-mish	Case's inlet, &c	19	21	40		
S'Kosle-ma-mish	Case's inlet, &c	14	13	27		
Se-heh-wa-mish	Hammersly's inlet, &c	11	12	23		
Sa-wa-mish	Totten's inlet, &c	2	1	3		
Squa-aitl	Eld's inlet, &c	22	23	45		
Stell-cha-sa-mish	Budd's inlet, &c	–	–	20	–	Estimate
Nov-seh-chatl	South bay	–	–	12	– 170	Estimate

Squalli-ah-mish - six bands	Nisqually river and vicinity.	84	100	184		
Steila-coom-a-mish	Steilacoom creek and vicinity	–	–	25	1700	
Pu-yallup-a-msih	Mouth of Puyallup river, &c	–	–	50	–	Estimate
T'Qua-qua-mish	Heads of ....do.......do...	–	–	50	– 100	Estimate
Su-qua-mish	Peninsula between Hood's canal and Admiralty inlet	215	270	485		
S'slo-ma-mish	Vashon's island	18	15	33	518	
D'Wamish	Lake Fork, D'Wamish river	89	73	162		
Sa-ma-mish S'kel-tehl-mish	D'Wamish lake, &c	71	30	101		
Smul-ka-mish	Head of White river	–	–	8		
Skope-ah-mish	Head of Green river	–	–	50		
Se-ka-mish	Main of White river	–	v	30		
				----	351	
Sin-a-ho-mish		161	138	350	–	Part of the women omitted, but included in the total
Qunk-ma-mish Sky-wa-mish	Upper branches, north side Sinahomish river					
Sky-wa-mish Sk-tah-le-gum	Upper branches, N. side Sinahomish river	–	–	300	–	Estimate
Snow-qual-	South fork, north	–	–	195		

mook	side Sinahomish river					
				v	275	
Sto-luch-wa-mish	Sto-luch-wa-mish river, &c	–	–	200		
Kikiallis	Kik-I-allis river, L. Whidbey's island	–	–	75	275	
Skagit	Skagit river and Penn's Cove	–	–	300	–	Estimate
N'qua-cha-mish Sma-lih-hu Mis-kai-whu Sa-ku-me-hu	Branches of Skagit river	–	–	300	– 600	Estimate
Squi-na-mish Swo-da-mish Sin-a-ah-mish	North end Whidby's island	–	–	–	300	Estimate
Samish	Samish river and Bellingham bay	–	–	–	150	
Nook-sank	South fork of Lummi river	–	–	–	450	
Lum-mi	Lummi river and peninsula	–	–	–	450	
Skim-i-ah-moo	Between Lummi Point and Fraser's river	–	–	–	250	
Total					7,559	

FORM OF CENSUS RETURN. -- GENERAL INSTRUCTIONS, [436]

The census should be taken every year at the time when the Indians are most collected together. The easiest method of obtaining it, and liable to least chance of confounding different tribes, is to employ the chief or head man to count by tallies of sticks. Special pains should be taken to ascertain correctly the number of bands into which each tribe is divided, and the names of the petty as well as the principal chief. Any other statistical details may be stated under the head of general remarks.

The report must be forwarded to the superintendent, with the estimates of the agency for the service of the ensuing year.

Census of _____ band belonging to the _____ tribe of Indians, living at _____,in Washington Territory, taken _____ 185 , by _____, agent,

Names of bands and tribes	Names of chiefs and sub-chiefs	Principal residence	Men	Women	Boys	Girls	Slaves	TOTAL	Canoes	Horses	Cattle	Bushels of potatoes	Remarks

INDIANS TRIBES of WASHINGTON TERRITORY by George Gibbs, LLD

originally published in the Reports of Explorations and Surveys to Ascertain **United States Geographical and Geological Survey of the Rocky Mountain Region** Washington, 1855.

OLYMPIA, WASHINGTON TERRITORY
March 4, 1854.

SIR: Herewith I have the honor to submit my report upon the subject of the Indian inhabitants of Washington Territory; and to be,

Very respectfully,

GEORGE GIBBS

Capt GEORGE B MCCLELLAN,
Commanding Western Division NP Railroad Exploration

PLACE NAMES

Method of Pronunciation

a	as a in "father" except that at the end of a word it has the same sound as in peninsula
aā	as a in the word "mass"
eh	as a in "mate"
e	unaccented as in e in "merry" "when"
i	as e short, or as i in "magnitude"
ai	has the prolonged sound of i as in the Spanish "pais"
u	has the sound of oo unless followed by a consonant when it is sounded as in "fun" "hut" etc
ew	as u in the word "puke"
y	as in English "my" etc before a vowel it becomes a consonant as in "you"
ay	as in "may"
ow	as in "how"
au	as in "maul"
aii	like the sound of ahw or aāw
ch	before a vowel as in "church" at the end of a syllable or word it gives the guttural sound of the gaelic as in "loch" or of the German unless preceded by t when it takes the hard sound as in "scratch" {č}
gh	at the end of a syllable is also guttural
j ~ jh	as in jail
g	as in give
s'	followed by an apostrophe signifies a simple sibilant very common before other consonants, particularly h & k as or example "s'huts kus"
h'	followed as in the preceding case by an apostrophe denotes an aspirate not guttural,, as in the word "hah'tl" "s'hah'tl"
tkl ~ tlk ~ tl	represent the peculiar clucking of the gutturals
z	as in the English "gaze"

the letters r f v are wanting. b and m are used indiscriminately, also d and n. By the Kwantlen's d is changed into l, as also n. [p2]

Nomenclature

Bellingham Bay and Gulf of Georgia

what com[152]	the outlet of the lake
squod li cum	small creek at Ind[ian] village
klik a toh nud	prairie at Military Station
chah choo sen	island in delta of Lummi River
swul leh sen	portage to straits above Pt Francis
seh liss	Point Francis
keh mook oom	outer bend of *do* [ditto, same "]
whn cht lan	under the bluff on Hale's Passage
tom whik sen	Ind[ian] village
taā la pie	white man's house above it
mah mo lie	a little above
maā chan ilp	lower mouth of Lummi
skul hah nutl	upper *do* [ditto] "
sut eh nus	bight inside Sandy Point
slai uks	Sandy Point
tuts e nuts	beach above the point
tul tul o	}
kwulch tun nus	} various points on the shore
hoo tchich hum	}
hul lech tan	point below Whitehome, rocks off is[land]
whee ess en itch	bight above the last
whul kwāan	indentation just south of Whitehome
now uk sen	Point Whitehome
tsau wuch	Birch Bay
tsult laāltch	within Pt Whitehome
shkwaām	small creek on SE side of bay

---

[152] Nasals {m n ŋ} indicate Straits Coast Salish languages. *jm*

Appendices ~ Place Names

klun kun nup	locality East of last
tut kum aā la	creek in Birch Bay
shka ahl	}
ma lach han	} other localities in the bay
hoi a mit hlaā la	small bight on N side
mook mook kwch kun	west of do " [p3]
kwul luk an	}
hoos chaā kutl	points on shore, above Birch Bay
al aā alum	Stony Point visible from Camp
salleht lus	Ind[ian] vill[age] at upper end of Sand Spit
she litsh ~ tcheh litch	Sand Spit, Simiahmoo Bay
sim i ah moo	Name of the tribe {Semiamhoo}
kluk 'h	brook inside of the bay
kwul lah hoom	creek at head of bay
see es sus	Shaw's Point
tah ta lo	creek at Camp Simiahmoo
pe kahlps	present Indian Camp
kwo ma is	Pt west of camp "slight ocare" Slytscans J SH
too wahk	the Sandy Point inside
no ku meh hil	creek heading in Langley Prairie
tsum tun num	" " " near Fraser R
kwus so wutl	" " " tule swamp
taā na kun	bight inside Pt Roberts
chul tun num	Point fishery
smah kwuts	prairie at Pt Roberts
che was sen	(properly S'cho ah sen) Ind[ian] vill[age] outside?? {Tsawwaussen}

Interior Custer's Route[153]

---

[153] Named for Henry Custer, Swiss topographer on the US Northwest boundary survey team, also AW Custer was first postmaster at this locale. *jm*

Appendices ~ Place Names

sow el loh wuch	pr[airi]e at head of no ku meh hil {Nicomtl}
tsaāts kwai yem	branch of creek at the prairie
tsut laāng	branch where Ind[ian] house is
stul tuch til	fork of Tsutlaāng
ta ang ten	branch at beaver pond
ho hwah kwutl	first branch of Tahtalo
pehl han	potato patch
ahnowutl	little prairie on *do* "
ha pai elt hu	larger " " "
so sai	head of Tahtalo
se es sys	Shaw's Point
tuch tuch hum	first large branch of Kwul lah hoom ~ con lahm
ka lah wul leh	second *do* "
kal kalk ku	first creek running to Nooksaak
she ku mich	second " " "
tsah ming	creek running to Seh ku mich
noo kope	larger fork of *do* "
kwool laām	~~creek~~ fork of the last
kweh sa litsch	first prairie on Nooksaak
kwo las ta meh	second *do* "
mah moo koom	prairie at Skul leh itl house
koh kwoon nes tum	branch of seh ku mich above
set she no wa	branch of kwool laām
ko kwa ahm	an upper branch of Kwool laām
pehp she	[ ]
seet leh whutsh	head of kwool laām
noo ko kwum	small lake at head of 'kwaachem ??
see it leh hu	1st creek running into Soomass
tah ta la o	riv[er] entering Soomass Lake {Sumas lake, drained 1915}
skum mehn	}

165

swah leh whai	} points or localities on the creek, coming in from the west, from the ?? up [3b]
stuk ah niss	} heading in a swamp
ne oh ku nooch tan	} three heads on the last creek
hood maāts	} small house on it
shahs ma koom	the swamp
tsech lehm	small stream from mtn into lake
shwum mut	place of Custer's camp
seetsh tan	high peak ascended?? by him
klaā lum	creek emptying into lake beyond tahtalao
kwud stanss	another *do* "
yuch wun neh ukw	1st small prairie on tahtalao
hoo mah so snelp	2nd *do* "
kwil tel lum un	prairie near Nooksaak
koh yohtl	creek running through it
tum mehw tan	creek entering tahtalao below pr[airi]e
chah a la sum	prairie on head of it
ne see sa ahk	small pr[airi]e at mouth of tum mehw
ne oh ku nooh tan	2nd prairie on *do* "

Fraser River & C[anyon] (Kwantlan Language)

kuk a teh niis	the Cowichan fishery near mouth
keh kait ~ keh kite	the skwaunish *do* "{fishery} south side
cheh tch lus	small creek opposite <added as insert>
kwio kwut lum	stream behind Misskweum [Musquem] village
miss kwe um	small village on the island
keht sie	Pitt R and Lake
hul chahm	buttes at mouth of Lake
chul chul	site of old Ft Langley
kwai e tass ~ kwi e tass	stream opposite *do* "
chil o wheh ying	stream below present Fort

sah na satl	a tributary of Pitt R
skwah lutsh	Ind[ian] vill[age] opposite Fr Langley
silts ahss	the Langley Buttes
sai yah al ten	small stream above Ft L[angley]
hai yuks ~ s'hai yuks	Kwantlen R
kwa ah num	small stream above *do* "
mams hweh	lower Masskwee [Matsqui] R
pook chen nus	fishing villages on island
kwaā chem	Upper Masskwee R
yeht sehm	first branch of *do* "
skow ak sen	Mass kwee Prairie
oke iaā koonw	high point on prairie
me maāk teb	} branches of kwaa chem R
klaht hlo	}
skwah na watl	}
so mo sakw	}
shum a hum set	prairie at camp No 5
skah na	masskwe [Matsqui] vill[age] on Upper pr[air]e
haāt suk	a stream on N side Fraser R, above the Kwaa chum
hul whai elt hu	prairie on Masskweh R
stehtch	} right hand branch *do* " ascending
o weh tum	} right hand branch *do* " ascending
yeech yill	} two below Soomass
tsah mahtl	} two below Soomass [4b]
klatl hwass	a large slough on N side Fraser R
tso ho mass	a stream putting into it
stuch kehn	Soomass mtns [mountains]
kwee ah matsh	stream on N side Nukatsum territory ??
mass li tel la	a creek
hel hul ahss	a mountain
laā how ic	creek & mtn above Soomass flat

Appendices ~ Place Names

ko meh litsh	center hill of the map, mouth of Chik [k] ?? {Chilliwack}
ko mut hoom	mountain on N side Fraser's R
swehl tcha	mountain between Pekosie & the Lake
sehs kul la kun	slough on northern side
skow un nicts	village a mouth of Isehniss } Harrison's R & L {river & lake}
tseh niss	Harrison's river & lake
nuk um men	a small stream running into little lake
steh mwa	higher peak on west do "
kweh kwuch hum	mtn between Harrison's & Fraser's R
kluk tuk sen	the small lake
choo choo waā sen	village at head of rapids
yaalsh tun [ā]	large village on the strait
shu pah peh lum	upper village
s'hah ha	creek from west at upper vill[age]
tsuk wil la	sloping rock on right bank of river
kwah lis	stream at camp no 8 ??
saāt sla	snow peak & creek on lake
sho waātl	small lake on trail to Fraser's R
h'kwai ukw	first island in lake
hwehw kwaā sun	the Persis ?? island
noos kah la	first creek about camp No 9
kt chess ~ kul chess	island, opposite camp 9
hoot sah lo ka litsh	mtn east of the peninsula
sip shum	a stream on west side behind klchess I[sland]
ne huk wutsh	mtn seen up gap of lake fr[om] C[am]p 9
le laā le wutsh	mtn east of lakes seen?? Fr[om] C[am]p No 9
h'tasm a hoom	do west " " " [4c]
nooksh kwum wutl	} creek at camp No 9 on Harrison's L
what hoom	} creek & cascade west of S point Kulchess
shpet kehl	} little I[sland] west side of Lake
shoo up ohls	} creek at place of Musi obs[ervation] N c[am]p [#] 10

168

choo choo wulp	} brook at gravelly flat, W side of Lake
koo what sew	} ″ opposite head of first island
shook shook o meh	} ″ the birch trees" Camp No 10 I[sland]?? three
s'haalt chum [ā]	} the rapids of Harrison's R
shmah lakw	}
shpah pel tum	} creeks putting into W side ?? below s'hah ha
ass hu	} "the seal" {L> ′asx^w =hair seal}

Fraser R continued

tum me a hai	}
la yome sun	} two mountains S of Chiloweguk R
kleht lw keh	"snow peak"
s'yeh yuk	point of rocks at Camp No 11
kech keh shum	creek entering slough above Cp No 11
hach tcha	Pelalthu village on the island
semehn	creek on south opposite it
kwaiss	small lake at its source
keh ka la hum	mtn on Soomass lake S of stuch kehn
see ah la	Camp No 12 on island
kum kweh niis	mtn opposite it
skah met shin	high mtn between Harrison's & L Francis
skah ka enet shin	village on opposite Island
kwa lee ta kum	village on the slough under the mtn
she am a wis	island below, coming out of trail fr[om] lake
shweh lits	village opposite
show hah mil	mountain over it
hwa leht	village / on island / at place of ?? kur obsn [observation] Mch 21st
shnah se la	exit of trail from the lake
ka hahl 'hs	high peak below the trail behind hill
yuk kwah la wun	stream moving into slough from trail [4d]
see sa sum	creek on N side

skwah wahl kum	high bluff mtn above L before it
skow aāl hu	Ind[ian] vill[age] next above that of mtn?? observ
ko kweh niss	a stream on South side
stet hwaā sum	very precipitous mtn over it
se shehk	high mtn on south side
~~ks kweh~~ ~ wa hus sum	Camp No 13
keh ka al	mtn opposite Camp 13
ts'kah lis	site of Ft Hope
wool kum mech	hill on island of camp 14
ai h'yew	" " " opposite
kleh kwun nuw	stream below Ft Hope
nuk a lah woom	snow mtn in gap of *do*
koomt seh niss	mtn behind Ft Hope
ste teh mia	mtn on S side up & below Ft H[ope]
slept h'yel luk	" " " kusikwunnum
kwee kwee ah len	stream fr[om] south above Ft
hooks hah sum	branch of Nooksahk
noo teh a kwoom	" " "
noo whai yum	south f[or]k Nooksahk
ko la wheh	north " " "
te ko meh	Mt Baker
smamt lek	mtn between Chiloweyuck & Nooksahk
ee shal tul luk	mtn in gap of kwee kwee ah len
kleh lah woom	East frk of " " also a mtn & lakes of the same name
skehm	small creek ~~on left~~ near C[am]p Mch 28[th] behind Pt of rocks
kwee ach	snow mtn between Ft Hope & Yale S riv
kwāat se tose [ā]	{ park of same name
whee ah koom	{
klehs kum kum sum	knob on NW end of koomt seh niss
ktitl tah lits	Ind[ian] vill[age] at mouth of kwu kwe ah la [p5]

Fraser R continued

s'haht la koom	rapid stream fr[om] west Mch [March] 26[th]
tsim e kwehm	hill below Ft Yale
hwah hu lalp	at the Ft
che wehlp	above the creek & the creek
sche inn	last Ind[ian] vill[age] on right b[an]k below falls
me tul la	Ind[ian] house opposite chewehlp
s'hen niss	mtn on right bank above Ft
hut lalh	" " " in center ?? of gap
kl patl	" " " on left bank
lahs kotes	a mtn seen down the river, also from lake
shoot leht luts	small stream from north riv (April 1)
skwaala [ā]	a prairie on it
ten eh scii	"leaning mountain" S of Chiloweyuck
smehm ku	} a range of snow mts east of kleht la keh {visible fr mouth of Fraser's R
mam ook wum	large prairie between Soomass & chilow[k]
skwo aā litsh	"signal peak" <added at end> [p6]

Adopted Spelling of the *Names of Camps* Etc (Official)

man sel pan ik	creek heading with Chuchehum
kle sil kwu	" " " klehkwunum
wai haist	mtn on upper Skagit
shah wa tum	" " " Skagit
ne po pe eh kum	creek, branch of *do* "
che cheet hu	Skagit cache
ho zo meen	mt near Camp Skagit
chu chu wan ten	creek of Haig's camp
skwai kwi eht	mt at head of *do* "
pa say ten	creek of Harris camp
yakl to le min	mouth of Pasayten

171

nais nio loh	south fork Similkameen
si mil ka meen	{Similkameen}
okin a kane	{Okanogan, Okanagan}
tcho pahk	mt back of C[am]p Similkameen
haip wil	the lake " " "
o so yoos	
sah lilt kwu	the forks
te kum whehl tin	Archer's (Camp of Oct 9th)
se hai yak kan	Camp of Oct 10th
se hai uks	the creek
twai yeep	upper forks of Ne hoi al pit kwu
ne hoi al pit kwu	} [7b]
in chu in tum	}
stat a poos tin	}
en chahm	} lakes below Statapoostin
sin pail hu	creek running south to Columbia R [Sanpoil]
show yet pi	Kettle Falls
stle kehm	Mill Creek
pep tah shin	creek at Depot
chow a wee za	Fool's prairie
an i aht wha	kamass
che laws kan	Little Pend Oreille
chem a kane	Walkers prairie & creek
kai seet lin	crossing of Spokane [crofsing]
kal is pelm	Pend Oreille Lake
yome tsin	White Sheep Creek
en kwool ch la	mouth of Clark's Fork

NW Boundary Com Jno G Parke
Colville Depot W T chief act & sec
Jany 7 1860   [p8]

Appendices ~ Place Names

kit lat laā nook	creek heading east of Mt Wilson, empties into lower [lake]
a kwote katl nam	name of the upper lake
kin nook kleht nan na	creek running east from divide ?? to lake
a kam i na	east fork of kish e nehn ka min na a watushi ??
kish e nehn	
kish ne neh na	
kint la	
a kin is sahtl	Flathead River
a kin kwo nah ki	branch of *do* heading with Tobacco River
kat lak woke	creek running to Flathead through pass
kaisin	a branch of the last
yak in a kahk	name of the pass
ak o no ho	creek running to Kootenay
skits ooh nan na	small creek running to Kootenays above it
ak swak	creek from south at bend of Kootenay
yaks koo nak he	first creek below bend of *do* " from north
ak kaph kleh	Falls of Kootenay
yak took i na	third creek from north
ka yak ka	creek from south below falls, a large lake on it
yakh	
moo yie	
yak kwoo kah keh	} the Chelemta cache
skwoots kose	}
chuk kose	the Mooyie lakes
ha cha atl	Ind[ian] village below Aklew cache
aktlaka	creek above kishenehn [p9]

Adopted Spellings of the *Names of Camps* etc (Official)

Simiahmoo

Sumass

Chiloweyuck

Tummeahai

Chuch che hum

Skagit

Similkameen

Okinakane

Fraser

Nooksahk

Swehl tcha

Pekosie

La yome sin

Sen eh say

En saaw kwatch

COWLITZ

\# 726   George Gibbs to Warbass, Semiahmoo Bay, 7 December 1857, Inquiry concerning Klickitat and Cowlitz Indians.

UG Warbass to Gibbs, Cowlitz Landing, 14 February 1858, Klickitat and Cowlitz terminology, map of Cowlitz river with native place names.

Camp of the North West Boundary Survey
Semiahmoo Bay Dec 7th 1857

Dr Warbass (Direct to Fort Steilacoom)

My Dear Sir
    The question which I am desirous of obtaining answers to are as follows:

The name and location of the Klickatat tribe, on the Cowlitz River. I understand them to be called Ti-tin-a-pam or perhaps that is merely the name of their village? What is the name of the tribe itself, and the Indian name of the Klickatat prairie?
    What is the name of the North fork of the Cowlitz which heads in Mt Rainier – the one which Mr Hurd and your brother Edward called Tilton's River.
    What was the precise location of the Cowlitz tribe – was it at the Hudson's bay farm, or whence used if not what was the Indian name of this farm?
    What did they call the landing?

Can you get Hoh-hoh or some of the rest to make a rough map of the Cowlitz River and give the name & location of the various bands, which formerly occupied its course?

Please get the Indian names of the various Kinds of Salmon, Salmon trout & brook trout, that frequent the river, both in Chinook & Cowlitz, & the Seasons of the year that they arrive, or are abundant.

On the other side you will also find some words which on looking over my Cowlitz vocabulary I find missing. I have written the corresponding ones in Chinook (not Jargon) which may assist in getting the true meanings in Cowlitz. Will you be good enough to fill them up.

Your brother paid us a visit a few days ago and was in good condition. Please give my compliment to Mrs Warbass & believe me,

Very Truly Yours,
George Gibbs [2]

Selish

Cowlitz Landing 14 February 1858
To: George Gibbs, Esq

Dear Sir

I have been unable to comply with your request of December 7th until now, and I hasten to make known the result.

The name of the Klickatat tribe is Ti-tin-a-pam {taidnapam}, the Cowlitz Indians call them Wah-nookts, the Klikatats call their prairie Quailt. They call the Cowlitz River, Te-quil-i-pam-cha-wah; Cha-wash means water, that is the name of the River at this place. They call the River above as far as their possessions extend on the River, Ti-tin-a-pam.

The Cowlitz Indians call the River above the same Ti-tiu-a-pam, and the balance of the way down to Monticello nu-che-lip

The location of the Cowlitz tribe was 2 miles above the Hudson Bay Farms. They call the Farms the same as all prairie land Now-ok. The Nowakum River they call Nulk-tsulk. The name of this place in Cowltiz is Klac-olks. Our little Prairie they call ow-well-kenkh or Paint ellahai {Wawa > *Ilahee* = land} because they procured an herb to make paint of.

They call a Mountain smuck
Large Salmon which run after harvest is qul-a { }
Dog Salmon is called pu-natch, Chinook Salmon running in Summer are called tsow-olt. Middle Size Salmon such as we salt with silver sides are called Sal-a-wah. A large speckled Salmon with stripes or belts around it are called Snoon-ocht. That are very scarce. [3]

All trout are called Tsow-olts

The within information was obtained from Hoh-hoh and Bonaparte Plummond. I could not get them to make a sketch of the Cowlitz River but with their assistance I send a representation in order to give the names of the Branches and places along the River. They know but little of the River about the Klickitat Branch.

The course of the river is not made with any intention of being accurate but merely to obtain points and names. They have names for every prominence or foot of land upon the River but I thought it unimportant. (Any other information I may obtain for you will be done cheerfully – hoping the rough manner in which this is conveyed will prove satisfactory.)

I remain your
abst Srvt
UG Warbass

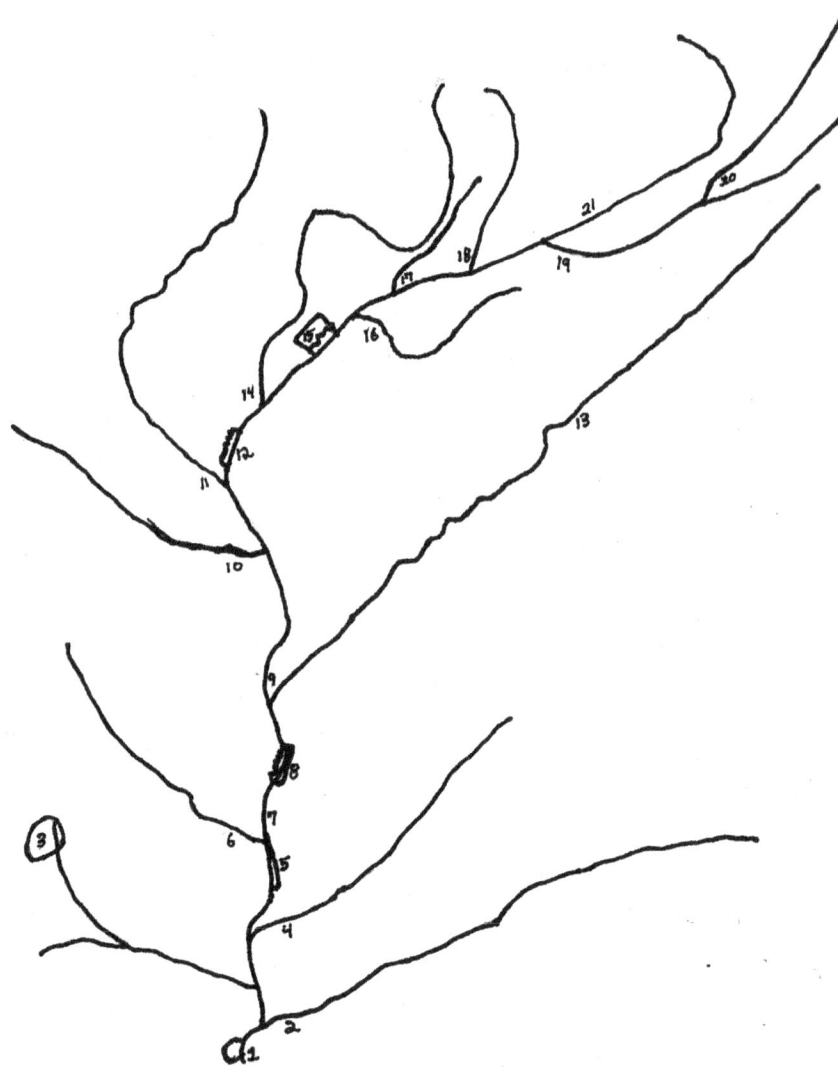

Warbass Map of Cowlitz River

14 Nov 1858

1	now-oo-tsou	Monticello	
2	cowee-men		
3	tsalkh	'lake'	
4	tsop		MJ < t̓u•′s
5	ts-ka-lump	rapids	JH < sá•ʔkilɑmɑx
6	neth-nee		MJ niłhwi′
7	cayles [eagles?]		
8	ne-yam-a-tikh	rapids	JH < wɪya•mtɪx
9	tse-qual-i-sen	forks	

Appendices ~ Place Names

10	cow-mat-tsen		JH < k̇αmαts'ı
11	mock-taults	Mill creek	
12	tun-ta-malk	Grand Rapids	
13	se-a-kt		JH < si•q̇ʷk (Toutle)
14	cla-quil		JH < tαkwαl
15	klac-olts	Cowlitz Landing	
16	ma-tap-p-lw		matə'p
17	che-wap-pow-lik		TA tcawp'
18	sol-cum		MJ sa'lkum
19	scow-wow-woulk		
20	cha-chin		
21	ti-tin-a-pam	river above Landing	

JH = John P Harrington MJ = Melville Jacobs TA = Thelma Adamson

The within information was obtained from Hoh-hoh and Bonaparte Plumondon. I could not get them to make a sketch of the Cowlitz River, but with their assistance I send a representation in order to give the names of the branches and places along the River. They know but little of the River above the Klikatat Prairie.

COWLITZ PLACE NAMES

Yoke*	Costima	Location	Sources*
	ctci'l	Cowltiz River	
qawi'mən		Coweeman R	JH, EC
mansa'la	mansa'la	Kelso	JH
ṫu•'s		Strander Creek?	MJ
cɛ•'q̇ʷkᵘ	ci'q̇ʷk	Toutle R	TA, MDK
niɬhwi'	niɬhwi'	Arkansas? Whittle? Crk	
wi'lapsas		"sturgeon place"	EC? < c'iwq,sƛ̇e?qk̇ʷu
k̇a'matsi	k̇a'matsi	Olequa	JH, EC, TA
ənə'n	< wəx̣kn cz	"horn, antler"	JH,TA,MDK

177

Appendices ~ Place Names

matə′p	matə′ʙ	Salmon Crk	JH,EC,TA,MDK
	tsali′tsalitən	a creek ?	
k̓ʷalsa′lyals		creek 5 mi above Toledo	
pcwa′pcwa		a creek ?	
łəqa′tcq̓ən	łəka′tcq̓ən	"white fir" creek	
suspa′nas		"strawberry place" 2-3 mi below Salkum	
sa′lkum	sa′lkum	Mill creek @ Salkum	
t̓ca′lt̓calc	t̓calt̓ca′lc	Winston creek, below Mayfield	
	tsi′qls		
	tsi•′x̣iwun	Silver Creek	
cqwɛ•′litam	cqwɛ•′litəm	Klickitat Creek	< qʷila = bleed cz
lala′lx̣	lala′lx̣	Tieton R	JH
t̓cqa′łənł		"falls above the farm"	
ala′layac		"place of nettles", prairie opp Mossy Rock	
kwɛ•′lt	qwɛ•′lt	Mossy Rock prairie	EC
tca′luwaik		a valley ?	
iya′nc		"driftwood, log jam"	
nu′cnu		"nose" creek, near Mossy Rock	
cq̓ilq̓i′lt		"skunk cabbages" 1 mi W of Riffe	
cx̣u′mtani	cx̣u′mtani		

* Yoke = Jim   Castima = Lewy to MJ   EC = Edward Curtis   JH = John P Harrington
MDK = Dale Kinkade   MJ = Melville Jacobs   TA = Thelma Adamson

[Route] *Cowlitz to Olympia & Steilacoom*

Newaukum R	nook-tsahl
People of Ford's Prairie	kwai-ai-ilts
Skookum Chuck people	teh-a-woot
Ford's prairie	tahol-shin
Boisfort prairie	chis-le-tah (owhillapsh)

Upper Chehalis R   too-tah-pa

Grand Mound Prairie   klak-ai-aktl

Prairie at Linklater's   te-nal-quet. Te-nal-quuhl

Chambers Prairie   kl-ko-minn

Creek from plains   muck

GRAYS HARBOR –

Rivers, Creeks, Streams, and Features

North Side of Bay

Pt Brown

  Oyhut

  Sampson

North Bay

  Campbell Slough

  Jessie Slough "named for an Indian, who rafted logs on the slough, and whose nickname was 'Humptulips Jesse'" (Hitchman 1985: 137).

Humptulips = xʷəmtulapš < /apš/ 'stream' (Bright 2004: 175)[154]

    Burg Slough

  Gillis Slough

  Chenois Creek = čənus, name of a Lower Chehalis leader (Bright 2004: 93); qi'əsqalʔux (James and Martino 1986: 44)

  Grass Typso Creek [Latin name for cattails]

  James Rock aka Neds Rock, Lone Rock, Point New, Brackenridge Bluff; shoreline there is named = ɬəmim̓ (James and Martino 1986: 44)

Pt. New

Bowerman Basin

Hoquiam = x̌ʷəqʷyamc < x̌ʷəqʷ- 'hungry' + yamc Douglas fir, wood = driftwood 'hungry for wood' (Bright 2004: 173)

Fry Creek chominim (James and Martino 1986: 42; Van Syckle 1982: 370)

---

[154] The angled bracket < means "derived from" *jm*

Cow Pt

Big bluff near Aberdeen = qaysáləbeš, questing site for wealth spirit who gifted sons of chiefs with the song to summon whales to beach themselves

Wishkah = xʷəšqaÍ < xʷəš- stink + qaÍ water = 'stinking water' (Bright 2004: 572). Its epic involves a huge rotting whale dropped by a Thunderbird which lived on nearby Mount Olympus.

South Side of Bay

Pt Chehalis
  South Bay
    Andrews R

Elk River Nushiatska (James and Martino 1986: 40)

Beardslee Slough

Dempsey Creek

Redman Slough

John's River < "Uncle" John Hale land claim, Wilkes called it Dinsmas River (Hitchman 1985: 138); two cabins, burials, prairie above high tides (James and Martino 1986: 39)
    Beaver Creek camas beds (James and Martino 1986: 40)

Stearns Bluff ~ a/k/a Roundtree Point, Judsons Point, Crabapple Point, Jones Point, South Arbor (James and Martino 1986: 39)

O'Leary plankhouse, weir (James and Martino 1986: 39)

Stafford < a settler; Wilkes called it Typha Creek (Hitchman 1985: 267)

Indian

Chapin

Newskah = "good water", with tidal weir nearby (Van Syckle 1982: 370)

Charley

Riverine

Chehalis River mouth from Cow Point to Cosmopolis = nsulapalucn

Chehalis River nsulapš

Cosmopolis = qaysalməs

North Side of River

Elliott Slough
Max Slough
Higgins Slough
Peels Slough
Wynoochee = xʷənuɬč (Bright 2004: 576)
Camp
Sylvia Creek
Satsop = sacapš < /sa'a-/ 'make, do' + /capš/ stream = 'made stream' (Bright 2004: 422)
Newman Creek
Mox Chehalis < Chinuk Wawa 'two, twin, double' + Lower Chehalis 'sand' (Bright 2004: 299)
Porter
Gibson
Shelton
Cedar
Black

South Side of River

Blue Slough
Preachers Slough < 1859 transit of Rev JS Douglass, a Methodist Episcopal minister (Hitchman 1985: 240)
Stevens
Elizabeth
Workman < settler, ~ a/k/a Mason's Creek
Delezine
Eaton
Gaddis

Coastal

Quinault < k̓ʷinayɬ (Bright 2004: 405)
Wreck
Moclips = nəw̓muɬapš > beginning syllable has dropped off (Bright 2004: 292)
Joe
Elk
Boone
Copalis = k̓ʷpils < /-ils/ 'rock' (Bright 2004: 121)
Connor
Oyhut < Chinuk jargon "portage, cross over"

Grays Harbor	Chihalis River	Chihalis Language cn't
Cedar River	chahnitot	
Creek S side just above Cedar	tsh-chol	
Vill[age] ditto	klak-wah-nuhl	
Black R at mouth	Saht-sall	
On N side above Black R	ta-ow-wun	
Mound prairie	kluk-ai-a-kl	
Skukum Chuck Village	the-a-woot-en	
Mouth of Newaukum	noochts-saal	
Tho[ma]s Ford	nich-yeo-nuchtl	
Boisfort Pr[airi]e	tah-lal	} Owillapah
Above the forks	tsa-wah-sen	} villages
Upper Chehalis, above Ford's	noo-so-lup = "rapid water"	
Mt St Helens	she-kwi-ukl	
Mt Rainier	ne-shah-kwi-ukl	
Small prairie on W side R	nah-chal	

Below Ford's, where noises are heard

These native place names express inherent qualities or attributes of these spots, while the English ones rely on the personal names of explorers, first settlers, notables, or nostalgia for places in Europe.

Of all these names, only the Wishkah involves an epic with profound spiritual and religious consequences. Outside of Grays Harbor, Ronald Olson (1936: 17-22) recorded similar names in Quinault territory, showing that the Wishkah epic is consistent with the region.

VOCABULARY

Of 180 {basic} words, which it is desired to collect in the different languages and dialects throughout the Pacific coast, for publication by the Smithsonian Institute of Washington.

The Indian words should be spelled carefully, particular care being taken to divide the syllables according to the sound, and written as legibly as possible. The name of the tribe, the district of country which it occupies, and the number of individuals of which it consists, as near as can be estimated, should be given, with the name and residence of the person by whom it is taken. Any other words may be added, together with further general information. The conjugation of the verb, at least in the present, past and future tenses, would also be very desirable.

Replies may be addressed to Captain GB McClellan, US Engineers, care of the US Quartermaster, Columbia Barracks, Washington Territory, endorsed "official business".

1 man
2 woman
3 boy
4 girl
5 infant
6 father
7 mother
8 husband
9 wife
10 son
11 daughter
12 brother
13 sister
14 Indians~people
15 head
16 hair
17 face
18 forehead
19 ear
20 eye
21 nose

22 mouth
23 tongue
24 teeth
25 beard
26 neck
27 arm								1/
28 hand
29 fingers
30 nails
31 body
32 leg
33 foot
34 toes
35 bone
36 heart
37 blood
38 town~village
39 chief
40 warrior
41 friend
42 house
43 kettle
44 bow
45 arrow
46 axe
47 knife
48 canoe
49 shoes
50 pipe
51 tobacco
52 sky

53 sun
54 moon
55 star
56 day
57 night
58 light adj
59 dark adj
60 morning
61 evening /3
62 spring
63 summer
64 autumn
65 winter
66 wind
67 thunder
68 lightning
69 rain
70 snow
71 hail
72 fire
73 water
74 ice
75 earth~land
76 sea
77 river
78 lake
79 valley/prairie
80 hill~mt
81 island
82 stone
83 salt

84 iron
85 tree
86 wood
87 leaf
88 bark
89 grass
90 pine (fir)
91 flesh~meat
92 dog
93 buffalo
94 bear
95 wolf /4
96 deer
97 elk
98 beaver
99 tortoise
100 fly
101 mosquito
102 snake
103 bird
104 egg
105 feather
106 wings
107 duck (mallard)
108 pigeon
109 fish
110 salmon
111 sturgeon
112 name
113 affection
114 white

*116 black

115 red

117 blue

118 yellow

119 green

120 great

121 small

122 strong

123 old

124 young

125 good

126 bad

127 handsome

128 ugly

129 alive /6

130 dead

131 cold

132 warm

133 I

134 Thou

135 He

136 We

137 Ye

138 They

139 This

140 That

141 All

142 Many~much

143 Who

144 Near

145 To-day

146 Yesterday
147 To-morrow
148 Yes
149 No
150 One
151 2
152 3
153 4
154 5
155 6
156 7
157 8
158 9
159 10
160 11
161 12
162 20
163 30
164 100
165 1000
166 I/To Eat
167 I/To drink
168 I/To run
169 I/To dance
170 I/To sing
171 I/To sleep
172 I/To speak
173 I/To see
174 I/To love
175 I/To kill
176 I/To sit

177 I/To stand
178 I/To go
179 I/To come
180 I/To walk

APS/Gibbs 180 word list {*116 out of order}

Following dictionary extracts are each arranged in three lines, 1ˢᵗ = modern spelling, 2ⁿᵈ = Gibbs original entry, 3ʳᵈ = parsed etymology into units of meaning {morphemes} and grammatical aspects.

ARTIFACTS & TOOLS

Analysis and updated spellings
by Zalmai Zahir, University of Oregon

{ʔáakʷal *wattles, lattice of a fish weir* }:
    A'-a-kwul, *the lattices of a fish weir*
        {ʔáakʷal *wattles* (Ballard 1957)

{ʔálʔal *house* }
    A'-lal, *a house*
        {ʔálʔal *'house', 'home'*}.

{sxʷʔáx̌ʷad *basket* }:
    swa'-hwɑd , *a bag*
        {sxʷʔáx̌ʷad *'basket'* < sxʷ- (pervasive) + ʔáx̌ʷad (root √)}.

{ʔəʔútx̌s *Nootka style canoe* }:
    O-ōt-hus, *a canoe* (Makah pattern)
        {ʔəʔútx̌s *'Nootka style canoe (also called Chinook canoe and family canoe)'*}.

{ʔəxʷádᶻad *drag net*}:
    Akh-hwɑd'-zad, *a seine, net*
        {ʔəxʷádᶻad *'drag net'* }.

{ʔíčəb *blanketed, clothed, covered* }:
    As sit'-sum, *clothed, dressed*
        {ʔəsʔíčəm[155] *'someone is wearing a blanket', 'someone is covered or clothed'*
        < ʔəs- (stative) + ʔíčəm/ʔíčəb (root) *blanketed, clothed, covered*}.

{ʔúlal *cattail, Typha latifolia* }:
    O-lal, *the cat-tail rush*
        {ʔúlal *'cattail', 'Typha latifolia'*}.

{ʔúləx̌ *gather* }:
    So-lɑkh, so-lukh, *the smaller sizes of dentalium shells*
        {sʔúləx̌ *'dentalium'*} < s- (nominalizer) + ʔúləx̌ (root) *gather*}.
    so-lukh-ti slug-wa'-di, *pendants of dentalium shells* (so-lukh, *dentalium*)

---

[155] Classic Lushootseed, with M.

{sʔúləx̌ ti sx̌ʼəgʷádiʔ *'the earrings are dentalium'* < s- (nominalizer) + ʔúləx̌ (root) *gather* s- (nominalizer) + x̌ʼəgʷ (root (variant) *stitch; make cattail mat(s) with needle* + -adiʔ (lexical suffix for) *Ear, side of head; side*}.

{sbəkʷ *ball, small wooden ball for shinny game* }:

    S'bo-kwɑlts, *fine or small shot*

        {sbəkʷalc *'shot for rifle~gun'* < s- (nominalizer) + bəkʷ (root) + -alc (lexical suffix for) *cylindrical object*}.

{caq̓ *spear, jab* }:

    Ut-satsk', *to spear or pierce*

        {ʔucácq̓/ʔucícq̓ *'act of spearing big game on saltwater'* < ʔu- (stative) + ca-/ci- (reduplication) + c(a)q̓ (root) *spear, jab*}.

    Tsa'-kad, *to spear, pierce, stab*

        {cáq̓ad *'spear or jab something'* < caq̓ (root) *spear, jab* + -a- (infix) + -d (transitive)}.

{cil *bear up, support from beneath, place on or in a receptacle* }:

    Hut-se'-lup-id, *a saddle*

        {*xʷcíləpəd *'saddle'* < xʷ- (pervasive) + cil (root) *bear up, support from beneath, place on or in a receptacle; dish up* + -ap/-əp (lexical suffix for) *bottom, base, buttocks* + -ə- (infix) + -d (transitive)}.

{ciq *poke, jab* }:

    T'hut-se'-uk-ud, *a ramrod*

        {txʷcíqəd *'ramrod'* < txʷ- (pervasive) + ciq (root) *poke, jab* + -ə- (infix) + -d (transitive)}.

{čácus *archery bow* }:

    Saus, sa'-sʊs, *a wooden bow*

    S't-sa'-sʊs, tsa'-tsʊts, *a bow*

    Tsa'-tsʊts, st-sa'-sʊs, *a bow*

        {čácus *'archery bow'*}.

        {sčácus *archery 'bow'* < s- (nominalizer) + čácus (root)}.

{čakʷ *wash* }:

    Tsa-gwut, tsɑkw-tsakw, *to wash clothes*

    Tsɑkw-tsɑkw, tsa'-gwut, *to wash clothes*

        {čágʷad *'wash something'* < čagʷ/čakʷ (root) *wash* + -a- (infix) + -d (transitive). čakʷčakʷ *'wash clothes', 'wash'* < čakʷ- (reduplication) + čakʷ (root) *wash*}.

    Huts-go-sud, *soap*

{xʷč̓(a)gʷúsəb *'soap'* < xʷ- (pervasive) + č̓(a)gʷ/č̓akʷ (root) *wash* + -us (lexical suffix for) *face, head, upper part* + -əb (reflexive)}.

Tut-sa'-gwus-sub, *to wash the face*
{dxʷč̓agʷusəb *'wash own face'* < dxʷ- (pervasive) + č̓agʷ/č̓akʷ (root) *wash* + -us (lexical suffix for) *face* + -əb *reflexive*}.

Tuts-a'-gwo-litsh, *to wash dishes*
{dxʷč̓agʷulč *'wash dishes'* < dxʷ- (pervasive) + č̓agʷ/č̓akʷ (root) *wash* + -ulč (lexical suffix for) *container*}.

{c̓əs *peck, nail, drive into wood*}:

Ot-sus'-sud, *to drive nails*
{ʔuc̓ə́səd *'someone nailed it'*, *'someone/something pecked at it'*, *'he nailed it'*, *'she is nailing it'*, *'it pecked at it'* < ʔu- (stative) + c̓əs (root) *nail, peck* + -ə- (infix) + -d (transitive)}.

Ot-salt-hu, *to hammer, to pound*
{*ʔuc̓(ə)sál̓ʔtxʷ *'someone hammered on the house'* < ʔu- (stative) + c̓ə́s (root) *peck, nail, drive into wood* + -al̓ʔtxʷ (lexical suffix for) *house, building*}.

Sukh-w't-s'halt'-hu, *a hammer*
{*səxʷc̓(ə)sál̓ʔtxʷ *'hammer'*, *'by means of nailing a house/building (literal)'* < səxʷ- (lexical prefix for) *by means of* + c̓əs (root) *peck, nail, drive into wood* + -al̓ʔtxʷ (lexical suffix for) *house, building*}.

Sus-el-tud, *a stone adze*
{*c̓əsəltəd *'stone adze'* < c̓əs (root) *peck, nail, drive into wood* + -əl- *on, at, in, by* + -təd (lexical suffix for) *implement for*}.

Tsus-tud, *a nail (for boards)*
{c̓ə́stəd *'a nail'* < c̓əs (root) *peck, nail* (verb) + -təd (lexical suffix for) *implement for*}.

{č̓ə́bəʔ *carry on back, backpack*}:

O cho'-ba, as-chu-ba, *to carry*

As-chub-ba, *to bring wood and water. wait on (?)*

As-chub'-ba, *to carry*
{ʔuč̓ə́bəʔ{156} *'something was being carried on someone's back'* < ʔu- (stative) + č̓ə́bəʔ (root) *carry on back, backpack*.
   {ʔəsč̓ə́bəʔ *'something is carried on someone's back'* < ʔəs- (stative) + č̓ə́bəʔ (root) *carry on back*}.

{čəƛ̓áq *'rough mat in cedar-bark checker work'*}:

Chit-lak, es-chɑt, *a bark mat*
{čəƛ̓áq *'rough mat in cedar-bark checker work'*.

{156} If the word is ʔučúbəʔ rather than ʔučəbəʔ, then this would mean *someone or something is going/gone landward away from the water*. zz

ʔəsčaat *'fine mat of inner bark of cedar, from British Columbia'* (Waterman 1973: 28, 29)}.

{sčádiʔ *small fish hook* (Zahir~McCleary: MS)}:
    S'cha'-de, *a wooden fish-hook*
        {sčádiʔ *'small fish hook'* < s- (**nominalizer**) + čadiʔ (**root**)}.

{sčádᶻəb *skirt, cedar bark skirt*}:
    S'chɑd zub, *a woman's fringed petticoat*
        {sčádᶻəb *'skirt'*, *'cedar bark skirt'* < s- (**nominalizer**) + čadᶻəb (**root**)}.

{čaxʷ *club, hit with a stick, whip*}:
    O-cha'-hwud-sid, *to whip*
        {ʔučáxʷad *'someone whipped/is whipping someone/something'*, *'someone clubbed/is clubbing someone/something'* < ʔu- (**stative**) + čaxʷ (**root**) *whip, club* + -a- (**infix**) + -d (**transitive**)}.
    Cha'-wa-tub, cha'-hwut, *to cut, to chop*
        {čáxʷatəb *'someone club someone'*, *'he whip something/someone'* < čaxʷ (**root**) *club, hit with stick* + -a- (**infix**) + -təb (**third person**).
        čáxʷad *'club'*, *'hit with a stick'*, *'he whip someone/something'* < čaxʷ (**root**) *club, hit with a stick* + -a- (**infix**) + -d (**transitive**)}.
    O-tla'-hwud-dab, *to drum, to pound with sticks*
        {ʔučáxʷadəb *'someone pounded something'*, *'someone was drumming'*, *'someone is drumming'*, *'he is drumming'*, *'she is pounding something'* < ʔu- (**stative**) + čaxʷ (**root**) *club, whip* + -a- (**infix**) + -d (**transitive**) + -əb (**experiencer and middle voice**)}.
    Hu-cha'-hwo-pud, *a whip*
        {xʷčáxʷapəd *'whip'*, *'something to whip someone on the buttocks* (literal)*'* < xʷ- *that which* + čaxʷ (**root**) *whip, club* + -ap (**lexical suffix for**) *buttocks*}.

{čəlp *twist, turn sprain*}:
    As-chulp, *twisted*
        {ʔəsčəlp *'it is twisted'*, *'it is turned'*; *'it is sprained'* < ʔəs- (**stative**) + čəlp (**root**) *twist, turn; sprain*}.
    ikh-hwu-chulp, *twisted*
        {ʔəxʷčəlp *'kind of twisted/turned/sprained'* < ʔəxʷ- + čəlp (**root**) *twist, turn*},
    Chelp'-lin, *a gimlet*
        {*čəlptən *'gimlet'*, *'an implement for twisting'* < čəlp (**root**) *twist, turn, sprain* + -tən/-təd (**lexical suffix for**) *implement for*}.
    Chul-put-tud, *to bore (as with a gimlet)*
        {*čəlpətəb *'someone bore something* < čəlp (**root**) *twist, turn; sprain* + -ə- (**infix**) + -təb (**third person**)}.

Hu-chil-pe'-gwud, *a gun-screw*
> {*xʷčə́lpigʷəd *'gun-screw'*, *'something to turn inside of something especially a small tight area'*; *'emotions are upset'*, *'you're all upset '* < xʷ- *that which* + čəlp (root) *turn, twist, sprain* + -igʷəd **(lexical suffix for)** *inside small, tight-fitting area; inside human or animal body, the insides; mental processes; side of body*}.

Tu-chul-pud, *to twist, bore as with a gimlet*
> {dxʷčə́lpəd *'something that has been caused to be twisted'* < dxʷ- **(pervasive)** + čəlp **(root)** *twist, turn, sprain* + -ə- **(infix)** + -d **(transitive)**}.

{čə́x̌əʔ *rock, boulder, stone* }:
> Chet'-la, *a rock or stone*
> > {čə́x̌əʔ *'rock'*, *'boulder'*}. (* Name of Gibb's Donation Land Claim)
>
> Chet-la hōltsh, *an iron pot*
> > {čə́x̌əʔulč *'iron pot "* < čə́x̌əʔ **(root)** *rock, boulder* + -ulč **(lexical suffix for)** *container*}.

{čə́šayʔ *salmon spear*}:
> Chish ai', *a fishing pole*
> > {čə́šayʔ *'salmon spear'*}.

{čə́wayʔ *Shell* }:
> Chau ai, *shells*
> > {čə́wayʔ *'shell'*}.

{sčič *mussel* }:
> S'chĕts, *the blue mussel*
> > {sčič *'mussel'* < s- **(nominalizer)** + čič **(root)**}.
>
> As-chitsh, *studded with brass nails*
> > {**Possibly** ʔəsčič < ʔəs- **(stative)** + či- **(reduplication)** +čič **(root)**. Possibly ʔəsčič < čič *it sticks on, goes on* (DK: p. 41)}.

{dəkʷ~dəgʷ *inside something relatively small, inside something confining* }:
> Dekhw, de-ukh, *in, within*
> > {dəkʷ *'inside something relatively small'*, *'inside something confining'*}.
>
> As-dɛkhw', as-dukhw', *in, within*
>
> As-dɛkhw', as-dukhw, *within*
>
> Us-de'-ʊkh, *in*
> > {ʔəsdə́kʷ *'something is inside of something'* < ʔəs- **(stative)** + dəkʷ **(root)** *inside something confining*}.
>
> O-dug-wus, *to put into (as into a bowl)*

{ʔudə́gʷəš *'someone put something into something'* < ʔu- (**stative**) + dəgʷ (**root**) *inside something relatively small, inside something confining* + -ə- (**infix**) + -š (**transitive**)}.

tʊkh-dug-wush, *loaded gun*
{dxʷdə́gʷəš *put something inside of something* < dxʷ- (**pervasive**) + dəgʷ (**root**) *inside something relatively small, inside something confining* + -ə- (**infix**) + -š (**transitive**)}

Na'-gwa-bet, *an echo*
{nə́gʷbid[157] *'in between'* < nəgʷ (**root**) *inside something relatively small, inside something confining* + -b- (**experiencer and middle voice**) + -i- (**infix**) + -d (**transitive**)}.

Dug-kus-sed, *to hook or fasten (as a dress)*
{də́gʷqsəd *'fasten hook and eye'* < dəgʷ (**root**) *inside something relatively small or confining* + -qs (**lexical suffix for**) *point, nose* + -ə- (**infix**) + -d (**transitive**)}.

T'hud-duk-shid, *to bend (as a bow)*
{Possibly *dxʷdə́kʷšəd *'put* < dxʷ- (**pervasive**) + dəkʷ (**root**) *inside something confining* + -šəd (**lexical suffix for**) *foot, lower leg*}.

{duukʷ *iron, knife* }:

Snokw, *iron, a knife*
{snuukʷ[64] *'iron', 'knife'* < s- (**nominalizer**) + nuukʷ (**root**)}.

No-kwɛd, *an iron arrow-head*
{núu(kʷ)qʷid[158] *'iron arrow head'* (Daniels Metcalf Zahir: *Mink* MS) < nuukʷ/duukʷ (**root**) *iron, knife* + -qʷid (**lexical suffix for**) *head; top, summit*}.

sno-do-kwɑl'-li, *sheath*
{snudúukʷali *'sheath for a knife'*, < s- (**nominalizer**) + nu-/du- (**reduplication**) + nuukʷ/duukʷ (**root**) *iron, knife* + -ali (**lexical suffix for**) *place of*}.

{dᶻakʷ *rock, shake* }:

Dza'-a-gwut, *to rock (as a cradle)*
{dᶻágʷəd *'rock it', 'shake it'* < dᶻagʷ/dᶻakʷ (**root**) *rock, shake* + -ə- (**infix**) + -d (**transitive**)}.

Od-za'-kwut, *to quiver, rock, "teeter."*
{ʔudᶻákʷad *'someone is shaking/rocking something'* < ʔu- (**stative**) + dᶻakʷ (**root**) *shake, rock* + -a- (**infix**) + -d (**transitive**)}.

dzɑkw'-ted'-ĕtl, *The cradle-stick, to which it is hung* (Snoh.)

---

[157] The use of "N" in place of "D" in combination with "B" and "D" indicates that the word is in transition between prior classic and post contact Lushootseed. zz

[158] Classic Lushootseed, with N.

{dᶻakʷtədiʔɬ 'cradle stick', 'rocker' < dᶻakʷ (root) *rock, shake*+ -təd (lexical suffix for) *implement for* + -iʔɬ (lexical suffix for) *infant, child* }

Dzud-duk-ted-ɛd, *the cradle-stick or rocker*
{dᶻədᶻákʷtədiʔɬ 'cradle stick', 'rocker' < dᶻə- (reduplication) dᶻakʷ (root) *rock, shake*+ -təd (lexical suffix for) *implement for* + -iʔɬ (lexical suffix for) *infant, child*}.

{dᶻəq̓, *grind, sharpen* }:
Dzuk-kud, dzɑ kad, *the sound of whetting on a stone*
{dᶻə́q̓əd 'grind it', 'sharpen it' < dᶻəq̓ (root) *grind, sharpen* + -ə- (infix) + -d (transitive)}.

Od-zuk'-kud, *to whet (as a knife on a stone)*
{ʔudᶻə́q̓əd 'someone ground/sharpened something' > ʔu- (stative) + dᶻəq̓ *ground, sharpen*+ -ə- (infix) + -d (transitive)}.

{dᶻúləq̓ *spindle whorl* }:
Dzo'-lak, *a distaff*
{dᶻúləq̓ 'spindle whorl'}.

{gəx̌ *loosen, bail out (of jail); unraveled, untie* }:
Gukh-had, gukh-hɛd, *unstrung (as a bow), untied, loose*
O-ghɑt, *to unstring, untie*
{gə́x̌əd 'loosen it', 'untie it' < gəx̌ (root) *loosen, bail out (of jail); unraveled, untie* + -ə- (infix) + -d (transitive)}.

{gʷal *capsize* }: [also world transformation, begin a new era ~ age]
O-gwɑl', *to upset*
{ʔugʷál 'it capsized' < ʔu- (stative) + gʷal (root) *capsize*}.

{gʷə́sub *bark on cattail* }:
Gwus-sōb, *a species of grass, a coarse thread*
{gʷəsub 'bark on cattail'}.
Uk-so'-bus, *small baskets*
{ʔugʷəsúbus 'make a small closely woven basket of cattail' (gʷəsúbus *small closely woven basket of cattail* (Waterman 1973: 9) < ʔu- (stative) + gʷə́sub (root) *bark on cattail* + -us (lexical suffix for) *face, head, upper part*}.

{gʷəx̌ʷ *loose, unraveled* }:
As-gwi-ha'-had, *fringed*
{ʔəsgʷəx̌ʷáx̌ad 'it is fringed'' < ʔəs- (stative) + gʷəx̌ʷ (root) *loose, unraveled* + -ax̌ad (lexical suffix for) *at the side, edge, side appendage*}.

{-gʷiɬ (lexical suffix for) *canoe, boat* }:
> Gwitl (meaning unknown)
>> { -gʷiɬ (lexical suffix for) *canoe, boat, waterway; curved side; narrow passage way*}.

{huʔƛ̣ *large dentalium* }:
> Hōtl, *the larger dentalium shells*
>> {huʔƛ̣ *'large dentalium'*} (Waterman 1973: 78).

{sǰadᶻ *necklace, large kerchief that can be tied about the neck; draped*}:
> As-jʊdsh {As-jɑdsh (see *Neck* in Section II)}, *the neck*
>> {*ʔəsǰádᶻ *'neck, place for a necklace'* < ʔəs- (stative) + ǰadᶻ (root) *necklace, large kerchief that can be tied about the neck; draped*}.

> Jɑd-shib, *a necklace*
>> {ǰádᶻəb ~ sǰádᶻəb *'necklace'* < s- (nominalizer) + ǰadᶻ (root) *necklace, large kerchief that can be tied about the neck; draped* + -əb (experiencer and middle voice)}.

{kaw̓x̌ʷ *tin can* }:
> Kaukh, *tin, tin ware*
>> {kaw̓x̌ʷ *'tin can'*}.

{k̓agʷalxʷ *flax* }:
> Ka-gwɑl'hw, *flax*
>> {k̓agʷalxʷ *'flax'* (Ballard~Zahir, *Plants*, MS)}.

{k̓aw *touch, bump* }:
> Ka-hōs, ka ho' sin, *a club*
>> {*k̓ax̌ús *'club for fish'* < k̓a(w) (root) *touch, bump* + -us (lexical suffix for) *face, surface*.
>> *k̓ax̌úsən *'club for fish'* (see *fishing-gear, seines, nets*) < k̓a(w) (root) *touch, bump* + -us (lexical suffix for) *face, surface* +-ən/-əd (transitive).
>> k̓ax̌ústədad *'club for killing fish made of maple or alder '* (Haeberlin ~ Gunther 1976: 26) < k̓a(w) (root) *touch, bump* + -us (lexical suffix for) *face, surface* +-ən/-əd (transitive) + -ad}.

[k̓əplaš ~ k̓əplač *club*]:
> Kup-lush, *a slung-shot, a loaded stick*
>> {k̓əplaš *'club'* (Zahir~McCleary: MS, Kinkade 1991: 192), k̓əplač *'club'* (Beavert~Zahir 2008: MS)}.

{kʷal *weave* }:
> Kl'-pɑt', *the figures on baskets*

{kʷaləpád *'figures on basket'* (Waterman, 1973. 10) < kʷal (**root**) *weave* + -əp/-ap (**lexical suffix for**) *bottom, base, buttocks* + -ad}.

Kwe-lo'-litsh, *a basket*
{kʷalúlč *'basket'* < kʷal (**root**) *weave* + -ulč (**lexical suffix for**) *container, belly*}.

As-kwɑl'-gwus, *crosswise*
{ʔəskʷálgʷəs *'weave crosswise'* < ʔəs- (**stative**) + kʷal (**root**) *weave* + -gʷəs (**lexical suffix for**) *pair*}.

{kʷəd *take, get, catch* }:

O-kwud-dud, *to take, to catch, to gather*
{ʔukʷə́dəd *'someone took~caught something'*, *'he took it'*, *'she took it'* < ʔu- (**stative**) + kʷəd (**root**) *take, get, catch* + -ə- (**infix**) + -d (**transitive**)}.

Skōd, *a water-bucket*
{skʷəd *'container'*, *'bucket'*; *'something to take'* < s- (**nominalizer**) + kʷəd (**root**) *take, get, catch*}.

O-kwɑd-datsh, *to take back a gift*
{ʔukʷə́dač *'someone took something* (not specific)*'* < ʔu- (**stative**) + kʷəd *take, catch, get, carry in hand* + -ač}.

Kwɛd-i-gwus, *to wrestle*
{kʷədigʷəs *'wrestle'*, *'a pair takes each other'* (**literal**) < kʷəd (**root**) *take, get* + -i- (**infix**) + -gʷəs/-gʷas (**lexical suffix fir**) *pair*}.

Kwid-do-bai'-o-ched, kwud-dub-ba'-lōb, *the handle of anything*
Kwud-dub-ba'-lōb, kwid-do-bai'-o-chid, *the handle of anything*
{*kʷədəbáyučəd *'handle'* < kʷəd *take, get, catch* + -əb (**experiencer and middle voice**) + -ay- (**infix**) + -uč + -ə- (**infix**) + -d (**transitive**).
   kʷə́dəbálap *'straight handle* (as on a dipper, pan or axe)*'* < kʷəd *take, get, catch* + -əb (**experiencer and middle voice**) + -alap}.
   {kʷədubáyučəd, kʷə́dəbálap *'straight handle* (as on a dipper, pan or axe)*'* < kʷəd *take, get, catch;* suf.: -alap}.

Kwid-dats-shuds, *shake hands* (imperative)
{kʷədáčic *'shake my hand* (imperative)*'* < kʷəd (**root**) *take, get, catch* + -ačiʔ (**lexical suffix for**) *hand, lower arm;* -c (**lexical suffix for**) *me~I* (**patient**)}.

O-kwi-dat-chi, o-kwid-dat-shud, *to take the hand, shake hands*
{ʔukʷədáčiʔ *'someone shook hands'*, *'he shook hands'*, *'she shook hands'* < ʔu- (**stative**) + kʷəd (**root**) *take, get, catch* + -ačiʔ (**lexical suffix for**) *hand*.
   ʔukʷədáčid *'someone shook someone's hand'*, *'he shook her hand'*, *'she shook his hand'* < ʔu- (**stative**) + kʷəd (**root**) *take, get, catch* + -ačiʔ (**lexical suffix for**) *hand* + -d (**transitive**)}.

O-ke'-a-kait, *to hold*
{ʔukʷíʔkʷəd *'someone kind of took it'*, *'someone took a little bit'*, *'someone sort of caught it* (a ball)*'*, *'he sort of took it'*; *'someone kind of got it'*; *'she took*

a little bit' < ʔu- (**stative**) + kʷiʔ- (**reduplication**) kʷəd (**root**) *take, catch, hold, carry in hand*}.

Skwe'-a-kwōd, *a water-bucket*
{skʷíʔkʷəd *'a small container or object for taking something'* < s- (**nominalizer**) + kʷíʔ- (**reduplication**) + kʷəd (**root**) *take, get, catch, hold*}.

{kʷuʔt *small cattail mat for sleeping* }:
Kōt, *a mat of flat rushes*
{kʷuʔt *'small cattail mat for sleeping'*}.
Skwe'-gwut, *a mat of the tule rush*
{skʷikʷuʔt *'small mat', 'kind of cattail sleeping mat', 'mat for fisherman's lap while trolling '* (Waterman 1973: 28) < s- (**nominalizer**) + kʷi- (**reduplication**) + kʷuʔt (**root**) *small cattail mat used for sleeping*}.

{ḱʷás *burn body, roast, barbecue* }:
O-kwɑslt, o-hod, *to burn* {ʔuḱʷás *'something was burned~roasted~barbecued', 'it was roasted', 'it was barbecued'* < ʔu- (**stative**) + ḱʷas *burn body, roast, barbecue*. ʔuhúd *'something was burned, it was burned', 'someone got burned', 'he burned', 'she burned'* < ʔu- (**stative**) + hud *fire, burn*}.

{sḱʷásəb *hide, pelt* }:
Skwa'-sub, *the skin of an animal with the hair on*
skwa'-sum, *the skin of an animal with hair on*
{sḱʷásəb *'animal skin', 'hide'* < s- (**nominalizer**) + ḱʷasəb (**root**)}.
{sḱʷásəm *'animal skin', 'hide'* < s- (**nominalizer**) + ḱʷasəm (**root**)}.
Skwa'-se-buts, *a scalp*
{sḱʷásəbəč *'scalp'* < s- (**nominalizer**) + ḱʷásəb (**root**) + -ač/-əč (**lexical suffix for**) *head*}.

{sḱʷíḱʷaac *tule rush* }:
Kwe'-kwɑts, *the tule rush*
{sḱʷíḱʷaac *'tule rush'* < s- (**nominalizer**) + ḱʷíḱʷaac (**root**)}.

{ḱʷilp *root* }:
Kwelp, *roots of trees*
{ḱʷilp *'root'* (Snyder 1968: 192 > sḱʷilp *root*)}.

{laʔb *see, watch, look* }:
He'-lɑb, lɑbt, *see* (imperative)
Labt, la-bid'-tli, he-lɑb, *see! see ye* (imperative)
{hílab *'look* (**imperative**)' < hílaʔ *look* (**imperative**) + -b (**experiencer and middle voice**).

láʔbəd *'see', 'watch', 'look'* < laʔb *see, watch, look* + -ə- (infix) + -d (transitive).

labtxʷ *'someone looks at someone/ something', 'look at it (imperative)'* < laʔb (root) *see, watch, look* + -txʷ (transitive).

láʔbəd ƛi *'you folks look' (imperative)* < laʔb (root) *see, watch, look* + -ə- (infix) + -d (transitive) ƛi *you folks* (imperative)}.

O-la'-bit, *to see, to show*
{ʔuláʔbəd *'someone saw something', 'he saw it', 'she saw him', 'it (an animal) saw her'* < ʔu- (stative) + laʔb (root) *see* + -ə- (infix) + -d (transitive)}.

S'hu-lal'-bus, *a looking-glass*
{sxʷlálbus *'mirror', 'window '* < s- (nominalizer) + xʷ- (pervasive) + la- (reduplication + lʔ(a)b (root) *see, watch* + -us (lexical surface for) *face, surface*}.

{slágʷac *inner bark of red cedar* }:
Sla'-gwuts, *inside bark of thuja*
{slágʷac *'inner bark of red cedar'* < s- (nominalizer) + lagʷac (root)}.

{ləq̓ʷáyʔ *plate, platter* }:
Luk-wai, *a dish or stone or crockery*
{ləq̓ʷáyʔ *'plate', 'platter'*}.

Lil-kwi, *a wooden dish or plate*
{líĺq̓ʷayʔ *'small dish or plate'* < li- (reduplication) + l(ə)q̓ʷayʔ (root) *plate, platter*}.

{ləxʷ *stab, cut up* }:
As-lokh, *split*
{ʔasləxʷ *'something is stabbed, cut up'* < ʔəs- (stative) + ləxʷ (root) *stab, cut up*}.

La-hōd, *to stab*
{ĺəxʷud *'someone stab~cut up something'* < ləxʷ (root) *stab, cut up* + -ə- (infix) + -d (transitive)}.

O-lakh-hwōd, *to strike with a weapon, stab*
{ʔuláxʷud *'someone stabbed someone~something', 'someone cut something up', 'someone is stabbing~cutting someone/something', 'he stabbed him', 'she stabbed it'* < ʔu- (stative) + ləxʷ (root) *stab, cut up* + -u- (infix) + -d (transitive)}.

{ləx̌ *light* }:
Lakh, *light* {ləx̌ *'light'*}.
As-lʊkh, *light*
{ʔəsləx̌ *'it is lit'* < ʔəs- (stative) + ləx̌ (root) *light*}.

A-ti-lα'-hi, te-la'-hi, *presently (in the course of the day)*
A-ti-slαkh'-hel, *to-day, to-night*
> {ʔal ti ləx̌i(l) *'presently'*, *'today'*, *'on this day '* < ʔal *on, at, in* (time or space) ti *this, the* ləx̌ *light* + -il (lexical suffix for) *becoming*.
>> ti ləx̌i(l) *'presently'*, *'today','* this day' < ti *this, the* ləx̌ *light* + -il (lexical suffix for) *becoming*}.
>> ʔal ti sɬáx̌il *'on this night, tonight '* < ʔal *on, at, in* (time or space) + ti *this, the* + ɬax̌ *night*}.

Te-lakh-hi, a-ti-lαkh-hi, *presently, during the day*
Tes-lαkh'-hi, *to-day*
Tu-tel-hi, tel-h'ye, *presently*
> {ti sləx̌i(l) *'this day'*, *'presently'* < ti *this, the* s- (nominalizer) + ləx̌ (root) *light* + -il (lexical suffix for) *becoming*.
>> ... ʔə ti sləx̌i(l) *'presently'*, *'…on this day'*, *'…now days'* < ʔə (determiner) + ti *this, the* < s- (nominalizer) + ləx̌ (root) *light* + -il (lexical suffix for) *becoming*}.

tel'-he, tel-hɛtsh, tel-h'ye, *presently*
> {ti ləx̌i(l) *'presently'*, *'these days'* < ti *this, the* + ləx̌ (root) *light* + -i(l) (lexical suffix for) *becoming*.
>> ti ləx̌ič *'presently'*, *'these days'* < ti *this, the* + ləx̌ (root) *light* + -ič (lexical suffix for) *cover(ing), surface, on top of, over, series of items on a string, string, cord; spine*}.

O-la'-hel, o-la'-hil-lukh, *to dawn*
> {ʔuləx̌il *'it became day'* < ʔu- (stative) + ləx̌ (root) *day, light* + -il (lexical suffix for) *become*.
>> ʔuləx̌iləxʷ *'to become day now'* < ʔu- (stative) + ləx̌ (root) *day, light* + -il (lexical suffix for) *become* + -əxʷ *now*}.

Shla'-hel, sla'-hel, *day*
> {sləx̌il *'day'*, *'light '* < s- (nominalizer) + ləx̌ (root) *light* + -il (lexical suffix for) *become*}.

Le-he'-lel-lʊs, *the morning star*
> {ləx̌ílalus *'morning star'* < ləx̌ *light* + -il (lexical suffix for) *become* + -alus (lexical suffix for) *eye, constellation*}.

Lukh'-shid, *a torch or candle*
> {ləx̌šad *'light'*, *'lamp'*, *'torch'*, *'candle '* < ləx̌ *light* + -šad (lexical suffix for) *foot, foot and shank, leg*}.

{lilwáʔs *sleeping platform* }:
  Hul-lo-a'-sed, hul-wa'-sed, *a bed or bed-place in a lodge*
  Lul-wa'-sed, hul-lo-a'-sed, *a bed, bed-place in a lodge*
> {xʷliɬwaʔsəd *'sleeping platform'*}.

  Le-le'-ye-was, *the constellation Orion*

{*liʔliyiwaʔs *'constellation Orion, little sleeping platform'*, < liʔ- (reduplication) + liyiwaʔs (root (variant of lilwáʔs) sleeping platform}.

{luʔ *hole (in something but not through)* }:

    As-lo, *a hole*

        {ʔəslúʔ *'hole (in something but not through)'* < ʔəs- (stative) + luʔ (root) *hole (in something but not through)*}.

    as'-lo-hul-de', *the ear-holes for rings, &c.* (from as'-lo, *a hole*)

        {ʔəslúʔaldiʔ *'the ears are pierced'* < ʔəs- (stative) + luʔ (root) *hole (in something but not through)* + -adiʔ (lexical suffix for) *ear, side of head; side*},

    as-hwulo'-uks, *the holes for the nose-ornament*

        {*ʔəsxʷlúʔqs *'holes for the nose ornament'* < ʔəs- (stative) + xʷ- (pervasive) + luʔ (root) *hole (in something but not through)* + -qs (lexical suffix for) *nose, point*}

{luẋ *old person, old* }:

    Lōt-lil, *to grow large*

        {lúẋil *become old* < luẋ (root) *old* + -il (lexical suffix for) *become*}.

    Wul-lōt-lil, *a youth, young man*

        {ʔulúẋil *'someone or something getting older'* < ʔu- (stative) + luẋ (root) *old* + -il (lexical suffix for) *become*}.

    Us-hlōt'-lil, *to grow large*

        {ʔəslúẋil *'someone/something is getting older'* < ʔəs- (stative) + luẋ (root) *old* + -il (lexical suffix for) *becoming*}.

    Lo'-lʊtl, *old (of persons)*

        {lúluẋ *very old person, very old* < lu- (duplication) luẋ (root) *old person, old*)}.

    Slo-tlalk-shid, slut-lalk-shid, *the big toe*

        {sluẋalq(s)šəd *'big toe'* < s- (nominalizer) + luẋ (root) *old* + -al- (lexical affix for) *on, at, in* + q(s)šəd (lexical suffix for) *toe*}.

{łáč̕ *extinguish* }:

    O-klatch, *to extinguish, put out (as a candle)*

        {ʔułáč̕ *'(the fire) went out'* < ʔu- (stative) + łač̕ (root) *extinguish*}.

{słágʷid *sleeping mat* }:

    Sla'-gwid, *the under mat or sheet of a bed*

        {słágʷid *'sleeping mat'* < s- (nominalizer) + łágʷid *lay out mats to sleep on*}.

{łə́b *bail or splash something out with a swishing motion* }:

    Kleb'-bud, tsub'-bed, *a spoon*

    Tsub-bɛd, kleb-bud, *a spoon*

{ɬə́bəd *bail or splash something out with a swishing motion*, 'spoon' < ɬəb (root) *bail or splash something out with a swishing motion* + -ə- (infix) + -d (transitive)}.

{*ɬə́b(b)id 'spoon' < ɬəb (root) *bail or splash something out with a swishing motion* + -b- (experiencer and middle voice) + -i- (infix) + -d (transitive).

{ɬə́gʷɬ *leave, leave behind* }:

O-klug-wul, ot-hlug-wutl, *to leave a person or thing intentionally*

Ot-hlug-wutl, o-klug-wutl, *to leave a person or thing intentionally*

{ʔuɬə́gʷil 'someone left', 'he left', 'she left' < ʔu- (stative) + ɬəgʷ(ɬ) (root) *leave, leave behind* + -il (lexical suffix for) *to become*.

ʔuɬə́gʷɬ 'someone left', 'he left', 'she left' < ʔu- (stative) + ɬəgʷɬ (root) *leave, leave behind*}.

Kla'-gwits-ɑb, *to strip one's self*

{ɬágʷič̓əb *take clothes off'* < ɬəgʷ(ɬ) (root) *leave, leave behind* + -ič̓aʔ/-ič̓əʔ (lexical suffix for) *clothes, wear, support from shoulder* + -b (reflexive)}.

As-la'-gwit-sa, *naked*

{ʔəsɬágʷič̓aʔ 'someone is naked', 'someone is without clothes' < ʔəs- (stative) + ɬagʷ(ɬ) (root) *leave, leave behind* + -ič̓aʔ (lexical suffix for) *clothes, cloth, blanket*}.

Hut'-lu-gwul-le'-gwud-dub, *a posthumous child*

{dxʷɬəgʷəlígʷədəb 'posthumous child' < dxʷ- (pervasive) + ɬəgʷ (root) *leave, leave behind* + -əl- (lexical suffix for) *on, at, in* + -igʷəd (lexical suffix for) *inside, inside a human or animal body*}.

{ɬəṗəgʷásəd *fold up* (**as a blanket**) (Kuipers 2002: 59)}:

Ikh-hup'-a-gwa, t'hup-a-gwa'-sud, *to fold up (as a blanket)*

{ɬəṗəgʷásəd *fold up (as a blanket)'* < ɬəṗ *hang folded* + -ə- (infix) + -gʷas (lexical suffix for) *pair*}.

{ɬəq̇ *to one side* }:

tʊtl-ka'-lʊs, *one-eyed*

{*txʷɬ(ə)q̇álus 'one eye' < txʷ- (pervasive) + ɬəq̇ (root) + -alus (lexical suffix for) *eye*}.

tu-t'hluk-a-wai-yʊs, *the "Half-faced," the name of a fabulous being, half dog, half woman*

{*dxʷɬəq̇əwayus 'half faced' < dxʷ- (pervasive) + ɬəq̇ (root) + -ə- (infix) + -way- (infix) + -us (lexical suffix for) *face, cliff*}.

{ɬič̓ *cut* }:

O-kle'-chid, o-klɛts, *to cut*

{ʔuɬíč̓id 'someone cut something', 'someone is cutting something', 'he cut it', 'she cut it' < ʔu- (stative) + ɬič̓ (root) *cut* + -i- (infix) + -d (transitive).

Ancient Tool Names

ʔutɬič 'something was cut', 'it was cut' < ʔu- (stative) + ɬič (root) *cut*}.

Wut-le-chal'-e-kwu, *to cut with scissors*

{ʔutɬičalikʷ *'cut continuatively'* < ʔu- (stative) + ɬič (root) *cut* + -alikʷ (**continuative action**)}.

Sukh-lɛtsh, *a saw*

{səxʷɬič *'saw', 'scissors' (literal)'* < səxʷ- (**lexical prefix for**) *by means of* + ɬič (root) *cut*}.

Kle-chil'-ke-dub, *to cut the hair*

{ɬičalqidəb *'cut own hair'* < ɬič (root) *cut* + -alqid (**lexical suffix for**) *hair* + -əb (**reflexive**)}.

{ɬid *tie* }:

Kle'-did, *tied*

{ɬídid *'tie something'* < ɬid (root) *tie* + -i- (**infix**) + -d (**transitive**)}.

Klɛd'-gwild, klɛd-ted, *a rope*

kled-tid, *thread of spider*

{ɬídgʷild *'tie a canoe/boat'*, < ɬid (root) *tie* + -gʷil (**lexical suffix for**) *canoe, waterway; curved side; narrow passage* + -d (**transitive**).

ɬídtəd *'rope, 'thread'*, < ɬid (root) *tie* + -təd (**lexical suffix for**) *implement for*}.

kle'-datl-datl {ɬídaʔɬəɬ *'rope bridle'* < ɬid (root) *tie* + -aʔɬəɬ (**lexical suffix for**) *parts of mouth*}.

Sle-dal'-shid, st-kwɑl-shid, *the head-band for carrying loads*

{sɬidálšəd *'tumpline'* < s- (**nominalizer**) + ɬid (root) *tie* + -al- (**lexical affix for**) *on, at, in* + -šəd (**lexical suffix for**) *foot*.

sɬ(ə)q̓ʷálšəd *'tumpline'* < s- (**nominalizer**) + ɬ(ə)q̓ʷ (root) *snap a flexible object in two* + -al- (**lexical affix for**) *on, at, in* + -šəd (**lexical suffix for**) *foot*}.

klĕt'-shid, *moccasin-strings*

{ɬídšəd *moccasin strings, shoe strings* < }.

Kle-dɑb, *fishing line*

{ɬidab *'fish* (**verb**)'}.

Kle-dɑp, *halibut-hook*

{ɬidap *'halibut hook', 'trawling'* < ɬid (root) *tie* + -ap (**lexical suffix for**) *bottom, base, buttocks*)}.

{ɬik̓ʷ *hook* (**verb**) }:

Kle-kwɑl'-litsh, *to catch on (as on a thorn)*

{ɬik̓ʷálič *'to catch on* (as on a thorn)' < ɬik̓ʷ (root) *hook* + -alič (**lexical suffix for**) *pack, bundle*}.

Kl-kwɑp-sub-tub, chi-kwup-sub, *to choke, strangle.*

{ɬik̓ʷápcəbtəb *'hook someone around the neck'* < ɬik̓ʷ (root) *hook* + -apcəb (**lexical suffix for**) *throat* + -təb (**third person**).

čikʷápcəb *'someone is choking'* < čikʷ (**root**) *stuff into, caulk; swallow something* + -apcəb (**lexical suffix for**) *throat*}.

Kle-kwud, *an iron fish-hook*
Kli-uk' wud, *a halibut-hook (of wood)*
{ƛ́ikʷ(t)əd *'iron fish hook, gaff'*, < ƛ́ikʷ (**root**) *hook* + –təd (**lexical suffix for**) *implement for, tool*}.

Ut-likhl'-kwu, *to fish with a hook*
{ʔuƛiƛ́kʷ *'sort of hook something'*, *'fish with a hook'* < ʔu- (**stative**) + ƛi- (**reduplication**) + ƛ́ikʷ (**root**) *hook something*}.

As-hu-le'-a-kwɑtl-dutl, *to pull the lip down*
{*ʔəsxʷƛikʷaʔƛdəƛ *'the lip is hooked'* < ʔəs- (**stative**) + xʷ- (**pervasive**) + ƛ́ikʷ (**root**) *hook something* + -aʔƛdəƛ (**lexical suffix for**) *part of mouth*}.

{ƛq̓áli *digging stick* }:

Kl'ka-lid, *a kamas-stick, a stick for digging roots, &c*
{ƛq̓áli *'digging stick'*}.

{ƛ̓ač *cinch* }:

Klat'-sup-pud, *a buckle, belt*
{ƛ̓ačəpəd *'belt'*, *'buckle'* < ƛ̓ač (**root**) *cinch* + -əp/-ap (**lexical suffix for**) *bottom, base, buttocks* + -ə- (**infix**) + -d (**transitive**)}.

{ƛ̓ač *belly* }:

Klatch, *the belly* {ƛ̓ač *'belly'*}.

{ƛ̓akʷ *stitch; make cattail mat* }:

Klɑkw'-tid, *a mat-needle*
{ƛ̓ákʷtəd *'mat needle'* < ƛ̓akʷ (**root**) *stitch; weave a mat with a mat needle* + -təd (**lexical suffix for**) *implement for*}.

Ast-lug-wa'-di, *an ear-pendant*
{ʔəsƛ̓əgʷádiʔ *'someone is wearing an earring'* < ʔəs- (**stative**) + ƛ̓əgʷ (**root (variant)**) *stitch; make cattail mat(s) with needle* + -adiʔ (**lexical suffix for**) *ear, side of head; side*}.

Sklug-wa'-di, slet-lo-a'-di, *earrings*
{sƛ̓əgʷádiʔ *'earrings'* < s- (**nominalizer**) + ƛ̓əgʷ (**root (variant)**) *stitch; make cattail mat(s) with needle* + -adiʔ (**lexical suffix for**) *Ear, side of head; side.*
{* sƛ̓əƛ̓wádiʔ *'ear ornaments of abalone shell'* (Waterman 1973: 78) < s- (**nominalizer**) + ƛ̓əƛ̓w- (**root**) + -adiʔ (**lexical suffix for**) *side; ear, side of head*}.

so-lukh-ti slug-wa'-di, *pendants of dentalium shells* (so-lukh, *dentalium*)
{sʔúləx ti sƛ̓əgʷádiʔ *'the earrings are dentalium'* < s- (**nominalizer**) + ʔúləx (**root**) *gather*   s- (**nominalizer**) + ƛ̓əgʷ (**root (variant)**) *stitch; make cattail mat(s) with needle* + -adiʔ (**lexical suffix for**) *ear, side of head; side*}.

{x̣al² *put away; put on clothing* }:

    O-tlalsh', o-tluls', *to put away, to put on (as a hat)*

        {ʔux̣álš '*someone put something away*', '*he put it away*', '*she put it away*'; '*someone put something on (clothing)*', '*he put it on*', '*she put it on*' < ʔu- (**stative**) + x̣al (**root**) *put away; put on clothing* + -š (**transitive**)}.

{x̣əláyʔ *shovel nose canoe* }:

    Klai, *a shovel nose or burden canoe*

        {x̣əláyʔ '*shovel nose canoe*'}.

{x̣əlíls *prepare rocks for cooking* }:

    Tlul-ɛlts, *cooking with hot stones*

        {x̣əlíls '*prepare rocks for cooking*'}.

{* sx̣əx̣wádiʔ '*ear ornaments of abalone shell*' (Waterman 1973: 78)}:

    slet-lo-a'-de, ***ear-rings or pendants***

        {* sx̣əx̣wádiʔ '*ear ornaments of abalone shell*' < s- (**nominalizer**) + x̣əx̣w- (**root**) + -adiʔ (**lexical suffix for**) *side; ear, side of head*}.

{x̣əp *deep, down, below, beneath* }:

    Klap, *to hide, cache anything*

    Klip, tlip. See "Klep."

    Klep, klip, kle-pa'-buts, *beneath, under*

    Tlip, klip, *under, beneath*

    st'lup, *Deep, sunken*

        {x̣əp '*deep*', '*down*', '*below*', '*beneath*'.

        x̣əpábac '*underneath*', '*beneath*' < x̣əp (**root**) *deep, down, below, beneath* + -abac (**lexical suffix for**) *solid object*}.

        {sx̣əp '*something deep*', '*down*', '*below*', '*beneath*' < s- (**nominalizer**) + x̣əp (**root**) *deep, down, below, beneath*}.

    Skle-pai'-yʊt sid, *the under lip and chin*

        {sx̣əpáyucid '*under lip*', '*under chin*' < s- (**nominalizer**) + x̣əp (**root**) *deep, down, below, beneath* + -ayucid (**lexical suffix for**) *chin, jaw*}.

    St'lup, *deep*

        {sx̣əp '*deep*' < s- (**nominalizer**) + x̣əp (**root**) *deep, beneath*}.

    Kletl-pikw, *a woman's dress (modern)*

        {*x̣ix̣(ə)pikʷ '*undershirt*', '*petticoat*' (McCleary~Zahir: MS) > łáday=ikʷ *woman's garment*) < x̣i- (**reduplication**) + x̣əp (**root**) *deep, down, below, beneath* + -ikʷ}.

{x̣ič *tattoo* (**verb**) (Snyder 1968: 179)}:

    Sklel-litsh, *tattooing*

{sƛ̓ič *'tattoo'* < s- (**nominalizer**) + ƛ̓ič (**root**) *tattoo* (**verb**)}.

As-tletl, *tattooed*

{ʔəsƛ̓íč *'someone is tattooed'* < ʔəs- (**stative**) + ƛ̓ič (**root**) *tattoo*}.

{ƛ̓iq *emerge, take something out, come out of hiding, emerge from thick brush, come out of water* }:

Pet'-lo-ki, *the spring*

{pədƛ̓iqi(l) *'spring (time)'* < pəd- (**lexical prefix for**) *time of* + ƛ̓iq (**root**) *'emerge'*, *'take something out'*; *'come out of hiding'*, *'emerge from thick brush'*, *'come out of the water'* + -i(l) (**lexical suffix for**) *become*}.

{ƛ̓uč *pull together, bunch up; tie, knot, wrap up package* }:

Ot-tlots, *a knot, a tangle*

{ʔuƛ̓úč *'something was tied'*, *'it was tied'*, *'it was knotted up'* < ʔu- (**stative**) + ƛ̓uč (**root**) *together, bunch up; tie, knot, wrap up package*}.

Ot-tlots-ot, *to tie, to knot*

{ʔuƛ̓účud *' someone tied something up'*, *'someone wrapped up a package'*, *'he tied it'*, *'she packaged it'* < ʔu- (**stative**) + ƛ̓uč (**root**) *pull together, bunch up; tie, knot, wrap up package* + -u- (**infix**) + -d (**transitive**)}.

Klots-a-lekw', *to tie*

{ƛ̓učalikʷ *'continuatively tie or wrap something'* < ƛ̓uč (**root**) *together, bunch up; tie, knot, wrap up package* + -alikʷ (**continuative action**)}.

{pəd *earth, soil; dirt, dust; bury* }:

Puds, *to cook underground*

{pəd *'cook underground'* < pəd (**root**) *earth, soil, dirt, dust; bury*}.

As-pud, *the roots of plants, a heap of earth*

{ʔəspə́d *'something is buried'*, *'covered with dirt'* < ʔəs- (**stative**) + pəd (**root**) *earth, soil; dirt, dust; bury*}.

O-pud-dud, *to bury*

{ʔupə́dəd *'someone buried something~someone'*, *'he buried it'*, *'he buried him'*, *'she buried it'* < ʔu- (**stative**) + pəd (**root**) *bury* + -ə- (**infix**) + -d (**transitive**)}.

Ot-hu-pud'-dud, *to become muddy*

{ʔudxʷpə́dəd *'it became muddy'* < ʔu- (**stative**) + dxʷ- (**pervasive**) + pəd (**root**) *earth, soil, dirt, dust; bury* + -ə- (**infix**) + -d (**transitive**)}.

Pi-da'-likw, *to plant or sow*

{pədálikʷ *'plant (verb)'* < pəd (**root**) *earth, soil, dirt, dust, bury* + -alikʷ (**continuative action**)}.

{puʔ *blow, wind* }:

O-po'-ōd, *to blow (with breath)*

{ʔupúʔud *'someone blew something'*, *'he blew it'*, *'she blew it'* < ʔu- (stative) + puʔ (root) *blow* + -u- (infix) + -d (transitive)}.

Shi-pōt-ai'-li, *the mast of a canoe or boat*
{šxʷpútali *'mast'* < šxʷ- (pervasive) + pu(ʔ) (root) *blow* + -t (transitive) + -ali (lexical suffix for) *place of*}.

O-po'-a-lekw, *to blow (as the wind)*
{ʔupúʔalikʷ *'the wind is blustery'*, *'the wind was blustery'*; *'someone is continuously blowing something'* < ʔu- (stative) + puʔ (root) *blow* + -alikʷ (continuative action)}.

Chil-po'-ted, *to make sail*
{čəɬpúʔtəd *'to make a sail'*, *'make sail'* < čəɬ- (lexical prefix for) *make* + puʔ (root) *blow, wind* + -təd (lexical suffix for) *implement for*}.

Po'-tud, *a sail*
{pútəd *'sail'* < pu(ʔ) (root) *blow* + -təd (lexical suffix for) *implement for*}.

Shu'-put (English), *a shirt*
{sxʷpútxʷ *'shirt'* < s- (nominalizer) + xʷ- (pervasive) + pu(h) (root) *blow* + -tx (transitive)}.

Spimpt, *a calico shirt*
{sxʷpiptxʷ *'shirt'* < s- (nominalizer) + xʷ- (pervasive) + pi- (reduplication) + p(uh) (root) *blow* + -txʷ (transitive)}.

{p̓aʔkʷ **pipe (for stove or tobacco)**}:

Pɑkw, pa'-kwuts, *a pipe, a large pipe*
{p̓aʔkʷ *'pipe (for stove or tobacco)'*.
*p̓áʔkʷəc *'where pipes abounds'* < p̓aʔkʷ (root) + -ac (lexical suffix for) *plant, tree, bush, shrub*}.

{p̓aƛ̓ **sew** }:

Hɛkh-ka'-bats sukh-pɑts', *spool-thread*
{x̌əqábac səxʷp̓áƛ̓ *'spool of thread'*, < x̌əq (root) *bind, wrap* + -abac (lexical suffix for) *solid object* səxʷ- (lexical prefix for) *by means of* + p̓aƛ̓ (root) *sew*}.

O-pɑd-stad, *to sew*
{ʔup̓áƛ̓ad *'someone sewed something'*, *'someone is sewing something'*, *'he sewed it'*, *'she sewed it'*, *'she is sewing it'* < ʔu- (stative) + p̓aƛ̓ (root) *sew* + -a- (infix) + -d (transitive)}.

Pad-sted, pots'-ded, *a needle*
Pots-ded, pɑd-sted, *a needle*
{p̓áƛ̓təd *'needle'* < p̓aƛ̓ (root) *sew* + -təd (lexical suffix for) *implement for*}.

Sukh-pɑts, *thread*
{səxʷp̓áƛ̓ *'thread'*, *'by means of sewing (literal)'* < səxʷ- *by means of* + p̓aƛ̓ (root) *sew*}.

Pɑt-sub-uts, *a shirt of dressed skins*

{*p̓ac̓əbəc *'sewn solid object'* < p̓ac̓ (root) *sew* + -abac/-əbəc (lexical suffix for) *solid object, body*}.

{p̓ayəq *hew out, carve out, make a canoe* }:
    O-pai'-ak, *a carpenter, worker in wood*
        {ʔup̓áyəq *'someone hewed~carved something out'*, *'someone carved a canoe'*, *'he hewed it out'*, *'she carved it out'*, *'he made a canoe'* < ʔu- (stative) + p̓áyəq (root) *hew out, carve out, make a canoe*}.

{p̓əɬ *clear, make visible, reveal* }:
    O-pi-klo'-sub, *to comb*
        {ʔup̓əɬusəb *'someone combed their hair* < ʔu- (stative) + p̓əɬ (root) *clear, make visible, reveal* + -us (lexical suffix for) *face* + -əb (reflexive)}.

{p̓il *flat, flatten, broad* }:
    As-pel', *broad, thick*
        {ʔəsp̓íl *'something is flat, flatten, broad'* < ʔəs- (stative) + p̓il (root) *flat, flatten, broad*}.
    O-pe'-lap, *to rise, as the tide*
        {ʔup̓ílab *'the tide has risen'*, *'the tide was up'*, *'it was high tide'* < ʔu- (stative) + p̓il (root) *flat, broad* + -ab (method used to do something)}.
    spe'-lap, *flood tide*
        {sp̓ílab *'flood tide'* {"*tide, flood tide*"} < s- (nominalizer) + p̓il (root) *flat, broad* + -ab (method used to do something)}
    Ikh-pe'-lʊs, *a flattened head*
        {ʔəsp̓ílus *flatten forehead* ' < p̓il (root) *flatten* + -us (lexical suffix for) *face, head, upper part*}.
    as-hu-pɛlks, *flat-nosed*
        {ʔəsxʷp̓ílqs *'someone~something has a flat nose* < ʔəs- (stative) + xʷ- (pervasive) + p̓il (root) *flat* + -qs (lexical suffix for) *nose, point*}.

{p̓usəb *float* }:
    Pōp-sa-ba'-hat, *floats of a net or seine*
        {p̓úp̓(u)səbəx̌əd, p̓up̓(u)səbax̌ad *'floats for a net or seine {"seine net (floats for)", "floats for a net or seine"}* < p̓u- (reduplication) + p̓úsəb (root) *float* + -əx̌əd/-ax̌ad (lexical suffix for) *edge, side appendage*}.

{qəbə́təd *axe* }:
    Ko-bat'-it, *an axe*
        {qəbə́təd *'axe'*}.
    Skub-ut-ud-ul-li, *an axe-handle*
        {sqəbə́tədali *'axe handle'*, *'place of ax* (literal) < s- (nominalizer) + sqəbə́təd (root) *axe* + -ali *place of*}.

{q̓iis *the highest of four-point in dice* }
> Kɛs, *the highest or four-point in dice*
>> {q̓iis *'the highest of four-point in dice'*} (Waterman 1973: 74).

{q̓il *ride, load* }:
> Ke-lɑb, ke'-lo-bit, *a canoe (generic)*
>> {q̓ílab *'load vehicle'* < q̓il (root) *ride, load* + -ab (method used to do something).
>> q̓ílbid *'canoe (any kind)'*, *'vehicle of any kind including wagons and automobiles'* < q̓il (root) *ride, load* + -b (third person and middle voice) + -i- (infix) + -d (transitive suffix)}.
>
> O-ke'-la-gwil, *to get on or into (as a horse or canoe)*
>> {ʔuq̓ílagʷil *'someone got into a vehicle'*, *'someone got onto the horse'*, *'he got into the canoe'*, *'she got into the car'*, *'she got onto the wagon'* < ʔu- (stative) + q̓il (root) *get in/on any sort of conveyance either to travel oneself (get on board, mount, ride) or to load a vehicle (especially a canoe)* + -agʷil (doer put self in action)}.
>
> Swus-ke'-lʊs, *a swing*
>> {səxʷəsq̓ílus *'swing'* < səxʷ- (lexical prefix for) *by means of* + ʔəs- (stative) + q̓il (root) *load into vehicle* + -us (lexical suffix for) *face, surface*}.

{*qʷádᶻiladxʷ }:
> Kwɑds-a-lat' hu, *brass kettle*
>> {*qʷádᶻilaladxʷ *'brass kettle'*, *'brass'* (*qʷádᶻaladxʷ *brass, pail material* (Hilbert Miller Zahir 2001: 68), qʷádᶻiladxʷ *penny* (Thompson~Ramirez 1996: MS)}.

{qʷalalatxʷ *copper* }:
> Ku-la-lat'-hu, *brass*
>> {qʷalalatxʷ *'copper'*} (Bates Hess Hilbert 1994: 198).

{qʷályus *adze* }:
> Kwa'-li-ʊs, kwal'-yʊs, *an adze*
>> {qʷályus *'adze'*} (Zahir~McCleary: MS).

{qʷəq̓ʷ *white* }:
> Ho-kokw, *white*
>> {x̌ʷuqʷə́q̓ʷ *'white'* < x̌ʷu- (prefix denoting color) + qʷəq̓ʷ (root) *white*}.
>
> Ho-kōk, *dollar, silver*
>> {x̌ʷuqʷə́q̓ʷ *'white'*, *'dollar'*, *'silver'* < x̌ʷu- (prefix denoting color) + qʷəq̓ʷ (root) *white*}.
>
> Hok-ko-lit'-za, *a white blanket*

{x̌ʷuqʷə́q̇ʷulíčaʔ *'white blanket or cloth'* < x̌ʷu- (**prefix denoting color**) qʷə́q̇ʷ (**root**) *white* + -ul- (**infix**) + -ičaʔ (**lexical suffix for**) *cloth, clothes, wear, blanket*}.

K'ho'-hu-belts, *white pebbles*
{qʷə́q̇ʷəbilc *'white rocks'* < qʷə́q̇ʷ (**root**) *white* + -əb (**experiencer and middle voice**) + -ilc (**lexical suffix for**) *round thing, money, curved objects; rock*}.

tu-kwōk-wʊs, *Spotted-faced (as a piebald horse)*
{dxʷqʷə́q̇ʷus *'white face, spotted face'* (as a piebald horse) < dxʷ- (**pervasive**) + qʷə́q̇ʷ (**root**) *white* + -us (**lexical suffix for**) *face, cliff*}

{sqʷíƛ̓əb *spear for bottom fish*}:
    Skwɛt'-lub, *a fish-spear*
        {sqʷíƛ̓əb *'spear for bottom fish'* < s- (**nominalizer**) + qʷiƛ̓əb (**root**)}.

{qʷúʔqʷaʔ *drink*}:
    O-ko'-kwa, *to drink*
        {ʔuqʷúʔqʷaʔ *'someone drank', 'someone is drinking', 'he drank', 'she is drinking', 'something drank', 'it is drinking'* < ʔu- (**stative**) + qʷúʔqʷaʔ (**root**) *drink*}.

    Sko'-kwa, *a drink or draught of anything*
        {sqʷúʔqʷaʔ *'drink (noun)'* < s- (**nominalizer**) + qʷuʔqʷaʔ (**root**) *drink*}.

    Hu-kwe'-a-kʊd, *a cup*
        {xʷqʷíʔqʷaʔad *'cup', 'drink a little (literal)'* < xʷ- (**derivational**) + qʷíʔ- (**reduplication**) qʷúʔqʷaʔ (**root**) *drink* + -a- (**infix**) + -d (**transitive**)}.

    Sukh-ko'-kwa, *a cup*
        {səxʷqʷúʔqʷaʔ *'cup', 'by means of drinking (literal)'* < səxʷ- (**lexical prefix for**) *by means of* + qʷuʔqʷaʔ (**root**) *drink*}.

{qʷúbayʔ ~ sqʷúbayʔ *dog*}:
    Ko'-bai, sko'-bai, *a dog*
    Sko'-bai, ko'-bai, ko-mai, *a dog*
        {qʷúbayʔ *'dog'*.
        sqʷúbayʔ *'dog'* < s- (**nominalizer**) + qʷubayʔ (**root**) *dog*}.

    Ko-matl'-kɛd, *a dog's-hair blanket*
        {qʷumáyʔalqid[159] *'dog hair'* < qʷúmayʔ/qʷúbayʔ (**root**) *dog* + -alqid (**lexical suffix for**) *hair*}.

{q̇ʷaqʷyilc *shinny game*}:
    Kek-li ɛlsk, *a game similar to hockey or bandy*
        {q̇ʷaqʷyilc *'shinny game'*} (Snyder 1968: 162).

---

[159] Classic Lushootseed, with M.

{q̊ʷásdulíčaʔ *mountain goat wool blanket*}:
>   Kwɑs'-do lit' za, *a goat's-wool blanket*
>   {q̊ʷásdulíčaʔ 'mountain goat wool blanket' < q̊ʷásd + -ul- (**infix**) + -ičaʔ (**lexical suffix for**) ***blanket, cloth, clothes***}.

{saX̌ *scrape* }:
>   O-sa'-had-shid, *to scrape (as with a knife)*
>   {ʔusáX̌ad čəd[160] 'I scraped it', 'I am scraping it' < ʔu- (**stative**) + saX̌ (**root**) *scrape* + -a- (**infix**) + -d (**transitive**) čəd *I, me*}.
>   Sukh'hutl-kwɛd, *a razor*
>   {sáX̌ətqʷid 'razor' < saX̌ (**root**) *scrape* + -ət- (**infix**) + -qʷid (**lexical suffix for**) ***beard***}.
>   O-sukh-hutl-kwɛd, *to shave*
>   {ʔusáX̌ətqʷid 'he shaved whiskers', 'someone shaved facial hair', 'he is shaving a face', 'he shaved' < ʔu- (**stative**) + saX̌ (**root**) *scrape* + -ət- (**connecting affix**) + qʷid (**lexical suffix for**) ***facial hair***}.

{səlp *spin, twist, whirl* }:
>   O-sulp-tsut, *to whirl (as water)*
>   {ʔusə́lpcut 'someone spun themselves around', 'someone is spinning around', 'he is spinning around', 'she spun around' < ʔu- (**stative**) + səlp (**root**) *spin, twist* + -cut (**reflexive**)}.
>   Suld, sult, *yarn*
>   {səlp 'yarn', 'spin', 'whirl'
>   su-sulp'-tub, *vertigo (see "To whirl")*
>   {*səsəlptəb 'vertigo' < sə- (**reduplication**) + səlp (**root**) *twist, whirl* + -təb (**third person**)}

{súk̓ʷəb *cedar bark still on the tree; act of removing inner cedar bark from the outer bark* }:
>   So'-kwub, *the outside bark of the thuja*
>   {súk̓ʷəb 'cedar bark still on the tree'; 'act of removing inner cedar bark from the outer bark'}.

{šagʷ *push through* }:
>   Du-shɑkhw', *to string beads*
>   {dxʷšagʷ 'string beads' < dxʷ- (**derivational**) + šagʷ (**root**) *push through*}.
>   Tu-sha'-gweb, *to string beads*
>   {dxʷšágʷəb 'string beads' < dxʷ- (**pervasive**) + šagʷ (**root**) *push through* + -əb (**experiencer and middle voice**)}.
>   O-tu'-sha-shukw, *to embroider with beads*

---

[160] Gibbs analyzed čəd = *I ~ me* as a suffix. zz

{*ʔudxʷšašagʷ *'embroider with beads'* < ʔu- **(stative)** + dxʷ- **(pervasive)** + šagʷ **(root)** *push through*}.

Chuk-chuk-wɛts, *large beads*
{*šagʷšagʷic ~ *šagʷšagʷilc *'large beads'* < šagʷ- **(reduplication)** + šagʷ **(root)** *push through* + -ic/-ič **(lexical suffix for)** *cover(ing), surface, on top of, over, series of items on a string, string, cord; spine*}.

{šálbixʷ *outside* **(but near)** *the house* }:
    Shal-bɛkhw', shal-be'-ukh, *out of doors, out, without*
        {šálbixʷ *'outside* **(but near)** *the house'*}.

{šaẃ *bone* }:
    Shau-utsh, *the skull*
        {šáẃač *'skull'* < šaẃ **(root)** *bone* + -ač **(lexical suffix for)** *head*}.
    Shauks, *a bone arrow-head*
        {šaẃqs *'bone arrow-head', 'bone point'* < šaẃ **(root)** *bone* +-qs **(lexical suffix for)** *point, nose*}.

{šəbəd *seine net, trawl net, fish trap* }:
    Shub-ɛd, *a seine or net*
        {šə́bəd *'seine net', 'trawl net', 'fish trap'*}.
    Sheb-ɛdb, *the fish with a seine*
        {šə́bədəb *'fish with a seine'* < šə́bəd *seine net, trawl net, fish trap* + -əb **(experiencer and middle voice)**}.
    Shukh'-shukh-bud, she'-sha-bad, *a seine or net*
    She-sha'-bud, *a small seine or net*
        {šəšə́bəd *'seine nets'* < šə- **(reduplication)** + šə́bəd **(root)** *seine net, trawl net*.

        {šiʔšə́bəd *'small seine net'* < šiʔ- **(reduplication)** + šə́bəd **(root)** *seine net, trawl net*}.

{šə́dᶻəl *go outside* **(from house)** }:
    O-shɛd-zul, *to go out*
        {ʔušə́dᶻəl *'someone went outside', 'something* **(an animal)** *went outside', 'he went outside', 'she went outside'* < ʔu- **(stative)** + šə́dᶻəl **(root)** *go outside*}.

{šə́dᶻt *canoe bow* }:
    Shudst, *the bow of a canoe* {šə́dᶻt *'canoe bow'*}.

{šəgʷɬ *door, doorway, path, road* }:
    Shugw'tl, *a road, doorway*
        {šəgʷɬ *'door', 'doorway', 'path', 'road'*}.

{šic *rub* }:
    Shits-ted', *a file*
        {šíctəd *'a file'* < šic (**root**) *rub, file* + -təd (**lexical suffix for**) *implement for*}.
    Shɛd-zʊs, *the smelt*
        {šídᶻus *'rub on the cutting edge* (face) *in order to sharpen a knife'*, *'smelt'*
        < šidᶻ/šic (**root**) *rub, file* + -us (**lexical suffix for**) *face, head, upper part*}.
    Shi-its-ke'-dub, *to wash the hair*
        {šicqídəb *'wash hair'*, *'rub hair'* < šic (**root**) *rub, file* + -qid (**lexical suffix for**) *head* + -əb (**reflexive**)}.

{šič *stick into, stick through, sheathe, insert* }:
    Shis-chuck-sit'-chi, *a finger-ring*
    Skɛts-k'se'-chi, *a finger-ring*
        {šiščqsačiʔ *'ring for finger'* < ši- (**reduplication**) + š(i)č (**root**) *stick into, stick through, sheathe, insert* + -qsačiʔ *finger*}.
    Shʊt-sits-a'-lub, *the feathering of an arrow*
        {*šičičáləp *'feathering an arrow'* < šič *stick into, stick through, sheathe, insert* + -ič (**reduplication**) + -aləp *cylindrical object*}.

as-hu-shɛlts-k's-chʊkh, *You wear the nose-ornament*
    {*ʔəsxʷšíčqs čəxʷ *'you wear the nose-ornament'* < ʔəs- (**stative**) + xʷ- (**pervasive**) + šič (**root**) *stick into, stick through, sheathe, insert* + -qs (**lexical suffix for**) *nose, point*}.

{šuk̓ʷ *powder, grey* }:
    Skwe'-litsht, *gunpowder*
        {š(u)k̓ʷílič *'gunpowder'* < šuk̓ʷ (**root**) *powder* + -il (**lexical suffix for**) *become* + -ič (**lexical suffix for**) *cover(ing), surface, on top of, over, series of items on a string, string, cord; spine*}.

{šul *pass beneath, insert, slide between, sheathe, put beneath, go under, enter cramped area* }:
    Shu-lud, *to pierce*
        {šúlud *'pass something beneath'*, *'insert'*, *'slide between'*, *'sheathe'*, *'put beneath'*, *'go under'*, *'enter cramped place'* < šul (**root**) *pass something beneath, insert, slide between, sheathe, put beneath, go under, enter cramped place* + -u- (**infix**) + -d (**transitive**)}.
    Shel-shel'-a-wɑp, *a lizard*
        {šuĺšúləwap *'lizard'* ("It will can crawl under you when you sit down" (Zahir~Rimarez 1994-98: MS)) < šuĺ- (**reduplication**) + šul *pass beneath, insert, slide between, sheathe, put beneath, go under, enter cramped place* + -aw- (**infix**) –ap (**lexical suffix for**) *bottom, base, buttocks*}.

{taʔɫ *prong of a salmon spear* }:

Tɑtl, *a pointed spear-head*
> {taʔɬ *'prong of a salmon spear'*}.

{tab *thing, that* }:
> Stab, *what*
>> {stab *what* < s- (**nominalizer**) + tab (**root**)}.
>
> Sta-bɛwks, stab-dōp, *property, goods, things*
>> {stábigʷs *'possessions'*, *'prized possessions'*, *'belongings'*, *'treasures'*
>> < s- (**nominalizer**) + tab (**root**) + -igʷs *things, possessions*.
>> stábdup *'property'*, *'things of the land'* < s- (**nominalizer**) + tab (**root**) + -dup *ground, floor*}.
>
> Stɑb-o-ta', stɑb-ta', *what is that?*
>> {stábəxʷ taʔ *'what is that now?'*, *'What is this now?'* < s- (**nominalizer**) + tab (**root**) + -əxʷ *now* ta *this, that*.
>> stab taʔ *what is that/this?* < s- (**nominalizer**) + tab (**root**) ta *this, that*}.

{təs *hit with fist* }:
> O-tus'-sid, o-tut-so-shed, *to strike*
> O-tut'-so-shed, o-tus-sid, *to strike*
>> {ʔutə́səd *'someone struck someone with the fist'*, *'he struck him with his fist'*, *'she struck him with his fist'* < ʔu- (**stative**) + təs (**root**) *hit with fist* + -ə- (**infix**) + -d (**transitive**).
>> ʔutə́səd čəd[161] *'I struck him with my fist'*, *'I struck her with my fist'*
>> < ʔu- (**stative**) + təs (**root**) *hit with fist* + -ə- (**infix**) + -d (**transitive**) čəd *I/me*}.
>
> S'hu-tɛt-sʊt-shid, *to knock*
>> {ʔutít(ə)sucid *'someone knocked on the door'* < ti- (**reduplication**) + təs (**root**) *hit with fist* + -ucid (**lexical suffix for**) *body of water, river; mouth, language; doorway, opening; eat*}.
>
> Si-u'-tid-sōltsh, *to drum (as at dances, &c.)*
>> {ʔutít(ə)sulč *'someone is drumming'* < s- (**nominalizer**) + ti- (**reduplication**) + təs (**root**) *hit with fist* + -ulč (**lexical suffix for**) *container, stomach*}.

{təx̌ʷ *pull, haul* }:
> Tukh-hōd, *haul* (imperative)
> O-ta'-hwōt, *to haul*
>> {tə́x̌ʷud *'pull something'* < təx̌ʷ (**root**) *pull* + -u- (**infix**) + -d (**transitive**)}.
>> {ʔutə́x̌ʷud *'someone pulled something'*, *'someone is pulling something'*, *'he pulled it'*, *'she is pulling it'*, *'it is pulling it'* < ʔu- (**stative**) + təx̌ʷ (**root**) *pull, haul* + -u- (**infix**) + -d (**transitive**)}.
>
> Stukh, *Portage*
>> {stəx̌ʷ *'something pulled'*, *'portage'* < s- (**nominalizer**) + təx̌ʷ (**root**) *pull, haul*}

---

[161] Gibbs analyzed čəd = *I~me* as a suffix. zz

Tut-hwɛtsht, *strung (as a bow)*
    {tə́t(ə)x̌ʷič 'strung (as a bow)' < tə- (**reduplication**) + t(ə)x̌ʷ (**root**) *pull* + -ič (**lexical suffix for**) *cover(ing), surface, on top of, over, series of items on a string, string, cord; spine*}.

Shu-tukh'-hwitsh, tukh-hwitsh, *a bow-string*

Tukh'-hwitsh, shu-tukh-hwitsh, *a bow string*
    {šxʷtə́x̌ʷič 'bow string' < šxʷ- (**pervasive**) + təx̌ʷ (**root**) *pull* + -ič *string, cord*. tə́x̌ʷič 'bowstring' < təx̌ʷ (**root**) *pull* + -ič *string, cord*}.

Stukh-o-gwith, *a portage*
    {stəx̌ʷúgʷiɬ 'portage' < s- (**nominalizer**) + təx̌ʷu (**root**) *pull* + -gʷiɬ (**lexical suffix for**) *canoe, boat, vehicle*}.

Twɑlsh'-tub, *to pick feathers*
    {t(ə)x̌ʷílčtəb 'pick feathers' < təx̌ʷ (**root**) *pull* + -ilč (**lexical suffix for**) *shank* + -təb (**third person**)}.

{stídigʷəd *cedar limb, rope made from cedar limbs* }:

    Ste-di-gwut, *a twig-rope, a withe*
        {stídigʷəd 'cedar limb', 'rope made from cedar limbs' < s- (**nominalizer**) + tídigʷəd (**root**)}.

    Te'-de-gwud-dōltsh, *a twig-basket*
        {stídgʷədulč 'cedar limb basket' < s- (**nominalizer**) + tídigʷəd (**root**) + -ulč (**lexical suffix for**) *container, basket*}.

{tiǰ *sinew, muscle* }:

    Tetsh, tidsh, *the sinews of an animal*
    Tidsh, tetsh, *the sinews of an animal*
        {tiǰ 'sinew', 'muscle'}.

{stiwatɬ *Coast Salish style canoe* }:

    Ste'-wɑtl, *a canoe (northern pattern)*
        {stiwatɬ 'Coast Salish style canoe'[162] < s- (**nominalizer**) + tiwatɬ (**root**)}.

{tup *pound* }:

    To'-pʊd, *the pound in a mortar*
        {túpud 'pound something' < tup (**root**) *pound* + -u- (**infix**) + -d (**transitive**)}.

{ɬəbš *braid* }:

    O-tub-sid, *to braid*
        {ʔutə́bšəd 'someone braided something', 'someone is braiding something', 'he braided it', 'she is braiding it' < ʔu- (**stative**) + ɬəbš (**root**) *braid* + -ə- (**infix**) + -d (**transitive**)}.

---

[162] Large, for saltwater travel, with both ends raised diagonally out of the water.

Stub-shid-de', tob-she-dud, *braided*

Tob-she-dud, stub-shi-de', *twisted or braided, knotted hair*
> {stə́bšədiʔ *'braided hair'* < s- (nominalizer) + ɬəb (root) *braid* + -š- (transitive) + -adiʔ (lexical suffix for) *side of head, ear*.
>
> {ɬəbšə́dəd *'...as I braid'*, *'...when I braided'* < ɬəbs (root) + -a- (infix) + -d (transitive) + -əd (dependent phrase suffix for) *I, me*.

Ta-bɛtld', *rope*
> {ɬəbítəd *'rope'* < ɬəb (root) *braid* + -iɬəd}.

{ɬəd *in a row, line up* }:

Tu-du-gwɑlts, tukh-dug-wash, *to load a gun*

O-tu'-du-gwɑlts, *to load a gun*
> {ɬə́dəgʷalc *'load a gun'* < ɬəd (root) *line* + -əgʷ- (connecting affix) + -alc (lexical suffix for) *cylindrical object*}.
>
> {*ʔuɬə́dəgʷalc[163] *'someone loaded a gun'*, *'he loaded the gun'*, *'she loaded the gun'* < ʔu- (stative) + ɬəd (root) *in a row, line up* +-əgʷ- (connecting affix) + -alc (lexical suffix for) *cylindrical object*}.

{ɬə́ḵʷəb *hit with stick* }:

Uts-tukh'-hwōb, *to strike with a stick*
> {ʔuɬəḵʷəb *'hit with a stick'* < ʔu- (stative) + təḵʷ (root) *hit with a stick* + -əb (experiencer and middle voice)}.

Sti-kōp, stuk-ōp, *wood or sticks*

Stuk-wub, *a stick, a yard-measure, wood*
> {stə́ḵʷəb *'log'*, *'stick'*, *'wood'* < s- (nominalizer) + təḵʷ (root) *hit with stick* + -əb (experiencer and middle voice)}.

Stuk-hum, *trees* (generic)
> {stə́ḵʷəm[69] *'log'*, *'stick'*, *'wood'*, *'tree'*, *'yard stick'* < s- (nominalizer) + tə́ḵʷ (root) *hit with stick* + -əm (experiencer & middle voice)}.

Skuk'-e-dŏm, stuk-ti-kŏb, *forest, wooded country*

Stuk-te-kob, *forest country*
> {stəḵʷədəm *'forest'*, *'trees'*, *'logs'*, *'sticks'* < s- (nominalizer) + tə́ḵʷ(root) + -ə- (infix) + -d (transitive) + -əm/-əb (experiencer and middle voice)}.
>
> {stə́ḵʷt(ə)ḵʷəb *'forest'*, *'trees'*, *'logs'*, *'sticks'* < s- (nominalizer) + təḵʷ (reduplication) + tə́ḵʷ (root) *hit with stick* + -əb (experiencer and middle voice)}.

Ste-kwa'-mus, *a mark {mask} used at dances*
> {stiɬ(ə)ḵʷámus[164] *'mask'* < s- (nominalizer) + ti- (reduplication) + təḵʷ (root) *hit with stick* + -ab/-əb (experiencer ~ middle voice) + -us *face*}.

T'ko-boltsh, *a wooden spoon*

---

[163] Word refers to sequential packing of a gun with powder, ball, and wadding. *zz*
[164] Classic Lushootseed, with M.

{tək̓ʷábulč *'wooden spoon'*, *'wooden container'* < tə́k̓ʷ (root) *hit with stick* + -ab/-əb (experiencer and middle voice) + -ulč (lexical suffix for) *container*}.

T'kwɑb-shid, *leather shoes or boots*
{tək̓ʷábšəd *'shoes'*, *'boots'* < tə́k̓ʷ (root) *hit with stick* + -ab/-əb (experiencer and middle voice) + -šəd (lexical suffix for) *feet, foot*}.

{sƛə́ljixʷ *medicine*}:

Stul-ji-ʊkh, *medicine, physic*
{sƛə́ljixʷ *'medicine'* < s- (nominalizer) + ƛə́ljixʷ (root)}.

stul-jiʊkh ha-lekw-chid, *A doctor* {sƛəljixʷalikʷ čəd *'I am a doctor'* < s- (nominalizer) + ƛə́ljixʷ (root) + -alikʷ (continuative action) čəd *I, me*}

{ƛəq̓ʷ *snap a flexible object in two* }:

St-kwɑl'-shid, sle-dat-shid, *the head-band for carrying loads*
{sƛəq̓ʷálšəd *'tumpline'* < s- (nominalizer) + ƛəq̓ʷ (root) *snap a flexible object in two* + -al- (lexical affix for) *on, at, in, by* + -šəd (lexical suffix for) *foot, lower leg*.

sƛidálšəd *'tumpline'* < s- (nominalizer) + ƛid (root) *tie* + -al- (lexical affix for) *on, at, in* + -šəd (lexical suffix for) *foot, lower leg*}.

Tuk'-ke-te-kuts, *the vine maple, acer cercinnatum*
{ƛə́qƛ(ə)qac *'vine maple tree'* < ƛəq- (reduplication) + ƛ(ə)q (root) *thick; adhere* + -ac (lexical suffix for) *tree, bush, shrub, plant*}.

{ƛigʷ ~ ƛih *thank, pray* }:

Te'-hetsh. Qu. *to ask for*
{ƛíhič *'pray for'* < ƛigʷ/ƛih (root) *thank, pray* + -ič (lexical suffix for) *cover(ing), surface, on top of, over, series of items on a string, string, cord; spine*}.

{ƛilib *sing* }:

O-te'-lib, *to sing (speaking of people)*
{ʔuƛílib *'someone has sang'*, *'someone is singing'*, *'he is singing'*, *'she sang'* < ʔu- (stative) + ƛílib (root) *sing*}.

Ste'-lib, te'-lib, *a song*

Te-lib, ste'-lib, ste'-lim, *a song*

ste'-lim (from te'-lib, *a song*), *that of success with women*

Ste'-lim, *the magic of success with women*
{sƛílib *'song'* < s- (nominalizer) + ƛílib (root) *sing*. ƛílib (root) *sing*}.

*sƛilim[165] *'song'* < s- (nominalizer) + ƛilim~ƛilib (root) *sing*}.

---

[165] Classic Lushootseed, with M.

{t̓iq̓ʷ *smoke, murk* }:
>   Ste'-a-kwush, *smoke, fog*
>   >   {st̓iq̓ʷš 'smokey object' < s- (**nominalizer**) + t̓iq̓ʷ (**root**) *smoke, murk* + -š (**transitive**)}.
>
>   Ste'-uk-wil, *smoke or fog*
>   >   {st̓íq̓ʷil 'smoke' < s- (**nominalizer**) + t̓iq̓ʷil (**root**) *smoking*}.
>
>   Tʊs-te'-o-bil, tu-tewk-o-bil, *muddy, to muddy*
>   >   { dxʷt̓íqʷəbil 'turbid' < dxʷ- (**pervasive**) + t̓iqʷ *smoke, murk* + -əb (**experiencer and middle voice**) + -il (**lexical suffix for**) *become*}.

{t̓ísəd *arrow, bullet, stinger of an insect* }:
>   Te'-sid, te'-sud, te'-sum, *the sting of an insect, an arrow, a bullet*
>   >   {t̓ísəd 'arrow', 'bullet', 'stinger of an insect'. t̓ísən[71] 'arrow', 'bullet', 'stinger of an insect'}.

{stu?qʷ *small feathers* }:
>   stōkw, *feathers*
>   >   {stu?qʷ 'small feathers'}.

{t̓uč *shoot someone or something* }:
>   Ho-tōt'-so-hum, *to shoot (with gun or bow)*
>   >   {?ut̓účuhəm[166] 'someone shot someone or something' < ?u- (**stative**) + t̓uč (**root**) *shoot someone or something* + -əm/-əb (**experiencer and middle voice**)}.
>
>   O-tot-sil, o-tōt-sōd, *to shoot with gun or bow, to hit a mark*
>   >   {?ut̓účil 'someone fired (a gun)', 'someone shot (an arrow)', 'he fired', 'she shot' < ?u- (**stative**) + t̓uč (**root**) *shoot* + -il (**lexical suffix for**) *become*.
>   >   ?ut̓účud 'someone shot something', 'he shot it', 'she shot it' < ?u- (**stative**) + t̓uč (**root**) *shoot* + -u- (**infix**) + -d (**transitive**)}.
>
>   tōt-sa-de', *Shoot, to (with gun or bow)*
>   >   {t̓učadi? 'shoot' < t̓uč (**root**) *shoot* + -adi? (**lexical suffix for**) *side; ear, side of head*}.

{wə́q̓əb *box, chest, trunk* }:
>   wuk-kub', wo-kɑp', *a box, chest, trunk*
>   Wo-kɑp', wuk-kub', *a box, chest, trunk*
>   >   {wə́q̓əb 'box', 'chest', 'trunk'}.

{swup *bracelet* }:
>   Swop, *a bracelet of brass wire* {swup 'bracelet' < s- (**nominalizer**) + wup (**root**)}.

---

[166] Classic Lushootseed, with M.

{sxʷayʔs *hat, cap* }:
    Shwais', *hat or cap*
        {sxʷayʔs '*hat*', '*cap*' < s- (**nominalizer**) + xʷayʔs (**root**)}.

{xʷəc *remove* (**clothing**); *remove, empty* }:
    O-hwuts, *to clean*
        {ʔuxʷə́c '*something was cleaned*', '*a clothing item was removed*'; '*something was removed*' < ʔu- (**stative**) + xʷəc (**root**) *take* (**clothing**) *off; remove; empty*}.
    O-hwut-sid, *to take off (as a hat)*
        {ʔuxʷə́cəd '*someone removed an item of clothing*', '*someone removed something*', '*he removed it*', '*she removed it*' < ʔu- (**stative prefix**) + xʷəc (**root**) *take* (**clothing**) *off; remove; empty* + -ə- (**infix**) + -d (**transitive suffix**)}.
    Hwut-sɛd-tid to pōt-t'd, *take in sail* (**imperative**)
        {xʷə́cəd tə dxʷpútəd '*take in the sail* (**imperative**)' < xʷə́cəd *take* (**clothing**) *off; remove; empty* tə *the* dxʷpútəd *sail*}.
    As-hwat'-sab, *empty*
        {ʔəsxʷə́cab '*something is empty*' < ʔəs- (**stative prefix**) + xʷəc (**root**) *remove* (**clothing**); *remove, empty* + -ab (**method used to do something**)}.
    As-hwuls-hwut i-gwus (meaning unknown)
        {ʔəsxʷə́cxʷəcidgʷəs '*nothing to feed with*' < ʔəs- (**stative prefix**) + xʷə́c- (**reduplication**) xʷəc (**root**) *take off, empty, remove* + -idgʷəs (**lexical suffix for**) *torso, breast, chest*}.

{hikʷ sxʷúyub '*big sale*' < hikʷ *big, large* + s- (**nominalizer**) + xʷúyub (**root**) *sell* }:

{*x̌aʔliw *horn spoon* }:
    Ha-lekw', *a spoon*
        {*x̌aʔliw '*horn spoon*'} (Kuipers 2002: 155).

{x̌ac̓ *cover* (**something**) }:
    As-hat-sitch, *covered (As with a blanket)*
        {ʔəsx̌ác̓ič '*it is covered*' < ʔəs- (**stative prefix**) + x̌ac̓ (**root**) *cover* (**something**) + -ič (**lexical suffix for**) *cover(ing), surface, on top of, over, series of items open a string, string, cord; spine*}.
    Hats-a-be-dɑk, *skin leggings*
        {*x̌ac̓abidaq '*skin leggings*', '*something to cover the legs*' < x̌ac̓ (**root**) *cover* + -a- (**infix**) + -b- (**experiencer and middle voice**) + -i- (**infix**) + -d (**transitive**) + -aq (**lexical suffix for**) *forked, wedged~angle shape*}.

{x̌ádᶻax̌̓ *pry it up, pry it open* }:
    O-hadz'-ut-lud, *to prize as with a lever*
        {ʔux̌ádᶻax̌̓əd '*it was pried up/open*' < ʔu- (**stative prefix**) + x̌ádᶻax̌̓ (**root**) *pry it up, pry it open* + -ə- (**infix**) + -d (**transitive**)}.

{x̌al *write, mark* }:

 As-hɑl, *embroidered, figured, written*
  {ʔəsx̌ál *'it is written', 'it is marked', 'it is decorated'* < ʔəs- (**stative prefix**) + x̌al (**root**) *written, marked, decorated*}.

 O-hal, o-haʹ-lad, *to embroider, write, &c*
  {ʔux̌ál *'it was marked~written~embroidered'* < ʔu- (**stative prefix**) x̌al (**root**) *write, mark, decorate, embroider*.
   ʔux̌álad *'someone marked~wrote~embroidered something'* < ʔu- (**stative prefix**) x̌al (**root**) *write, mark, decorate, embroider* + -a- (**infix**) + -d (**transitive**)}.

 S'hɑl, *embroidery, needle-work, writing, anything figured*
  {sx̌al *'marking', 'embroidery', 'basket design', 'letter'* < s- (**nominalizer**) + x̌al (**root**) *write, mark, draw, paint*}.

 Sukh-hɑl, *pen or pencil, writing materials*
  {səxʷx̌ál *'pen', 'pencil'*, < səxʷ- (**lexical prefix for**) *by means of* + x̌al (**root**) *write, mark, decorate, embroider*}.

 Hul-lɛlʹ-do-pĕd, *the floor of a house*
  {x̌əlíldupəd *'floor'* < x̌əl (**variant (root)**) *mark, write, decorate* + -il (**lexical suffix for**) *becoming* + -dup (**lexical suffix for**) *floor, ground*}.

 Hul-lai-yʊt-sid, *large storage-baskets*
  {x̌aláyucid *'design at rim of basket* (Waterman 1973: 11)*'* < x̌al (**root**) *mark, write, decorate* + -ay- (**infix**) + - ucid (**lexical suffix for**) *body of water, river; mouth, language; doorway, opening; eat*}.

 as-kulkh-hulk as-hulʹ-hul-eltsʹ, *Striped (with broad stripes)*
  {*ʔəsx̌əqx̌əq ~ ʔəsx̌álx̌alilc *'something is wrapped and marked around a cylindrical object'* < ʔəs- (**stative**) + x̌əq (**reduplication**) + x̌əq (**root**) *bind, wrap around, tie* ʔəs- (**stative**) + x̌al (**reduplication**) + x̌al (**root**) *mark, write, decorate* + ilc (**lexical suffix for**) *round curved object, forehead; rock*}

{x̌al-/x̌əl- *cover with planks* (Kuipers 2002: 124) }:

 S'hal-tans, s'hal-ted-ĕtl, *a cradle*
  {sx̌áltən[167] *'cradle'* < s- (**nominalizer**) + x̌al/x̌əl- (**root**) *to cover with planks, board covering* + -tən/-təd *implement for*.
   sx̌áltədiʔɫ *'cradle'* < s- (**nominalizer**) + x̌al/x̌əl (**root**) *to cover with planks, board covering* + -tən/-təd (**lexical suffix for**) *implement for* + -iʔɫ *infant, child*}.

{x̌əd *push* }:

 O-had-dud, *to push*
  {ʔux̌ə́dəd *'something/someone was pushed/is being pushed'* < ʔu- (**stative prefix**) + x̌əd (**root**) *push* + -ə- (**infix**) + -d (**transitive**)}.

---

[167] Classic Lushootseed, with N.

Hud-shad'-bid, *a snowshoe*
>{x̌ədšádbid *'snowshoe'* < x̌əd (root) *push* + -šad (lexical suffix for) *foot, leg* + -bid + -b- (experiencer and middle voice) + -i- (infix) + -d (transitive)}.

Hʊt-sha'-to-bid, s'hʊd-sha'-bed, *foot-prints*

S'hʊd sha'-bid, hat-sha'-to-bid, *a foot-print*
>x̌ədšádəbid *'foot print'* < x̌əd (root) *push* + -šad (lexical suffix for) *foot, lower leg* + -əb (reflexive) + -i- (infix) + -d (transitive)}.
>
>{sx̌ədšádbid *'foot print'* < s- (nominalizer) + x̌əd (root) *push* + -šad (lexical suffix for) *foot, lower leg* + -(ə)b (reflexive) + -i- (infix) + -d (transitive).

hud-da'-lu-sid, *scraper for smoothing mats* (Niskwally),
>{x̌ədalusəd *'mat creaser'* < x̌əd (root) *push* + -al- (lexical infix for) *on, at, in, by* + -us (lexical suffix for) *face, surface* + -ə- (infix) + -d (transitive)}.

{x̌ək̓ʷ(u) *turn over, overturn* }:

>As-hukw, *upside down*
>>{ʔəsx̌ə́k̓ʷ *'it is upside down'* < ʔəs- (stative prefix) + x̌ək̓ʷ (root) *turn over, overturn*}.
>
>Huk-kɛd, huk-ke'-ud, *to pick up the tongs, &c*
>>{x̌ə́k̓ʷəd *'roasting sticks for cooking salmon on open fire'* < x̌ək̓ʷ (root) *turn over, overturn* + -ə- (infix) + -d (transitive)}.
>
>Huk-kɒt-sid, *covered, with the lid on*
>>{x̌ək̓ʷúcid *'cover', 'lid'* < x̌ək̓ʷ (root) *turn over, overturn* + -ucid (lexical suffix for) *mouth, language; doorway; opening in general*}.

{sx̌əláʔs *board, plank* }:

>S'hul-ɑs', *a plank or board*
>>{sx̌əláʔs *'board', 'plank', 'wall'* < s- (nominalizer) + x̌əláʔs (root)}.

{x̌əq *bind, wrap around, tie* }:

>Hukh-hud, *to lash or lace with a cord*
>>{x̌ə́qəd *'wrap string or cloth around something', 'wrap a package', 'wind something around it'* < x̌əq (root) *bind, wrap around, tie* + -ə- (infix) + -d (transitive)}.
>
>O-ha'-kut-tub, *to wind*
>>{ʔux̌ə́qətəb *'someone wrapped something', 'someone wound something around something'* < ʔu- (stative prefix) + x̌əq (root) *wrap, wind* + -təb (third person)}.
>
>Eskh-kos'-tum, *compress for flattening the head*

{ʔəsx̌əqúsəm[168] *compress for flattening the forehead* '*someone's head is being compressed*' < x̌əq (**root**) *bind, wrap around, tie* + -us (**lexical suffix for**) *face, surface* + -əm/-əb (**reflexive**)}.

Swus-huk-kōs, *the compress for the child's head in the cradle*
{səxʷəsx̌áqus '*compress for the forehead*' < səxʷ- (**lexical prefix for**) *by means of* + ʔəs- (**stative**) + x̌əq (**root**) *bind, wrap around, tie* + -us (**lexical suffix for**) *face*}.

Hɛkh-ka'-bats sukh-pɑts', *spool-thread*
{x̌əqábac səxʷp̓áč '*spool of thread*', '*an object wrapped for sewing* (literal)' < x̌əqábac *wrapped or bound object* (< x̌əq (**root**) *bind, wrap*; + -abac (**lexical suffix for**) *solid object*) + səxʷp̓áč *by means of sewing* (**literal**), *sewing machine* (< səxʷ- (**lexical prefix for**) *by means of* + p̓áč (**root**) *sew*)}.

{x̌páy *cedar* }:

Hi-paikhtl', h'pai'-ats, *Oregon cedar, thuja*
{x̌páyac '*western red cedar tree*', '*Thuja plicata*' < x̌páy (**root**) *cedar* + -ac (**lexical suffix for**) *tree, shrub, bush, plant*}.

Hɛkh-pai'-yʊltsh, *a large dish or plate*
{hikʷ x̌páyulč '*large cedar bowl or platter*' < hikʷ *big, large* x̌páyulč *cedar container* (<x̌páy (**root**) *cedar* + -ulč (**lexical suffix for**) *container*)}.

{x̌ʷəc *sharp; strong or tart taste* }:

Hwuls, *sharp edged*
{x̌ʷəcilc '*sharp edge*', '*sharp rocks*' < x̌ʷəc (**root**) *sharp* + -ilc (**lexical suffix for**) *round thing, money, curved objects; side, rock*}.

Hwōt-skus, *sharp-pointed*

Hwud-zuks, hwudsks, *sharp-pointed*
{x̌ʷəcqs '*sharp point*' < x̌ʷəc (**root**) *sharp; strong or tart taste* + -qs (**lexical suffix for**) *point, nose*}.

{x̌ʷəƛ̓t *pillow* }:

Hwɑtl, *a pillow*
{x̌ʷəƛ̓t '*pillow*'}.

{x̌ʷílab *thread* }:

Ho-elb, *thread*
{x̌ʷílab '*thread*'}.

---

[168] Classic Lushootseed, with M. Forehead compression to mold infant skulls as a mark of being born high-class. *zz*

{x̌ʷiq̓ʷ *wrap* }:

    Hwe-a-kwus'-sub, *to hang one's self*

        {x̌ʷiq̓ʷúsəb *'hang self'* < x̌ʷiq̓ʷ (root) *wrap* + -us (lexical suffix for) *face* + -əb (**reflexive**)}.

    Hwiʊkh'-kwi-ekw', kwi-ekw' {hwe' hw-kwi-ɛks}, *a sailor's "palm," a thimble*

        {*x̌ʷix̌ʷ(i)qʷiqs *'thimble'* < x̌ʷi- (**reduplication**) + x̌ʷ(i)qʷ *wrap* + -i- (**infix**) + -qs (lexical suffix for) *point, nose*}.

{x̌ʷubt *paddle* (**noun**) }:

    Hobt, *a paddle*

        {x̌ʷubt *'paddle'*}.

    Hɛk-hōbt, *an oar*

        {hikʷ x̌ʷubt *'oar', 'large paddle'* < hikʷ *big* x̌ʷubt *paddle*}.

    Hōb-ti, *the ash*

        {x̌ʷúbti(l) *'ash* (**tree**)*'* < x̌ʷubt *paddle* + -il (lexical suffix for) *becoming*}.

{x̌ʷuq̓ʷ *stick something into something into something* }:

    O-ho'-kot, o-ho'-kwut, *to prick as with a pin*

        {ʔux̌ʷúq̓ʷud *'someone stuck something into something'* < ʔu- (**stative prefix**) + x̌ʷuq̓ʷ (root) *stick something into something into something* + -u- (**infix**) + -d (**transitive**)}.

{yal~yəl *encompass* }:

    E'-la-chid, *to pull the hair*

        {yəláčəd *'gather hair from the scalp', 'pull the hair back'* < yəl (root) *encompass* + -ač (lexical suffix for) *head* + -ə- (**infix**) + -d (**transitive**)}.

    Yal'-shid, yel'-shid, *a pair of moccasins, shoes, or stockings*

        {yál̓šəd *'moccasins'* < yal̓~yal (root) *envelope* + -šəd (lexical suffix for) *foot, lower leg*}.

    Ye-la'-bit-shid, yel-ɑm'-tsen, *pantaloons of skin or cloth.* See "Yal-shid."

        {*yəlábidšəd *'pantaloons of skin or cloth'* < yəl~yal (root) *envelope* + -a- (**infix**) + -b- (**experiencer and middle voice**) + -i- (**infix**) + -d (**transitive**) + -šəd (lexical suffix for) *foot, lower leg.*

        yəlámcən[169] *'pants'* < yəl~yal (root) *envelope* + -amcən/-abcəd (lexical suffix for) *calf of leg*}

    yel-a-wɑkh *petticoat*

        {*yələwaq *'petticoat'* < yəl (root) *encompass* + -əw- (**infix**) + -aq (lexical suffix for) *forked, wedged~angle shape*}.

---

[169] Classic Lushootseed, with M & N.

{syalt *'cedar root water tight basket that can be used for cooking'* }:
> Si-αlt, *basket work kettle*
>> {syalt ~ siyalt *'cedar root water tight basket that can be used for cooking'* < s- (**nominalizer**) + yalt (**root**)}.

{yax̌ *fetch water* }:
> Wi-at-la-lekw, *to fish with a dip-net*
>> {yax̌alikʷ *'fish with dip-net'* < yax̌ (**root**) *fetch water, gore, dip out water* + -alikʷ (**continuative action**)}.

{yəlíx̌ʷəd *basket hat* }:
> yul-le'-a-kwud, *basket hat*
>> {yəlíx̌ʷəd *basket hat*} (Waterman 1973: 9).

{yə́x̌ʷəd *flint, arrow head* }:
> Yakh'-hwud, *a gun-flint*
> Yukh-hwud, *a stone arrow-head, a gun-flint*
>> {yə́x̌ʷəd *'flint', 'arrow head'*}.

{yídad *fish trap* }:
> E'-dαd, *a fish-weir, also one of the constellations so called*
>> {yídad **'fish trap'**}[170] (Ballard 1957).

{yidúʔ *Swing* }:
> Ye'-do, *a swing*
>> {yídúʔ *'swing'*}.
> Yai'-do-uts, *the honeysuckle*
>> {yidúʔac *'honeysuckle'* < yidúʔ (**root**) *swing* + -ac (**lexical suffix for**) *tree, bush, shrub, plant*}.

---

[170] Made of a wooden rectangular grid, and laid in a stream above the water. Weirs were constructed so fish had to jump onto the grid, where the fisherman could then catch them. See Ballard 1957.

SMITHSONIAN MISCELLANEOUS COLLETCIONS #160

INSTRUCTIONS
FOR RESEARCH RELATIVE TO THE
ETHNOLOGY AND PHILOLOGY
OF AMERICA
PREPARED FOR THE SMITHSONIAN INSTITUTION
BY GEORGE GIBBS

CONTENTS

Introductory Remarks	1	225
Ethnology	2	226
Crania	2	226
Specimens of art, etc.	4	227
Hints for Ethnological Inquiry	7	229
Philology	13	233
Introductory Remarks	13	233
Orthography	17	237
Vowels	18	237
Consonants	18	238
Comparative Vocabulary	20	239
Appendix A ~ Physical Character of Indian Races	34	253
Appendix B ~ Numeral Systems	40	256

INTRODUCTORY REMARKS

THE Smithsonian Institution is desirous of extending and completing its collections of facts and materials relative to the Ethnology, Archaeology, and Philology of the races of mankind inhabiting, either now or at any previous period, the continent of America, and earnestly solicits the cooperation in this object of all officers of the United States government, and travelers, or residents who may have it in their power **to** render any assistance. Full credit will always be given for contributions received.

JOSEPH HENRY
Secretary S. I.

Smithsonian Institution,
Washington, March 1, 1863

WASHIINGTON: SMITHSONAIN INSTITUTION   MARCH 1863

ETHNOLOGY.

CRANIA. — Among the first of the desiderata of the Smithsonian Institution, is a full series of the skulls of American Indians. {?!}

The jealousy with which they guard the remains of their friends renders such a collection in most cases a -difficult task, but there are others in which these objects can be procured without offence. Numerous tribes have become extinct, or have removed from their former abodes; the victims of war are often left where they fall; and the bones of the friendless and of slaves are neglected. Where, without offence to the living, acquisitions of this kind can be made, they will be gladly received as an important contribution to our knowledge of the race.

Various methods of disposing of the dead have prevailed among different tribes, as burning, burial, deposit in caves, in lodges, beneath piles of stone, and in wooden sepulchres erected above-ground, placing on scaffolds or in canoes, and attaching to the trunks of trees. In many instances the bones, after a season, are collected together and brought into a common cemetery. Where the first-mentioned form, that of burning, is followed, we must, of course, look to chance for the preservation of the remains. This method is, however, more rare than the others.

It is requisite, for the purpose of arriving at particular results, that the most positive determination be made of the nation or tribe to which a skull belongs. In extensive prairie countries, hunted over or traversed by various tribes, or where, as on the Pacific coast, several tribes and even stocks inhabit a district of limited extent, this is often difficult, or even impossible. Unless, therefore, information of a direct nature is obtained, the collector should be guarded in assigning absolute nationality to his specimens. It will be better to state accurately the locality whence they are derived, and the owners or frequenters of the neighborhood, to one of which they are likely to belong. Where several specimens are collected, each should be numbered to correspond with a catalogue in which the above points are mentioned; as also whether it was found in a grave or other place of deposit, [3] the character of the ornaments and utensils placed with it, and whether it was in its original place or had been combined with others. Finally, it should be ascertained whether the tomb was that of existing or recent inhabitants of the country, or of more ancient date, — such, for example, as the mound-builders of the Ohio; and, in this latter case, if the remains are those of the original-inhabitant, or have been since deposited. In this inquiry the character of the articles buried with the body will often furnish a. clue. The same precaution should be adopted where tribes have been removed from their native regions to a different locality. In short, where any doubt exists in the mind of the collector, all those circumstanced should be examined into which in the absence of direct testimony, will facilitate a conclusion as to origin.

It may be mentioned in this connection, that among some tribes it is the custom to marry out of the tribe, as a matter of policy. Skulls of women found in the cemeteries of one of these might therefore very probably belong to an adjoining tribe, and, possibly, to one of' an entirely different stock. In such cases, too, there can be no certainty that the men themselves are of the pure blood, of one race, and it is, therefore, important to ascertain if this custom exists. Among those tribes where flattening or altering the head is common to *both* sexes, particular suspicion should attach to any having the skull unaltered. This process is usually a mark of rank, or at least of freedom and an unaltered skull, if found in a burial-place or well-marked receptacle, may almost be assumed to be that of a stranger; if neglected, it is probably that of a slave. But as slaves were often buried with their owners, even this is not a positive conclusion. Among some of' the Pacific tribes, however, compression of the bead is confined to females or is, at any rate, only carried to any considerable extent among them. Slaves are sometimes of the same tribe with their owners, but they are more frequently purchased from others; and it should be noted that on the Pacific the course of the trade has been from south to north.

.In order to ascertain whether differences of form exist among different stocks, the accumulation of as many specimens as possible of each tribe is desirable, and duplicates moreover afford the means of extending the collection by exchange.

Skulls which have been altered in shape .possess a certain interest in themselves, though they are in other respects disadvantageous for comparison. The practice, in different forms, formerly existed more widely than at present, several tribes in the southern States, as the Natchez, &c., having been addicted to it. Two methods are still [4] employed in North America: that of flattening the head by pressure on the forehead, as practised among the Chinooks and other tribes in Oregon and Washington Territory, and that of elongating it, peculiar to a few on the northern end of Vancouver island.

SPECIMENS OP ART, ETC. — Another department to which the Institution wishes to direct the attention of collectors, is that of the weapons, implements, and utensils, the various manufactures, ornaments, dresses, &c, of the Indian tribes.

Such a collection may naturally be arranged under three periods. The first, that of the races which had already *passed* away before the discovery of the continent by Europeans, or whose extinction may be considered as coeval with that event; next, of the tribes who have *disappeared* with the settlement of the Atlantic States and the country between the Alleghanies and the Mississippi; and finally, that of the *present* time, or that of the yet existing nations, confined to the northern and western portions of the continent and to Mexico.

It is among the last that the greatest variety exists, and of which it is especially important to make immediate collections, as many articles are of a perishable nature, and the tribes themselves are passing away or exchanging their own manufactures for those of the white race. It is hardly necessary to specify any as of particular interest, for almost every thing has its value in giving completeness to a collection. Among the most noticeable, however, are dresses and ornaments, bows and arrows, lances, war-clubs, knives, and weapons of all kinds, saddles with their furniture, models of lodges, parflesh packing covers and bags, cradles, mats, baskets of all sorts, gambling' implements, models of canoes (as nearly as possible in their true proportions), paddles, fish-hooks and nets, fish-spears and gigs, pottery, pipes, the carvings in wood and stone of the Pacific coast Indians, and the wax and clay models of those of Mexico, tools used in dressing skins and in other manufactures, metates or stone mortars, &c., &c.

In making these collections, care should be taken to specify the tribes from which they are obtained, and where any doubt may exist, the particular use to which each is applied. Thus, for instance, among the Californians, one form of basket is used for holding water; another for sweeping the seeds from various plants and grasses; a third, as their receptacle during the process of collection; a fourth, for storage; still another, in which to pound the seeds; again, one to boil the porridge made from the flour; and finally, others as dishes from which the preparation is eaten. It will also be desirable to ascertain the Indian names given to each article [5]

Of the *second* class, the remains are also numerous, and are scattered through all the States east of the Mississippi, in the form of axes, arrow-heads, sinkers for nets, fleshing chisels, and other implements of stone, and in some cases fragments of rude pottery.

To the first class belong the only *antiquities* of America, and these are of various descriptions. They include the tools found in the northern copper-mines; the articles inclosed in the mounds at Ohio and elsewhere; the images common in Kentucky and Tennessee indicating, among other things, the worship of the Phallus; pottery, the fragments of which are abundant in Florida, the Gulf States, and. on the Gila, connecting an extinct with an existing art; and especially those specimens frequently disinterred in the Mexican States, belonging to the era of Aztec or Toltecan civilizations. It is especially important to ascertain the antiquity of these by careful observation of the circumstances under which they are discovered, in order not to confound ancient with modern utensils.

To this class also belong those articles found under conditions which connect archaeology with geology, and which, may be classed as follows:

1. The contents of shell beds of ancient date found on the sea-coasts and bays, often deeply covered with soil and overgrown with trees; among which, besides the shells themselves, implements of stone, bones of fish, animals, and birds used for food, are frequently met with. The examination of these collections in Denmark and other countries of northern Europe has led to the discovery of remains belonging to a period when a people having no other implements than those of stone or bone occupied the coast prior to the settlement there of the present race. It is possible that a similar investigation' in America may carry us back to a very remote period in aboriginal history.

2. Human remains, or implements of human manufacture, bones of animals bearing the marks of tools or of subjection to fire, found in caves beneath deposits of earth, and more especially of' stalagmite of stony material formed by droppings from the roof.

3. Spear and arrow heads, or other weapons, and evidences of fire discovered in connection with bones of extinct animals, such as mammoth, fossil elephant, &c., among superficial deposits, such as salt-licks, &c.

4. Implements of the same description found in deposits of sand and gravel, or other like material, exposed bluffs or steep-banks; such as have recently attracted the attention of 'European' geologists.

In all these cases the utmost care should be taken to ascertain with [6] absolute certainty the true relations of these objects. In the case of the shell-banks, the largest trees, where any exist, should, if practicable, be cut down and the annual rings counted. Next, the depth, of the superincumbent deposit of earth should be measured, and its character noted, whether of gravel, sand, or decomposed vegetable matter; as also whether it has been stratified by the action of water. Next, the thickness of the shell-bed should be ascertained, and the height of its base above present high-water mark; as also whether it exhibit any marks of stratification. Finally, the face of the bed having been uncovered, a thorough examination should be made, commencing at the top and carefully preserving all objects which exhibits [sic] signs of human art, and noting the depth in the deposit at which they were discovered. Specimens of each species of shell should be collected, and all bones or fragments of them saved. Evidences of the use of fire should be watched for and recorded.

In the search of caverns, the same system should be followed. First, the floor should be inspected for any recent remains either of men or animals; next, the superficial earth should be carefully removed over a considerable space and thoroughly examined at various depths, the results, if any, being kept separate, and marked accordingly. Where a stalagmite deposit, such as is common in limestone caverns, forms the floor, it must be broken up and its thickness measured. The underlying materials should then be cautiously removed and sorted over, each layer being kept by itself; and where any remains are discovered, the utmost precaution should be taken to determine their actual circumstances. If, for instance, they are bones of men, it should be ascertained whether the skeleton is entire and in a natural position, indicative of having been buried there, or scattered, as also its position relative to any other remains, whether under or over them; if of animals, whether they exhibit the marks of tools, and above all, evidences of the employment of fire. Every fragment of bone or other evidence of animal life should be preserved and. marked with the order of its succession in depth.

The same precautions should be taken in the other cases mentioned, the conditions under which the objects are found, and the depth and character of covering of each being noted, and full sets of specimens sent for examination.

Besides collecting the articles heretofore mentioned, persons able to make the investigations, are invited to report the information sought in the following paper prepared by the late Prof. W. W. Turner. [7]

HINTS FOR ETHNOLOGICAL INQUIRY.

Inquiries of this description have the two-fold object of ascertaining the present condition of these tribes and their past history. Although both branches of the investigation have of course a mutual bearing upon each other, yet the former has more of a practical, the latter more of a scientific character; the former is comparatively easy; the latter environed with difficulties. In examining into the numbers, physical and mental characteristics, and actual conditions of the Indian tribes, we are accumulating data for beneficent, legislative, and philanthropic action in their behalf. The work, moreover, is a mere matter of observation, to be accomplished with the requisite expenditure of time and labor to almost any degree of minute accuracy that may be desired. On the contrary, any reliable knowledge of ante-Columbian events, that is now attainable, can, from the nature of things, be only general in its character, and the fruit of laborious induction from the comparison of many diverse particulars. As none of the tribes of the continent, not even the most advanced; ever arrived at the grand and fruitful idea of an alphabetic character for commemorating their thoughts and deeds, almost their entire history previous to the advent of Europeans is left a mysterious blank. o ascertain, if possible, the origin of the aboriginal population of this portion of our globe, to trace the migrations and conquests of the various nations that composed it from one part of the continent to another, to disclose their superstitions, their manners and customs, their knowledge of the arts of war and peace — in short, to place before us a moving panorama of America in the olden time — such is the purpose which the scientific ethnologist has in view, and to accomplish which he neglects no source of information that promises to cast even a single ray of light into the obscurity with which the subject is surrounded.

Names of tribes. — In addition to the name by which a tribe calls itself, it is desirable to ascertain those which are given to it by surrounding tribes, together with the literal meaning of each name.

Geographical position. — Give as accurately as may be the size of the territory,- whether mainland or island, belonging to each tribe; its climate, soil, and general character; also its animal, vegetable, and mineral productions.

Number. — What is the number of individuals in the tribe. State, if you can, the number of adult males, females, and children respect [8] ively. Has the number of the tribe increased or diminished to any remarkable extent; and if so, to -what cause is the change owing.

Physical constitution. — It is essential to notice the general stature of the people, the form of their bodies generally, and the proportions of their limbs the form of the skull and the facial angle; the features; have these anything which distinguishes them from other people? What are the color and texture of their skin and hair? What beard have they? What is the color of their eyes? Are they generally handsome or ugly? Have they much or but little muscular strength? Are they remarkable for the peculiar perfection of any of their organs, as that of sight, of hearing, of smelling; or for any corporeal faculties, as speed in running, facility of climbing, of diving and remaining long under water, or for nimbleness and dexterity, or the reverse? What is, the ordinary duration of life among them? It is highly desirable, also, that photographs should be taken of individuals of each tribe.

Picture-writing, etc. — A full description is desirable of any modes that the natives may practise of recording events or communicating ideas by sensible signs, especially paintings or picture-writings, however rude, whether on pieces of bark or skin, on their dwellings or implements, on rocks, &c. When the object itself containing the record cannot be secured and brought away, exact drawings of the figures should be taken, colored after the originals. Every circumstance, respecting the locality and people among whom found should be noted down, together with the interpretations of the natives (endeavoring in all cases to have the independent testimony of more than one), when attainable.

Dress. — State the materials, colors, and fashion of their dresses and ornaments. Do they paint themselves; and if so, with what materials? Do they paint variously on different occasions, as on festivals and before going to war? Give specimens of the figures they employ, especially of any that may be distinctive of the tribe or band. The same of tattooing, if practised. Some tribes of the northwest make large incisions in the under lip, others flatten the heads of their infants by compression; all such things should be observed and accurately noted respecting each tribe.

Food. — Describe the materials of which it consists, with the mode of procuring it, as by hunting, fishing, collecting roots, berries, &c. Do they practise agriculture at all; if so, to what extent; and what grains, roots, etc., do they cultivate? Do they rear any domestic animals? Do they make any stimulating drinks of their own; and are they fond of tobacco or any other narcotic? [9]

Dwellings. — Are these permanent or movable; of what materials are they constructed, and how? Are they entirely above or partially under ground; what is their interior arrangement? Drawings of both exteriors and interiors should be made, so as to give an accurate idea of their peculiarities. On whom does the labor of construction fall, the men or the women; and in case of migration, is the entire structure removed, or only the outside covering? When a number of dwellings are placed near each other, as when a tribe encamp together on a spot, is any regular mode of arrangement observed? Have they any buildings set apart for public purposes, as business, amusement, or worship, and how are they constructed?

Arts. — An exceedingly interesting branch of inquiry, and one too often overlooked or but imperfectly attended to by travellers, is presented to us in the primitive industrial arts of the aborigines. Of what materials is the pottery composed; is any of it turned on a wheel; how are the materials compounded; is the ware burned completely or partially; is it glazed or not? How is it ornamented? Have they any utensils of stone; and if so, what is the material? Of what materials are their arrow and spear heads manufactured, and what is the process? Are there individuals whose business it is to make them? Do they make any articles of metal; and if so, of what metals, and what is their mode of working them? How and by what means do they produce fire? Their modes of spinning, weaving, and dyeing, and the materials and implements used, are of great interest. What are their modes of trapping animals and taking fish; and how are their implements for these purposes constructed? Do they still retain the bow and arrow, or have they wholly or partially abandoned them for the use of firearms? The construction and mode of using all their implements should be described, and complete collections made of them. Their performances, too, in the way of what may be called the fine arts, merit attention; such as their drawings and paintings on smooth rocks or the barks of trees, or their vessels, their dwellings, ' etc.; and their carvings in wood and stone, as on pipe-bowls, paddles, bows, etc., etc. If native melodies should be discovered among them, they should by all means be noted down, together with the words sung with them.

Trade. — Do they carry on any traffic with each other, or with the whites? If so, of what articles does it consist, and how is it conducted? Have they any common standard of value which .approaches the nature of money?

Religion. — What is the nature of their religious belief; as far as it [10] can be obtained. What are the objects of their worship? Have they any idea of a Creator of all things?; and do they give any account of the creation? Do they worship the sun, fire, or the serpent (What becomes of men and animals after death? Are there any persons of the character of priests set apart for the performance of religious ceremonials? If so, how are they supported, and in what general estimation are they held? Have they a sacred fire, and is it kept perpetually burning?

Government. — Is the tribe commanded by the same chief or chiefs, in peace and in war, or by different ones? What is the extent of a chief's authority; and how does he acquire it, by birth or by the choice of the people? What are the insignia of his office, and what his privileges. Who are entitled to speak in the councils of the tribe? What laws have they; for instance, what are the punishments for theft, for adultery, for murder; and by whom are punishments inflicted?

Social life. — Is slavery known among them? Is female chastity prized? What is the treatment of women by their husbands; of children by their parents? What is the division of labor between husband and wife? What festivals have they? [E]numerate them by their native names, and describe their import, and the manner in which they are celebrated. What ceremonies do they observe at births, marriages, and funerals? Are women obliged to live apart during their monthly terms, or after giving birth to a child? At what age do marriages take place, and what degrees of consanguinity are prohibited? May a man marry into the same band or tribe to which he belongs, or must he go to another for a wife? Do children belong to the tribe of the father or of the mother? Is polygamy practiced? Do the several wives stand on a footing of equality, or is one superior to the rest, and if so, why? How is the body disposed of after death; and what articles, if any, are buried with it?

War. — Do the warriors array themselves in a peculiar attire and adjoin in the war-dance before setting out? What are their weapons? What is their treatment of captives, especially if females? Do they practise scalping, and shave their own heads, all but the scalp-lock?

Medicine. — Are there any persons in the tribe whose profession it is to practise the cure of diseases, or is this a part of the business of the priest, or so-called "medicine-man?" What is their mode of treating the principal complaints? Do they practise blood-letting, tooth-pulling, or any other surgical operations? What plants do they use as remedies, and for what complaints is each one applied? It is [11] hardly necessary to say that collections of such plants and their seeds should be made for cultivation and experiment at home.

Literature. — Have they any thing partaking of the nature of a literature among them; that is, have they any songs, tales, fables, and especially any historical legends? If they have, an endeavor should be made to record and preserve them, not so much for the information they may directly convey, as for the insight they must necessarily afford into the mental idiosyncrasy of the people. If there is any one capable of writing the language, it is much to be wished that these things should be set down in the original words, as well as an English translation.

If the Indians, like many tribes in the older States, use pictorial images for the purpose of recalling to memory the themes and general tenor of their songs, &c., specimens should be collected and delineated, and accompanied by copies of the documents they are intended to illustrate.

Calendar and Astronomy. — What divisions of time are in use among the Indians? How many days do they reckon to a month, and how many months to the year? What names are given to these days, and to the months; and what are the literal meanings of the names! Have they any length of the natural year? What names do they give to individual stars and constellations, particularly to those of the zodiac; and how do they account for eclipses? How do they ascertain and name the points of the compass? Have they any theory respecting the nature and motions of the stars, and respecting the causes of wind, rain, hail, snow, thunder, &c.

History. — Have the tribe, as far as their knowledge extends, always lived on their present territory; if not, from what direction did they come, and to what other tribes do they state themselves to be related? What changes have been introduced among them by intercourse with the whites? With what tribes have they been, and are they now, at war? Give the name of their principal chief, and of any other eminent men among them, and of their predecessors, as far as they are remembered.

Antiquities. — Earthworks, of various forms and dimensions, and for various purposes, as for defence against enemies, for watch-towers, for funeral monuments, have been found in great numbers in the valley of the Mississippi and elsewhere; and an examination of their structure and contents has disclosed a variety of the most interesting facts respecting the races that erected them. If time and opportunity be afforded of properly examining one of them, it is highly desirable that [12] it should 'be done. When a mound is opened, every particular respecting its position, site, form, and structure, should be noted down on the spot, the description being assisted by drawings of the ground-plan and elevation; and an accurate list should be taken of all the articles found in it. Such as are taken should be properly labelled, and kept by themselves, with the same care that is observed with respect to objects of natural history. When, however, the work cannot be thoroughly done, it is better to leave the mound unopened for a more favorable opportunity. [13]

PHILOLOGY

In view of the importance of .a uniform system in collecting words of the various Indian languages of North America, adapted to the use of officers of the government, travellers, and others, the following is recommended as a STANDARD VOCABULARY. It is mainly the one prepared by the late Hon. Albert Gallatin, with a few changes made by Mr. Hale, the Ethnologist of the United States Exploring Expedition, and is adopted as that upon which nearly all the collections hitherto made for the purpose of comparison have been based. For the purpose of ascertaining the more obvious relations between the various members of existing families, this number is deemed sufficient. The remote affinities must be sought in a wider research, demanding a degree of acquaintance with their languages beyond the reach of transient visitors.

The languages spoken within the limits of the United States, in which the greatest deficiencies exist, are those of the tribes comprised in the States of California and Texas, and the Territories of Utah, Nevada, and New Mexico, and to these attention is particularly directed. It is not intended, however, to confine the collection to the languages of the United States. Those of British and Russian America and of Mexico, particularly the western coast, fall within the purpose of this circular; and the alphabet may, in fact, with certain local adaptations, be used in any region.

Some of the words contained in it will of course be found inapplicable in particular sections of the country; as, for example, ice, salmon, and sturgeon among the southern tribes, buffalo among the coast tribes of the Pacific, and such should at once be omitted.

Where several languages are obtained by the same person in one district, the inquirer may substitute for these the names of familiar things, taking care that the same are carried through them all, and that they are those of native and not imported objects. Such words as coat, hat, etc., are of course useless for purposes of comparison, unless it is explained that they refer to the dress of deer-skin, the hat of basket-work used by the natives, and of their own primitive manufacture. [14]

As the languagesof savage nations, being unwritten and without fixed standard, are subject to constant change, the number of dialects is everywhere considerable. The collector is therefore recommended to obtain vocabularies in each dialect; and for the greater certainty, to employ one of those already collected, on the correctness of which reliance can be, placed, as the medium of obtaining others.

Whenever leisure and opportunity offer for the collection of larger vocabularies than that here given, it will of course be desirable to procure them; as also information concerning the grammatical structure of the language, such as the modes of forming the plurals in nouns and adjectives, their declension, the conjugation of verbs, the character and use of pronouns, the number and employment of adverbs, prepositions, &c. Grammars and dictionaries, never yet published were made of many of the languages of Upper and Lower California and the Mexican States by the Spanish missionaries, and the Smithsonian Institution has been favored with the loan of several manuscripts which are in the course of publication. It is desired to procure others, or copies of them, whenever it is possible, from all parts of both the American continents, or of printed works on the same subject. The present form is issued for the use of travellers or merely transient residents among tribes where no such records are procurable.

In making collections, the utmost care is requisite to represent accurately the sounds of unfamiliar languages, particularly those which to us appear uncouth, and the inquirer, should satisfy himself, by repetition of the words to other individuals, that he has correctly acquired their pronunciation. While the assistance of interpreters conversant with the language is desirable to insure a correct understanding, the words themselves should be taken down from the lips of an Indian of the tribe. A great difference indeed exists among Indians in the purity with which they speak their own language, chiefs and men of note and women of good standing, as a general thing, speaking more correctly than common persons. Great patience is necessary to secure accuracy, as their attention soon becomes fatigued by being kept on the stretch. Whenever this is observed to be the case, it is best to postpone the subject for a time, if possible.

The character of the Indian mind is so essentially different from that of the white man, they think in so different a manner, that many precautions are necessary to avoid giving them wrong impressions of our meaning, and of course obtaining incorrect replies.

Indians not only distinguish by different names the degrees and [15] modifications of relationship, such as the elder from the younger brother and sister, but women use different words from men in dressing their relations; as, for instance, a man employs one word in saying "my father," and a woman another. Again, different words are, at least in some languages, used in speaking *of* one's parents from those used in speaking *to* them. It is, therefore, necessary either to give each form, or to specify by what sex and in what sense the words are used. Further to prevent uncertainty, it is preferable to employ the possessive pronoun in connection with the word, as given in the vocabulary, *e.g.,* "my father," &c., and this is, in fact, in consonant[c]e with Indian practice.

Their languages are deficient in *generic* terms, or those representing classes of objects. Thus very few possess words equivalent to "tree," "bird," "fish," &c., though names will be found for every particular species, as each kind of oak and pine, of duck or salmon; and of certain animals, such as deer, there will be found, besides the specific name, black or white-tailed deer, as the case may be, separate words signifying buck, doe, and fawn, as with us. It is, therefore, essential in obtaining such names, to ascertain definitively the object intended, and to note this in the vocabulary.

This tendency to particularize extends to almost every class of objects. In regard to parts of the body, it has been found that in many languages there is no one word for arm or leg, but separate ones for the upper arm, and that below the elbow; for the thigh, and that part below the knee. Even of the hands and feet there are often no names embracing the whole. So, too, the words "leaf," "bark," are represented by distinct names, according to their character, as broad and needle-shaped leaves, the woody and fibrous barks. Sheath and pocket knives and the various forms of canoes have in like manner each their specific names.

In respect to particular words, the following points may be noted:

Man. This must be carefully distinguished from the word "person," the collective of which is "people," *i.e.;* Indians.

Boy, Girl, Infant. The answer often given for these is simply "little man," "little woman," "little one."

Husband and *wife.* Distinct words exist in most languages for these relationships; in others, it would seem as if there was only "my man," "my woman."

Indians, people. Care must be taken that the name of the tribe is not given. [16]

Head. A very common mistake to be guarded against is the substitution of hair or scalp.

Face. The name for the forehead or. eyes is, in some cases, employed for the whole face.

Neck. Throat is apt to be given instead of neck.

In naming parts of the body, as well as relationship, it will be found a very common practice with Indians to prefix the pronoun "my" to each one, as " my head," &c. The recurrence of the same syllable at the beginning of each word will indicate this.

Town, village. Generally speaking, the same word is given as for house, or it is rendered "many houses." In New Mexico, *pueblo* would have a different meaning from the habitations of the wild tribes.

Warrior. Among the tribes of the Pacific coast, whore there is no distinctive class of warriors, this is frequently rendered "strong man," "quarrelsome," &c.

Friend is a word of very indefinite meaning. Instead of it, "cousin," or "one liked," will often be given.

Sun and *moon*. Curiously enough, these, among several tribes, bear the same name and are actually supposed to be the same. Others use for moon "night sun."

The Seasons. These words have been retained, though it is questionable if they have a very definite signification with Indians. The names of particular months, or "moons," warm or cold weather, or the periods in which particular occupations are followed probably, in most cases, replace them.

River, lake. For these simply the word "Water" will often be given, as among tribes of limited range, their own river or lake is "the water" which they best know.

Mountain. "Rock" is frequently the translation. Some tribes, again, apply a special name to snow peaks.

The colors. The idea of color seems to be indistinct, dark blue and dark green having, in many languages, the same name as. black, and yellow the same as light green.

Old and *young*. Care should be taken that the words for "old man," "young man," are not supplied; or, on the other hand, "worn out," and "new," as is often the case.

Alive is frequently rendered "not dead."

Cold, warm. Here, again, caution is requisite, as cold or warm weather may be given instead.

Yesterday and *to-morrow*. In some languages, a single word is used for both, the distinction being made only by the connection. [17]

Numerals. Many tribes go no farther in counting than ten, and among those of California, it is said, some have no names for numbers beyond five. Others, on the contrary, have different sets of numerals, or rather their numerals have different terminations, one class being used in ordinary (counting, the other applying to men, money, &c.

Pronouns. The personal pronouns are of two classes, one simple or absolute, the other variously called fragmentary and copulative. These last are used only in composition, as in the form of prefixes and suffixes to the verbs.

Verbs. It is a matter of dispute whether the Indian verb has any true infinitive mood, as " to go," " to eat," &c., and its simplest form appears to be, in all cases, the third person singular present, "he goes," "he eats." It will be better, therefore, to obtain either this form or that of the first person, "I go," &c. The last will be found often to be combined with the copulative pronoun.

ORTHOGRAPHY.

It is, of course, essential to the proper understanding by others of the words collected, especially in view of general comparisons, that a precise and fixed system of spelling should be used, and this is more so where the usual language of the collector is English than where French or Spanish, as there is far less certainty in the pronunciation of the first than of these last. In English, for instance, four different sounds are given as belonging to the letter *a*, viz.: those in *far, fall, fat, fate*. As regards the simple vowels, the difficulty can be partly remedied by employing the Spanish or Italian sounds, as given, below, and a further advantage will be found in separating the words into syllables and marking the principal one with an accent, thus Da-ko'-ta. There are, however, in every language, sounds peculiar to itself, and the different Indian tongues abound in them, many being almost beyond our capacity to imitate and certainly to write, without some addition to the ordinary alphabet. Various systems, contemplating a universal alphabet, or one applicable to all languages, have been devised, each having its peculiar merits; but the great, difficulty, never fully overcome, has been to represent intelligibly such unfamiliar sounds without confusing the inquirer with new characters or numerous marks, or, again, by employing several letters to represent a single sound. The alphabet here recommended for adoption, without pretending to remedy these defects, will at least prove an assistance to the collector in the field. Should it be necessary to represent [18] other sounds, not included below, it will be better for him to adopt some arbitrary mark of his own, describing fully its value or meaning.

VOWELS.

A	as long in *father*, and short in German *hat* (nearly as in English what).
E	as long in *they* ("long a" in *face*), short in met.
I	" " " *marine*, short in *pin*.
O	" " " *go*, short in *home, whole* (as generally pronounced in the northern States).
U	as long in *rule* (*oo* in *fool*), short in *full* (*oo* in *good*). U as in *union, pure*, &c.; to be written *yu*.
Â	as in *all* (*aw, au* in *bawl, taught*),
A	" " *fat*.
U	" " *but* (*o* in *love, oo* in *blood*).
AI	" " *aisle* (" *long* i" in *pine*).
AU	as *ow* in *now, ou* in *loud*.

The distinction of long and short vowels to be noted, as far as possible, by the division into syllables, joining a following consonant to a short vowel, and leaving the vowel open if long. Where this is insufficient, or where greater distinctness is desirable, a horizontal mark above, to indicate a long vowel, a curved mark a short one, thus: ā, ă, ē, ĕ, &c. A nasal syllable, like those found so commonly in French, to be marked by an index, n, at the upper right-hand corner of the vowel; thus o^n, d^n, a^n, u^n, will represent the sounds of the French *on, an* or *en, in*, and *un*, respectively.

CONSONANTS.

B	as in English *blab*.
C	not to be used excepting in the compound *ch*; write *k* for the hard sound, *s* for the soft.
D	as in English *did*.
F	" " " *fife*.
G	" " " *gig*, never for the soft sound, as in *ginger*; for this use always *j*.
H	as in English *how, hoe, handle*.
J	" " " *judge*.
K	" " " *kick*. [19]
L	as in English *lull*.
M	" " " *mimic*.
N	" " " *noon*.
P	" " " *pipe*.
Q	not to be used: for *qu* write *kw*.
R	as in English *rear*.
S	" " " *sauce*.
T	" " " *tight*.
V	" " " *vow*.
W	" " " *wayward*.
X	not to be used: write *ks* or *gz*, according to the sound, in *wax, for example*.
Y	as in English *you, year*.
Z	" " " *zeal, buzz*.
Ñ	as *ng* in English, *singing*.
SH	as in English *shall, shoe*.
ZH	as *z* in *azure*, *s* in *fusion*.
CH	as in English *church*.
TH	" " " *thin, truth*.
DH	as *th* in *the, with*.
KH	a surd guttural aspirate, the German *ch* in *ach, loch, buch*, and sometimes approaching that in *ich, recht, bucher*.
GH	a sonant guttural aspirate (Arabic *ghain*); other compounds; like the clucks occurring in Chinook, &c., to be represented by *kl, tkl, tlk*, &c , according to their analysis.

COMPARATIVE VOCABULARY. [20]

ENGLISH	SPANISH
Name of tribe	Nombre de la tribu
1 man	hombre
2 woman	mujer
3 boy	muchacho
4 girl	muchacha
5 infant	nino o nina
6 my father (said by son)	mi padre (dice el hijo)
7 my father (said by daughter)	mi padre (dice la hija)
8 my mother (said .by son)	mi madre (dice el hijo
9 my mother (said -by .daughter)	mi madre (dice la hija)
10 my husband	mi marido
11 my wife	mi esposa
12 my son (said by father)	mi hijo (dice el padre)
13 my son (said by mother)	mi hijo (dice la madre)
14 my daughter (said by father)	mi hija (dice el padre)
15 my daughter (said by mother)	mi hija (dice la madre)
16 my elder brother	mi hermauo mayor
17 my younger brother	mi hermano menor
18 my elder sister	mi hermana mayor
19 my younger sister	mi hermana menor
20 an Indian	Indio
21 people	gente
22 head	cabeza
23 hair	pelo
24 face	cara
25 forehead	frente
26 ear	oreja
27 eye	ojo
28 nose	nariz
29 mouth	boca

COMPARATIVE VOCABULARY. [21]

FRENCH	LATIN
Nom de tribu	Nomen nationis
1 homme	vir, homo
2 femme	mulier
3 garcon	puer
4 fille	puella
5 enfant	infans
6 mon pere (dit le fils)	pater meus (dicit filius)
7 mon pere (dit le fille)	pater meus (dicit filia)
8 ma mere (dit le fils)	mater mea (dicit filius)
9 ma mere (dit le fille)	mater mea (dicit filia)
10 mon mari	sponsus meus
11 mon epsouse	uxor mea
12 mon fils (dit le pere)	filius meus (dicit pater)
13 mon fils (dit la mere)	filius meus (dicit mater)
14 ma fille (dit la mere)	filia mea (dicit pater)
15 ma fille (dit la mere)	filia mea (dicit mater)
16 mon frere aine	frater meus natu major
17 mon frere cadet	frater meus natu manor
18 ma soeur ainee	soror mea natu major
19 ma soeur cadette	soror meea natu minor
20 sauvage	Indus
21 peuple	populus
22 tête	caput
23 cheveux	crinis
24 figure	facies
25 front	frons
26 oreille	auris
27 oeil	oculus
28 nez	nasus
29 bouche	os

COMPARATIVE VOCABULARY. [22]

ENGLISH	SPANISH
Name of tribe	Nombre de la tribu
30 tongue	lengua
31 teeth	dientes
32 beard	barba
33 neck	cuello
34 arm	brazo
35 hand	mano
36 fingers	dedos
37 thumb	dedo pulgar
38 nails	uñas
39 body	cuerpo
40 chest	pecho
41 belly	barriga
42 female breasts	pechos de mujer
43 leg	pierna
44 foot	pie
45 toes	dedos del pie
46 bone	hueso
47 heart	corazon
48 blood	sangre
49 town, village	pueblo, villa, aleea
50 chief	jefe
51 warrior	guerrero
52 friend	amigo
53 house	casa
54 skin lodge	casa de cueros
55 kettle	caldera
56 bow	arco
57 arrow	flecha
58 axe, hatchet	hacha
59 knife	cuchillo
60 canoe	canoa
61 moccasins	zapatos Indios
62 pipe	pipa

COMPARATIVE VOCABULARY. [23]

FRENCH	LATIN
Nom de tribu	Nomen nationis
30 langue	lingua
31 dents	dentes
32 barbe	barba
33 cou	collis
34 bras	brachium
35 main	manua
36 doigts	digiti
37 pouce	digitus pollex
38 ongles	ungues
39 corps	corpus
40 poitrine	sternum
41 ventre	venter
42 mamelles	ubera
43 jambe	crus
44 pied	pes
45 doigts du pied	digiti pedia
46 os	os
47 coeur	cor
48 sang	sanguis
49 bourg, village	oppidum, pagus
50 capitaine	dur
51 guerrier	miles
52 ami	amicus
53 maison	domus
54 loge de peaux	tentorium e pellibus
55 chaudiere	lebes
56 arc	arcus
57 fleche	sagitta
58 hache	ascia
59 couteau	culter
60 canot	scapha Indica
61 souliers de sauvage	calceamenta Indica
62 pipe	tubus nicotianus

COMPARATIVE VOCABULARY. [24]

ENGLISH	SPANISH
Name of tribe	Nombre de la tribu
63 tobacco	tabaco
64 sky	cielo
65 sun	sol
66 moon	luna
67 star	estrella
68 day	dia
69 night	noche
70 morning	mañana
71 evening	tarde
72 spring	primavera
73 summer	verano
74 autumn	otoño
75 winter	invierno
76 wind	viento
77 thunder	trueno
78 lightning	relampago
79 rain	lluvia
80 snow	nieve
81 fire	fuego
82 water	agua
83 ice	hielo
84 earth, land	tierra
85 sea	mar
86 river	rio
87 lake	lago
88 valley	valle
89 prairie	llano
90 hill, mountain	cerro, montaña
91 island	isla
92 stone, rock	piedra, roca
93 salt	sal
94 iron	hierro
95 forest	bosque, selva

COMPARATIVE VOCABULARY. [25]

FRENCH	LATIN
Name of tribe	Nombre de la tribu
63 tabac	nicotianum
64 ciel	coelum
65 sol	sol
66 lune	luna
67 étoile	stella
68 jou	dies
69 nuit	nox
70 matin	tempus matutinum
71 soir	vesper
72 printemps	ver
73 été	aestas
74 automne	autumnus
75 hiver	hibernus
76 vent	ventus
77 tonnerre	tonitru
78 éclair	fulgur
79 pluie	pluvium
80 neige	nix
81 feu	ignis
82 eau	aqua
83 glace	glacies
84 terre	terra
85 mer	mar
86 fleuve, riviére	flumen
87 lac	lacus
88 vallée	vallis
89 prairie	pratum
90 côte, montagne	collis, mons
91 ile	insula
92 pierre, roche	petra
93 sel	sal
94 fer	ferrum
95 forét	sylva

COMPARATIVE VOCABULARY. [26]

ENGLISH	SPANISH
Name of tribe	Nombre de la tribu
96 tree	árbol
97 wood	madera
98 leaf	hoja
99 bark	orteza
100 grass	zacate
101 pine	pino
102 maize	mais
103 squash	calabaza
104 flesh, meat	carne
105 dog	perro
106 buffalo	bisonte, bufalo
107 bear	oso
108 wolf	lobo
109 fox	zorra
110 deer	ciervo
111 elk	??
112 beaver	castor
113 rabbit, hare	conejo
114 tortoise	tortuga
115 horse	caballo
116 fly	mosca
117 mosquito	mosquito
118 snake	culebra, serpiente
119 rattlesnake	culebra de cascabel
120 bird	ave
121 egg	huevo
122 feathers	plumas
123 wings	alas
124 goose	ganso
125 duck (mallard)	pato
126 turkey	pavo, guanajo
127 pigeon	pichon
128 fish	pez

COMPARATIVE VOCABULARY. [27]

FRENCH	LATIN
Name of tribe	Nombre de la tribu
96 arbre	arbor
97 bois	lignum
98 feuille	folium
99 écorce	cortex
100 herbe	herba
101 pin	pinus
102 mais	zea mais {!!}
103 citrouille	cucurbitus
104 chair	caro
105 chien	canis
106 buffle	bison, bos americanus {!!}
107 ours	ursus
108 loup	lupus
109 renard	vulpes
110 cerf	cervus
111 élan	cervus canadiensis {!!}
112 castor	castor
113 lapin, liévre	lepus
114 tortue	testudo
115 cheval	equus
116 mouche	musca
117 maringouin	culex
118 serpent	serpens
119 serpent a sonnettes	crotalus
120 oiseau	avis
121 oeuf	ovum
122 plumes	plumae
123 ailes	alae
124 oie	anser
125 canard	anas boschas
126 dindon	pavo
127 tourte	columba
128 poisson	piscis

COMPARATIVE VOCABULARY. [28]

ENGLISH	SPANISH
Name of tribe	Nombre de la tribu
129 salmon	salmon
130 sturgeon	esturion
131 name	nombre
132 white	blanco
133 black	negro
134 red	colorado
135 light blue	azul celeste
136 yellow	amarillo
137 light green	verde
138 great, large	grande
139 small, little	pequeño
140 strong	fuerte
141 old	viejo
142 young	jóven
143 good	bueno
144 bad	malo
145 dead	muerto
146 alive	vivo
147 cold	frio
148 warm, hot	caliente
149 I	yo
150 thou	tú
151 he	él
152 we	nosotros
153 ye	vosotros
154 they	ellos
155 this	este
156 that	aquel
157 all	todo, todos
158 many, much	mucho, muchos
159 who	quien
160 far	lejos
161 near	cerca de

COMPARATIVE VOCABULARY. [29]

FRENCH	LATIN
Nom de la tribu	Nomen nationis
129 saumon	salmo
130 esturgeon	sturio
131 nom	nomen
132 blanc	albus
133 noir	niger
134 rouge	rubrum
135 bleu	coeruleum
136 jaune	amarillis
137 vert	viridis
138 grand	magnus
139 petit	parvus
140 fort	fortis
141 vieux	vetus
142 jeune	juvenis
143 von	bonus
144 mauvais	malus
145 mort	mortuus
146 vivant	vivus
147 froid	frigidus
148 chaud	calidus
149 je	ego
150 tu	tu
151 il	ille
152 nous	nos
153 vous	vos
154 ils	illi
155 ceci	iste
156 cela	ille
157 tout, tous	omnis, totus
158 beaucoup	multus
159 qui	qui
160 loin	longe
161 prés	prope

COMPARATIVE VOCABULARY. [30]

ENGLISH	SPANISH
Name of tribe	Nombre de la tribu
162 here	aqui
163 there	allá
164 to-day	hoy
165 yesterday	ayer
166 to-morrow	mañana (el dia de)
167 yes	sí
168 no	no
169 one	uno
170 two	dos
171 three	tres
172 four	cuatro
173 five	cinco
174 six	seis
175 seven	siete
176 eight	ocho
177 nine	nueve
178 ten	diez
179 eleven	once
180 twelve	doce
181 twenty	viente
182 thirty	treinta
183 forty	cuarenta
184 fifty	cincuenta
185 sixty	sesenta
186 seventy	sentena
187 eighty	ochenta
188 ninety	noventa
189 one hundred	ciento
190 one thousand	mil
191 to eat	comer
192 to drink	beber
193 to run	correr
194 to dance	bailer

COMPARATIVE VOCABULARY. [31]

FRENCH	LATIN
Nom de la tribu	Nom nationis
162 ici	hic
163 lá	illuc
164 aujourd'hui	hodie
165 hier	heri
166 demain	cras
167 oui	ita
168 non	minime
169 un	unus
170 deux	duo
171 trois	tres
172 quatre	quatuor
173 cinq	quinque
174 six	sex
175 sept	septem
176 huit	octo
177 neuf	novem
178 dix	decem
179 onze	undecim
180 douze	duodecim
181 vingt	viginit
182 trente	triginta
183 quarante	quadaginta
184 cinquante	quinquaginta
185 soixante	sexaginta
186 soixante-dix	septuaginta
187 quatre-vingts	octoginta
188 quatre-vingt-dix	nonaginta
189 cent	centum
190 mille	mille
191 manger	edere
192 boire	bibere
193 courir	currete
194 canser	saltare

COMPARATIVE VOCABULARY. [32]

ENGLISH	SPANISH
Name of tribe	Nombre de la tribu
195 to sing	cantar
196 to sleep	dormir
197 to speak	hablar
198 to see	ver
199 to love	amar
200 to kill	matar
201 to sit	sentarse
202 to stand	estar en pie
203 to go	ir
204 to come	venir
205 to walk	andar
206 to work	trabajar
207 to steal	robar
208 to lie	mentir
209 to give	dar
210 to laugh	reir
211 to cry	gritar

COMPARATIVE VOCABULARY. [33]

FRENCH	LATIN	
Nom de la tribu	Nomen nationis	
195 chantar	cantare	
196 dormir	dormire	
197 parler	loqui	
198 voir	videre	
199 aimer	amare	
200 tuer	caedere	
201 s'asseoir	sedere	
202 se tenir debout	stare	
203 aller	ire	
204 venir	venire	
205 marcher	ambulare	
206 travailler	operari	
207 voler	furare	
208 mentir	mentiri	
209 donner	dare	
210 rire	ridere	
211 crier	clamare	[34]

INSTRUCTIONS
RELATIVE TO THE
ETHNOLOGY AND PHILOLOGY OF AMERICA.

APPENDIX A.
PHYSICAL CHARACTER OF THE INDIAN RACES.

INVESTIGATIONS are now being made into the physical character of the soldiers composing the armies of the "United States, embracing a large number of measurements of different parts of the body, designed to ascertain the effect of climate, locality, and mode of life upon men, the average size and proportions of troops of the "United. States as compared with those of foreign countries, and those of the different States as compared with each other.

In connection with this inquiry it is deemed a matter of interest to extend the examination to the Indian tribes of America, and to ascertain the proportions of the aboriginal races as compared with those of European descent, and also the effects of different food, climate, and mode of life upon the various tribes of the former.

The measurements selected for this purpose are, for various reasons, limited to a smaller number than in the case of the army, and with the exception of that of weight, which as being variable is of the least consequence, are such as can be taken with a tape-measure. They should be made with great care in feet, inches, and tenths of an inch.

Persons familiar with the Indians are aware that a great difference exists in the complexion, not merely of individuals, but of tribes. In some cases that peculiar reddish tinge of the skin which has given to the race the name of "Red" or "Copper-colored Men" is predominant and marked; in others a light brown is the more common; again, a yellowish or somewhat orange hue exhibits itself; and, finally, some approach nearly to black. Among the lighter colored the red often shows in the {May, 1885 (p35)} [36] cheek. Nor were these diversities due altogether to climate or exposure. There seem to be well authenticated instances in which food also influences complexion. Thus it is said that among the Chepewyan tribes of British America, the Cariboo or Reindeer eaters are much darker than the cognate tribes who live on fish, and this, too, although they inhabit a far northern latitude. The texture of the skin is a noticeable feature. That of the younger Indians, where it can be perceived through the dirt, is, usually, exceedingly soft and delicate, but becomes wrinkled with middle age. An important difference in the color of the hair also occasionally shows itself. For instance, the Indians of the Nooksahk tribe, in the neighborhood of Mount Baker, Washington Territory, have often light-brown and even flaxen hair in youth, which, however, grows dark with age, and yet their blood is unmixed. When neglected and exposed to the sun the hair becomes of a rusty hue, and like that of whites loses its gloss. Among some of the Pueblo tribes of New Mexico albinos are not uncommon. Hazel eyes are frequent among the Indians of the lower Klamath.

Particular information should be given as to their food, whether consisting of game, fish, maize, roots, &c., and even as to the kinds of either, whether of buffalo, elk, deer, or cariboo, of salmon or other varieties of river fish, or of the various animal productions of the sea, such as the whale, walrus, seals, &c., as among the Esquimaux and some of the Northwest Coast Indians.

Their mode of life will, of course, influence the development of the form. Among the tribes who live almost altogether on horseback, or in canoes, we may expect to see the legs comparatively small, while in the latter the arms will be proportionately large. Among the mountain tribes, on the other hand, the legs will be more muscular and the chest expanded. As a general rule their limbs are rounded, and the separate muscles are not developed as in the white and black races. As to this, observations are requested.

The age of Indians it is very difficult, in most cases impossible, to ascertain, as they keep no record even in memory. An estimate founded on careful observation will, however, afford a reasonable approximation. Sometimes a reference to a known event as having occurred when they were of the size of some young boy will afford a guide. As the men usually marry young, [37] the age of their families furnishes often another. A great age, notwithstanding apparent decrepitude, is very rarely attained, especially by the male sex.

In the case of mixed breeds it is by all means desirable to ascertain and state whether either one or both parents were themselves mixed, and, if so, to what degree. Any observations on the comparative physical development, health, and length of life among the mixed breeds will be very gladly received.

Where the inquiry, is made by medical men, other points will naturally suggest themselves. Among them, it will be well to ascertain the number of regular pulsations and respirations per minute.

It is hardly necessary to add that these measurements should be confined to adult males. Observations on boys who have not attained their growth would have no value.

PARTICULARS OF INQUIRY.

In order to avoid the necessity of transcribing the questions, references may be made to the numbers and letters. Separate tables in quarto have been prepared, and will be furnished on application to the Smithsonian Institution.

1. Name of Indian.
2. Name of tribe.
3. If of mixed blood, in what proportion?
4. Country occupied by tribe.
5. Mode of subsistence, whether by hunting, fishing, &c.
    Habits, whether used to riding, foot, or canoe travel.
6. Articles of usual food.
7. Age (by estimation) between 20 and 30, 30 and 40, &c.
8. State of general health.
9. Weight in lbs. and half lbs.
10. General complexion, whether reddish, brown, yellowish, or black.
11. Hair, color of. [38]
12. Eyes, color of,

a. Whether oblique or not.
   b. Distance between outer angles over root of nose.
13. Teeth
    a. How many are lost?
    b. Are they much ground down by hard food?
    c. Do the opposing incisor teeth of the two jaws rest on each other, do they overlap?
14. Entire height without shoes,
15. Head.
    a. Largest circumference around.
    b. Distance between orifices of ears over top of head.
    c. Distance from root of nose over top of the head 'to base of skull.
16. Arm
    a. Length outside from point of shoulder cap to tip of middle finger.
    b. Length from 'same to point of elbow when bent.
    c. Length from point of elbow to lower end of ulna.
    d. Length from lower end of ulna to tip of middle finger.
    e. Largest girth of arm.
    f. Largest girth of forearm.
    g. Largest girth of hand.
17. Distance from upper centre of breast bone to end of middle finger, arm extended.
18. Breadth of shoulders behind.
19. Girth-of neck. [39]
20. Girth of chest around nipples.
    a. With full inspiration.
    b. After expiration.
21. Girth of waist.
22. Girth around hips on level with the head of the thigh bones.
23. Leg.
    a. Height from ground to top of '.hip-bone, outside.
    b. Height to knee-joint outside.
    c. Height to crotch inside.
    d. Largest girth of thigh.
    e. Largest girth of leg.
24. Foot.
    a. Length from tip of great toe to extremity of heel
    b. Girth of instep.
    c. Girth around heel and instep.

INSTRUCTIONS
RELATIVE TO THE
ETHNOLOGY AND PHILOLOGY OF AMERICA

APPENDIX B
NUMERAL SYSTEMS [40]

In the original circular of "Instructions" allusion was made to the fact that some of the Indian tribes use different sets of numerals, or rather modifications of the numerals, as applied to different objects. This fact, in connection with the various serial systems upon which their enumeration is based, presents a subject worthy pf particular .inquiry, the more especially as the same singularity exists among other distant and distinct barbarous nations.

Mr. Gallatin in his "Notes on the Semi-Civilised Nations of Mexico," &c., published in the Transactions of the American Ethnological Society (vol. ii. p. 54, et seq.), says: "Another peculiarity of the Mexican and Maya, and of which traces may be seen in other languages of the same group, is the alteration which the numerals undergo according to the nature of the object to be counted. The distinctions are not always easy to be understood; and the objects of the same class, that is to say in counting which the same altered numeral is used, are apparently of the same incongruous nature. Those stated by Father Alonzo de Molina for the Mexican language, are as follows:

1 ce, cem

2 ome

3 yey

4 naul

5 macuilli

6 chica-ce

7 chic-ome

8 chic-uey

9 chicu-naul

10 mat-lactli

20 cem-poualli [41]

I have excerpted only the first ten numerals and the word for twenty from Mr. Gallatln's Table *A*. He proceeds: —

"The numerals as laid down in Table *A*. are used in counting animated beings, manias, mats, paper, tortillas, ropes, skins, canoes, cycles, knives, and candles; but in counting several of these, the word *pilli* and sometimes *quimilli, is* substituted for *poualli* (20).

"The syllable *tetl* is added to the numerals, and these lose their last syllable *(matlactetl* for *matlacti, cem-poualtetl* for *cempoualli*) when counting fowls, eggs, cocoa, jars, frijoles, fruits, roots, rolls, or round things.

"The word *pantli* is added to the numeral when speaking of ridges made by the plough, of walls, files of men, and of other things arranged in length.

"*Tlementli* is added to the numeral when speaking of speeches, dishes, bags, shields, or when a thing is doubled above another, or when speaking of things differing one from the other."

No reference to such a system as to be found in the Grammatical sketch of the HEVE, translated by Mr. Buckingham Smith (No. 111 of Shea's Linguistics); in the Nevome Grammar (ibid. No. V), the Mutsun of Father Arroyo (ib. No. IV), or Father Sitjars vocabulary of the San Antonio (ib. No. VII), the only extended works at present accessible on the languages of Sonora and California, but it is very possible that it may exist there and have escaped notice.

In Father Pandosy's Grammar of the Yakama, a Sahaptin language of Washington Territory (Shea's Linguistics, No. V), the numerals are not specially referred to; but in the accompanying dictionary *metat* is given for three, *metao,* three persons; *pinept* for four, *pinapo* four persons; *parat* five, *par-nao,* five persons, and other numerals are given in duplicate or triplicate without explanation.

Father Meugarini, in his Grammar of the Selish, or Flathead of the Rocky Mountains (Shea, No. II.), Bays of the cardinal numbers, "they are duplex, one set relating to things, the other to persons, thus: — [42]

	Relating to things	*Relating to persons*
1	nko	schnaksi
2	esel	chesel
3	cheles	ch'cbeles
4	mus	ch'musms
5	zil	ch'zilzil
6	tackan	ch'tackan
7	sispel	ch'sispel
8	hehenem	ch'hehenem
9	ganut	ch'ganut
10	open	eh'open

Similar changes exist in other dialects of the Selish, of which the following from the Nisqually will serve as an instance: —

	Applied to men.	*Applied to money.*
1	dut-cho	che-elts
2	sale	sal-elts
3	klekhw	kle-hwelts
4	bos	bos-elts
5	tsa-lats	tslat-selts
6	dze-la-chi	dzlatch-elts
7	tsoks	tsok-selts
8	t'ka-chi	t'ka-chi-elts
9	hwul	hwul-elts

10	pa-duts	pa-dats-elts
20	sa-l-chi	

Zeisberger in his "Grammar of the Language of the Lenni-Lenape, or Delaware Indians" (Trans. Am. Phil. Soc., N. S., vol. iii), gives the list of numerals, without stating its application, as follows: —

1	ngutti	6	guttasch
2	nischa	7	nischasch
3	nacha	8	chasch
4	newo	9	peschkouk
5	palenmach	10	tellen

And then adds the following, used in respect to inanimate objects, as towns, rivers, houses, &c.

Mawat, ngutti, one, only one, and in the plural, *nischenol,* two; nechenol, three, &c., concerning which he observed, "When men, animals, or other things are spoken of, which among the [43] Indians are considered as belonging to the animated class of beings, they say: *mauchsa, mayauchsu,* one person, or a person; or living being. It is truly incorrect to say *ngutti lenno,* a man. And in the plural, *nischowak lennowak,* two men, &c.

All and *ak,* the terminations, of these last in the plural, are respectively applied, the former to inanimate, the latter to animate objects. But as exceptions, it is stated that among nouns, trees and the larger plants are considered animate, while fishes take the inanimate termination. It is thus evident that a similar idea has governed the form of the numeral adjective in the Delaware and the Mexican.

Other examples among the North American languages might be cited, but the above are sufficient to indicate the object of inquiry. The system appears, however, not to have been universal, as, according to Dr. Wilson, there is no distinction of numerals in the Seneca or other Iroquois languages.

Singularly enough, the same idea prevails in the numerals of other and far distant races, of which a few specimens may be useful.

The Hon. John Pickering, in "Memoirs of the American Academy," N. S., vol. ii, gives an account of the language and inhabitants of Tobi, or Lord North's Island, in the Indian Archipelago, derived from an American seaman, Horace Holden, who .spent two years upon it. This island is situated about lat. 3° 2' north and lon. 131° 4' east, and is of very small extent and sparsely inhabited. The different forms of the digits are thus given in the accompanying vocabulary; —

	General cardinals	For cocoanuts	For fish
1	yat	su	simŭl
2	guh-lu	guo	gwimŭl
3	ya	saru	srimŭl
4	van	vao	vamŭl
5	ni	limo	nimŭl
6	wor	waru	wawrimŭl
7	vish	vishu	vishi-emŭl

8	wawr	tin (?)	wawrimul
9	tiu	(wanting)	tuimul
10	se, sek	sek	sek

He adds, however, that in counting out fish, they proceed by pairs or couples, as, two, four, six, &c. [44]

In counting *fish hooks*, they nee still a different set of numerals, which were not recollected. It would appear farther that stones, birds, and days were counted by the same numerals as cocoa-nuts and men and women by those employed to enumerate fish. Mr. Hale, in the "Ethnography, &c., of the U. S. Exploring Expedition," copies Holden's vocabulary, which is also appended to a narrative of his captivity, published at Boston.

Dr. L. H. Gulick, in his notes on the Grammar of the Ponape dialect (12mo. Honolulu, 1858, pp. 39), states that "the enumeration of all objects is alike as far as *nine,* after which there is a singular variety." The difference is in —

I. The mode of counting all animated objects, and all kinds of sticks and timbers, and everything that to a native is connected in idea with separate sticks, as trees, canoes, &c.
II. The enumeration of yams, taro, and a few of the most costly articles.
III. The numbering of cocoanuts, bread-fruits, eggs, shells, stones, &c., in fact, probably, of all common, least valued objects, not included under the first head."

Examples are given, not necessary to repeat here, as also of 'peculiarities in the numerative particles.

The Island of Ponape, Paauopa, or, as written by Mr. Hale, Bonabe, is one of the central islands of Micronesia. That gentleman gives also a vocabulary of the language of Taputeoua, in the Kingsmill group, one of the most eastern, and separated from Tobi by 2600 miles. Speaking of the numerals, he says that the natives furnished the expedition with several sets or classes, which he conjectured were used in counting objects of different kinds, though he had no means of obtaining from them any explanation. There were five of them in all, and all given in the digits, or from one to ten. — Eth. of Ex. Esp. p. 440.

Leaving Micronesia for Polynesia, Mr. Hale states that some of the terms for the higher numbers are only used in counting particular articles. For *four,* the Hawaiians, for instance, have two terms, *ha* and *tauna.* For forty, they have *tanaha, iato,* and *ta'au.* The first of these, tanaha, is the general term; *iato* is used in counting pieces of *tapa* (native cloth), and *ta'au* in counting fish. (Ib. p. 250.)

It is remarkable that thus, in Tobi and Taputeoua, the distinction should extend to all the digits; and in Ponape, which [45] is between the two, and Hawaii, distant 3500 miles, it should be confined to the higher numbers.

The last example here presented is from Bowen's Yoruba Dictionary, in the 10th vol. Smithsonian Contributions. In this, an African Language, traces of the same system also appear. Thus in ordinary counting the first vowel is short, while among what the author terms "cardinals of price," up to forty, the vowel is long; thus *okay,* one, *edzi,* two; *okay, edzi.* The reason given for this is that the latter are contractions of *owo-kay, owo-edzi, i. e.* one cowrie, two cowries, &c.

It thus appears that this peculiar arithmetic is of wide distribution, and by no means confined to a single or even to cognate races. A more perfect knowledge of barbarian languages would probably show its still greater extension. In what process of the human mind it has its origin, and the reasons for the singular collocation of objects which different tribes embrace in the several forms of the numerals, are questions of curious speculation.

The division of objects, into animate and inanimate, or, as they have been termed by other writers, noble and ignoble, is a well-known feature in several of the languages of North America. Mr. Howse states that the Cree and Chippeway (Ojibwa) nouns are divisible into two classes, animate and inanimate, analogous to gender in European languages, but that many inanimate nouns, from possessing some real or imaginary excellence, are personified as animates. Perhaps a clue to this may be found in the pantheism, or rather pan-demonism of the Indian mythology. The Indians of Oregon, for example, believe that not only all animals were once people possessed of supernatural powers, or magicians, but that prominent mountains, isolated rocks, very old trees, and other remarkable objects, were so likewise, a belief which, in fact, seems to have characterized the superstitions of all the tribes of the continent. But, though this might account for a simple division into animate and inanimate, embracing all such objects, it would not explain the multiplicity of forms exhibited in some of the examples above given. The disposition to particularize, and the want of generic terms among barbarous races, may have had some connection with this division, for since to adopt a different system of counting every object would be impossible, the simple desire to be specific may have led to an anomalous form of classification. [46]

The second object in this investigation is to ascertain the series of numbers upon which enumeration is based among different tribes. The most natural, and, among barbarous nations, most common, is the quinary system, or that by fives, corresponding with the fingers of one hand. In this the first five digits are simple, that is to say, are all different, the second form compounds or modifications of these first, as will be seen by referring back to the example given of the Mexican. In many cases, however, it has happened that, in the lapse of time, new words have been adopted for a portion, while the old have become obsolete, or appear only occasionally in combination. In a number of vocabularies examined, it would appear that the numbers 7 and 8 most frequently retain the compound form, and 10 has oftenest changed. The 7 aud.8 usually contain the elements of the words 2 and 3, as representing the 3d and 3d fingers on the second hand. Nine is frequently "one less than ten."

Probably in almost all these languages the quinary system was the oldest, and the decimal, where it now exists, has been of subsequent introduction, or rather growth. In the Chinook, for example, the names of the digits are all simple with the exception of that for seven. Thus *makst* two, *sini-makst* seven, *sini* being, perhaps, an obsolete form of five. These obsolete forms are sometimes revealed in the numeral ten and its compounds and multiples. Thus the simple digit ten may have one name, while in eleven = 10+1, or twenty = 2 x 10, the word will be entirely different. In the Napa, of California, *hopen* signifies two, and m*a-ha-ish* ten, but twenty is *hopi-hol,* the other multiples retaining the syllable *hol* up to one hundred, which is *ma-ha-ish sol,* the *h* being changed to *S* for euphony.

Twenty is, in some languages, a translation of *two tens,* in others a distinct word exists, and this is in many the name for head, body, or person, as in the Opata, *seis dosme* (literally one person), signifying, of course, all the fingers and toes of one person. In the Nisqually the word for twenty, *s'ha-lat-chi,* means literally the fingers and toes. As to the other multiples of ten, they are usually expressed by the literal translation of 3 x 10, 4 x 10, &c. But in the Opata and kindred dialects this form, occurs, 20, *seis dosme;* 30, *seis dosme macoi tarewa,* i. e. ten more than one person; 40, *wodun dosme,* or two twenties, 50, [47] *wodun dosme macoi tarewa*; 60, *beidum dosme,* three twenties, &c.

A good many anomalous forms occur, unnecessary to repeat here, as, for instance, 2 x 4 for 8, 2 *x* 3 for six.

Besides the quinary and decimal series, the binary and vigintesimal are supposed .to be represented.

A sufficient number of extended, vocabularies of numerals have not been obtained to admit of *a*thorough examination and cor*m*pariso*n* of the different series in use, and the following table has, therefore been prepared, which will enable the collector to combine both subjects of inquiry in one, the figures having been *s*elect*e*d in reference to the latter, and the arrangement in parallel columns to the former. These are headed "Simple Cardinals," "Personal Cardinals," and "Cardinals of Value," merely as a guide, and not as indicating that they will in all cases convey the true idea. It is desired that as careful inquiry as possible should be made into the -facts in each one, and that the objects included in the separate classe*s* be enumerated. It is probable that in some languages other columns must be added.

Very few tribes, it will be found, count beyond 100, while some of the more ignorant have no numbers beyond five. It is desireable in all cases, if possible, to ascertain the meaning of the larger collective numbers, as 10, 30, and 100, and another point of inquiry may be the names of the different fingers, especially of the thumb, thus:
—

Little finger
Ring finger
Middle finger
Fore-finger
Thumb [48]

TABLE OF NUMERALS

	Simple cardinals	Personal cardinals	Cardinals of value	Other cardinals
1				
2				
3				
4				
5				
6				
7				
8				
9				
10				
11				
12				
13				
14				
15				
16				
17				
18				
19				
20				
21				
22				
23				
24				
25				
30				
40				
50				
60				
70				
80				
90				
100				

[49, 50, 51]

KE-KAI-SI-MI-LOOT
(1790s – 1875) Queen Chief[171]

Throughout the Northwest Coast, rank trumps gender, enabling elite women of the nobility to assume commanding roles throughout native communities and, sometimes, the region. A few have been remembered in the oral record, such as Queen Susan ~ *kwəntal'uc'ln* of the Chehalis and *Yag^wało* ~ *Yag^wałiw'* of the Skagit.[172] Best known in the written record is the woman named *Ki-kai-si-mi-loot*, nicknamed "Queen," supposedly by William Tolmie[173] at Fort Nisqually. Most recently and ironically she was dubbed Ms Chief by Murray Morgan (1979). She entered the historical record in the 1840s giving crucial aid to the Wilkes US Exploring Expedition, who called her (respectfully for that time) "squaw chief" during their survey of the coast (Joyce 2001, Ramsey 2015, Viola and Margolis 1985, Wilkes 1844).

As expedition captain, Lt. Charles Wilkes (1844: Volume 5), after another officer's insubordination, selected Passed Midshipman Henry Eld, assisted by George Colvocoresses, to take charge of the naval survey of Grays Harbor, departing from US ships anchored off Ft. Nisqually in Puget Sound, where Queen had agreed to provide horses and porters to carry their canoes and gear across the Black River portage into a tributary of the Chehalis River.

> On the same evening {19 July 1841} he arrived within a short distance of the portage; and the next morning Mr {George} Colvocoressis {sic} went, with the sergeant and boy, to an old squaw chief who had promised at Nisqually to be their guide to the Sachap {Satsop} river, and to furnish horses and men to cross the portage. They returned at an early hour, without either horses or Indians, but with a promise that they were to be furnished the next day. The next morning they found that the chief had arrived with five horses and a number of Indians, and was ready to transport the baggage. Some time, however, elapsed before an arrangement could be made for the large canoe, which was thought to be too heavy to transport; but this was finally settled by the same personage offering another in lieu of it, which, though of smaller dimensions, was accepted. Ten

---

[171] Thanks to John Mounts, Annabelle Mounts Barnett, Kelly McAllister, Kurt Reidinger, Jolynn Amrine Goertz, Ed Nolan, Steve Anderson, Nathan Reynolds, Vic Kucera, Donna Turnipseed, Dale Sadler, and, especially, her kinsman Del McBride. Curved brackets indicate additions by author {JM}.

[172] Pedigrees of these women indicate Queen Susan was sister of Chief *Yawnish*; *Yag^wałiw* ~ *Yag^wało*, daughter of the Skagit Prophet and wife of Samish Chief *Petius* at Bayview, traveled with body guards; Sally was widow of Tsenahmus, a Chinook chief; Lower Skagit *Sneatlum* women from Penn Cove married and traded widely, and "*Damasq*" led Puyallups at Minter Bay.

[173] Steve Anderson (2015) suggests that this "Queen" nickname more likely came from her time married into Klallam country since Straits natives at Port Townsend were commonly, if mockingly, named for English royalty. Native nicknames at Nisqually were usually biblical or common first names, like Tom and George, her brothers. He is currently tracing her close family ties with Lahalet, their famous contemporary and Nisqually leader.

Indians were furnished to transport it and the rest of the articles, and they were soon in a condition to move. This despatch {sic} was principally owing to the directions and management of this squaw chief, who seemed to exercise more authority than any that had been met with; indeed her whole character and conduct placed her much above those around her. Her horses were remarkably fine animals, her dress was neat, and her whole establishment bore the indications of Indian opulence. Although her {Klallam} husband was present, he seemed under such good discipline as to warrant the belief that the wife was the ruling power, or, to express it in more homely language "wore the breeches" [5: 121].

The companion report by Colvocoresses provides an estimate of her age in 1841 and more detail about her family and slaves:

8 P.M., we have just seen a Squaw Chief, of the Sachal tribe, who has promised to meet us at the first "Portage" and act as our guide to the Sachal River….
    On the following day we made an early start, and by 8 o'clock we reached the Portage. The chief woman was there awaiting us, with her horses, five in number; they were large, fine-looking animals, and in excellent condition, which is not generally the case with Indian horses. She also brought with her ten men, who were to assist in carrying the small canoe. The large one, she declared, was too heavy to transport, and if we would let her have it, she would give us a smaller one in return, when we arrived at the Sachal River, which offer we very thankfully accepted. In less than an hour all the arrangements had been completed, and we proceeded on our journey, the Indians bring up the rear.
    It is due to the Chief Squaw to say, that we owe this {speedy} dispatch principally to her; through her husband was present, she made all the bargains, and gave the Indians their directions. She is a woman of great energy of character and exercises greater authority over those around her than any man chief I have met with since I have been in the country. She is about fifty years of age {in 1841}, and dresses very neat for an Indian woman [1852: 240, 243].

About 5 P.M., we were overtaken and passed by our old friend, the Squaw Chief, and her husband. She informed us that they were going to pay a visit to a sister {Sophy}, who was resident on the banks of the Chapel River. Her canoe was large and handsomely painted, and was paddled by five slaves, two of whom were women. [1852: 246]

Wilkes added, as they tried to reach their goal, she again came to their rescue with better equipment and added manpower:

On the 31st, after passing two elbows in the river, the cape on the south of the entrance to Gray's Harbour was seen. The flood tide was very strong against them, so that they made but slow progress, and as they opened out the harbour and entered it, they found a strong southwest wind blowing, which caused a short and disagreeable sea, that very nearly swamped their small canoe, and obliged them to run for the lee shore. Here all the things were taken out and placed to dry, on one of the huge trees that had been brought down by the freshets. From this awkward situation they were relieved by the old squaw chief [5: 133 and her husband, who passed them quickly in a light canoe], who had preceded them from Nisqually. She came over in her large canoe, with ten Indians, and offered to carry the [5: 137] party over to the weather shore, where they could encamp in a less exposed place. The offer was gladly accepted and they were taken over to the village [5: 136-137].

Over a decade later, she came to know George Gibbs, who was compiling dictionaries and ethnographies of tribes along the proposed route of the US northern railroad, and was especially concerned with the more numerous tribes in Puget Sound and western Washington territory. Gibbs (1856, 1877a, 1877b) homesteaded at Steilacoom, taught his more precise alphabetic spelling of the native name of the town to other settlers, assembled words from his Nisqually cook Jack, and kept as a pet a native Salish woolly dog named Mutton, whose bones and pelt are in the collections of the Smithsonian in DC.

Though she provided Gibbs with her human and transformed spirit pedigrees, he associated her more with her residence than her ancestral blood ties, as shown below. Of special note, she narrated the foundational Moon[174] epic cycle of chiefly families of this region, and other stories dropped from half of his 1877 edited summary.

> *Ke-kai-si-mi-loot*, an old woman of the Nisqually, daughter of *To-was-tan*,[175] a former chief and related to half the nobility of the country on one side or the other, not content with her human pedigree, which, however, she could only carry back three generations, informed me that she was sprung from four generations of Skookams: *Tshit-no-wehtsh, Ai-yah-hose, Hutl-kwus-keh-nam, & Tsul-tsah-lup-*

---

[174] For many Puget Sound tribes, especially the Snoqualmie, this epic establishes the stellar pedigree of chiefly families throughout this region and beyond.

[175] In briefly (see chart), if *To-was-tan* was Nisqually, where his name would have been pronounced *Towastad*, and married to Cynthia ~ *Kwe'-caith*, sister of *Skanewa*, Queen would be, by English kin terms, first cousin of his son Tyee Dick. Among natives, however, all <u>cousins</u> are <u>siblings</u>, called brothers and sisters (= sibcuz). *Tyee* is a usual Chinuk Wawa title for a "boss, leader, chief." {For the record, one chart shows Cynthia > Lucy > famous Mary Kiona, but it is more than problematic given their known ages.}

Skanewah ~ *Scanewa* was Cowlitz high chief, murdered and beheaded in 1828 (See note 9). His father was *Xniva*, sister Cynthia (~ *Kwe'-caith*, who was struck forever mute at the sight of his returned corpse, according to Mounts family), and son Tyee Dick ~ *Elac-ac-ca* ~ *Kalapa Scanawah* married to Tyee Mary, a niece ~ daughter of *Leschi* (Fitzpatrick 2004: 126). Queen's close kin are sister Sophy (1815 – 1853) and two brothers: George ~ *Qun-us-up-am* ~ *Tum-ah-sun* ~ *Kwonesappa* and Tom ~ *Hky-you-yah*. Descendant Del McBride says Queen was niece of *Skanewa*; Cecelia Carpenter (1982, 1986: 169) names her as *What-co-blote*, Sophy as *Hup-ah-sootse*, and says Tom was killed by his father-in-law for abusing his wives (who were sisters). Murray Morgan (1979: 61) wrongly names her as Princess Charlotte, Chinook Chief Concomly's daughter married to a Cowlitz chief.

NB ~ Much against my own convictions, because it diminishes {kills} native language use, the English names of these four siblings precede here for a wider readership. To emphasis their significance, moreover, all native terms are always *italicized*.

tu,[176] after which they became Indians, *Ke-uch-keh-nam* being the first. How far back this was she could not say (Gibbs in Clark 1955: 315).

According to this account, *Spilyai* {Coyote} himself turned all the *Skookooms* {strong dangers} into animals, stones, etc. The version given below, received from a *Stakta-mish*,[177] or upper Chihalis woman, named *Kikai-si-mi-loot* {sic}, is the more popular one (Gibbs in Clark 1955: 145).

In his ethnographic (Haeberlin and Gunther 1930, Miller 1999, Suttles 1990) summary of western Washington tribes, Gibbs[178] (1877a: 185-6) noted:

In a few instances, matrons of superior character, "strong minded women", have obtained an influence similar to that of chiefs. Sally, the widow of Tsenahmus, a Tsinūk chief, well known on the Lower Columbia, enjoys great authority among the Indians and general immunity from the whites. The queen, an old lady of the Tsihalis {partially}, who patronized Captain Wilkes's party in 1841, yet rules her neighborhood with undisputed sway, and on occasion of the late {1855 Cosmopolis treaty} council "put in her oar" with considerable effect against a removal.

Greater details of her life and pedigree were provided a century later by Del McBride, a direct descendant, on a single page dated 18 July 1979 on file at the State Capitol Museum in Olympia, where he was long curator.

This woman's name was Kai-Kai-sume-lute, but Dr Tolmie, the factor at Fort Nisqually, nicknamed her "Queen" for her regal bearing, and her power over the local Indian groups.
    She was born about 1800, and George Gibbs refers to her as Chehalis, but Edward Huggins of Ft. Nisqually says she was half Cowlitz, half Nisqually. She

---

[176] *Skookum* is Chinuk WaWa for "strong, dangerous, powerful": *A-yah-hase* is "half deer and half snake with two heads and two pairs of {retractable} horns" (Miller 2015: 65).

[177] The Stak-ta-mish, "forest people," are commonly called Upper Chehalis. They "belonged to the coastal division of the Salishan linguistic family" (Swanton 1952: 426.) They lived along the upper Chehalis River, in what is now southwestern Washington, and have a reservation set up by executive order around the confluence of Black and Chehalis Rivers in the aftermath of the aborted treaty council at Cosmopolis in 1855. Speakers of a Coast Salish language of the Tsamosan branch, they were especially adapted to prairies, maintaining huge camas and oak gardens.
    A detailed variant of this Moon epic is included in Thelma Adamson's <u>Folk-Tales of the Coast Salish</u> 1934: 158-72. The inclusion of specific names and places in Queen's account indicate that it is the privileged version belonging to a noble family which was thereby entitled to pass on these names to its members.

[178] Gibbs was secretary at the aborted Cosmopolis treaty, where tribal dislocation was the divisive issue, and already knew Queen, who is not mentioned in the written treaty record, nor is her sister-in-law, the wife of George.

had strong affiliations with all three Indian groups, also the Puyallup, Chehalis, and Quinault. Her husband was high born Klallam.

"Queen's" mother was the only sister {Cynthia ~ *Kwe'-caith*} of Chief *Skanewah*, one of the major early figures of the Cowlitz tribe. Probably born in the 1770s, he was killed by hostile Indians[179] on Puget Sound about 1829 {1828} while on a mission for the Hudson's Bay Co. between Ft. Vancouver and Ft. Langley.

"Queen" had a number of finely kept horses, also fine canoes, which she rented out to the white men.[180] After the establishment of Fort Nisqually in 1833, she became the forelady or "straw-boss" of the work force in the potato, and vegetable, fields around the Fort, along Sequalitchew Creek. Once, when dissatisfied with the rations given to her workers, she called what was probably the first organized labor strike in the Northwest and refused to let her people go back to work until the Hudson Bay Company improved the food for the workers.

"Queen" had a sister, *Kup-ah-sootse*, or "Sophy," born about 1815. Sophy died about 1853, and was buried at Fort Nisqually, according to Edward Huggins, with considerable pomp. Gold coins and trade beads were buried with her, and a fine horse was ceremonially slaughtered over the grave.

There were also two brothers, somewhat younger. One was *Hky-yo* or "Tom" and the other *Tum-ah-shun* {*Qun us up am* ~ George}. "Tom" had a daughter, Mary, who first married James Chipman, a Nisqually, then John

---

[179] Though a Cowichan or Klallam murderer is sometimes blamed, Nathan Reynolds searched the contemporary Fraser River Ft. Langley journals for details. Our joint reading of these records follows: *Skanewah* used his friendship and employment to carry letters and provide horses to the HBC, who safeguarded his sometimes haughty but miserly dealings. Though Ft Vancouver was much closer to his home, the HBC insisted *Skanewah* trade at Ft Langley in the interest of lessening intertribal hostilities. In September 1827, he ransomed a Klallam sister in law from Lekwiltok ~ Yukeltaws ~ southern Kwakiutls of the BC Inside Passage, and took her as another wife. In February 1828, an Okanogan man staying at *Skanewah*'s lodge at Ft Langley fell through the ice and drowned, weighted down by three blankets and a steel trap, on his way from trying to buy a slave at Katzie. His Duwamish widow was generously compensated with two beaver pelts by a chief of the local Kwantlens to absolve their tribal territory (land is willful) of any blame in his death. *Skanewah*, though quasi-responsible as host, was less generous and soon criticized across the region. For protection and transport, he bought a second slave, a Lekwiltok held at Katzie, who was likely the same one intended for the Okanogan man. This slave soon escaped, probably because of this threatening gossip, but he was retaken and needed to be distanced from that area, so, in May, *Skanewah* left the river with his wife and baby, carrying a wealth of blankets, kettles, traps, axes, new clothes, and a gun. At Pt Roberts, he was killed, supposedly by a Skykomish, an upriver Lushootseed tribe closely related to inland Salish, including Okanogan, and to Duwamish, thus implicating the widow. A search of the Skykomish's gear when he visited Ft Langley on 10 May 1829, however, provided no evidence and he was allowed his continued freedom (Maclachlan 1998: 36, 63, 65; Suttles 1998: 199).

[180] HBC 1848 Indian Blotters indicate that her brother George did the same, as well as carried messages from Ft Nisqually to Ft Vancouver {below}.

Longfred, a Quinault. In 1917, when the Nisquallies were evicted from the Pierce County side of the Reservation by the U.S. Army etc., the Longfreds moved to Oakville and Chehalis Reservation, where she died in the 1920s.

My relationship with "Queen," her sister and brothers is a little remote by "white-man" standards, but she was the niece of *Sce-ne-wah*, my great-great-great-grandfather. By Indian standards, she was much closer, and acted as an aunt to my great-grandmother, Catherine Mounts. "Queen" was buried on the hill above the farm of her "niece," Mrs Daniel {Catherine} Mounts, on Mounts Road.

Queen's Cowlitz pedigree is all the more impeccable since this tribe was regarded as "blue bloods" (Roblin 1919) across the region, regardless of their trafficking in livestock and slaves. Her father *To-was-tan* {Nisqually} and mother Cynthia ~ *Kwe'-caith* were prestigious, like her widely-traveled uncle *Skenewa*, whose widely-respected son and Medicine Creek Treaty signer, Tyee Dick, is buried under an impressive granite plinth in the Puyallup cemetery. Her own siblings were equally prominent, but died in mid-life, sometimes violently. Her last days were spent with Mounts kin at Nisqually Delta, and she was buried in an uphill cemetery. Throughout her life, she was, as a good leader, concerned for the welfare of others,[181] especially those she employed as "straw boss" supplying native foods, labor, or cash income. Indeed, Tolmie does say she led the first successful labor strike in the Northwest to get better food for the native women working in HBC fields.

Additional family details and incidents are supplied by British tenant farmer Joseph Heath's diary, and letters written by HBC factor Edward Huggins (1903) in Tacoma to Historian Clarence Bagley in Seattle. Memories of living Mounts family members appear in footnote 4.

Joseph Heath (1805 - 1849), oldest of thirteen siblings, gambled away family fortunes, forcing the sale of their ancestral estate called The Rookery, Great Marlow, Buckinghamshire. Banished, he became a HBC tenant farmer at Steilacoom (1844-49), rigorously applying productive farming techniques his irate father insisted he learn to take over the estate whose forfeit he caused. Dr William Tolmie oversaw Heath's accounts at Ft Nisqually, settling him on 170 acres remaining from a failed HBC colony moved from Red River (Winnipeg, Manitoba). As gentleman farmer, Heath employed native workers, training them in "painstaking" English farming standards.

He spelled the native name of his factotum or manager *Klapat*,[182] but renamed *Klapat*'s brother as Tom, after his own sibling who had paid Joseph's passage to the Northwest. Of Heath's own brothers, William already worked for HBC in the Northwest as a shipmate; Charles became English tutor to the Czar of Russia; and Tom settled in New Zealand, becoming head of

---

[181] Gibbs, as expected from his keen language skills, provides the best transcription of Queen's native name, Huggins is partial, and, given the M ~ B shifts in Lushootseet, *-blote* = *-mi-loot*, leaving *What-* to be reconciled with *ke-kai* by quite a stretch. Sophy's native name written with initial K or H probably began with X, pronounced at the back of the throat.

[182] "*Klap-at*" might derive from the Chinuk WaWa word klap = "to find; to catch" as in *mika klap kuitan* = Did you catch the horse? (Gill 1933:55, Long 1909: 23, Johnson 1978), or, more likely, from ƛp < the Cowlitz particle that refers to themselves, derived from ƛəp "deep" (Kinkade 2004: 47, 47), suggesting his nickname is an ethnic designation rather than a personal name, applicable to a variety of key people of that tribe.

the Wellington Public Library. Other family members became headmasters at Eton and Harrow. Equally highly educated, Joseph kept diaries, but only the one from 1845-49 survived to be printed, after it was found in a trunk in England, transcribed in 1934, and long languished at Tacoma (McDonald 1979).

Of these workers, *Klapat* might be identified as double-named *Klapat Skanawah* ~ Richard Scanawa ~ Tyee Dick, but we assume he is single-named George ~ *Quan-us-up-am* ~ *Tum-ah-shun* ~ *Kwonesappa* (aged about 40), who, along with Tom ~ *Hky-you-yah* (aged about 30) were brothers of the sisters Queen ~ *Kekaisimiloot* (1790-1860s) and Sophy ~ *Khup-ah-sootse* (1815-53). As noted, all four were the children of *Towastan* and Cynthia ~ *Kwe'-caith*, sister of Cowlitz high chief *Scanewa*. *Kwonesappa* is listed as a Cowlitz subchief at the aborted 1856 Cosmopolis treaty council, and was killed when one of his shamanic patients died in treatment and the mourning family took revenge on the Cowlitz trail {below}.

George attended the treaty with one of his wives. Famed elder Emma Millet Luscier told John P Harrington that, amplifying his cryptic abbreviations, *k'aysalams* {now Cosmopolis} was the locale of the big conference with Governor Isaac Stevens, too bad Gov Stevens did not finish his work for the Indians before he died. My mother had had her 1st baby at the time of this conference {1856}. Cowlitz Indians at this conference were *Imtatʃ* {Umtuch}, *wahhawx*, {Howhow}, Henry *ts'ixxu•ł* {Cheholtz}, *k'wa•nasa•ppam* {George}, and *hwunhwântʃ'* (his wife at that time). *Wahhawx* had to go first from *nawq'w* (the Catholic Mission at Cowlitz Prairie, the name means a big prairie = *nawaq^{w}m*) up to *k'alamx* to tell his daughter to come home to *nawq'w* to take care of her little brother named *ayya•l*, who was Emma's mother's younger brother.) Of note, neither George's sister nor wife are mentioned in the treaty meeting notes by George Gibbs.

Tom was married to two sisters (aged 18, 25), until killed with a dull axe by his father-in-law *Tay-lush-kyne* for abusing them. Reasons why appear briefly in the Heath diary for early June of 1845 {below}. Of Tom's widows, one married a Kanaka ~ Hawaiian named *Keava'haccow* ~ *Heavehaccon* and the other sister married Tyee Dick ~ her deceased husband's sibcuz (cousin ~ brother). Tom's daughter was Mary, who first married James Chipman, then John Longfield, moving to Oakville when the US Army took Nisqually tribal lands.

Klapat is mentioned much more frequently, often involving errands to Ft Nisqually. The diary itself begins with *Klapat* and Heath returning from New Years imbibing at Dr Tolmie's table, extracted below, beginning with page number, weekday, and date; along with more personal details in direct quotes. Occasional references to Catholicism derive from the first Catholic Mission (Schoenberg 1962) north of the Columbia River (Jessett 1959), founded on Cowlitz Prairie, and explains why these polygamous brothers moved north to Ft Nisqually away from monogamy-enforcing priests.

13 Wednesday 1 January 1845 ~ *Klapat* who had taken too freely of the Jolly God and had much difficulty in keeping his seat on his horse, entertained me greatly, being the only Indian I had ever seen in that state, sometimes singing Indian songs, from which he would break into Catholic hymns, then go through the "Pater noster" and all the English words he could make use of, most anxious to see his wives, of whom he is bless with two; one too many, I think.

16 Saturday 18 January '45 ~ *Klapat*, the beau ideal of an Indian dandy, went off this evening to visit friends.
Tuesday 21 January '45 ~ His child, about two months old, not likely too live.

18 Friday 31 January '45 ~ *Klapat* a most invaluable servant, a good ploughman, carpenter, in fact, everything. Don't know what I should have done without him, a lucky thing for he that he has two wives, the reason for his being turned away from the Cowlitz Farm.

22 Sunday Feb 23 '45 ~ *Klapat* is at the Fort to talk with the Doctor about turning one of his (wives) off.

36 Thursday April 24 '45 ~ *Klapat* idle as possible, doing scarcely anything the whole day. High winds, heavy hailstorms and piercing cold; cuts the lambs up sadly – three more dead.

41 Sunday May 25 '45 ~ Found that Doctor {Tolmie} is much prejudiced against *Klapat* {because of a false report}.

43 Tuesday June 3 '45 ~ *Klapat* preparing to start for Cowlitz.

43 Wednesday June 4 '45 ~ *Klapat* set off for the Cowlitz with two of his wives {suggesting more than two}.

46 Friday June 20 '45 ~ *Klapat* returned from the Cowlitz with plough timbers.

54 Tuesday 12 August '45 ~ *Klapat*'s wife – one of them – produced a little girl, with which he seems very proud. Wish it had come after harvest, as I lose his services, as nothing would induce an Indian to work at such times {suggesting couvade to claim fatherhood, and perhaps the 1875 mother and newborn buried in Mounts cemetery}.

95 Friday April 2 1847 ~ Finished *Klapat*'s clothes.

Tom's accident that likely led to his domestic difficulties and death is also noted:

47 Friday June 4 '45 ~ raising one of the posts {barn beams}, and in doing so it fell and broke both of poor little Tom's thighs. At first we thought he was dead.

48 Saturday June 5 '45 ~ in no pain except for his head, where he was thrown to the ground. *Klapat*, his brother, is in better spirits today and most attentive.

In 1846, *Quanasapam* ~ George provided a rifle and pistol to free two native ox thieves from jail after they had been flogged (Ramsey 2015: 224). In the 1848 Indian Blotter, he is paid trade goods (flour, stroud, milk, tobacco) for rental of his horse, and carrying letters to Cowlitz. He also rented out large Klallam canoes.

Edward Huggins (1903), who left London to become a HBC clerk, then the last factor at Ft Nisqually, and became an American citizen to claim the fort land as his own homestead, described this family, but with shortened names and at least one misstep at {sic}.

There was a family of Nisqually's considered to be quite aristocratic, were good looking, and always dressed neatly. The head of the family was an old woman named *Kai-sum-lute*, she was also called Queen. I think she was a cousin {sic} of *Laghlet*, the last Nisqually Chief. My wife {Letitia Work, daughter of HBC John Work ~ Wark} just told me that she was *Laghlet*'s {*Lahalet*'s} sister, and cousin to Dan Mounts wife's mother. She the (Queen) had a remarkable good-looking sister named Sophie, who died when she was 40 or 45 yrs. of age. Another member of the family was named *Qun-us-up-um*, a great medicine man, who lived part of the time at Nisqually and part at Cowlitz. He got into a difficulty (one of his patients died, and the defunct's relations killed him on the Cowlitz River trail. Another Nisqually named Tom, a relative {brother} of Queen's, took two sisters wives. He treated them badly and they left him. He went, one night, to the lodge of the two women. He was drunk and fell asleep. The father of the two girls took an axe, blunt, and tried to cut off his head, but failed. They brought the body to the fort and 'twas an awful sight, his head half sawed off. Ezra Meeker doesn't know, and 'twould be better to not tell him. EH

In a separate account called "The Story of Tom," Huggins (1904) details Tom's end. After mentioning Tom's siblings, he dismisses as lazy, *cultus* {Chinuk WaWa: "worthless, bad"} cousin *Elac-ac-ca ~ Skah-ni-wah*, who married into *Leschi*'s family and fought with them during the Treaty Wars, then moved to Puyallup and reformed to become known as Tyee Dick.

Tom was handsome, fond of hunting, trading horses, and alcohol, especially with Jennie, a cousin who lived with a NCO officer at Fort Steilacoom, who could legally buy booze. After one excessive binge, Tom rode up to the *Tlithlow* home of *Tay-lush-kyne*, his father-in-law, who had taken back his two daughters married to Tom after too many of his violent outbursts. Tom was very drunk, and quickly fell asleep on a mat bed. Without a word, *Tay-lush-kyne* reached for a heavy square headed HBC axe and swung it to cut off Tom's head but the blade was too blunt, leaving a fatal, gruesome, gaping neck wound. A horse and cart took the body to Ft Nisqually for burial. Protracted negotiations settled on a few horses and blankets in lieu of blood revenge. Tom's pretty wives soon remarried, one to Tyee Dick and one to a Hawaiian (native *Kanaka*) named *Heave'haccon*, a "master mechanic" who worked for the Puget Sound Agricultural Company and was among the 20 men Huggins took to farm at Muck during the Treaty War. Later he worked for the Tacoma Mill company until he died. Both second marriages produced many children, who settled among Puyallups.

In a follow up letter of 20 October 1903, Huggins added "When Sophy died, she was given a grand funeral and a lot of horses (eight or ten) were supposed to be killed over her grave for her to use in the spirit land, but a half breed, with whom she – at one time – lived, is said to have killed a couple of old and useless *kuitans* {horses in Chinuk WaWa} and walked off with the remainder. She was buried near the fort, and a cedar split-board house put over her grave, but in the 1860s her remains were removed to the Nisqually reservation {Mounts} cemetery."

Queen

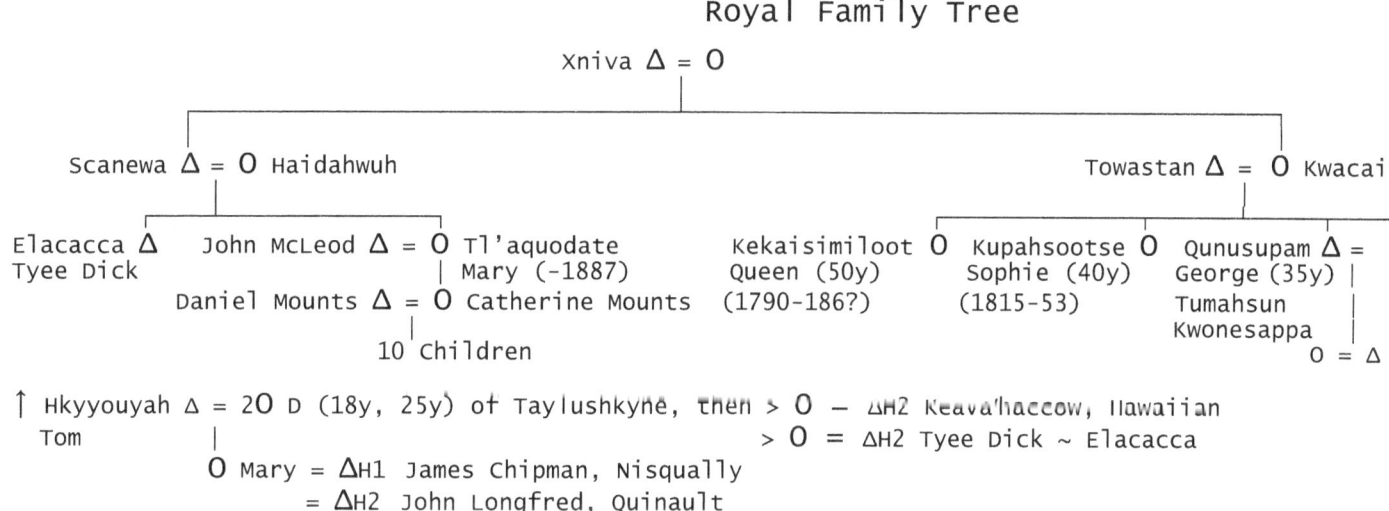

Royal Family Tree

```
                            Xniva △ = O
        ┌───────────────────────┴───────────────────────┐
Scanewa △ = O Haidahwuh                        Towastan △ = O Kwacait
    ┌────────┴────────┐                    ┌──────────┬──────────┬──────────┐
Elacacca △   John McLeod △ = O Tl'aquodate  Kekaisimiloot O  Kupahsootse O  Qunusupam △ =
Tyee Dick                |   Mary (-1887)   Queen (50y)      Sophie (40y)   George (35y) |
          Daniel Mounts △ = O Catherine Mounts (1790-186?)   (1815-53)       Tumahsun
                         |                                                   Kwonesappa
                    10 Children                                                        O = △
```

↑ Hkyyouyah △ = 2O D (18y, 25y) of Taylushkyne, then > O — △H2 Keava'haccow, Hawaiian
  Tom | > O = △H2 Tyee Dick ~ Elacacca
       O Mary = △H1 James Chipman, Nisqually
              = △H2 John Longfred, Quinault

Codes: O female △ male, ~ also known as, = marriage, | descendants, children;
-F -M > father mother, -S -D > son daughter, -B -Z > brother sister.

Plural wives are assumed but not indicated in this chart.

These names seem to be in Cowlitz, one of the four languages in the Tsamosan Branch of Coast Salish, which uses M and N sounds. Nisqually belongs to the Lushootseed ~ Puget Salish Branch, which shifted sounds M to B and N to D instead of these M N nasals.

Summary

Throughout, my arguments rely on various interconnections based on this fourfold "sibling set," where Queen is the best known, and Tom, because of his English name, readily identifiable. Earlier in his life Tyee Dick was known by the double name of "*Klapat Scad-a-wah*", and this brother (by native kinship) ~ first cousin (by American kinship) is sometimes mixed into this sibling ~ sibcuz set, as is *Lahalet*, but the marriage of Tom's widow to Dick speaks to their separate families. The marriage might have been a levirate, if single name George ~ *Klapat* ~ *Qun-us-up-a*m ~ *Tum-ah-shun* ~ *Kwonesappa* had already been killed, with Dick becoming kinsman next in affinal line.

Modern Mounts family members (McAllister and Barnett 2011) recall that *Tl'aquodote* ~ Mary (the first Mrs. John McLeod ~ McCloud) died June 15, 1887 and was buried on the Muck claim. She was youngest daughter of Cowlitz chief *Scanewa* with his wife *Haidawah*, said to be *Humptulips*. In 1905, after John McLeod died, her remains were removed from Muck to join his at the Steilacoom Masonic Cemetery. At that time of exhuming, her coffin was opened, checking on its valued contents and also revealing that she was notably well preserved, proving her residual spiritual powers. A tree and a depression marked the site of her former grave on a rise near the barn at Muck. In time, Daniel and Catherine Mounts were also buried among the same Masons, though some of their children are buried at Bethany Lutheran across the road from the McLeod homestead. Other children are buried in the huge South Tacoma Way cemetery.

Uphill from the Mounts home were four landmarks: a road, a small cemetery, a spring, and a school house built near it by the Mounts for neighborhood children. The teacher roomed in the large Mounts home, and teacher Katherine Jensen, who arrived with her own camera, married Frank Mounts and they had two sons and a daughter. For a time, John McLeod lived in a room attached to the school house in order to satisfy the residence requirement to validate his own homestead claim. Later, this land was transferred to his daughter Catherine Mounts in order to keep it within the family when his crofters woolen cooperative (Anderson 2010) was being sued. When the army took over the hillside in 1917, the school house was moved down the hill and converted into a home where several families lived until it was torn down. Construction of I-5 rerouted the road, so only the spring survives as a landmark.

Queen, or "Queenie" as she is still known to the family, lived in a cabin where Washburn Creek met Red Salmon Creek, and was buried beside her sister Sophy on the hill, near the southbound lanes of I-5 on a bluff above the Nisqually Delta.[183] Family memory is that the graves of other "aunts" of Catherine were in this small plot surrounded by a white picket fence. Sophy was probably the first grave dug there for her 1860s reburial (aside from possible stillbirths). Also within the pickets was a grave shared by a grandniece (daughter of George and wife of *Tenas LaPlate*[184] ~ *Yuckton*) and her baby who died from childbirth complications in 1875 while living at the Mounts. Local rumor says construction workers looted all these graves for their valuables, long before federal laws provided some protections and tribal officials had the legal authority to safeguard their ancestral remains and cemeteries. Yet looting should not be total oblivion, so some traces should remain.

---

[183] Directions are not intuitive here because, as Kelly McAllister notes, though paralleling the Pacific coast, Interstate 5 in this stretch runs east-west. Similarly, the Nisqually River flows north so the Mounts farm was on the east side of it, not what seems to be north.

[184] *Tenas* is "little," *La Plate* is from French "prêtre = priest," both are Chinuk WaWa.

The Mounts family lost this land and cemetery when it was confiscated for Camp Lewis Army Post in 1917, later Ft Lewis Army Base and now Joint Base Lewis McChord. Gaul and Braget neighbors were allowed to graze cows there until about 1939, when a golf course – then Ft Lewis and now Eagles Pride links – was built along that ridge, currently at the intersection of Mounts Road and I-5.[185] By then, most members of the Mounts family had moved away, though at least one granddaughter worked in the pro shop with her baby sometimes resting under the sales desk. Neighborhood memory attributes the incentive for this course to Dwight Eisenhower, later Supreme Allied Commander in WW II, US President, and famous golfer. Given his historic significance, local memory has inflated his 1940-41 position as Chief of Staff of IX Corps. His son John, who attended Tacoma's Stadium High School with Mounts children, reports "Ike" never played this course. No trace of Queen's grave plot has yet been located, and the only evidence remaining for the huge Mounts farmstead and out buildings is its root cellar, sprouting a tight cluster of fruit trees.

Queen's version of the Moon epic told to George Gibbs, the most detailed on record for the entire region, serves to continue her memory and cultural legacy. Sadly, it was left out of the 1877 publication that is actually only half of Gibbs's 1856 written manuscript. It finally appeared a century later (Clark 1955), though edited for folklore rather than its ethnographic, ethnohistoric, and pedigreed genealogical content.

---

[185] Carl Gaul, who herded cattle on the hillside as a boy, recalled the location of these graves: "Jensen kids showed me ... it was over the fence from the golf course property on Katy's {Mounts Easterday's} portion. If so it may well be that they are still there" ~ Carl Gaul email to Annabelle Mounts Barnet, Sunday, 16 September 2001, 5:55PM. By phone 4 August 2016, Thursday, 11am, Carl noted the cemetery with picket fence was on the brow of the hill directly above the Mounts big house, and the looters were WPA workers.

REFERENCES

Adamson, Thelma 1934 Moon. <u>Folk-Tales of the Coast Salish</u>. NY: Memoirs of the American Folk-Lore Society 27: 158-72.

Anderson, Steve 2010 A Crofter's Tale. <u>Columbia</u>. Summer: 27-33.

    2015 Email. Sat, Oct 31, 2015, 01:33 PM.

Ballard, Arthur 1957 The Salmon-Weir on Green River in Western Washington. <u>Davidson Journal of Anthropology</u> 3: 37-53.

Bates, Dawn, Thom Hess, and Vi Hilbert 1994 <u>Lushootseed Dictionary</u>. Seattle: University of Washington Press.

Beavert, Virginia, and Sharon Hargus 2009 <u>Ichishkiin Sinwit</u> ~ <u>Yakama / Yakima</u> ~ <u>Sahaptin Dictionary</u>. Seattle: University of Washington Press.

Beckham, Stephen 1969 George Gibbs, 1815-1873: Historian and Ethnologist. UCLA: History PhD Dissertation.

Boas, Franz, and Pliny Goddard 1924-5 Vocabulary of an Athapascan Dialect of the State of Washington, <u>International Journal of American Lingustics</u> III: 39-45.

Bouchard, R. and D. Kennedy. 1984. Indian history and knowledge of the Lower Similkameen River – Palmer Lake Area. British Columbia Indian Language Project, Victoria, B.C.

Boyd, Robert 1999 <u>The Coming of the Spirit of Pestilence</u>: Introduced Infectious Diseases and Population Decline among Northwest Coast Indians, 1774-1874. Seattle: University of Washington Press.

    2011 Cathlapotle and Its Inhabitants, 1792-1860: a report prepared for the U.S. Fish and Wildlife Service, Region 1. Cultural Resource Series #15, Portland, OR.

Bright, William, ed 2004 <u>Native American Placenames of the United States</u>. Norman: University of Oklahoma Press.

Butler, B Robert 1978 Bison Hunting in the Desert West Before 1800: The Paleo-Ecological Potential and the Archaeological Reality. <u>Plains Anthropologist Memoir</u> 14 : 108-112.

Carpenter, Cecilia Svinth 1982 A Source Book on the Indian History of Ft Nisqually ~ Dupont Site. Tahoma Research Service.

    1986 <u>Fort Nisqually: A Documented History of Indian and British Interaction</u>. Tacoma: Tahoma Research.

Carstensen, Vernon 1953 Pacific Northwest Letters of George Gibbs. <u>Oregon Historical Quarterly</u> LIV ~ 54 (Sept): 190-99.

Clark, Ella 1953 <u>Indian Legends of the Pacific Northwest</u>. Illustrations by Robert Bruce Inverarity. Berkeley: University of California Press.

    1955 George Gibbs' Account of Indian Mythology in Oregon and Washington Territories, Part I. <u>Oregon Historical Quarterly</u> 56 (4): 293-325. December.

    1956 George Gibbs' Account of Indian Mythology in Oregon and Washington Territories, Part II. <u>Oregon Historical Quarterly</u> 57 (2): 125-167. June.

Collins, June 1949 John Fornsby: The Personal Document of a Coast Salish Indian. <u>Indians of the Urban Northwest</u>. Marian Smith, ed. Columbia University Contributions to Anthropology 36: 287-341.

    1950   The Indian Shaker Church. <u>Southwestern Journal of Anthropology</u> 6: 399-411.

    1966   Naming, Continuity, and Social Inheritance among the Coast Salish of Western Washington. <u>Papers of the Michigan Academy of Science, Arts, and Letters</u> 51: 425-36.

    1974   <u>Valley of the Spirits</u> ~ <u>The Upper Skagit Indians of Western Washington</u>. Seattle: University of Washington Press.

Colvocoresses, George 1852 <u>Four Years in a Government Exploring Expedition</u>: to the island of Madeira, Cape Verd Islands, Brazil, coast of Patagonia, Chili, Peru, Paumato group, Society Islands, Navigator group, Australia, Antarctic continent, New Zealand, Friendly Islands, Fejee group, Sandwich Islands, Northwest Coast of America, Oregon, California, East Indies, St Helena, &c., &c. New York: Cornish, Lamport. <u>Chapter Xix. From Nisqually To Columbia River, By Land</u> 239-262 (255-278) Http://Pds.Lib. Harvard.Edu/ Pds/View/8550387?N=259&Imagesize=1200&Jp2res=.5&Printthumbnails=No.

Duff, Wilson 1975 Images: Stone: BC: 30 Centuries of Northwest Coast Indian Sculpture. Seattle: University of Washington Press.

Doig, Ivan 1980 <u>Winter Brothers</u> ~ <u>A Season at the Edge of America</u>. NY.

Donnelly, Joseph, SJ, ed. 1967 <u>Wilderness Kingdom</u> ~ <u>Life in the Rocky Mountains</u>: 1840-1847. The Journals & Paintings of Nicolas Point, SJ. Chicago: Loyola University Press.

Dunn, John 1995 <u>Sm'algyax</u> / A Reference Dictionary and Grammar for the Coast Tsimshian Language. Seattle: University of Washington Press for Sealaska Heritage Foundation. [1978, 1979 Canadian Museum of Civilizations]

Erikson, Patricia Pierce, with Helma Ward & Kirk Wachendorf 2002 <u>Voices of a Thousand People</u> ~ <u>The Makah Cultural & Research Center</u>. Lincoln: University of Nebraska Press.

Fitzpatrick, Darlene 2004 <u>We Are Cowlitz</u> ~ <u>A Native American Ethnicity</u>. Lanham: University Press of America.

Gaul, Carl 2016 Phone call, 11pm, 4 August. + Emails to Annabelle Mounts Barnett.

Gibbs, George > See p 9.

Gill, John K. 1933 Gill's Dictionary of the Chinook Jargon, With Examples of Use in Conversations and Notes Upon Tribes and Tongues. Portland: JK Gill Co.

Gunther, Erna 1927 <u>Klallam Ethnography</u>. University of Washington Publications in Anthropology 1 (5): 171-314.

Haeberlin, Herman, and Erna Gunther 1930 The Indians of Puget Sound. <u>University of Washington Publications in Anthropology</u> 4 (1), pp. 1-84.

John Peabody Harrington Papers: Quinault/Chehalis/Cowlitz/Yakima/Chinook/Chinook Jargon, 1942-1943: p88, frame # 3; http://collections.si.edu/search/slideshow_embedded?xml =%22http://sirismm.si.edu/naa/viewer/Harrington_mf1_r18_Gallery/viewer_Harrington_mf 1_r18.xml%22.

Hilbert, Vi, Jay Miller, and Zalmai Zahir 2001 Puget Sound Geography. sdaʔdaʔ gʷəɬ dibəɬ ləšucid ʔacaciɬtalbixʷ. A Draft Study of the Thomas Talbot Waterman Place Name Manuscript and Other Sources, Edited with Additional Material. Lushootseed Press.

Hitchman, Robert 1985 Place Names of Washington. Washington State Historical Society.

Huggins, Edward 1903 Letters to Clarence B Bagley Esquire, page 19 ~ Oct 1903, University of Washington Suzzallo Library Special Collections, Clarence Bagley Collection, Folder 2/4 - 17, 1903 – 1907, 186 letters total.

    1904 The Story of Tom. University of Washington Suzzallo Library Special Collections, Clarence B. Bagley Collection.

James, Karen, and Victor Martino 1986 Grays Harbor and Native Americans. Seattle: US Army Corps of Engineers, DACW67-85-0093. October.

Jessett, Thomas 1959 Reports and Letters of Herbert Beaver, Chaplain to the HBC and missionary to the Indians at Ft Vancouver. Champoeg Press.

Johnson, Samuel 1978 Chinook Jargon: A Computer-Assisted Analysis of Variation in an American Indian Pidgin. Lawrence: University of Kansas, Linguistics PhD.

Joyce, Barry Alan 2001 The Shaping of American Ethnography ~ The Wilkes Exploring Expedition, 1838 - 1842. Lincoln: University of Nebraska Press.

Keyes, General Erasmas Darwin 1988 Fighting Indians in Washington Territory. Fairfield: Ye Galleon Press, extract of Fifty Years' Observation of Men and Events. NY: Scribner, 1884.

Kinkade, Dale 1991 Upper Chehalis Dictionary. Missoula: University of Montana Occasional Papers in Linguistics 7.

    2004 Cowlitz Dictionary and Grammatical Sketch. Missoula: University of Montana, Occasional Papers in Linguistics 18.

Long, Frederick 1909 Dictionary of the Chinook Jargon. Seattle: Lowman and Hanford.

Mapes, Lynda 2009 Breaking Ground ~ Lower Elwa Klallam and Unearthing of Tse-whit-zen Village. Seattle: University of Washington Press.

McDonald, Lucille, ed. 1979 Memoirs of Nisqually Joseph Heath. Fairfield, WA: Ye Galleon.

Maclachlan, Morag 1998 The Fort Langley Journals 1827-30. Vancouver: UBC Press.

McAllister, Kelly, and Annabelle Mounts Barnett 2011 Catherine McLeod Mounts ~ A young girl of mixed race growing up in the midst of two cultures colliding. Columbia Summer: 3-8.

McBride, Del 1979 Queen Info Sheet. State Capitol Museum. 18 July.

Miles, Charles 2003 James Swan ~ Cha-tic of the Northwest Coast. New Haven: Yale Press.

Miller, Jay 1998 Middle Columbia River Salishans. Plateau. Deward Walker, ed. DC: Smithsonian Handbook of North American Indians, Volume 12: 253-270.

    1999 Lushootseed Culture and the Shamanic Odyssey: An Anchored Radiance. University of Nebraska Press.

    2005 Dibble Cultivating Prairies to Beaches: The Real All Terrain Vehicle. Journal of Northwest Anthropology (JONA) 39 (1): 33-39, Spring.

2011 First Nations Forts, Refuges, and War Lord Champions around the Salish Sea. <u>JONA</u> 45 (1): 71-87, Spring.

2012 <u>Honne ~ Spirit of the Chehalis</u>. Lincoln: University of Nebraska, Bison Books.

2015 <u>Herman Haeberlin Regained</u>. Seattle: Amazon [2005 Lushootseed Press].

2015 <u>Pacific Plateau Portrayal</u>. Seattle: Amazon.

Morgan, Murray 1979 <u>Puget's Sound ~ A Narrative of Early Tacoma and the Southern Sound</u>. Seattle: University of Washington Press.

Moulton, Gary E, ed. 2002 The Definitive <u>Journals of Lewis and Clark</u>: Down the Columbia to Fort Clatsop. Volume 6. Lincoln: University of Nebraska Press.

Norton, Helen 1979 The Association between Anthropogenic Prairies and Important Food Plants in Western Washington. <u>Northwest Anthropological Research Notes</u> (<u>NARN</u>) 13 (20): 434-49.

1980 Evidence for Bracken Fern as a food for Aboriginal Peoples of Western Washington. <u>Economic Botany</u> 33 (4): 384-396.

Olson, Ronald 1936 <u>The Quinault Indians</u>. University of Washington Publications in Anthropology 6 (1): 1-190.

Owens, Kenneth, ed. 1985 <u>The Wreck of the *Sv Nikolai* ~ Two Narratives of the First Russian Expedition to the Oregon Country</u> 1808-1810. Alton Donnelly, trans. Portland: Oregon Historical Society Press.

Palmer, Katherine Van Winkle 1925 <u>Honne ~ The Spirit of the Chehalis</u>. The Indian Interpretation of the Origin of the People and Animals – as Narrated by George Sanders. Geneva, NY: Press of W. F. Humphrey. Reprint: 2012 George Sanders <u>Honne ~ The Spirit of the Chehalis</u> ~ The Indian Interpretation of the Origin of the People and Animals. Jay Miller, ed. Lincoln: University of Nebraska Press, Bison Books.

Peterson, Jacqueline, with Laura Peers 1993 <u>Sacred Encounters ~ Father De Smet and the Indians of the Rocky Mountain West</u>. Norman: University of Oklahoma Press.

Prucha, Francis Paul 1994 <u>Indian Peace Medals in American History</u>. Norman: University of Oklahoma Press.

Ramsey, Jerry 2015 <u>Stealing Puget Sound, 1832-1869</u>. Gorham.

Ray, Verne 1960 The Columbia Indian Confederacy: A League of Central Plateau Tribes: 177-89. <u>Culture in History</u>: <u>Essays in Honor of Paul Radin</u>. Stanley Diamond, ed. Columbia.

Reynolds, Nathaniel 2007 "More Dangerous Dead than Living": The Killing of Chief Umtuch. Longview, WA: Cowlitz Indian Tribe: Past and Present, Volume II: June 1.

Roblin, Charles 1919 Roblin's Schedule of Unenrolled Indians. DC: National Archives I, RG 75, BIA, Quinault Agency files.

Ross, John Alan 2011 <u>The Spokan Indians</u>. Spokane, Washington: Michael Ross.

Ruby, Robert, and John Brown 1965 <u>Half-Sun on the Columbia</u>: <u>A Biography of Chief Moses</u>. Norman: University of Oklahoma Press.

Scheuerman, Richard, and Michael Finley 2008 Finding Chief Kamiakin ~ The Life and Legacy of a Northwest Patriot. Pullman: WSU Press.

Schoenberg, Wilfred 1962 A Chronicle of the Catholic History of the Pacific Northwest, 1743-1960. Arranged after the manner of certain medieval chronicles and annotated with copious notes for further reference. Portland: Catholic Sentinel Printery.

Schoolcraft, Henry 1851-57 Historical and Statistical Information Respecting the History, Condition and Prospects of the Indian Tribes of the United States. 6 volumes. Philadelphia: Lippincott Grambo.

Snyder, Sally 1964 Skagit Society and Its Existential Basis: An Ethnofolkloristic Reconstruction. Seattle: University of Washington, Anthropology, PhD Dissertation.

    1975 Quest For the Sacred in Northern Puget Sound: An Interpretation of Potlatch. Ethnology 14 (2): 149-161.

Stern, Theodore 1993 Chiefs & Chief Traders ~ Indian Relations at Fort Nez Perce, 1818-1855. Volume 1. Corvallis: Oregon State University Press.

    1996 Chiefs & Change in the Oregon Country ~ Indian Relations at Fort Nez Perce, 1818-1855. Volume 2. Corvallis: Oregon State University Press.

Stone, Harold Otho
    1959 Resurrection of Chief Atwin: An Eyewitness Tells of the Weird Indian Ceremony He Attended Half-A-Century Ago. Seattle Times 8 March: J-1.

Suttles, Wayne, ed. 1990 Northwest Coast. Handbook of North American Indians 7. DC: Smithsonian Press.

    1998 The Ethnographic Significance of The Fort Langley Journals: 163-210. The Fort Langley Journals 1827-30. Vancouver: UBC Press.

Swan, James 1870 The Indians of Cape Flattery. DC: Smithsonian Contributions to Knowledge 16: 1-105.

    1972 The Northwest Coast: or, Three Years Residence in Washington Territory; Seattle: University of Washington Press. [NY 1857]

Swanton, John 1952 The Indian Tribes of North America. Bureau of Ethnology, Bulletin 145.

Van Syckle, Edwin 1982 The River Pioneers. Early Days on Gray's Harbor. Pacific Search Press.

Viola, Herman, and Carolyn Margolis 1985 Magnificent Voyagers ~ The U.S. Exploring Expedition, 1838-1842. Smithsonian Institution Press.

Wilkes, Charles 1844 Narrative of the US Exploring Expedition, During the Years 1838, 39, 40, 41, 42. 5 volumes + atlas. Philadephia: Lea & Blanchard.

THANKS

Final editing of Gibbs was facilitated by a grant from 4Culture, aid from Lushootseed Research, and consultations with fellow scholars, natives, elders, and adepts.

Viola Garfield, Erna Gunther, Ann Bates, Carol Eastman, Andie Palmer, Robin Wright, Bill Holm, Greg Watson, Marjorie Halpin, Marilyn Richen, Tammy Jackson, Ann Schuh, Bob & Christine Keyes-Back, Tom & Donna Steinburn, Ellen Lowe, Nancy Griffin, Kurt Reidinger, Patt O'Flaherty, Laurel Sercombe, Bill Seaburg, Gerald Eck, Diana Riesky, Gerry DeLay, Larry & Michiko Epstein, Hiroko Roe, Andie Palmer, Alf Shepard, Carolyn Marr, Brad Burns, Carolyn Michael, Barbara Brotherton, Dean Reiman, Robert Rudine, Janet Yoder, Chris Roth, Pam Cahn, Joe & Joanne Kfouri.

Florence Hawley Ellis, Mary Elizabeth Smith, Cynthia Irwin-Williams, Philip Bock, Nibs Hill, Stanley Newman, James, Charlotte, Carmie Lynn, Laura Lee, Charlotte Mary, Jeremy Alan, Tamaya Lynn, Trent Toulouse, Marie, Ella Mae, John Dunn, Luceen Latorre Dunn, Michael Hittman, Amelia Susman Schultz, Guy Gibeau, Jean Mulder, Marie-Lucie Tarpent, Bruce Rigsby, Alfonso Ortiz, Robin Fox, Esther Goldfrank & Karl Wittfogel, Margaret Bacon, Yehudi Cohen, Warren Shapiro, Mark Leone, Elizabeth Brandt, Wick Miller, Tom Windes, Steve Lekson, Anna Sofaer, John Stein, Terry Strauss, Colin Calloway, Raymond De Mallie, Douglas Parks, Harvey Markovitz, Ruth Hamilton, Violet Brown, Donald Fixico, Merle Williams, Richard O'Connell, Linda Dombrowski, LaVonne Brown Ruoff, & Blue, Sherry, Sanger Clark.

Glenn & Dorothy Williams, Andrew & Nancy Core, Roland Wildman, Janet Pollak, Michele Teitelbaum, Cheryl Wase, Edward Deal, Nina Versaggi, Nancy Trembly, Kenneth Wilkie, Corinne Black, Karen &Tom Reynolds, Janet Pollak, Michele Teitelbaum, Cheryl Wase, Edward Deal, Nina Versaggi, Fiona Anders, Corinne Black, Patrick Twohy SJ, Ray Bucko, SJ, Mike Fitzpatrick SJ, Isabel Arcasa, Larry & Adeline Fredin, Guy Moura, Mary Marchand, Charles Chaz Charlie Monty Nelson, David Rice, Fred van Ronk, Mark DeLeon, Bill Layman, Pam Amoss, Carl & Charlene Gustafson, Brian & Suzie Holmes, Darby Stapp & Julie Longenecker, Robert Walls & Laura Dassow Walls, Jack & Deborah Fiander, Ken Tollefson, Wayne Suttles, Dale Kinkade, JV Powell, Dell & Virginia Hymes, Warren Snyder, Esther Goldfrank, Karl Wittfogel, Raymond Fogelson, Helen Tanner, Sam & Janet Stanley, William Fenton, Fred & Joan Eggan, Alice Kehoe, Don & Kay Fowler, Sven & Astrid Liljeblad, Don, Lois, Ron, Jay, Bedelia, Damas, Lily, Jill, John, Sasha, Vi.

Many Thanks to Nora Thompson Dean, Lucy Blalock, Lillie Whitehorn, Isabel Arcasa, Ed Davis, Lawrence Webster, Isadore & Jackie Tom, Martin & Susie Sampson Peter, Morris Dan, Theresa Willup, Helen Ross, Lottie Sam, Walter Sam, and Dewey Mitchell, Gladys Tantaquidgeon, Adeline & Larry Fredin, Jim Rementer, Linda Poolaw, TB & Pearl Charlie, Christine Sam, Fred Bruner, Barney Leader, Agnes Wagosh, Frances Ashanany, Christine & Charles Quintasket, Juliann Timentwa, Herman Friedlander, Sue Matt, Jerome & Mary Miller, Shirley Palmer, Lucy Covington, Emily Peone, Richard & Nora Dauenhauer, John & Helen Clifton, Oliver & Kristi Clifton, Ernest, Lynne, Cameron, Max & Jodie Hill, Ernie & Margie Hill, Mildred Wilson, Violet & Peter Neasloss, Tom Brown, Melvin Lucei, Rex & Angela Buck, Ted & Deborah Isham.

Throughout, my families of Millers, Toulouses, Dunns, Liebers, Chesnins, and, especially, Monday Nite & Ashland Annuals.

Index

A

Abernethy, A, 70
Adamson, Thelma, 92, 177, 178
Admiralty Inlet, 21, 28, 109, 110
Agassiz, Louis, 9, 11
Alaska, 2, 5, 11
Alm-cot-ti ~ Nisqually story teller, 101
American Geographical Society, 4
Amotken, 62f
Anderson, Alexander, 5
An-nan-in-ta, 48
Astoria, 4, 5, 73, 113, 124, 140

B

barn beams, 271
Bellingham, 21, 29, 83, 152, 154, 160; names 163
Black Hand, 85
Blessing, Matthew T, 9
Budd Inlet, 28, 93 #111, 158

C

Cameron, Mr, 43, 57
Cape Disappointment, 140
Cape Flattery, 20f, 43, 74, 82, 114, 148f, 158
Cascades, 18f, 20f, 30f, 43, 55f, 69f, 96f, 117f, 127f, 140f, 154
Cathlamet, 87
Champoeg, 56, 140
Charley, 74, 96, 180
Chelan Falls, 91
Chelan Lake, 22, 128
Chetlah, 2, 6, 7
Chief Atwin Stockum, 34 #19
Chief Chow-its-hoot, 83
Chief Concomly, 13, 266 #175
Chief Elsakweoit, 27
Chief Ka-ko-an, 23
Chief Ke-powh-kan, 118
Chief Klekahkahi, 130
Chief Ko-bakh-sat, 48
Chief Toke, 44, 148
Chief Tow-e-toks, 121, 126
Chief Tsin-nit-ieh, 24
Chief Tū-le'-uk, 24
Chief Umtuch, 55 #41, 270
Chief Victor ~ Kwi-kwi-kal-sih, 132
Chief Wiyawiikt, 123
Chieftess *Damasq*, 13 #5, 264 #172
Chimakum, 150, 152, 158
Chinuk Wawa, 4, 15 #9, 68 #64, 181, 267 #176, 269 #182
Chipman, James, 268, 270f
Chole-swoeh, 94
Columbia River, 4, 19f, 29f, 35f, 40f, 52, 61, 71f, 94, 111, 138, 271
Colvocoresses, George, 13f, 264f
Coquille River, 49
Cox, Ross, 36, 41, 111
cultus ~ bad, 272
Curtin, Jeremiah, 59
Curtis, Edward, 59 #49, 85 #97, 178
Custer, Henry, 164 #153
Czar of Russia, 269

D

Dart, Dr Anson, 117f, 132, 136
De Smet, Fr PJ, 132f
dentalia, 5, 22, 41, 45 #28, 50, 68 #66, 114, 124 #133, 190, 197, 205; also *haiqua*, *haikwa*
dogs, 7, 25, 39, 48f, 55f, 71, 79, 120, 152, 203, 211; woolly 7, 15, 25f, 55f, 113, 266
Dr Kuykendall, 59 #48, 62 #54, 69 #67, 72 #73, 87 #101, 89 #103, 103 #121
drum, drumming, 45, 193, 215
Dunn, J, 11, 47 #34

E

Eells, Myron, 66, 70
Eells, Rev E, 130, 131, 141
Eisenhower, Dwight, 275
Eld, Henry, 13, 264
Elip Tilikum ~ First Folks, 56 #42, 61f, 71f, 83, 103, 122

Elwa, 21, 27, 150
Enumclaw, 69 #67
Esquimalt Harbor, 43
Eton, 270

F

Finlayson, 31
fir log wife, 78
Flattery Jack, 150
Ford, Sidney, 34 #19, 69, 72, 79
Fort Colville, 5, 126f, 130f, 139, 140f, 144f
Fort Steilacoom, 5, 6, 152, 174, 166, 272f
Fort Vancouver, 4, 72, 119, 126, 138, 140f
Fr G Mengarini, 12, 60, 62, 73, 77, 132
Fr MC Pandosy ~ Pandozy, 5, 10, 124, 258
Fr Joset, 5, 130
Franchère, G, 56, 61, 111, 112
Fremont, John, 4

G

Gallatin, Albert, 3, 4, 234, 257
Ganey, WH, 66
George, 1, 2, 3, 4, 5, 6, 7, 9, 10, 11, 12, 13, 15, 16, 17, 22, 26, 27, 46, 52, 59, 70, 74, 151, 161, 265, 267, 269, 271, 272, 275
Goldsborough, HA, 25, 52
Goliah, 29, 153 #150
Gov Douglas, 57, 70
Grand Coulee, 132
Gray, Asa, 11
Gray, WH, 73, 74, 86
Gulick, Dr LH, 260

H

haikwa ~ dentalia, 5, 22, 41, 45 #28, 50, 68 #66, 114, 124 #133, 190, 197, 205; also *haiqua*
Hai-ya-watst, 113
Hale, Horatio, 18, 19, 22, 29, 31, 51, 58, 110, 234, 260
Harvard, 2, 4, 8, 11
Healey, Caroline Wells, 11
Heath, Joseph, 269f
Hitchcock, Dr CM, 47
Hood Canal, 22, 27, 28, 92, 106, 110

Hudson Bay Company ~ HBC, 4, 7, 11, 31, 32, 40, 47, 68, 70, 77, 123, 124, 126, 138, 142, 145, 155, 175, 268
Huggins, Edward, 267f

I

ictahs, 94
ignis fatuus, 35
incantations, 32, 45, 79, 82, 88, 121
Indian Blotters, 271
Irving, W, 4, 30, 111, 124

J

Jack ~ Gibb's cook, 7
Jennie, 272
Jesuits, 62, 130, 132, 141
Joint Base Lewis McChord ~ JBLM, 275

K

Kanaka ~ Hawaiian, 138, 140, 270, 272
Kathlapūtl, 20, 23, 55
Katzie, 268
Kautz, Lt AV, 7, 58 #45
Kettle Falls, 5, 91 #105, 128, 130, 139, 172
Kwi-han ~ Satsop, 83

L

Lakh-kanam, 113, 114
Lander, Edward, 65
Lane, William ~ Gibb's farmer, 6, 7
Lawetlat'ła ~ Smoker ~ Mt St Helens,
Lewis & Clark, 19, 30, 31, 39, 37, 42, 47, 52, 56, 81, 97, 111, 113, 118, 124, 133
Lewis River, 20, 23
Longfield, John, 269f
Lummi, 7, 10, 21, 29, 45, 83, 115, 152, 154, 160, 163

M

Makah, 21f, 30f, 43, 51f, 66, 74, 75 #79, 79 #86, 81, 105, 114, 241, 149, 150, 158, 190
Manhattan, 3
Mason, Charles, 6
McClellan, Capt George, 5, 22, 30, 46, 118, 126f, 155, 161, 183

McDonald, 130, 139, 270
McGrath, Mrs JJ, 59 #46
McKee, Redick, 4
McLeod, John, 273, 274, 275
measures, 6 #2, 17, 50f
Meeker, Ezra, 272
metis, 32
Missouria, 6
moon, 15, 21, 51, 61f, 74f, 92f, 237, 245, 266, 275
Mount Baker, 19, 77, 97, 154, 170, 254
mountain beaver, 54
Mounts, 15, 269, 271f, 275f
mouse wife, 121f
moxa, 47
Mt St Helens, 19, 68, 77, 97 #119, 118 #126, 121f, 182; see *Lawetlat'ła*
Mullan, Lt J, 64 #58
Mutton ~ Gibb's woolly dog, 7, 15, 266

N

necromancers, 83
New Dungeness, 27, 105f, 113f, 150, 157f
New York Historical Society, 4, 8, 12
Newell, Dr R, 56f
Newport, RI, 3, 282
Nisqually Delta, 15, 269, 274
Nooksack, 21, 29, 154, 165f, 254

O

Oak Pt, 70
Oblates, 7, 125, 141
ogresses, 67f #68
Olympia, WA, 6, 16, 92f, 156, 268
Opata, 262
Oregon City, 4, 70, 139f, 178
Orphan Tsunami, 27 #16
Owen, John, 132
Ozette, 27 #16

P

Pahtoo ~ Mt Adams, 96 #116
Pambrun,, 139
Patkanam, 28
Penn Cove, 13 #5, 43, 52, 265 #172
Pickering, John, 259

Pickett, Lt G, 7
Pickett, Jim, 7
Pillar Rock, 71
Pilling, JC, 12
Pishtst, 21, 27, 71, 78, 150
polygamy, 33, 121, 233
Pomerania, 55
Ponape, 260
Port Discovery, 27, 30, 43, 106f, 113f, 150, 157f
Port Ludlow, 27, 152
Port Townsend, 21, 26f, 37, 150f, 157f, 265
potatoes, 26, 39, 48, 67, 119, 123, 126f, 146, 150f
prock, 7
prostitution, 25, 33, 41, 149
Puget Sound Agricultural Company, 7, 68 #63, 140

R

Reidinger, Kurt, ii, 264
robes, 26, 54, 152
Round Hill School, 3

S

S'Hotlemamish, 28, 115
Sacramento, 4, 38, 57, 125
Sah-hali Tyee, 60
Sally, 13, 32, 264 #172, 267
Satsop, 13, 20f, 57, 83, 148f, 157, 181, 264
Scarborough Hill, 85
Schoolcraft, H, 4, 10, 16 #10, 37, 124
Scotam, 66
Seattle, 28, 269
Sequalitchew Creek, 268
Sheridan, Lt P, 7
shibboleth, 151
Shoalwater, 6, 10, 19f, 42f, 71, 77f, 81f, 111, 148, 157
Siberia, 11
Simmons, Col M, 20, 27f, 30f, 39, 46
Simpson, Gov Sir George, 131
Sitka, 53
Skagits, 13, 21f, 29f, 44, 56, 77f, 110, 154
Skomeltem, 62f
Skookams, 15, 62f, 70f, 91f, 267f #176

Skookumchuck, 5
sk^{w}ənt ~ waterfall, 129
Slaht-la-kwo ~ Screech Owl, 102f
Slawntehus, 131, 139f
Slocum, John, 34 #19
Sm'algyax ~ Tsmsyan, 11
Smalleh, 93
smallpox, 66, 117, 120, 124, 129f, 148f
Smee-ow, 66
Smith, Buckingham, 258
Smith, Jedediah, 4, 141
Smith, Solomon H, 112
Sneetlum, 33, 44, 52
Spanish, 25, 27, 56, 110, 113, 162, 238
Spilyai ~ Coyote, 61f, 68, 73, 76, 89, 90f, 92 #110, 99f, 122, 267
Split Sun, 123 #132, 128 #140
Spokan Garry, 56, 73, 131
sqəlalitut, 82
Squu-shum ~ Smoke ~ Fog, 48
Stak-ta-mish, 24, 92 #109, 267 #177
Starling, Edward A, 4
stars, 66, 74f, 79, 99, 201, 235
Steilacoom Masonic Cemetery, 274
Stevens, Isaac, 5f, 79, 116, 270f
Stevens, John Austin, 12
Sucker, 93
Suckley, Dr G, 46, 56f, 86
Sunswick Manor, 3
Swaal, 5, 19 #13, 23, 148
Swak-keuk ~ Frogess, 94
Swan, James, 6, 74, 79, 82

T

Tacoma Mill, 273
tah ~ spirit, 66 #60, 80 #88, 165
Taitinapam, 19, 23, 115, 149, 154
Thoreau, Henry David, 11
Thunderbirds, 69 #67, 80f #88, 180
Tinkham, A, 71
Tis-ai-luck-han, 18, 103
Tolmie, Dr William, 6, 12f, 31, 35, 49, 68, 72, 83, 101, 155f, 264f, 269f
Treaty War, 6, 8, 272
tsiatko ~ Sasquatch, 71f
Tsihalis, 19f, 30f, 44f, 51f, 111f, 267

Tsinnite'h, 48
Tsinūk ~ Chinook, 19f, 30f, 41f, 51f, 113
Tsitz-a-mah-han ~ Duke of York, 27, 113, 151
Tulalip Bay, 29
Tū-tū-ten, 58
Tyee Dick, 13 #6, 15 #8, 266 #175, 269f, 275

U

Umtuch, 55, 271

V

Vaqueros, 4
Vashon Island, 28, 102, 153, 159

W

Wa-kwin-nam, 48
Walker, Rev E, 130f, 141
Warbass, UG, 6, 174f
Watteetash, 61f, 68, 91f, 100
Whidbey Island, 21f, 44, 82, 110, 114, 146, 153f,
Whitman, Rev Dr M, 74, 133, 141
Whyeema, 94f
Willamette Valley, 4, 19, 23, 38, 50, 57, 118, 128, 139f
Wisconsin Historical Society, 2, 8, 16
Wolcott, Oliver, 3
Work, John, 32, 271

X

$x^w dab$ ~ Dr, 83

Y

Yag^{w}ałiw, 13, 264 #172
Yahotowit, 70f
Yahpohalla ~ Water Spider, 18, 98, 99
Yallakūb ~ Flattery Jack, 25
Yuknkwalt-tum ~ blind woman, 93

Z

Zugwa, 69

E sites

Gibbs Web Sites

US Boundary Survey

http://www.biodiversitylibrary.org/item/175282#page/12/mode/1up

http://www.biodiversitylibrary.org/bibliography/95245#/details = Forest growth

Gibbs grave site:

http://www.findagrave.com/cgi-bin/fg.cgi?page=gsr&GScid=285361&GSln=gibbs

Saint Marys Episcopal Churchyard, Portsmouth, Newport County, Rhode Island, USA

http://biodiversitylibrary.org/page/8817843#page/846/mode/1up

Sold @ Amazon.com

Jay Miller's books & E-books @ Amazon.com

ACCULTURATING AMELIA ~ Round Valley 1937 California
ALASKA EDGE ISLAND ~ Siberian Yupiks of St Lawrence Island
ALLIED MOUNDS ~ Touching the Earth, Modeling the World, Reaching the Sky
ANIMAL PEOPLE ADVENTURES ~ Native North American Tribal Stories
AT BAY ~ Cultures Converging through Southwest Washington > 5
BALLARD BULWARK ~
CHACO ECHOES ~ Pervasive Keresan Priesthoods
CHACOKIA ~ Chaco, Cahokia, Cities & Ceremonies ~ Bundles & Blood Lines Centuries Ago
CHINOOK CONCERNS ~ Emma Millett Luscier, Isabella Bertrand, Verne Ray
CIRCLING FOUR CORNERS ~ Re-Viewing Native American Indiens > 10
CROSSING ~ LINES: An Educational Memoir of Native North America
DEL-AWARE ~ Lenape Legacies
DELAWARE INTEGRITY ~ Rituals, Removals, Reforms by Lenape Indiens
DISCLAIMING TREATIES I ~ Puget Tribes 1927 Testimonies
DISCLAIMING TREATIES II ~ Puget Tribes 1927 Testimonies > 15
ELDERS' DIALOG ~ Ed Davis & Vi Hilbert Discuss Native Puget Sound Language, Culture, & Heritage
EVERGREEN ETHNOGRAPHIES ~ Hoh, Chehalis, Suquamish, and Snoqualmi of Western Washington
FEDERAL FISH FILES ~ Swindell 1942 Treaty Rights Report
GEORGE GIBBS NORTHWEST ARRAY ~ Full Reports, Place Names, Word List, Artifact Names, and Guide
GRASSROOTS JANET ~ Advancing Salish and Traditional Cultures > 20
HERMAN HAEBERLIN REGAINED ~ Anthropology and Artifacts of Puget Sound 1916-17
HERSTORY NW ~ Women Upholding Native Traditions
INDIEN ~ ETHNOGRAPHY: Cultural Traditions of Native North America
INDIEN ~ ETHNOLOGY: Grounded, Gendered, Meaningful Cultural Traditions
LESCHI IN LOVE ~ A Novel of Native Puget Sound > x2 > 25
MARCO MUCK MASKS ~ Frank Cushing on Marshes and Mounds
MINTER BAY ~ Land, Lore, Loss, and Lucre in the South Salish Sea
NATIVE MET HOW ~ Improving Posterity
OLD LUKH ~ A Novel of Native Puget Sound Daily Life, Places, and Stories
OVER THE FALLS ~ Sdoqwalbixw Survivance Surrounding Seattle > 30
PACIFIC PLATEAU PORTRAYALS ~ People Places Ponderings
RAY'S ARRAY ~ Raymond D Fogelson's Works
RIGHTING NATIVE PLACES ~ Adventures in Northwest Geography
SAHAPTINS STUDIES ~ Columbia River Plateau, Cora Du Bois, Homer Garner Barnett, Gerald Raymond Desmond
SDOQWALBIXW > 35
SOUND SALISH STRAITS ~ Central Salish Sea Cultures
UNSETTLING SEATTLE ~ Arresting Local Talent and Academic Illiteracy
WRITING WORDS IN WARY WORLDS ~ World Wide Improved Spellings of Native America Languages

JONA Memoirs

RESCUES, RANTS, & RESEARCHES ~ A Re-View of Jay Miller's Writings on Northwest Indien Cultures ~ #9
TRIBAL TRIO of the Northwest Coast by Kenneth D Tollefson ~ #10 > 40
INTERWEAVING COAST SALISH CULTURAL SYSTEMS ~ Collected Works of Pamela Thorsen Amoss ~ #14

University of Nebraska Press

ANCESTRAL MOUNDS ~ Vitality and Volatility Crossing Native North America 2015
HONNE ~ The Spirit of the Chehalis 2015

www.ingramcontent.com/pod-product-compliance
Lightning Source LLC
Chambersburg PA
CBHW081058290526
45795CB00006B/1906